Do's and Don'ts Around the World:
A Country Guide to Cultural and Social Taboos and Etiquette

By Gladson I. Nwanna, Ph.D

AFRICA

World Travel Institute
Baltimore, Maryland

Library of Congress Cataloging-in-Publication Data

Nwanna, Gladson I.
        Do's and don'ts around the world : a country guide to cultural and social taboos and etiquette : Africa / Gladson I. Nwanna.
            p.   cm. -- (International traveler's resource guide)
      ISBN 1-890605-04-2
         1.   Travel etiquette--Africa--Handbooks, manuals, etc.
      2. Africa-Social life and customs--Handbooks, manuals, etc. I. Title.
      II. Series.
      BJ2137.N832 1998
395'.096--dc21   97-19166
                                              CIP

Cover Design by Adrienne Waite

Printed in Canada

Acknowledgement

A lot of people have helped me with this project, giving me everything from encouragement and typesetting to editorial advice and help. I would especially, like to thank, Mrs. Phyllis Desbordes, Dr. Sydney E. Onyeberechi and Mr. Thomas J. Wilcox for their relentless assistance in editing parts of the chapters, and for other valuable suggestions, Ms. Bernadette R. Rose for her wonderful typing and editing skills, and Ms. Miatta Dabo and Adrenne Waite for their assistance in numerous ways.

A special thanks goes to the various personnel of foreign embassies and foreign government tourist bureaus in the U.S. and to government ministries abroad whose efforts in completing the exceedingly lengthy questionnaire made it all possible.

Preface

Several countries are at the crossroads of economic, social and cultural change and are undergoing profound changes. The trend towards globalization and integration of world economies are all a part of the forces transforming and changing social and cultural practices through out the world. One obvious outcome of this evolving and dynamic process is the change in social and cultural norms and practices; changes that have in some countries resulted in relaxation and/or accommodation of, and in other countries led to re-affirmation and tightening of the status quo with respect to social and cultural practices and other rules of etiquette.

Every year people travel out of their countries to one or more foreign countries. For the majority of these travelers their utmost wish is for an exciting and incident-free stay in the host country. Unfortunately, many of these travelers do not have an incident-free stay abroad. Even among those for whom safety is not a major issue, there is almost always the one spoiler, an embarrassing moment or encounter. Seasoned travelers have not escaped this spoiler, nor have they come up with a permanent solution to this seemingly unimportant, but unconformable nuisance. One can only think of a partial cure that, at best, guarantees the chance of minimizing part of such episodes. That cure is this book; a book that catalogues important and often forgotten **do's and don'ts** around the world.

In this book, I provide a country-by-country **DO's and DON'TS**. The aim of this book is to highlight areas and topics that, as a traveler to a foreign country, you may want to watch out for and take appropriate precautions against. I suggest that before traveling or upon arrival at your destination, you re-verify those topics and practices you hold so dearly. An important source of such a verification process will be the embassies, consulates and tourism bureaus representing those countries or regions.

This book is unique in many ways, not the least being the format. Some topics in the book may even appear to be repeated. This was deliberate on the part of the author. It was also deliberate to leave the various topical items as presented instead of arranging and/or grouping them by topics. This arrangement underlies the importance and emphasis the author chose to attach to every topical item and the conviction that all of the items warrant a glance or two by every foreign-bound traveler.

Other unique features of the book include the broad headings used to address the various topical items such as "Is customary, Is allowed...Is disallowed, Is a crime etc". Again this was deliberate. But importantly, it was done so as to reflect the difficulty in addressing the issue of **DO's and DON'TS** among countries. This arrangement is intended to also serve as a cautionary note to potential users of this book. This is more so, considering that even within countries a wide range of different and sometimes conflicting cultures and practices exist and in many cases there is only a fine line between what is acceptable or not acceptable. In essence, disagreements abound.

In effect, while the information conveyed in this book is useful and should help relieve some anxiety among foreign travelers, extreme caution should also be taken in interpreting any particular response for any given country. Ideally, this book should be taken only as a reference guide aimed at alerting you and increasing your awareness to issues, practices and behavior in other countries.

Not withstanding readers who may disagree with my choice of headings or with the responses to the topical items despite my earlier cautions, this book also carries the benefit of drawing information from sources I considered reliable and official. Virtually all of the information contained in this book in response to the various topical issues or questions came via a questionnaire and was provided by the embassies and/or representatives of the respective countries.

Another unique feature of this book is its wide appeal. Most of the information should be useful to every international traveler, irrespective of the country of origin or country of destination. This goal was of particular interest to me and provided the driving force in the search for questions and issues to include in the questionnaire.

Every effort was made to include important questions, issues and areas of potential concern to international travelers and to seek answers and guidance for you, the traveler. As I compiled and concluded my questionnaire and put the final touches to this book, it became very obvious that some issues of equal or greater importance are bound to be left out. It also became clear that certain items in this book may become contentious, controversial and may even generate heated arguments and debate. This, of course is not the intended purpose of the book.

Neither the issues nor the questions raised, nor items and topics treated in this book was expected to be exhaustive. I appeal to those of you who may have other concerns and comments about this book to kindly send them to me. Similarly, I ask the same for those who may detect errors that may have slipped my attention. Such feedback will help me immensely in improving future editions. It is virtually impossible to embark on a project, and a subject matter as this without anticipating concerns, particularly given the differences in customs, contents and social practices and norm even within the same national boundaries.

It is my expectation that the information contained in this book will make a big difference, particularly in ensuring a safe, enjoyable, rewarding and hitch-free trip for millions of overseas-bound travelers. It certainly should save you numerous embarrassing moments and hopefully provide you with more fun-filled times and happy memories. Suggestions and letters should be mailed to Public Relations Department, WTI, P.O. Box 32674 Baltimore, Maryland 21282-2674, USA.

POSTSCRIPT

Some Important Assumptions & Observations to keep in mind as you read this book, and as you travel abroad.

As I traveled through various foreign countries, I made some personal observations that should help you understand and better appreciate the contents, style and coverage of this book. They include:

The response to the various topical items in this book was intended to address the social and cultural norms and etiquette expected to prevail in <u>largely urban centers</u> of the countries profiled. While they should apply equally well in rural and suburban centers, I have observed that

(a) urban residents are generally more tolerant and understanding of foreigners than rural, particularly on issues dealing with social and cultural norms and decorum. This may be due to the degree and frequency of exposure and contact between foreigners and urban residents than with the rural residents. This, however, may not be the case with law enforcement issues. (see section c)

(b) you stand a greater chance of being stared, looked at with curiosity in rural areas or by rural residents than in urban areas or those exposed to urban living. In some areas, expect some rural residents, particularly children, to walk along with you or even want to touch you. It is all part of the curious feeling you should expect. This is likely the case when you have some "foreignness" in you, often due to your color or some other outstanding and distinguishing features. While this may seem awkward and discomforting at times to the foreigner, similar feelings, are often shared by the other parties. My suggestion is to feel relaxed now that you've been alerted. Most of the times it usually doesn't signify danger as you may be apt to think or feel. A good friendly smile from you may just do the magic. You may also notice that rural residents tend to be reserved and often shy.

Having made these observations, I caution that because of the more culture-minded nature of rural residents and their less tolerant attitude towards any form of contravention or violation of strongly held cultural norms and decorum, you can expect in some cases, strong negative feelings and even hostility from some quarters. Interestingly, the signs of such contravention are often clear to an alert international traveler. Either a Good Samaritan citizen will quickly alert you or you will find both children and some adults making threatening signals or physically attempting to harass you. Under such a circumstance, you may be better of stopping and asking for anyone around who understands your language to seek some understanding or clarification. Alternatively, cease and desist from doing whatever you are doing or may have been doing. For the most part, misunderstandings often stem from doing something as opposed to saying something, unless you are attempting to communicate in the local dialect or language.

(c) I have also observed that law enforcement authorities in rural areas tend to be more sympathetic and tend to forgive easily. In other words, despite the higher tolerance level and higher degree of understanding of foreigners, you stand a greater chance of getting into trouble with the law and getting arrested when you contravene the law in urban areas than in the rural areas. This should not be a reason or an excuse to want to deliberately test or flaunt the system during your visit to rural areas.

(d) Expect to be stopped and questioned by law enforcement when you stray into areas that are either prohibited to foreigners or appear segregated e.g. by color, or class or other distinct characteristics of which you do not appear to fit. Stating your case or claiming your ignorance calmly, and politely may be your best move.

(e) If you need assistance (outside law enforcement), expect mixed reactions from both urban and rural sector residents. How much real help you get will depend on the country, as much as where in the country you may be located. Deliberate attempts to misdirect a foreigner is not unusual. It is not unusual to find acts of hospitality and effort to assist a foreigner either. I have experienced both. Generally, rural residents tend to do better. You should rely more on law enforcement officers.

(f) Surprising as it may sound to many readers, life and activities in several countries of the world are still male-dominated and this permeates the prevailing culture. As a female international traveler, expect this state of affairs to manifest itself in the manner that may not only run contrary to your upbringing and expectations, but may be a source of unwarranted attention and embarrassment to your person. Although you may not be able to change things, at least you can learn to be aware of them and to place them to your own comfort level. The idea and trend towards equal rights of the sexes is hardly taken seriously in several developing countries, and you are better of not pushing it and not expecting much of it during your brief stay abroad. Similarly, keep in mind that once in a foreign country, you are subject to the, rules, regulations and laws of that country, including their constitution and not those of your country. To think or act otherwise is to expose yourself to potential risks of all types.

(g) If you love taking photographs as many international travelers do, particularly, first-timers, you need to be cautious of where you go to photograph and who or what you photograph. One of the most common incidents encountered by international travelers stems from taking photographs. In almost every country, taking photographs of military installations, barracks, posts, hardware (in fact, anything military) is prohibited. If you are caught, you are most likely to be detained, questioned, jailed or tortured. You can also bet your camera or video camera that the film or tape will be confiscated or destroyed. Similarly, while the taking of personal photographs inside the airport is allowed in several countries, there is equally a large number of countries where it is prohibited. It is safer to inquire first at the airport information desk if it is ok to take photographs. I will also suggest the same precautions if you must take a photograph of a sacred site, object or of someone. While some people in some countries may not object, photographing a person without asking permission may be an invitation for trouble. When such permission is sought and granted, do not be surprised if the person demands money (before or after) in return as compensation.

(h) Finally, always remember that you are a foreigner and not a citizen of the country or local. This means taking extra precautions in what you say and do, how you say and do things, as well as when and where you say and do them. Things that a local may get away with, you may not be so fortunate as to get away with. Hence, avoid feeling like a resident and be alert to locals who try to con or trick you into committing a crime or an offense. Furthermore, remember that several countries are still ruled by the military who are usually less tolerant of so many things, including their perception of foreigners and their interpretation of rules of laws.

(More of these observations can be found in the book (**Practical Tips for American Traveling Abroad: Ignore them at Your own Risk.** ISBN #: 1-890605-09-3; 263 pages, $19.99; Also available on-line for purchase and downloading at www.worldtravelinstitute.com)

DISCLAIMER:

OTHER RESOURCES

As a web or internet-accessible international traveler, you may find the following web sites useful, particularly, their links to several other instructive travel and country-related sites: **http://travel.state.gov/travel_pubs.html;**
http://travel.state.gov/travel_warnings.html. I encourage you to explore other country, travel and culture-related sites.

TABLE OF CONTENTS

ALGERIA	Is customary Is allowed Is permissible Is used. Is OK	Is not customary Is frowned upon	Is disallowed Is forbidden Is a crime	(See last page for comments on items referenced here)
Smoking in public	✓			
Eating in public		✓		
Not flushing public toilet			✓	
Spitting in public		✓		
Feeding animals & birds in public	✓			
Whistling in public		✓		
Drinking alcohol in public			✓	
Kissing in public		✓		
Breast feeding in public		✓		
Drunkenness (in public)			✓	
Cursing in public		✓		
Religious preaching in public	✓			
Begging (panhandling) in public	✓			
Giving money to beggars/panhandlers	✓			
Giving food/drink to beggars/panhandlers	✓			
Brushing teeth in public (other than in restrooms)		✓		
Strolling with pets in major public roads/streets	✓			
Chewing gum in public	✓			
Chewing gum in government offices		✓		
Combing hair in public (other than in toilets/restrooms)		✓		
Undressing/dressing in public			✓	
Wearing of dark glasses indoors in public places		✓		
Public display of wealth	✓			
Praying openly in public in non-designated areas		✓		
Walking bare feet in public	✓			
Chewing tobacco in public	✓			
Trimming one's finger or toe nails in public		✓		
Laughing aloud in public		✓		
Mingling of the sexes in public				n/a
Mixed bathing in public swimming pools				n/a
Distributing religious pamphlets (literature) in public/side streets		✓		

1

ALGERIA

	Is customary Is allowed Is permissible Is used. Is OK	Is not customary Is frowned upon	Is disallowed Is forbidden Is a crime	(See last page for comments on items referenced here)
Dancing on side street		✓		
Nude bathing			✓	
Littering			✓	
Binge Drinking			✓	
Hitchhiking		✓		
Jaywalking			✓	
Drunk driving			✓	
Speeding			✓	
Skating on side streets (side-walk)		✓		
Graffiti painting			✓	
Pilfering			✓	
Prostitution			✓	
Haggling in the market place				n/a
Consumption of alcoholic beverages in bars and restaurants				n/a
Gambling		✓		
Possession of pornographic materials			✓	
Possession of the Christian Bible		✓		
Possession of the Moslem Koran	✓			
Possession of bullet-proof vest		✓		
Possession of toy gun	✓			
Possession of fire crackers and firework			✓	
Possession of prescription drugs (without doctor's note)			✓	
Possession of regulated drugs (narcotics)			✓	
Possession of firearms (by foreigners)			✓	
Possession of pocket knife in public			✓	
Using walkie talkies			✓	
Using of "boom boxes"(loud sounding stereo system)				n/a
Using "walkman" (very small radio/cassettes with ear plugs) in public places	✓			
Using "walkman" (very small radio/cassettes with ear plugs) while driving or riding			✓	

2

ALGERIA

	Is customary Is allowed Is permissible Is used Is OK	Is not customary Is frowned upon	Is disallowed Is forbidden Is a crime	(See last page for comments on items referenced here)
Use of cellular phone	✓			
Use of binoculars/periscopes other than in sports arena		✓		
Taking photographs of people (without their permission)		✓		
Taking photographs at airports, train and bus stations	✓			
Taking photographs of airports	✓			
Taking photographs of churches and synagogues	✓			
Taking photographs of religious statues	✓			
Taking photographs of public buildings				n/a
Taking photographs of bridges				n/a
Tipping (gratuity)	✓			
Tipping (when service is rendered)	✓			
Tipping (when service is not rendered)		✓		
Tipping waiters/waitresses at restaurants and hotels				n/a
Tipping taxi/cab drivers				n/a
Tipping baggage handlers, porters, door persons				n/a
Tipping of hair dressers/barbers		✓		
Overtipping	✓			
Undertipping		✓		
Spilling cigarette butt (ash) on side streets/on the floor		✓		
Men wearing lipstick		✓	✓	
Wearing visible tattoo marks		✓		
Men painting/coloring their finger or toe nails		✓		
Cross dressing (men dressed like women & vice versa)		✓	✓	
Walking in public without a shirt (i.e., with the upper half of the body naked)		✓		
Men wearing braided hair		✓		
Men wearing earrings		✓		
Men wearing dreadlock hair style		✓		
Homosexuality			✓	
Lesbianism			✓	

3

ALGERIA

	Is customary Is allowed Is permissible Is used Is OK	Is not customary Is frowned upon	Is disallowed Is forbidden Is a crime	(See last page for comments on items referenced here)
Females covering their hair (wearing headgear) in public	✓			
Females exposing their full face in public	✓			
Females driving automobiles		✓		
Females riding motorcycles		✓		
Females riding bicycles		✓		
Females smoking in public		✓		
Women wearing bras (braziers) in public		✓	✓	
Use of lipstick by women	✓			
A woman extending her hands first when introduced		✓		
Female bashing			✓	
Females wearing trousers	✓			
Females wearing minis (short dresses)		✓		
Females wearing bikinis		✓		
Females wearing shorts		✓		
Persons of opposite sex holding hands in public	✓			
Persons of same sex holding hands in public		✓		
Handshake between opposite sex	✓			
Hugging in public by same sex	✓			
Hugging in public by opposite sex	✓			
Men and women walking side by side in public	✓			
Man walking ahead (in public), with the woman following	✓			
Woman walking ahead (in public), with the man following		✓		
Men opening doors for women	✓			
Sitting with legs crossed in the presence of elders		✓		
Talking to an elderly person with one's hat/cap on		✓		
Talking to an elderly person with hands positioned on both sides of one's waist		✓		
Blowing one's nose in public	✓			
Blowing one's nose in the presence of others	✓			
Addressing people by their title	✓			

4

ALGERIA

	Is customary Is allowed Is permissible Is used. Is OK	Is not customary Is frowned upon	Is disallowed Is forbidden Is a crime	(See last page for comments on items referenced here)
Addressing people by their family name/surname/last name/given name	✓			
Addressing people by their first name/ given name	✓			
Women going through doors first	✓			
Men helping women with their coats	✓			
Men extending their hands to women first during greetings		✓		
Taking off one's hat when entering a private home	✓			
Removing one's shoes when entering a private home		✓		
Invited guests bringing food at social gatherings	✓			
Guests bringing drinks at social gatherings	✓			
Shaking hands when leaving a small group	✓			
Shaking hands with everyone present, upon arrival at a social gathering	✓			
Eating with the right hand	✓			
Eating with the left hand	✓			
Eating with both hands		✓		
Presenting a gift or passing on an object with the left hand	✓			
Asking a man about his wife	✓			
Asking a woman about her husband	✓			
Making prior appointments before a meeting or visit	✓			
Addressing an audience with one or both hands in the pocket		✓		
Carrying on conversation during meals		✓		
Females sitting with legs crossed		✓		
People discussing their wealth		✓		
Asking someone his or her age, or how old the person is	✓			
Complementing someone on his/her physical looks	✓			
Complementing someone on his/her attire	✓			
Use of both hands in handshake	✓			
In greeting, a handshake accompanied by a slight bow		✓		

5

ALGERIA

	Is customary Is allowed Is permissible Is used. Is OK	Is not customary Is frowned upon	Is disallowed Is forbidden Is a crime	(See last page for comments on items referenced here)
Salutations such as "Good morning", "good afternoon", "Good evening"	✓			
The completion of a business deal with a handshake	✓			
Starting a negotiation session with a handshake	✓			
A gift for the host/hostess	✓			
Giving a business gift	✓			
A gift of money (use of money as gift)			✓	
Use of flowers as a gift	✓			
Use of business cards	✓			
Accepting/presenting gifts with both hands	✓			
Burning of the country's flag			✓	
Mutilation of the national currency			✓	
Casual wearing of clothings made with colors & marks of the national flag			✓	
Wearing of look-alike military (camouflage) fatigues (attire)		✓	✓	
Sitting on the floor (on floor mats)	✓	✓		
Discussion of religion	✓			
Discussion of politics	✓			
Discussion of sex	✓			
Patting/slapping someone on the buttocks		✓		
Patting/slapping someone on the back	✓			
Touching or patting someone's head/hair		✓		
Casual touching of any part of someone's body		✓		
Drinking directly out of a bottle/can		✓		
Placing one's leg(s) on the table or chair		✓		

ALGERIA

	Is customary Is allowed Is permissible Is used. Is OK	Is not customary Is frowned upon	Is disallowed Is forbidden Is a crime	(See last page for comments on items referenced here)
Showing the sole of one's foot (feet)		✓		
People standing very close when talking		✓		
Maintaining steady eye contact (direct gaze) when talking to someone	✓			
Kissing or exchange of kisses on the cheek	✓			
Counting money (change) in someone's palm		✓		
Finger pointing in public (in a daring manner)		✓		
Seeking attention by winking the eyes		✓		
Tapping the head to indicate someone is crazy		✓		
Twirling the head to indicate someone is crazy		✓		
Whistling as a way of requesting something/seeking attention		✓		
Using "thumbs-up" sign to mean OK	✓			
Forming a circle with the thumb and index finger (forefinger) to mean OK		✓		
Using the fingers to make a "V" sign for victory	✓			
Beckoning to someone with the index finger (forefinger)	✓			
The left to right waving of the hand with open palms facing outward to indicate "Good bye"	✓			
The use of a nod to show acknowledgement	✓			
Stopping/beckoning a taxi using a stretched hand with the thumb pointing upward		✓		
Using the thumb finger pointed to a direction, to request a ride or a hike	✓			
Raising one's hand/waving with an open fist to summon a taxi	✓			
Tapping one's foot/feet on the floor in a public gathering		✓		
Wiggling one's leg(s) when in a sitting position		✓		
Use of the hand (by motorists and cyclists) to signal direction of traffic	✓			

ALGERIA

		(See last page for comments on items referenced here)
Foreign tourists are welcome in the country.	yes	
The use of seat belt is mandatory.	yes	
International driving license is accepted.	yes	
Foreign drivers license is accepted.	no	
It is considered impolite to yawn in public.	yes	
Death penalty for drug trafficking is the law.	no	
Life imprisonment for drug trafficking is the law.	yes	
Guilty until proven innocent in court is the law.	no	
Innocent until proven guilty in court is the law.	yes	
Pedestrians always have right of way.	yes	
Exit visas are required of visitors.		n/a
Crash helmet is mandatory for motor cyclist.	yes	
Hanging is used as a form of legal punishment.	no	
Decapitation of a limb is used as a form of punishment.	no	
Caning is used as a form of legal punishment.	no	
Electric shock is used as a form of legal punishment.	no	
One is expected to stand up during the playing of the national anthem.	yes	
Crash helmet is mandatory for bicyclists.	yes	
Guests are expected to eat every thing on their plates.	no	
Table manners are very informal.	yes	
One is expected to cover one's mouth when laughing.	no	
A vertical nod of the head means YES (OK).	yes	
A horizontal shaking of the head means NO (Not OK).	yes	
Prostitution is allowed only in designated areas.	no	
One is expected to take off one's hat during playing of national anthem.	yes	
Separate seating arrangements (between sexes) are maintained at movies.	no	
Separate seating arrangements (between sexes) are maintained at churches.	yes	
Uninvited visitors or guests may not be welcome, even among acquaintances.	no	
Pets (e.g. cats, dog) are allowed in some hotels and restaurants.	no	
Couples invited for a meal may be separated during meals according to their sex.	no	
Punctuality is the order of business.	yes	
Automobiles are driven with headlights always turned on.	no	
Motorcycles are driven with headlights always turned on.	no	
Visitors with expired visa face mandatory jail time.	yes	
Visitors without exit visa face jail time.	no	
Visitors without entry visa face mandatory (automatic) jail time.	yes	

ADDITIONAL COUNTRY INFORMATION

(A)	The types of gifts to avoid:	pork based food items, drugs, alcohol, money from corruption.
(B)	Appropriate gifts for a foreigner to give:	Any type of gift that is representative of the foreign visitor's country.
(C)	Best time to present gifts (at the beginning or at the end of a visit?):	at the beginning
(D)	Best time to present gifts (on initial or later visits?):	during celebrations
(E)	Best place to present gifts (in private or in public?):	host's house or party house
(F)	Number(s) with certain connotations and/or myths attached to them:	Friday (13) bad luck
(G)	Basic shape(s) with negative connotations:	n/a
(H)	Basic color(s) with negative connotations:	n/a
(I)	Traditional greeting methods include:	hugging, kisses, handshake
(J)	Safe topics for discussion include:	weather, fashion, travel art, family religion, domestic politics, food, sports, irrational politics, sex, social conditions, money and personal wealth.
(K)	Best time for conversations (before, during, after meals?):	n/a
(L)	Forms of legal punishment:	jailing, public service
(M)	Approximately length of time one could be detained by law and order authorities before being charged in court:	48 hours
(N)	January 15, 1999, for example, will normally be written as:	15/1/99
(O)	Emergency code number:	19
(P)	Ambulance code Number:	62.33.33
(Q)	Police code number:	72
(R)	Telephone (country) code:	213
(S)	Telex (country) code:	61.12.201 28
(T)	Electricity requirements:	220 v 150 hz
(U)	Legal drinking age:	18/21
(V)	Systems of weights and measures:	metric
(W)	Legal age of incarceration:	18
(X)	Driving side of the road:	right
(Y)	Minimum expenditure expected of foreign visitors? $	yes
(Z)	Name of currency:	dinar
(Za)	Some places off-limits to foreign visitors:	Security installation
(Zb)	Some places, structures and items prohibited from being photographed:	Security installation

REPUBLIC OF ANGOLA	Is customary Is allowed Is permissible Is used. Is OK	Is not customary Is frowned upon	Is disallowed Is forbidden Is a crime	(See last page for comments on items referenced here)
Smoking in public	✓			
Eating in public			✓	
Not flushing public toilet		✓		
Spitting in public		✓		
Feeding animals & birds in public	✓			
Whistling in public	✓			
Drinking alcohol in public		✓		
Kissing in public	✓			
Breast feeding in public	✓			
Drunkenness (in public)		✓		
Cursing in public			✓	
Religious preaching in public		✓		
Begging (panhandling) in public	✓			
Giving money to beggars/panhandlers	✓			
Giving food/drink to beggars/panhandlers	✓			
Brushing teeth in public (other than in restrooms)			✓	
Strolling with pets in major public roads/streets	✓			
Chewing gum in public	✓			
Chewing gum in government offices		✓		
Combing hair in public (other than in toilets/restrooms)		✓		
Undressing/dressing in public			✓	
Wearing of dark glasses indoors in public places		✓		
Public display of wealth		✓		
Praying openly in public in non-designated areas			✓	
Walking bare feet in public	✓			
Chewing tobacco in public	✓			
Trimming one's finger or toe nails in public		✓		
Laughing aloud in public		✓		
Mingling of the sexes in public				
Mixed bathing in public swimming pools	✓			
Distributing religious pamphlets (literature) in public/side streets	✓			

ANGOLA

	Is customary Is allowed Is permissible Is used. Is OK	Is not customary Is frowned upon	Is disallowed Is forbidden Is a crime	(See last page for comments on items referenced here)
Dancing on side street		✓		
Nude bathing			✓	
Littering			✓	
Binge Drinking	✓			
Hitchhiking	✓			
Jaywalking	✓			
Drunk driving			✓	
Speeding		✓		
Skating on side streets (side-walk)		✓		
Graffiti painting	✓			
Pilfering			✓	
Prostitution		✓		
Haggling in the market place	✓			
Consumption of alcoholic beverages in bars and restaurants	✓			
Gambling		✓		
Possession of pornographic materials		✓		
Possession of the Christian Bible	✓			
Possession of the Moslem Koran	✓			
Possession of bullet-proof vest		✓		
Possession of toy gun	✓			
Possession of fire crackers and fireworks		✓		
Possession of prescription drugs (without doctor's note)	✓			
Possession of regulated drugs (narcotics)		✓		
Possession of firearms (by foreigners)		✓		
Possession of pocket knife in public	✓			
Using walkie talkies	✓			
Using of "boom boxes"(loud sounding stereo system)		✓		
Using "walkman" (very small radio/cassettes with ear plugs) in public places	✓			
Using "walkman" (very small radio/cassettes with ear plugs) while driving or riding			✓	

ANGOLA

	Is customary Is allowed Is permissible Is used Is OK	Is not customary Is frowned upon	Is disallowed Is forbidden Is a crime	(See last page for comments on items referenced here)
Use of cellular phone	✓			
Use of binoculars/periscopes other than in sports arena	✓			
Taking photographs of people (without their permission)	✓			
Taking photographs at airports, train and bus stations		✓		
Taking photographs of airports		✓		
Taking photographs of churches and synagogues	✓			
Taking photographs of religious statues	✓			
Taking photographs of public buildings	✓			
Taking photographs of bridges	✓			
Tipping (gratuity)	✓			
Tipping (when service is rendered)	✓			
Tipping (when service is not rendered)		✓		
Tipping waiters/waitresses at restaurants and hotels	✓			
Tipping taxi/cab drivers	✓			
Tipping baggage handlers, porters, door persons	✓			
Tipping of hair dressers/barbers	✓			
Overtipping	✓			
Undertipping			✓	
Spilling cigarette butt (ash) on side streets/on the floor			✓	
Men wearing lipstick		✓		
Wearing visible tattoo marks	✓			
Men painting/coloring their finger or toe nails		✓		
Cross dressing (men dressed like women & vice versa)		✓		
Walking in public without a shirt (i.e., with the upper half of the body naked)		✓		
Men wearing braided hair		✓		
Men wearing earrings		✓		
Men wearing dreadlock hair style				
Homosexuality		✓		
Lesbianism		✓		

ANGOLA

	Is customary Is allowed Is permissible Is used Is OK	Is not customary Is frowned upon	Is disallowed Is forbidden Is a crime	(See last page for comments on items referenced here)
Females covering their hair (wearing headgear) in public	✓			
Females exposing their full face in public	✓			
Females driving automobiles	✓			
Females riding motorcycles	✓			
Females riding bicycles	✓			
Females smoking in public	✓			
Women wearing bras (braziers) in public		✓		
Use of lipstick by women	✓			
A woman extending her hands first when introduced	✓			
Female bashing				
Females wearing trousers	✓			
Females wearing minis (short dresses)	✓			
Females wearing bikinis	✓			
Females wearing shorts	✓			
Persons of opposite sex holding hands in public	✓			
Persons of same sex holding hands in public	✓			
Handshake between opposite sex	✓			
Hugging in public by same sex	✓			
Hugging in public by opposite sex	✓			
Men and women walking side by side in public	✓			
Man walking ahead (in public), with the woman following	✓			
Woman walking ahead (in public), with the man following	✓			
Men opening doors for women	✓			
Sitting with legs crossed in the presence of elders		✓		
Talking to an elderly person with one's hat/cap on		✓		
Talking to an elderly person with hands positioned on both sides of one's waist	✓			
Blowing one's nose in public	✓			
Blowing one's nose in the presence of others	✓			
Addressing people by their title	✓			

DO'S AND DON'TS AROUND THE WORLD: A COUNTRY GUIDE TO CULTURAL AND SOCIAL TABOOS AND ETIQUETTE
ANGOLA

	Is customary / Is allowed / Is permissible / Is used. / Is OK	Is not customary / Is frowned upon	Is disallowed / Is forbidden / Is a crime	(See last page for comments on items referenced here)
Addressing people by their family name/surname/last name/given name	✓			
Addressing people by their first name/ given name	✓			
Women going through doors first	✓			
Men helping women with their coats		✓		
Men extending their hands to women first during greetings	✓			
Taking off one's hat when entering a private home			✓	
Removing one's shoes when entering a private home	✓			
Invited guests bringing food at social gatherings	✓			
Guests bringing drinks at social gatherings	✓			
Shaking hands when leaving a small group	✓			
Shaking hands with everyone present, upon arrival at a social gathering	✓			
Eating with the right hand	✓			
Eating with the left hand	✓			
Eating with both hands	✓			
Presenting a gift or passing on an object with the left hand		✓		
Asking a man about his wife	✓			
Asking a woman about her husband	✓			
Making prior appointments before a meeting or visit	✓			
Addressing an audience with one or both hands in the pocket		✓		
Carrying on conversation during meals	✓			
Females sitting with legs crossed	✓			
People discussing their wealth	✓			
Asking someone his or her age, or how old the person is	✓			
Complementing someone on his/her physical looks	✓			
Complementing someone on his/her attire	✓			
Use of both hands in handshake	✓			
In greeting, a handshake accompanied by a slight bow	✓			

14

ANGOLA

	Is customary Is allowed Is permissible Is used. Is OK	Is not customary Is frowned upon	Is disallowed Is forbidden Is a crime	(See last page for comments on items referenced here)
Salutations such as "Good morning", "good afternoon", "Good evening"	✓			
The completion of a business deal with a handshake	✓			
Starting a negotiation session with a handshake	✓			
A gift for the host/hostess	✓			
Giving a business gift	✓			
A gift of money (use of money as gift)	✓			
Use of flowers as a gift	✓			
Use of business cards	✓			
Accepting/presenting gifts with both hands	✓			
Burning of the country's flag			✓	
Mutilation of the national currency			✓	
Casual wearing of clothings made with colors & marks of the national flag	✓			
Wearing of look-alike military (camouflage) fatigues (attire)		✓		
Sitting on the floor (on floor mats)	✓			
Discussion of religion	✓			
Discussion of politics	✓			
Discussion of sex	✓			
Patting/slapping someone on the buttocks			✓	
Patting/slapping someone on the back		✓		
Touching or patting someone's head/hair		✓		
Casual touching of any part of someone's body	✓			
Drinking directly out of a bottle/can		✓		
Placing one's leg(s) on the table or chair		✓		

15

ANGOLA

	Is customary Is allowed Is permissible Is used. Is OK	Is not customary Is frowned upon	Is disallowed Is forbidden Is a crime	(See last page for comments on items referenced here)
Showing the sole of one's foot (feet)		✓		
People standing very close when talking		✓		
Maintaining steady eye contact (direct gaze) when talking to someone	✓			
Kissing or exchange of kisses on the cheek		✓		
Counting money (change) in someone's palm	✓			
Finger pointing in public (in a daring manner)		✓		
Seeking attention by winking the eyes		✓		
Tapping the head to indicate someone is crazy	✓			
Twirling the head to indicate someone is crazy	✓			
Whistling as a way of requesting something/seeking attention		✓		
Using "thumbs-up" sign to mean OK	✓			
Forming a circle with the thumb and index finger (forefinger) to mean OK	✓			
Using the fingers to make a "V" sign for victory	✓			
Beckoning to someone with the index finger (forefinger)	✓			
The left to right waving of the hand with open palms facing outward to indicate "Good bye"	✓			
The use of a nod to show acknowledgement	✓			
Stopping/beckoning a taxi using a stretched hand with the thumb pointing upward	✓			
Using the thumb finger pointed to a direction, to request a ride or a hike		✓		
Raising one's hand/waving with an open fist to summon a taxi	✓			
Tapping one's foot/feet on the floor in a public gathering		✓		
Wiggling one's leg(s) when in a sitting position	✓			
Use of the hand (by motorists and cyclists) to signal direction of traffic	✓			

16

ANGOLA

		(See last page for comments on items referenced here)
Foreign tourists are welcome in the country.	yes	
The use of seat belt is mandatory.	yes	
International driving license is accepted.	yes	
Foreign drivers license is accepted.	yes	
It is considered impolite to yawn in public.	yes	
Death penalty for drug trafficking is the law.	no	
Life imprisonment for drug trafficking is the law.	n/a	
Guilty until proven innocent in court is the law.	no	
Innocent until proven guilty in court is the law.	yes	
Pedestrians always have right of way.	no	
Exit visas are required of visitors.	yes	
Crash helmet is mandatory for motor cyclist.	yes	
Hanging is used as a form of legal punishment.	yes	
Decapitation of a limb is used as a form of punishment.	no	
Caning is used as a form of legal punishment.	no	
Electric shock is used as a form of legal punishment.	no	
One is expected to stand up during the playing of the national anthem.	yes	
Crash helmet is mandatory for bicyclists.	yes	
Guests are expected to eat every thing on their plates.	no	
Table manners are very informal.	no	
One is expected to cover one's mouth when laughing.	no	
A vertical nod of the head means YES (OK).	yes	
A horizontal shaking of the head means NO (Not OK).	yes	
Prostitution is allowed only in designated areas.	n/a	
One is expected to take off one's hat during playing of national anthem.	yes	
Separate seating arrangements (between sexes) are maintained at movies.	no	
Separate seating arrangements (between sexes) are maintained at churches.	no	
Uninvited visitors or guests may not be welcome, even among acquaintances.	yes	
Pets (e.g. cats, dog) are allowed in some hotels and restaurants.	yes	
Couples invited for a meal may be separated during meals according to their sex.	no	
Punctuality is the order of business.	yes	
Automobiles are driven with headlights always turned on.	no	
Motorcycles are driven with headlights always turned on.	no	
Visitors with expired visa face mandatory jail time.	yes	
Visitors without exit visa face jail time.	yes	
Visitors without entry visa face mandatory (automatic) jail time.	yes	

ADDITIONAL COUNTRY INFORMATION

(A)	The types of gifts to avoid:	n/a
(B)	Appropriate gifts for a foreigner to give:	depends
(C)	Best time to present gifts (at the beginning or at the end of a visit?):	at the beginning
(D)	Best time to present gifts (on initial or later visits?):	initial
(E)	Best place to present gifts (in private or in public?):	anywhere
(F)	Number(s) with certain connotations and/or myths attached to them:	n/a
(G)	Basic shape(s) with negative connotations:	n/a
(H)	Basic color(s) with negative connotations:	n/a
(I)	Traditional greeting methods include:	handshake
(J)	Safe topics for discussion include:	weather, fashion, travel, art, family, religon, domestic politics, food, sports, international politics, social conditions, money and perosnal wealth, sex
(K)	Best time for conversations (before, during, after meals?):	during meals
(L)	Forms of legal punishment:	jailing
(M)	Approximately length of time one could be detained by law and order authorities before being charged in court:	48 hours
(N)	January 15, 1999, for example, will normally be written as:	15/1/99
(O)	Emergency code number:	113 or 391479
(P)	Ambulance code Number:	336346-383362
(Q)	Police code number:	113 or 391479
(R)	Telephone (country) code:	224
(S)	Telex (country) code:	224
(T)	Electricity requirements:	220v
(U)	Legal drinking age:	18
(V)	Systems of weights and measures:	kg and metrics
(W)	Legal age of incarceration:	18
(X)	Driving side of the road:	right
(Y)	Minimum expenditure expected of foreign visitors? $	n/a
(Z)	Name of currency:	Kwanza
(Za)	Some places off-limits to foreign visitors:	n/a
(Zb)	Some places, structures and items prohibited from being photographed:	military objectives

REPUBLIC OF BENIN	Is customary Is allowed Is permissible Is used. Is OK	Is not customary Is frowned upon	Is disallowed Is forbidden Is a crime	(See last page for comments on items referenced here)
Smoking in public	✓			
Eating in public	✓			
Not flushing public toilet				n/a
Spitting in public	✓			
Feeding animals & birds in public	✓			
Whistling in public				n/a
Drinking alcohol in public	✓			
Kissing in public		✓		
Breast feeding in public	✓			
Drunkenness (in public)	✓			
Cursing in public	✓			
Religious preaching in public	✓			
Begging (panhandling) in public	✓			
Giving money to beggars/panhandlers	✓			
Giving food/drink to beggars/panhandlers	✓			
Brushing teeth in public (other than in restrooms)	✓			
Strolling with pets in major public roads/streets		✓		
Chewing gum in public	✓			
Chewing gum in government offices	✓			
Combing hair in public (other than in toilets/restrooms)		✓		
Undressing/dressing in public		✓		
Wearing of dark glasses indoors in public places	✓			
Public display of wealth				n/a
Praying openly in public in non-designated areas	✓			
Walking bare feet in public	✓			
Chewing tobacco in public	✓			
Trimming one's finger or toe nails in public	✓			
Laughing aloud in public	✓			
Mingling of the sexes in public				n/a
Mixed bathing in public swimming pools				n/a
Distributing religious pamphlets (literature) in public/side streets				n/a

BENIN

	Is customary Is allowed Is permissible Is used. Is OK	Is not customary Is frowned upon	Is disallowed Is forbidden Is a crime	(See last page for comments on items referenced here)
Dancing on side street	✓			
Nude bathing				n/a
Littering	✓			
Binge Drinking				n/a
Hitchhiking	✓			
Jaywalking				n/a
Drunk driving			✓	
Speeding			✓	
Skating on side streets (side-walk)		✓		
Graffiti painting	✓			
Pilfering				n/a
Prostitution			✓	
Haggling in the market place				n/a
Consumption of alcoholic beverages in bars and restaurants				n/a
Gambling		✓		
Possession of pornographic materials				n/a
Possession of the Christian Bible	✓			
Possession of the Moslem Koran	✓			
Possession of bullet-proof vest		✓		
Possession of toy gun	✓			
Possession of fire crackers and fireworks		✓		
Possession of prescription drugs (without doctor's note)	✓			
Possession of regulated drugs (narcotics)		✓		
Possession of firearms (by foreigners)		✓		
Possession of pocket knife in public		✓		
Using walkie talkies		✓		
Using of "boom boxes"(loud sounding stereo system)		✓		
Using "walkman" (very small radio/cassettes with ear plugs) in public places	✓			
Using "walkman" (very small radio/cassettes with ear plugs) while driving or riding				n/a

BENIN

	Is customary Is allowed Is permissible Is used Is OK	Is not customary Is frowned upon	Is disallowed Is forbidden Is a crime	(See last page for comments on items referenced here)
Use of cellular phone		✓		
Use of binoculars/periscopes other than in sports arena		✓		
Taking photographs of people (without their permission)	✓			
Taking photographs at airports, train and bus stations		✓		
Taking photographs of airports		✓		
Taking photographs of churches and synagogues		✓		
Taking photographs of religious statues				n/a
Taking photographs of public buildings				n/a
Taking photographs of bridges				n/a
Tipping (gratuity)	✓			
Tipping (when service is rendered)	✓			
Tipping (when service is not rendered)	✓			
Tipping waiters/waitresses at restaurants and hotels				n/a
Tipping taxi/cab drivers				n/a
Tipping baggage handlers, porters, door persons				n/a
Tipping of hair dressers/barbers				n/a
Overtipping	✓			
Undertipping	✓			
Spilling cigarette butt (ash) on side streets/on the floor	✓			
Men wearing lipstick		✓		
Wearing visible tattoo marks	✓			
Men painting/coloring their finger or toe nails				n/a
Cross dressing (men dressed like women & vice versa)		✓		
Walking in public without a shirt (i.e., with the upper half of the body naked)				n/a
Men wearing braided hair				n/a
Men wearing earrings				n/a
Men wearing dreadlock hair style				n/a
Homosexuality				n/a
Lesbianism				n/a

21

BENIN

	Is customary Is allowed Is permissible Is used Is OK	Is not customary Is frowned upon	Is disallowed Is forbidden Is a crime	(See last page for comments on items referenced here)
Females covering their hair (wearing headgear) in public	✓			
Females exposing their full face in public	✓			
Females driving automobiles	✓			
Females riding motorcycles	✓			
Females riding bicycles	✓			
Females smoking in public				n/a
Women wearing bras (braziers) in public	✓			
Use of lipstick by women	✓			
A woman extending her hands first when introduced	✓			
Female bashing				n/a
Females wearing trousers	✓			
Females wearing minis (short dresses)	✓			
Females wearing bikinis	✓			
Females wearing shorts				n/a
Persons of opposite sex holding hands in public	✓			
Persons of same sex holding hands in public		✓		
Handshake between opposite sex				n/a
Hugging in public by same sex		✓		
Hugging in public by opposite sex	✓			
Men and women walking side by side in public				n/a
Man walking ahead (in public), with the woman following				n/a
Woman walking ahead (in public), with the man following				n/a
Men opening doors for women				n/a
Sitting with legs crossed in the presence of elders			✓	
Talking to an elderly person with one's hat/cap on				n/a
Talking to an elderly person with hands positioned on both sides of one's waist				n/a
Blowing one's nose in public		✓		
Blowing one's nose in the presence of others		✓		
Addressing people by their title	✓			1

22

BENIN

	Is customary Is allowed Is permissible Is used. Is OK	Is not customary Is frowned upon	Is disallowed Is forbidden Is a crime	(See last page for comments on items referenced here)
Addressing people by their family name/surname/last name/given name	✓			
Addressing people by their first name/ given name	✓			
Women going through doors first		✓		
Men helping women with their coats				2
Men extending their hands to women first during greetings	✓			
Taking off one's hat when entering a private home	✓			
Removing one's shoes when entering a private home				n/a
Invited guests bringing food at social gatherings	✓			3
Guests bringing drinks at social gatherings	✓			3
Shaking hands when leaving a small group	✓			
Shaking hands with everyone present, upon arrival at a social gathering	✓			
Eating with the right hand	✓			
Eating with the left hand		✓		
Eating with both hands		✓		
Presenting a gift or passing on an object with the left hand		✓		
Asking a man about his wife	✓			
Asking a woman about her husband	✓			
Making prior appointments before a meeting or visit				n/a
Addressing an audience with one or both hands in the pocket	✓			
Carrying on conversation during meals				n/a
Females sitting with legs crossed				n/a
People discussing their wealth				n/a
Asking someone his or her age, or how old the person is				n/a
Complementing someone on his/her physical looks				n/a
Complementing someone on his/her attire				n/a
Use of both hands in handshake	✓			
In greeting, a handshake accompanied by a slight bow	✓			

23

BENIN

	Is customary Is allowed Is permissible Is used. Is OK	Is not customary Is frowned upon	Is disallowed Is forbidden Is a crime	(See last page for comments on items referenced here)
Salutations such as "Good morning", "good afternoon", "Good evening"	✓			
The completion of a business deal with a handshake				n/a
Starting a negotiation session with a handshake				n/a
A gift for the host/hostess	✓			
Giving a business gift				4
A gift of money (use of money as gift)	✓			
Use of flowers as a gift				5
Use of business cards	✓			
Accepting/presenting gifts with both hands	✓			
Burning of the country's flag			✓	
Mutilation of the national currency		✓		
Casual wearing of clothings made with colors & marks of the national flag				n/a
Wearing of look-alike military (camouflage) fatigues (attire)		✓		
Sitting on the floor (on floor mats)		✓		
Discussion of religion	✓			
Discussion of politics	✓			
Discussion of sex	✓			
Patting/slapping someone on the buttocks				n/a
Patting/slapping someone on the back				n/a
Touching or patting someone's head/hair				n/a
Casual touching of any part of someone's body				n/a
Drinking directly out of a bottle/can	✓			
Placing one's leg(s) on the table or chair		✓		

BENIN

	Is customary Is allowed Is permissible Is used. Is OK	Is not customary Is frowned upon	Is disallowed Is forbidden Is a crime	(See last page for comments on items referenced here)
Showing the sole of one's foot (feet)				n/a
People standing very close when talking	✓			
Maintaining steady eye contact (direct gaze) when talking to someone	✓			
Kissing or exchange of kisses on the cheek	✓			
Counting money (change) in someone's palm				n/a
Finger pointing in public (in a daring manner)	✓			
Seeking attention by winking the eyes				n/a
Tapping the head to indicate someone is crazy				n/a
Twirling the head to indicate someone is crazy				n/a
Whistling as a way of requesting something/seeking attention				n/a
Using "thumbs-up" sign to mean OK				n/a
Forming a circle with the thumb and index finger (forefinger) to mean OK				n/a
Using the fingers to make a "V" sign for victory				n/a
Beckoning to someone with the index finger (forefinger)				n/a
The left to right waving of the hand with open palms facing outward to indicate "Good bye"				n/a
The use of a nod to show acknowledgement				n/a
Stopping/beckoning a taxi using a stretched hand with the thumb pointing upward				n/a
Using the thumb finger pointed to a direction, to request a ride or a hike				n/a
Raising one's hand/waving with an open fist to summon a taxi				n/a
Tapping one's foot/feet on the floor in a public gathering				n/a
Wiggling one's leg(s) when in a sitting position				n/a
Use of the hand (by motorists and cyclists) to signal direction of traffic				n/a

25

		(See last page for comments on items referenced here)
Foreign tourists are welcome in the country.	yes	
The use of seat belt is mandatory.	no	
International driving license is accepted.	yes	
Foreign drivers license is accepted.	yes	
It is considered impolite to yawn in public.	n/a	
Death penalty for drug trafficking is the law.	yes	
Life imprisonment for drug trafficking is the law.	no	
Guilty until proven innocent in court is the law.	yes	
Innocent until proven guilty in court is the law.	yes	
Pedestrians always have right of way.	yes	
Exit visas are required of visitors.	yes	
Crash helmet is mandatory for motor cyclist.	yes	
Hanging is used as a form of legal punishment.	n/a	
Decapitation of a limb is used as a form of punishment.	n/a	
Caning is used as a form of legal punishment.	n/a	
Electric shock is used as a form of legal punishment.	n/a	
One is expected to stand up during the playing of the national anthem.	yes	
Crash helmet is mandatory for bicyclists.	yes	
Guests are expected to eat every thing on their plates.	yes	
Table manners are very informal.	no	
One is expected to cover one's mouth when laughing.	no	
A vertical nod of the head means YES (OK).	yes	
A horizontal shaking of the head means NO (not OK).	yes	
Prostitution is allowed only in designated areas.	no	
One is expected to take off one's hat during playing of national anthem.	yes	
Separate seating arrangements (between sexes) are maintained at movies.	no	
Separate seating arrangements (between sexes) are maintained at churches.	no	
Uninvited visitors or guests may not be welcome, even among acquaintances.	no	
Pets (e.g. cats, dog) are allowed in some hotels and restaurants.	n/a	
Couples invited for a meal may be separated during meals according to their sex.	yes	
Punctuality is the order of business.	no	
Automobiles are driven with headlights always turned on.	n/a	
Motorcycles are driven with headlights always turned on.	n/a	
Visitors with expired visa face mandatory jail time.	no	
Visitors without exit visa face jail time.	no	
Visitors without entry visa face mandatory (automatic) jail time.	n/a	

ADDITIONAL COUNTRY INFORMATION

(A)	The types of gifts to avoid:	n/a
(B)	Appropriate gifts for a foreigner to give:	money
(C)	Best time to present gifts (at the beginning or at the end of a visit?):	beginning
(D)	Best time to present gifts (on initial or later visits?):	n/a
(E)	Best place to present gifts (in private or in public?):	n/a
(F)	Number(s) with certain connotations and/or myths attached to them:	n/a
(G)	Basic shape(s) with negative connotations:	n/a
(H)	Basic color(s) with negative connotations:	n/a
(I)	Traditional greeting methods include:	n/a
(J)	Safe topics for discussion include:	all topics, including wealth, sex, social conditions and domestic politics
(K)	Best time for conversations (before, during, after meals?):	n./a
(L)	Forms of legal punishment:	jailing
(M)	Approximately length of time one could be detained by law and order authorities before being charged in court:	n/a
(N)	January 15, 1999, for example, will normally be written as:	15/1/95
(O)	Emergency code number:	n/a
(P)	Ambulance code Number:	n/a
(Q)	Police code number:	n/a
(R)	Telephone (country) code:	n/a
(S)	Telex (country) code:	n/a
(T)	Electricity requirements:	n/a
(U)	Legal drinking age:	n/a
(V)	Systems of weights and measures:	n/a
(W)	Legal age of incarceration:	n/a
(X)	Driving side of the road:	right
(Y)	Minimum expenditure expected of foreign visitors? $	n/a
(Z)	Name of currency:	CFA Franc
(Za)	Some places off-limits to foreign visitors:	n/a
(Zb)	Some places, structures and items prohibited from being photographed:	n/a

ENDNOTES

Item Number: *COMMENTS/EXPLANATIONS*

n/a: Not applicable/Not available/No response

(1)   Sometimes

(2)   No coats in Benin

(3)   But not always

(4)   Yes and No

(5)   OK, but not common and not everywhere

BOTSWANA	Is customary Is allowed Is permissible Is used. Is OK	Is not customary Is frowned upon	Is disallowed Is forbidden Is a crime	(See last page for comments on items referenced here)
Smoking in public	✓			
Eating in public	✓			
Not flushing public toilet		✓		
Spitting in public		✓		
Feeding animals & birds in public	✓			
Whistling in public	✓			
Drinking alcohol in public			✓	
Kissing in public	✓			
Breast feeding in public	✓			
Drunkenness (in public)		✓		
Cursing in public		✓		
Religious preaching in public	✓			
Begging (panhandling) in public		✓		
Giving money to beggars/panhandlers	✓			
Giving food/drink to beggars/panhandlers	✓			
Brushing teeth in public (other than in restrooms)		✓		
Strolling with pets in major public roads/streets	✓			
Chewing gum in public	✓			
Chewing gum in government offices		✓		
Combing hair in public (other than in toilets/restrooms)		✓		
Undressing/dressing in public		✓		
Wearing of dark glasses indoors in public places	✓			
Public display of wealth		✓		
Praying openly in public in non-designated areas	✓			
Walking bare feet in public	✓			
Chewing tobacco in public	✓			
Trimming one's finger or toe nails in public	✓			
Laughing aloud in public	✓			
Mingling of the sexes in public				n/a
Mixed bathing in public swimming pools				n/a
Distributing religious pamphlets (literature) in public/side streets				n/a

BOTSWANA

	Is customary Is allowed Is permissible Is used. Is OK	Is not customary Is frowned upon	Is disallowed Is forbidden Is a crime	(See last page for comments on items referenced here)
Dancing on side street	✓			
Nude bathing		✓		
Littering			✓	
Binge Drinking				n/a
Hitchhiking	✓			
Jaywalking		✓		
Drunk driving			✓	
Speeding			✓	
Skating on side streets (side-walk)	✓			
Graffiti painting			✓	
Pilfering				n/a
Prostitution			✓	
Haggling in the market place				n/a
Consumption of alcoholic beverages in bars and restaurants	✓			
Gambling			✓	
Possession of pornographic materials			✓	
Possession of the Christian Bible	✓			
Possession of the Moslem Koran	✓			
Possession of bullet-proof vest	✓			
Possession of toy gun	✓			
Possession of fire crackers and fireworks	✓			
Possession of prescription drugs (without doctor's note)	✓			
Possession of regulated drugs (narcotics)			✓	
Possession of firearms (by foreigners)	✓			
Possession of pocket knife in public	✓			
Using walkie talkies	✓			
Using of "boom boxes"(loud sounding stereo system)	✓			
Using "walkman" (very small radio/cassettes with ear plugs) in public places	✓			
Using "walkman" (very small radio/cassettes with ear plugs) while driving or riding	✓			

BOTSWANA

	Is customary Is allowed Is permissible Is used Is OK	Is not customary Is frowned upon	Is disallowed Is forbidden Is a crime	(See last page for comments on items referenced here)
Use of cellular phone	✓			
Use of binoculars/periscopes other than in sports arena	✓			
Taking photographs of people (without their permission)	✓			
Taking photographs at airports, train and bus stations	✓			
Taking photographs of airports	✓			
Taking photographs of churches and synagogues	✓			
Taking photographs of religious statues	✓			
Taking photographs of public buildings				n/a
Taking photographs of bridges				n/a
Tipping (gratuity)	✓			
Tipping (when service is rendered)	✓			
Tipping (when service is not rendered)		✓		
Tipping waiters/waitresses at restaurants and hotels	✓			
Tipping taxi/cab drivers	✓			
Tipping baggage handlers, porters, door persons	✓			
Tipping of hair dressers/barbers	✓			
Overtipping	✓			
Undertipping	✓			
Spilling cigarette butt (ash) on side streets/on the floor		✓		
Men wearing lipstick		✓		
Wearing visible tattoo marks		✓		
Men painting/coloring their finger or toe nails		✓		
Cross dressing (men dressed like women & vice versa)		✓		
Walking in public without a shirt (i.e., with the upper half of the body naked)	✓			
Men wearing braided hair		✓		
Men wearing earrings		✓		
Men wearing dreadlock hair style	✓			
Homosexuality			✓	
Lesbianism			✓	

31

BOTSWANA

	Is customary Is allowed Is permissible Is used Is OK	Is not customary Is frowned upon	Is disallowed Is forbidden Is a crime	(See last page for comments on items referenced here)
Females covering their hair (wearing headgear) in public	✓			
Females exposing their full face in public	✓			
Females driving automobiles	✓			
Females riding motorcycles	✓			
Females riding bicycles	✓			
Females smoking in public		✓		
Women wearing bras (braziers) in public		✓		
Use of lipstick by women	✓			
A woman extending her hands first when introduced	✓			
Female bashing			✓	
Females wearing trousers	✓			
Females wearing minis (short dresses)	✓			
Females wearing bikinis	✓			
Females wearing shorts	✓			
Persons of opposite sex holding hands in public	✓			
Persons of same sex holding hands in public	✓			
Handshake between opposite sex	✓			
Hugging in public by same sex	✓			
Hugging in public by opposite sex	✓			
Men and women walking side by side in public	✓			
Man walking ahead (in public), with the woman following	✓			
Woman walking ahead (in public), with the man following	✓			
Men opening doors for women	✓			
Sitting with legs crossed in the presence of elders	✓			
Talking to an elderly person with one's hat/cap on		✓		
Talking to an elderly person with hands positioned on both sides of one's waist		✓		
Blowing one's nose in public		✓		
Blowing one's nose in the presence of others		✓		
Addressing people by their title	✓			

32

BOTSWANA

	Is customary Is allowed Is permissible Is used. Is OK	Is not customary Is frowned upon	Is disallowed Is forbidden Is a crime	(See last page for comments on items referenced here)
Addressing people by their family name/surname/last name/given name	✓			
Addressing people by their first name/ given name	✓			
Women going through doors first	✓			
Men helping women with their coats	✓			
Men extending their hands to women first during greetings	✓			
Taking off one's hat when entering a private home	✓			
Removing one's shoes when entering a private home	✓			
Invited guests bringing food at social gatherings	✓			
Guests bringing drinks at social gatherings	✓			
Shaking hands when leaving a small group	✓			
Shaking hands with everyone present, upon arrival at a social gathering	✓			
Eating with the right hand	✓			
Eating with the left hand		✓		
Eating with both hands		✓		
Presenting a gift or passing on an object with the left hand		✓		
Asking a man about his wife	✓			
Asking a woman about her husband	✓			
Making prior appointments before a meeting or visit		✓		
Addressing an audience with one or both hands in the pocket		✓		
Carrying on conversation during meals	✓			
Females sitting with legs crossed	✓			
People discussing their wealth	✓			
Asking someone his or her age, or how old the person is	✓			
Complementing someone on his/her physical looks	✓			
Complementing someone on his/her attire	✓			
Use of both hands in handshake	✓			
In greeting, a handshake accompanied by a slight bow	✓			

33

BOTSWANA

	Is customary Is allowed Is permissible Is used. Is OK	Is not customary Is frowned upon	Is disallowed Is forbidden Is a crime	(See last page for comments on items referenced here)
Salutations such as "Good morning", "good afternoon", "Good evening"	✓			
The completion of a business deal with a handshake	✓			
Starting a negotiation session with a handshake	✓			
A gift for the host/hostess	✓			
Giving a business gift	✓			
A gift of money (use of money as gift)	✓			
Use of flowers as a gift	✓			
Use of business cards	✓			
Accepting/presenting gifts with both hands	✓			
Burning of the country's flag			✓	
Mutilation of the national currency			✓	
Casual wearing of clothings made with colors & marks of the national flag	✓			
Wearing of look-alike military (camouflage) fatigues (attire)	✓			
Sitting on the floor (on floor mats)	✓			
Discussion of religion	✓			
Discussion of politics	✓			
Discussion of sex		✓		
Patting/slapping someone on the buttocks	✓			
Patting/slapping someone on the back	✓			
Touching or patting someone's head/hair	✓			
Casual touching of any part of someone's body	✓			
Drinking directly out of a bottle/can	✓			
Placing one's leg(s) on the table or chair		✓		

BOTSWANA

	Is customary Is allowed Is permissible Is used. Is OK	Is not customary Is frowned upon	Is disallowed Is forbidden Is a crime	(See last page for comments on items referenced here)
Showing the sole of one's foot (feet)		✓		
People standing very close when talking	✓			
Maintaining steady eye contact (direct gaze) when talking to someone	✓			
Kissing or exchange of kisses on the cheek	✓			
Counting money (change) in someone's palm	✓			
Finger pointing in public (in a daring manner)		✓		
Seeking attention by winking the eyes	✓			
Tapping the head to indicate someone is crazy	✓			
Twirling the head to indicate someone is crazy	✓			
Whistling as a way of requesting something/seeking attention	✓			
Using "thumbs-up" sign to mean OK	✓			
Forming a circle with the thumb and index finger (forefinger) to mean OK	✓			
Using the fingers to make a "V" sign for victory	✓			
Beckoning to someone with the index finger (forefinger)	✓			
The left to right waving of the hand with open palms facing outward to indicate "Good bye"	✓			
The use of a nod to show acknowledgement	✓			
Stopping/beckoning a taxi using a stretched hand with the thumb pointing upward	✓			
Using the thumb finger pointed to a direction, to request a ride or a hike	✓			
Raising one's hand/waving with an open fist to summon a taxi	✓			
Tapping one's foot/feet on the floor in a public gathering	✓			
Wiggling one's leg(s) when in a sitting position		✓		
Use of the hand (by motorists and cyclists) to signal direction of traffic	✓			

35

		(See last page for comments on items referenced here)
Foreign tourists are welcome in the country.	yes	
The use of seat belt is mandatory.	yes	
International driving license is accepted.	yes	
Foreign drivers license is accepted.	yes	
It is considered impolite to yawn in public.	no	
Death penalty for drug trafficking is the law.	no	
Life imprisonment for drug trafficking is the law.	no	
Guilty until proven innocent in court is the law.	no	
Innocent until proven guilty in court is the law.	yes	
Pedestrians always have right of way.	no	
Exit visas are required of visitors.	no	
Crash helmet is mandatory for motor cyclist.	yes	
Hanging is used as a form of legal punishment.	yes	
Decapitation of a limb is used as a form of punishment.	no	
Caning is used as a form of legal punishment.	yes	
Electric shock is used as a form of legal punishment.	no	
One is expected to stand up during the playing of the national anthem.	yes	
Crash helmet is mandatory for bicyclists.	no	
Guests are expected to eat every thing on their plates.	no	
Table manners are very informal.	yes	
One is expected to cover one's mouth when laughing.	yes	
A vertical nod of the head means YES (OK).	no	
A horizontal shaking of the head means NO (Not OK).	yes	
Prostitution is allowed only in designated areas.	no	
One is expected to take off one's hat during playing of national anthem.	yes	
Separate seating arrangements (between sexes) are maintained at movies.	no	
Separate seating arrangements (between sexes) are maintained at churches.	no	
Uninvited visitors or guests may not be welcome, even among acquaintances.	no	
Pets (e.g. cats, dog) are allowed in some hotels and restaurants.	yes	
Couples invited for a meal may be separated during meals according to their sex.	no	
Punctuality is the order of business.	yes	
Automobiles are driven with headlights always turned on.	no	
Motorcycles are driven with headlights always turned on.	yes	
Visitors with expired visa face mandatory jail time.	no	
Visitors without exit visa face jail time.	no	
Visitors without entry visa face mandatory (automatic) jail time.	no	

ADDITIONAL COUNTRY INFORMATION

(A)	The types of gifts to avoid:	n/a
(B)	Appropriate gifts for a foreigner to give:	anything that is foreign is acceptable.
(C)	Best time to present gifts (at the beginning or at the end of a visit?):	n/a
(D)	Best time to present gifts (on initial or later visits?):	anytime
(E)	Best place to present gifts (in private or in public?):	any place
(F)	Number(s) with certain connotations and/or myths attached to them:	n/a
(G)	Basic shape(s) with negative connotations:	n/a
(H)	Basic color(s) with negative connotations:	n/a
(I)	Traditional greeting methods include:	shaking hands
(J)	Safe topics for discussion include:	weather, fashion, travel, art, family, religion, domestic politics.
(K)	Best time for conversations (before, during, after meals?):	n/a
(L)	Forms of legal punishment:	jailing, flogging, canning, hanging.
(M)	Approximately length of time one could be detained by law and order authorities before being charged in court:	24 hours
(N)	January 15, 1999, for example, will normally be written as:	15/1/99
(O)	Emergency code number:	999
(P)	Ambulance code Number:	999
(Q)	Police code number:	999
(R)	Telephone (country) code:	267
(S)	Telex (country) code:	267
(T)	Electricity requirements:	220/240 volts
(U)	Legal drinking age:	18 years
(V)	Systems of weights and measures:	metric systems
(W)	Legal age of incarceration:	18 years
(X)	Driving side of the road:	left
(Y)	Minimum expenditure expected of foreign visitors? $	yes
(Z)	Name of currency:	Pula
(Za)	Some places off-limits to foreign visitors:	n/a
(Zb)	Some places, structures and items prohibited from being photographed:	n/a

BURKINA FASO	Is customary Is allowed Is permissible Is used. Is OK	Is not customary Is frowned upon	Is disallowed Is forbidden Is a crime	(See last page for comments on items referenced here)
Smoking in public	✓			
Eating in public	✓			
Not flushing public toilet			✓	
Spitting in public		✓		
Feeding animals & birds in public	✓			
Whistling in public		✓		
Drinking alcohol in public	✓			
Kissing in public	✓			
Breast feeding in public	✓			
Drunkenness (in public)			✓	
Cursing in public			✓	
Religious preaching in public	✓			
Begging (panhandling) in public	✓			
Giving money to beggars/panhandlers	✓			
Giving food/drink to beggars/panhandlers	✓			
Brushing teeth in public (other than in restrooms)		✓		
Strolling with pets in major public roads/streets			✓	
Chewing gum in public	✓			
Chewing gum in government offices	✓			
Combing hair in public (other than in toilets/restrooms)		✓		
Undressing/dressing in public			✓	
Wearing of dark glasses indoors in public places	✓			
Public display of wealth		✓		
Praying openly in public in non-designated areas		✓		
Walking bare feet in public		✓		
Chewing tobacco in public	✓			
Trimming one's finger or toe nails in public		✓		
Laughing aloud in public	✓			
Mingling of the sexes in public	✓			
Mixed bathing in public swimming pools	✓			
Distributing religious pamphlets (literature) in public/side streets	✓			

BURKINA FASO

	Is customary Is allowed Is permissible Is used. Is OK	Is not customary Is frowned upon	Is disallowed Is forbidden Is a crime	(See last page for comments on items referenced here)
Dancing on side street	✓			
Nude bathing			✓	
Littering			✓	
Binge Drinking			✓	
Hitchhiking	✓			
Jaywalking		✓		
Drunk driving			✓	
Speeding			✓	
Skating on side streets (side-walk)	✓			
Graffiti painting			✓	
Pilfering	✓			
Prostitution			✓	
Haggling in the market place	✓			
Consumption of alcoholic beverages in bars and restaurants	✓			
Gambling	✓			
Possession of pornographic materials	✓			
Possession of the Christian Bible	✓			
Possession of the Moslem Koran	✓			
Possession of bullet-proof vest			✓	
Possession of toy gun		✓		
Possession of fire crackers and fireworks		✓		
Possession of prescription drugs (without doctor's note)	✓			
Possession of regulated drugs (narcotics)			✓	
Possession of firearms (by foreigners)			✓	
Possession of pocket knife in public			✓	
Using walkie talkies		✓		
Using of "boom boxes"(loud sounding stereo system)		✓		
Using "walkman" (very small radio/cassettes with ear plugs) in public places	✓			
Using "walkman" (very small radio/cassettes with ear plugs) while driving or riding	✓			

BURKINA FASO

	Is customary Is allowed Is permissible Is used Is OK	Is not customary Is frowned upon	Is disallowed Is forbidden Is a crime	(See last page for comments on items referenced here)
Use of cellular phone	✓			
Use of binoculars/periscopes other than in sports arena		✓		
Taking photographs of people (without their permission)	✓			
Taking photographs at airports, train and bus stations			✓	
Taking photographs of airports			✓	
Taking photographs of churches and synagogues	✓			
Taking photographs of religious statues	✓			
Taking photographs of public buildings			✓	
Taking photographs of bridges	✓			
Tipping (gratuity)	✓			
Tipping (when service is rendered)	✓			
Tipping (when service is not rendered)	✓			
Tipping waiters/waitresses at restaurants and hotels	✓			
Tipping taxi/cab drivers	✓			
Tipping baggage handlers, porters, door persons	✓			
Tipping of hair dressers/barbers	✓			
Overtipping	✓			
Undertipping	✓			
Spilling cigarette butt (ash) on side streets/on the floor			✓	
Men wearing lipstick		✓		
Wearing visible tattoo marks	✓			
Men painting/coloring their finger or toe nails		✓		
Cross dressing (men dressed like women & vice versa)		✓		
Walking in public without a shirt (i.e., with the upper half of the body naked)	✓			
Men wearing braided hair		✓		
Men wearing earrings		✓		
Men wearing dreadlock hair style		✓		
Homosexuality			✓	
Lesbianism			✓	

40

BURKINA FASO

	Is customary Is allowed Is permissible Is used Is OK	Is not customary Is frowned upon	Is disallowed Is forbidden Is a crime	(See last page for comments on items referenced here)
Females covering their hair (wearing headgear) in public	✓			
Females exposing their full face in public	✓			
Females driving automobiles	✓			
Females riding motorcycles	✓			
Females riding bicycles	✓			
Females smoking in public	✓			
Women wearing bras (braziers) in public		✓		
Use of lipstick by women	✓			
A woman extending her hands first when introduced		✓		
Female bashing		✓		
Females wearing trousers		✓		
Females wearing minis (short dresses)		✓		
Females wearing bikinis		✓		
Females wearing shorts	✓			
Persons of opposite sex holding hands in public	✓			
Persons of same sex holding hands in public	✓			
Handshake between opposite sex	✓			
Hugging in public by same sex	✓			
Hugging in public by opposite sex	✓			
Men and women walking side by side in public	✓			
Man walking ahead (in public), with the woman following	✓			
Woman walking ahead (in public), with the man following	✓			
Men opening doors for women	✓			
Sitting with legs crossed in the presence of elders	✓			
Talking to an elderly person with one's hat/cap on	✓			
Talking to an elderly person with hands positioned on both sides of one's waist		✓		
Blowing one's nose in public	✓			
Blowing one's nose in the presence of others	✓			
Addressing people by their title		✓		

BURKINA FASO

	Is customary Is allowed Is permissible Is used. Is OK	Is not customary Is frowned upon	Is disallowed Is forbidden Is a crime	(See last page for comments on items referenced here)
Addressing people by their family name/surname/last name/given name	✓			
Addressing people by their first name/ given name	✓			
Women going through doors first		✓		
Men helping women with their coats		✓		
Men extending their hands to women first during greetings	✓			
Taking off one's hat when entering a private home		✓		
Removing one's shoes when entering a private home		✓		
Invited guests bringing food at social gatherings		✓		
Guests bringing drinks at social gatherings		✓		
Shaking hands when leaving a small group	✓			
Shaking hands with everyone present, upon arrival at a social gathering	✓			
Eating with the right hand	✓			
Eating with the left hand		✓		
Eating with both hands		✓		
Presenting a gift or passing on an object with the left hand		✓		
Asking a man about his wife	✓			
Asking a woman about her husband	✓			
Making prior appointments before a meeting or visit		✓		
Addressing an audience with one or both hands in the pocket		✓		
Carrying on conversation during meals	✓			
Females sitting with legs crossed	✓			
People discussing their wealth		✓		
Asking someone his or her age, or how old the person is		✓		
Complementing someone on his/her physical looks	✓			
Complementing someone on his/her attire	✓			
Use of both hands in handshake	✓			
In greeting, a handshake accompanied by a slight bow	✓			

42

BURKINA FASO

	Is customary Is allowed Is permissible Is used. Is OK	Is not customary Is frowned upon	Is disallowed Is forbidden Is a crime	(See last page for comments on items referenced here)
Salutations such as "Good morning", "good afternoon", "Good evening"	✓			
The completion of a business deal with a handshake	✓			
Starting a negotiation session with a handshake	✓			
A gift for the host/hostess	✓			
Giving a business gift	✓			
A gift of money (use of money as gift)	✓			
Use of flowers as a gift	✓			
Use of business cards	✓			
Accepting/presenting gifts with both hands	✓			
Burning of the country's flag			✓	
Mutilation of the national currency			✓	
Casual wearing of clothings made with colors & marks of the national flag		✓		
Wearing of look-alike military (camouflage) fatigues (attire)		✓		
Sitting on the floor (on floor mats)	✓			
Discussion of religion	✓			
Discussion of politics	✓			
Discussion of sex		✓		
Patting/slapping someone on the buttocks	✓			
Patting/slapping someone on the back	✓			
Touching or patting someone's head/hair		✓		
Casual touching of any part of someone's body		✓		
Drinking directly out of a bottle/can	✓			
Placing one's leg(s) on the table or chair		✓		

43

BURKINA FASO

	Is customary Is allowed Is permissible Is used. Is OK	Is not customary Is frowned upon	Is disallowed Is forbidden Is a crime	(See last page for comments on items referenced here)
Showing the sole of one's foot (feet)		✓		
People standing very close when talking	✓			
Maintaining steady eye contact (direct gaze) when talking to someone		✓		
Kissing or exchange of kisses on the cheek	✓			
Counting money (change) in someone's palm		✓		
Finger pointing in public (in a daring manner)			✓	
Seeking attention by winking the eyes	✓			
Tapping the head to indicate someone is crazy	✓			
Twirling the head to indicate someone is crazy	✓			
Whistling as a way of requesting something/seeking attention		✓		
Using "thumbs-up" sign to mean OK	✓			
Forming a circle with the thumb and index finger (forefinger) to mean OK	✓			
Using the fingers to make a "V" sign for victory	✓			
Beckoning to someone with the index finger (forefinger)	✓			
The left to right waving of the hand with open palms facing outward to indicate "Good bye"	✓			
The use of a nod to show acknowledgement	✓			
Stopping/beckoning a taxi using a stretched hand with the thumb pointing upward	✓			
Using the thumb finger pointed to a direction, to request a ride or a hike	✓			
Raising one's hand/waving with an open fist to summon a taxi	✓			
Tapping one's foot/feet on the floor in a public gathering		✓		
Wiggling one's leg(s) when in a sitting position	✓			
Use of the hand (by motorists and cyclists) to signal direction of traffic	✓			

44

BURKINA FASO

		(See last page for comments on items referenced here)
Foreign tourists are welcome in the country.	yes	
The use of seat belt is mandatory.	no	
International driving license is accepted.	yes	
Foreign drivers license is accepted.	yes	
It is considered impolite to yawn in public.	yes	
Death penalty for drug trafficking is the law.	no	
Life imprisonment for drug trafficking is the law.	no	
Guilty until proven innocent in court is the law.	no	
Innocent until proven guilty in court is the law.	no	
Pedestrians always have right of way.	yes	
Exit visas are required of visitors.	yes	
Crash helmet is mandatory for motor cyclist.	no	
Hanging is used as a form of legal punishment.	no	
Decapitation of a limb is used as a form of punishment.	no	
Caning is used as a form of legal punishment.	no	
Electric shock is used as a form of legal punishment.	no	
One is expected to stand up during the playing of the national anthem.	yes	
Crash helmet is mandatory for bicyclists.	no	
Guests are expected to eat every thing on their plates.	no	
Table manners are very informal.	yes	
One is expected to cover one's mouth when laughing.	no	
A vertical nod of the head means YES (OK).	yes	
A horizontal shaking of the head means NO (Not OK).	yes	
Prostitution is allowed only in designated areas.	yes	
One is expected to take off one's hat during playing of national anthem.	yes	
Separate seating arrangements (between sexes) are maintained at movies.	yes	
Separate seating arrangements (between sexes) are maintained at churches.	no	
Uninvited visitors or guests may not be welcome, even among acquaintances.	no	
Pets (e.g. cats, dog) are allowed in some hotels and restaurants.	no	
Couples invited for a meal may be separated during meals according to their sex.	no	
Punctuality is the order of business.	yes	
Automobiles are driven with headlights always turned on.	no	
Motorcycles are driven with headlights always turned on.	no	
Visitors with expired visa face mandatory jail time.	no	
Visitors without exit visa face jail time.	no	
Visitors without entry visa face mandatory (automatic) jail time.	no	

ADDITIONAL COUNTRY INFORMATION

(A)	The types of gifts to avoid:	any gift is welcome
(B)	Appropriate gifts for a foreigner to give:	any gift is o.k. Gift is considered a symbol of friendship.
(C)	Best time to present gifts (at the beginning or at the end of a visit?):	at the beginning or at the end of a visit
(D)	Best time to present gifts (on initial or later visits?):	at any time
(E)	Best place to present gifts (in private or in public?):	at home
(F)	Number(s) with certain connotations and/or myths attached to them:	none
(G)	Basic shape(s) with negative connotations:	none
(H)	Basic color(s) with negative connotations:	none
(I)	Traditional greeting methods include:	removing the hat off; bending to greet old people
(J)	Safe topics for discussion include:	weather, fashion, travel, art, family, religion, domestic politics, food, sports, international politics, social conditions.
(K)	Best time for conversations (before, during, after meals?):	it depends on the places, time,
(L)	Forms of legal punishment:	fines, jailing
(M)	Approximately length of time one could be detained by law and order authorities before being charged in court:	48 or 72 hours for simple misdemeanors or longer for serious crimes.
(N)	January 15, 1999, for example, will normally be written as:	15/1/99
(O)	Emergency code number:	31-25-54 ext. 385
(P)	Ambulance code Number:	30-02-71 or 33-34-42.
(Q)	Police code number:	30-07-80 or 84.
(R)	Telephone (country) code:	226
(S)	Telex (country) code:	895
(T)	Electricity requirements:	220 volts
(U)	Legal drinking age:	21
(V)	Systems of weights and measures:	metric system
(W)	Legal age of incarceration:	21
(X)	Driving side of the road:	right
(Y)	Minimum expenditure expected of foreign visitors? $	$2500 or $4500
(Z)	Name of currency:	CFA Franc
(Za)	Some places off-limits to foreign visitors:	some administrative buildings, president's house, work places, some traditional places
(Zb)	Some places, structures and items prohibited from being photographed:	a list giving by the ministry of territorial administration.

CAMEROON	Is customary Is allowed Is permissible Is used. Is OK	Is not customary Is frowned upon	Is disallowed Is forbidden Is a crime	(See last page for comments on items referenced here)
Smoking in public	✓			
Eating in public	n/a			
Not flushing public toilet	✓			
Spitting in public		✓		
Feeding animals & birds in public	✓			
Whistling in public		✓		
Drinking alcohol in public	✓			
Kissing in public	✓			
Breast feeding in public		✓		
Drunkenness (in public)		✓		
Cursing in public	✓			
Religious preaching in public	✓			
Begging (panhandling) in public		✓		
Giving money to beggars/panhandlers	✓			
Giving food/drink to beggars/panhandlers	✓			
Brushing teeth in public (other than in restrooms)		✓		
Strolling with pets in major public roads/streets	✓			
Chewing gum in public	✓			
Chewing gum in government offices		✓		
Combing hair in public (other than in toilets/restrooms)		✓		
Undressing/dressing in public		✓		
Wearing of dark glasses indoors in public places		✓		
Public display of wealth		✓		
Praying openly in public in non-designated areas		✓		
Walking bare feet in public		✓		
Chewing tobacco in public	✓			
Trimming one's finger or toe nails in public		✓		
Laughing aloud in public	✓			
Mingling of the sexes in public			✓	
Mixed bathing in public swimming pools	✓			
Distributing religious pamphlets (literature) in public/side streets	✓			

CAMEROON

	Is customary Is allowed Is permissible Is used. Is OK	Is not customary Is frowned upon	Is disallowed Is forbidden Is a crime	(See last page for comments on items referenced here)
Dancing on side street		✓		
Nude bathing			✓	
Littering		✓		
Binge Drinking	✓			
Hitchhiking		✓		
Jaywalking	✓			
Drunk driving			✓	
Speeding			✓	
Skating on side streets (side-walk)		✓		
Graffiti painting			✓	
Pilfering			✓	
Prostitution	✓			
Haggling in the market place	✓			
Consumption of alcoholic beverages in bars and restaurants	✓			
Gambling	✓			
Possession of pornographic materials		✓		
Possession of the Christian Bible	✓			
Possession of the Moslem Koran	✓			
Possession of bullet-proof vest			✓	
Possession of toy gun			✓	
Possession of fire crackers and fireworks			✓	
Possession of prescription drugs (without doctor's note)	✓			
Possession of regulated drugs (narcotics)			✓	
Possession of firearms (by foreigners)			✓	
Possession of pocket knife in public	✓			
Using walkie talkies	✓			
Using of "boom boxes"(loud sounding stereo system)	✓			
Using "walkman" (very small radio/cassettes with ear plugs) in public places	✓			
Using "walkman" (very small radio/cassettes with ear plugs) while driving or riding	✓			

CAMEROON

	Is customary Is allowed Is permissible Is used Is OK	Is not customary Is frowned upon	Is disallowed Is forbidden Is a crime	(See last page for comments on items referenced here)
Use of cellular phone	✓			
Use of binoculars/periscopes other than in sports arena		✓		
Taking photographs of people (without their permission)			✓	
Taking photographs at airports, train and bus stations	✓			
Taking photographs of airports			✓	
Taking photographs of churches and synagogues	✓			
Taking photographs of religious statues	✓			
Taking photographs of public buildings			✓	
Taking photographs of bridges			✓	
Tipping (gratuity)	✓			
Tipping (when service is rendered)	✓			
Tipping (when service is not rendered)	✓			
Tipping waiters/waitresses at restaurants and hotels	✓			
Tipping taxi/cab drivers	✓			
Tipping baggage handlers, porters, door persons	✓			
Tipping of hair dressers/barbers	✓			
Overtipping	✓			
Undertipping	✓			
Spilling cigarette butt (ash) on side streets/on the floor		✓		
Men wearing lipstick		✓		
Wearing visible tattoo marks		✓		
Men painting/coloring their finger or toe nails		✓		
Cross dressing (men dressed like women & vice versa)		✓		
Walking in public without a shirt (i.e., with the upper half of the body naked)			✓	
Men wearing braided hair		✓		
Men wearing earrings	✓			
Men wearing dreadlock hair style		✓		
Homosexuality			✓	
Lesbianism		✓		

49

CAMEROON

	Is customary Is allowed Is permissible Is used Is OK	Is not customary Is frowned upon	Is disallowed Is forbidden Is a crime	(See last page for comments on items referenced here)
Females covering their hair (wearing headgear) in public	✓			
Females exposing their full face in public	✓			
Females driving automobiles	✓			
Females riding motorcycles	✓			
Females riding bicycles	✓			
Females smoking in public	✓			
Women wearing bras (braziers) in public	✓			
Use of lipstick by women	✓			
A woman extending her hands first when introduced		✓		
Female bashing	✓			
Females wearing trousers		✓		
Females wearing minis (short dresses)		✓		
Females wearing bikinis	✓			
Females wearing shorts	✓			
Persons of opposite sex holding hands in public	✓			
Persons of same sex holding hands in public	✓			
Handshake between opposite sex	✓			
Hugging in public by same sex	✓			
Hugging in public by opposite sex	✓			
Men and women walking side by side in public	✓			
Man walking ahead (in public), with the woman following	✓			
Woman walking ahead (in public), with the man following	✓			
Men opening doors for women	✓			
Sitting with legs crossed in the presence of elders		✓		
Talking to an elderly person with one's hat/cap on		✓		
Talking to an elderly person with hands positioned on both sides of one's waist		✓		
Blowing one's nose in public	✓			
Blowing one's nose in the presence of others	✓			
Addressing people by their title	✓			

50

CAMEROON

	Is customary Is allowed Is permissible Is used. Is OK	Is not customary Is frowned upon	Is disallowed Is forbidden Is a crime	(See last page for comments on items referenced here)
Addressing people by their family name/surname/last name/given name	✓			
Addressing people by their first name/ given name		✓		
Women going through doors first	✓			
Men helping women with their coats	✓			
Men extending their hands to women first during greetings	✓			
Taking off one's hat when entering a private home	✓			
Removing one's shoes when entering a private home	✓			
Invited guests bringing food at social gatherings	✓			
Guests bringing drinks at social gatherings	✓			
Shaking hands when leaving a small group	✓			
Shaking hands with everyone present, upon arrival at a social gathering	✓			
Eating with the right hand	✓			
Eating with the left hand		✓		
Eating with both hands		✓		
Presenting a gift or passing on an object with the left hand		✓		
Asking a man about his wife	✓			
Asking a woman about her husband	✓			
Making prior appointments before a meeting or visit	✓			
Addressing an audience with one or both hands in the pocket		✓		
Carrying on conversation during meals	✓			
Females sitting with legs crossed		✓		
People discussing their wealth	✓			
Asking someone his or her age, or how old the person is		✓		
Complementing someone on his/her physical looks	✓			
Complementing someone on his/her attire	✓			
Use of both hands in handshake	✓			
In greeting, a handshake accompanied by a slight bow		✓		

CAMEROON

	Is customary Is allowed Is permissible Is used. Is OK	Is not customary Is frowned upon	Is disallowed Is forbidden Is a crime	(See last page for comments on items referenced here)
Salutations such as "Good morning", "good afternoon", "Good evening"	✓			
The completion of a business deal with a handshake	✓			
Starting a negotiation session with a handshake	✓			
A gift for the host/hostess	✓			
Giving a business gift	✓			
A gift of money (use of money as gift)	✓			
Use of flowers as a gift	✓			
Use of business cards	✓			
Accepting/presenting gifts with both hands	✓			
Burning of the country's flag			✓	
Mutilation of the national currency			✓	
Casual wearing of clothings made with colors & marks of the national flag	✓			
Wearing of look-alike military (camouflage) fatigues (attire)			✓	
Sitting on the floor (on floor mats)	✓			
Discussion of religion	✓			
Discussion of politics	✓			
Discussion of sex	✓			
Patting/slapping someone on the buttocks		✓		
Patting/slapping someone on the back	✓			
Touching or patting someone's head/hair	✓			
Casual touching of any part of someone's body	✓			
Drinking directly out of a bottle/can	✓			
Placing one's leg(s) on the table or chair		✓		

52

CAMEROON

	Is customary Is allowed Is permissible Is used. Is OK	Is not customary Is frowned upon	Is disallowed Is forbidden Is a crime	(See last page for comments on items referenced here)
Showing the sole of one's foot (feet)	✓			
People standing very close when talking				n/a
Maintaining steady eye contact (direct gaze) when talking to someone				
Kissing or exchange of kisses on the cheek	✓			
Counting money (change) in someone's palm	✓			
Finger pointing in public (in a daring manner)		✓		
Seeking attention by winking the eyes	✓			
Tapping the head to indicate someone is crazy	✓			
Twirling the head to indicate someone is crazy	✓			
Whistling as a way of requesting something/seeking attention		✓		
Using "thumbs-up" sign to mean OK	✓			
Forming a circle with the thumb and index finger (forefinger) to mean OK	✓			
Using the fingers to make a "V" sign for victory		✓		
Beckoning to someone with the index finger (forefinger)	✓			
The left to right waving of the hand with open palms facing outward to indicate "Good bye"	✓			
The use of a nod to show acknowledgement	✓			
Stopping/beckoning a taxi using a stretched hand with the thumb pointing upward	✓			
Using the thumb finger pointed to a direction, to request a ride or a hike	✓			
Raising one's hand/waving with an open fist to summon a taxi	✓			
Tapping one's foot/feet on the floor in a public gathering		✓		
Wiggling one's leg(s) when in a sitting position	✓			
Use of the hand (by motorists and cyclists) to signal direction of traffic	✓			

53

		(See last page for comments on items referenced here)
Foreign tourists are welcome in the country.	yes	
The use of seat belt is mandatory.	yes	
International driving license is accepted.	yes	
Foreign drivers license is accepted.	no	
It is considered impolite to yawn in public.	yes	
Death penalty for drug trafficking is the law.	no	
Life imprisonment for drug trafficking is the law.	yes	
Guilty until proven innocent in court is the law.	yes	
Innocent until proven guilty in court is the law.	no	
Pedestrians always have right of way.	yes	
Exit visas are required of visitors.	yes	
Crash helmet is mandatory for motor cyclist.	yes	
Hanging is used as a form of legal punishment.	no	
Decapitation of a limb is used as a form of punishment.	no	
Caning is used as a form of legal punishment.	no	
Electric shock is used as a form of legal punishment.	no	
One is expected to stand up during the playing of the national anthem.	no	
Crash helmet is mandatory for bicyclists.	no	
Guests are expected to eat every thing on their plates.	no	
Table manners are very informal.	yes	
One is expected to cover one's mouth when laughing.	n/a	
A vertical nod of the head means YES (OK).	yes	
A horizontal shaking of the head means NO (Not OK).	yes	
Prostitution is allowed only in designated areas.	no	
One is expected to take off one's hat during playing of national anthem.	no	
Separate seating arrangements (between sexes) are maintained at movies.	no	
Separate seating arrangements (between sexes) are maintained at churches.	no	
Uninvited visitors or guests may not be welcome, even among acquaintances.	yes	
Pets (e.g. cats, dog) are allowed in some hotels and restaurants.	yes	
Couples invited for a meal may be separated during meals according to their sex.	no	
Punctuality is the order of business.	yes	
Automobiles are driven with headlights always turned on.	no	
Motorcycles are driven with headlights always turned on.	no	
Visitors with expired visa face mandatory jail time.	yes	
Visitors without exit visa face jail time.	yes	
Visitors without entry visa face mandatory (automatic) jail time.	yes	

ADDITIONAL COUNTRY INFORMATION

(A)	The types of gifts to avoid:	n/a
(B)	Appropriate gifts for a foreigner to give:	something from the visitor's country
(C)	Best time to present gifts (at the beginning or at the end of a visit?):	at the beginning
(D)	Best time to present gifts (on initial or later visits?):	at the end of visit
(E)	Best place to present gifts (in private or in public?):	in private
(F)	Number(s) with certain connotations and/or myths attached to them:	none
(G)	Basic shape(s) with negative connotations:	none
(H)	Basic color(s) with negative connotations:	black
(I)	Traditional greeting methods include:	a handshake, kiss
(J)	Safe topics for discussion include:	weather, fashion, travel, art family, religion, domestic politics, food, sports, international politics, social conditions, money and personal wealth, sex.
(K)	Best time for conversations (before, during, after meals?):	n/a
(L)	Forms of legal punishment:	jailing
(M)	Approximately length of time one could be detained by law and order authorities before being charged in court:	72 hours, but sometimes longer
(N)	January 15, 1999, for example, will normally be written as:	15/1/99
(O)	Emergency code number:	Yaounde: 20.21.44, Douala: 37.02.53
(P)	Ambulance code Number:	Yaounde: 22.38,11, Douala: 42.52.25
(Q)	Police code number:	n/a
(R)	Telephone (country) code:	237
(S)	Telex (country) code:	n/a
(T)	Electricity requirements:	110-220 KW 20
(U)	Legal drinking age:	20
(V)	Systems of weights and measures:	metric
(W)	Legal age of incarceration:	n/a
(X)	Driving side of the road:	right
(Y)	Minimum expenditure expected of foreign visitors? $	no minimum
(Z)	Name of currency:	CFA
(Za)	Some places off-limits to foreign visitors:	airport, military barracks, presidency
(Zb)	Some places, structures and items prohibited from being photographed:	military installations

REPUBLIC OF CAPE VERDE	Is customary Is allowed Is permissible Is used. Is OK	Is not customary Is frowned upon	Is disallowed Is forbidden Is a crime	(See last page for comments on items referenced here)
Smoking in public	✓			
Eating in public	✓			
Not flushing public toilet		✓		
Spitting in public		✓		
Feeding animals & birds in public		✓		
Whistling in public		✓		
Drinking alcohol in public		✓		
Kissing in public		✓		
Breast feeding in public		✓		
Drunkenness (in public)		✓		
Cursing in public		✓		
Religious preaching in public	✓			
Begging (panhandling) in public	✓			
Giving money to beggars/panhandlers	✓			
Giving food/drink to beggars/panhandlers	✓			
Brushing teeth in public (other than in restrooms)		✓		
Strolling with pets in major public roads/streets	✓			
Chewing gum in public	✓			
Chewing gum in government offices		✓		
Combing hair in public (other than in toilets/restrooms)		✓		
Undressing/dressing in public		✓		
Wearing of dark glasses indoors in public places	✓			
Public display of wealth	✓			
Praying openly in public in non-designated areas		✓		
Walking bare feet in public				n/a
Chewing tobacco in public	✓			
Trimming one's finger or toe nails in public		✓		
Laughing aloud in public		✓		
Mingling of the sexes in public	✓			
Mixed bathing in public swimming pools	✓			
Distributing religious pamphlets (literature) in public/side streets	✓			

CAPE VERDE

	Is customary Is allowed Is permissible Is used. Is OK	Is not customary Is frowned upon	Is disallowed Is forbidden Is a crime	(See last page for comments on items referenced here)
Dancing on side street		✓		
Nude bathing			✓	
Littering		✓		
Binge Drinking	✓			
Hitchhiking	✓			
Jaywalking		✓		
Drunk driving			✓	
Speeding				n/a
Skating on side streets (side-walk)	✓			
Graffiti painting		✓		
Pilfering		✓		
Prostitution			✓	
Haggling in the market place	✓			
Consumption of alcoholic beverages in bars and restaurants	✓			
Gambling			✓	
Possession of pornographic materials			✓	
Possession of the Christian Bible	✓			
Possession of the Moslem Koran	✓			
Possession of bullet-proof vest	✓			
Possession of toy gun		✓		
Possession of fire crackers and fireworks		✓		
Possession of prescription drugs (without doctor's note)			✓	
Possession of regulated drugs (narcotics)			✓	
Possession of firearms (by foreigners)	✓			
Possession of pocket knife in public			✓	
Using walkie talkies	✓			
Using of "boom boxes"(loud sounding stereo system)	✓			
Using "walkman" (very small radio/cassettes with ear plugs) in public places	✓			
Using "walkman" (very small radio/cassettes with ear plugs) while driving or riding		✓		

CAPE VERDE

	Is customary Is allowed Is permissible Is used Is OK	Is not customary Is frowned upon	Is disallowed Is forbidden Is a crime	(See last page for comments on items referenced here)
Use of cellular phone	✓			
Use of binoculars/periscopes other than in sports arena	✓			
Taking photographs of people (without their permission)		✓		
Taking photographs at airports, train and bus stations	✓			
Taking photographs of airports	✓			
Taking photographs of churches and synagogues	✓			
Taking photographs of religious statues	✓			
Taking photographs of public buildings	✓			
Taking photographs of bridges	✓			
Tipping (gratuity)	✓			
Tipping (when service is rendered)	✓			
Tipping (when service is not rendered)	✓			
Tipping waiters/waitresses at restaurants and hotels	✓			
Tipping taxi/cab drivers	✓			
Tipping baggage handlers, porters, door persons	✓			
Tipping of hair dressers/barbers	✓			
Overtipping	✓			
Undertipping	✓			
Spilling cigarette butt (ash) on side streets/on the floor		✓		
Men wearing lipstick	✓			
Wearing visible tattoo marks	✓			
Men painting/coloring their finger or toe nails	✓			
Cross dressing (men dressed like women & vice versa)		✓		
Walking in public without a shirt (i.e., with the upper half of the body naked)		✓		
Men wearing braided hair	✓			
Men wearing earrings	✓			
Men wearing dreadlock hair style				n/a
Homosexuality			✓	
Lesbianism			✓	

58

CAPE VERDE

	Is customary Is allowed Is permissible Is used Is OK	Is not customary Is frowned upon	Is disallowed Is forbidden Is a crime	(See last page for comments on items referenced here)
Females covering their hair (wearing headgear) in public	✓			
Females exposing their full face in public	✓			
Females driving automobiles	✓			
Females riding motorcycles	✓			
Females riding bicycles	✓			
Females smoking in public			✓	
Women wearing bras (braziers) in public	✓			
Use of lipstick by women	✓			
A woman extending her hands first when introduced			✓	
Female bashing	✓			
Females wearing trousers	✓			
Females wearing minis (short dresses)	✓			
Females wearing bikinis	✓			
Females wearing shorts	✓			
Persons of opposite sex holding hands in public		✓		
Persons of same sex holding hands in public	✓			
Handshake between opposite sex	✓			
Hugging in public by same sex	✓			
Hugging in public by opposite sex	✓			
Men and women walking side by side in public	✓			
Man walking ahead (in public), with the woman following	✓			
Woman walking ahead (in public), with the man following	✓			
Men opening doors for women	✓			
Sitting with legs crossed in the presence of elders	✓			
Talking to an elderly person with one's hat/cap on	✓			
Talking to an elderly person with hands positioned on both sides of one's waist		✓		
Blowing one's nose in public	✓			
Blowing one's nose in the presence of others	✓			
Addressing people by their title	✓			

	Is customary Is allowed Is permissible Is used. Is OK	Is not customary Is frowned upon	Is disallowed Is forbidden Is a crime	(See last page for comments on items referenced here)
Addressing people by their family name/surname/last name/given name	✓			
Addressing people by their first name/ given name	✓			
Women going through doors first	✓			
Men helping women with their coats	✓			
Men extending their hands to women first during greetings	✓			
Taking off one's hat when entering a private home	✓			
Removing one's shoes when entering a private home		✓		
Invited guests bringing food at social gatherings	✓			
Guests bringing drinks at social gatherings	✓			
Shaking hands when leaving a small group	✓			
Shaking hands with everyone present, upon arrival at a social gathering	✓			
Eating with the right hand	✓			
Eating with the left hand	✓			
Eating with both hands		✓		
Presenting a gift or passing on an object with the left hand		✓		
Asking a man about his wife		✓		
Asking a woman about her husband	✓			
Making prior appointments before a meeting or visit	✓			
Addressing an audience with one or both hands in the pocket		✓		
Carrying on conversation during meals	✓			
Females sitting with legs crossed	✓			
People discussing their wealth	✓			
Asking someone his or her age, or how old the person is		✓		
Complementing someone on his/her physical looks	✓			
Complementing someone on his/her attire	✓			
Use of both hands in handshake		✓		
In greeting, a handshake accompanied by a slight bow	✓			

CAPE VERDE

	Is customary Is allowed Is permissible Is used. Is OK	Is not customary Is frowned upon	Is disallowed Is forbidden Is a crime	(See last page for comments on items referenced here)
Salutations such as "Good morning", "good afternoon", "Good evening"	✓			
The completion of a business deal with a handshake	✓			
Starting a negotiation session with a handshake	✓			
A gift for the host/hostess	✓			
Giving a business gift	✓			
A gift of money (use of money as gift)		✓		
Use of flowers as a gift	✓			
Use of business cards	✓			
Accepting/presenting gifts with both hands	✓			
Burning of the country's flag			✓	
Mutilation of the national currency			✓	
Casual wearing of clothings made with colors & marks of the national flag			✓	
Wearing of look-alike military (camouflage) fatigues (attire)			✓	
Sitting on the floor (on floor mats)	✓			
Discussion of religion	✓			
Discussion of politics	✓			
Discussion of sex	✓			
Patting/slapping someone on the buttocks			✓	
Patting/slapping someone on the back			✓	
Touching or patting someone's head/hair			✓	
Casual touching of any part of someone's body		✓		
Drinking directly out of a bottle/can		✓		
Placing one's leg(s) on the table or chair	✓			

61

CAPE VERDE

	Is customary Is allowed Is permissible Is used. Is OK	Is not customary Is frowned upon	Is disallowed Is forbidden Is a crime	(See last page for comments on items referenced here)
Showing the sole of one's foot (feet)		✓		
People standing very close when talking	✓			
Maintaining steady eye contact (direct gaze) when talking to someone	✓			
Kissing or exchange of kisses on the cheek	✓			
Counting money (change) in someone's palm		✓		
Finger pointing in public (in a daring manner)		✓		
Seeking attention by winking the eyes	✓			
Tapping the head to indicate someone is crazy	✓			
Twirling the head to indicate someone is crazy	✓			
Whistling as a way of requesting something/seeking attention	✓			
Using "thumbs-up" sign to mean OK	✓			
Forming a circle with the thumb and index finger (forefinger) to mean OK	✓			
Using the fingers to make a "V" sign for victory	✓			
Beckoning to someone with the index finger (forefinger)	✓			
The left to right waving of the hand with open palms facing outward to indicate "Good bye"	✓			
The use of a nod to show acknowledgement	✓			
Stopping/beckoning a taxi using a stretched hand with the thumb pointing upward	✓			
Using the thumb finger pointed to a direction, to request a ride or a hike	✓			
Raising one's hand/waving with an open fist to summon a taxi	✓			
Tapping one's foot/feet on the floor in a public gathering		✓		
Wiggling one's leg(s) when in a sitting position		✓		
Use of the hand (by motorists and cyclists) to signal direction of traffic		✓		

CAPE VERDE

		(See last page for comments on items referenced here)
Foreign tourists are welcome in the country.	yes	
The use of seat belt is mandatory.	yes	
International driving license is accepted.	yes	
Foreign drivers license is accepted.	yes	
It is considered impolite to yawn in public.	yes	
Death penalty for drug trafficking is the law.	no	
Life imprisonment for drug trafficking is the law.	no	
Guilty until proven innocent in court is the law.	no	
Innocent until proven guilty in court is the law.	yes	
Pedestrians always have right of way.	yes	
Exit visas are required of visitors.	no	
Crash helmet is mandatory for motor cyclist.	yes	
Hanging is used as a form of legal punishment.	no	
Decapitation of a limb is used as a form of punishment.	no	
Caning is used as a form of legal punishment.	no	
Electric shock is used as a form of legal punishment.	no	
One is expected to stand up during the playing of the national anthem.	yes	
Crash helmet is mandatory for bicyclists.	yes	
Guests are expected to eat every thing on their plates.	no	
Table manners are very informal.	no	
One is expected to cover one's mouth when laughing.	yes	
A vertical nod of the head means YES (OK).	yes	
A horizontal shaking of the head means NO (Not OK).	yes	
Prostitution is allowed only in designated areas.	no	
One is expected to take off one's hat during playing of national anthem.	yes	
Separate seating arrangements (between sexes) are maintained at movies.	no	
Separate seating arrangements (between sexes) are maintained at churches.	no	
Uninvited visitors or guests may not be welcome, even among acquaintances.	yes	
Pets (e.g. cats, dog) are allowed in some hotels and restaurants.	no	
Couples invited for a meal may be separated during meals according to their sex.	no	
Punctuality is the order of business.	yes	
Automobiles are driven with headlights always turned on.	no	
Motorcycles are driven with headlights always turned on.	no	
Visitors with expired visa face mandatory jail time.	no	
Visitors without exit visa face jail time.	no	
Visitors without entry visa face mandatory (automatic) jail time.	no	

ADDITIONAL COUNTRY INFORMATION

(A)	The types of gifts to avoid:	n/a
(B)	Appropriate gifts for a foreigner to give:	n/a
(C)	Best time to present gifts (at the beginning or at the end of a visit?):	beginning
(D)	Best time to present gifts (on initial or later visits?):	initial
(E)	Best place to present gifts (in private or in public?):	public
(F)	Number(s) with certain connotations and/or myths attached to them:	13-black luck
(G)	Basic shape(s) with negative connotations:	square, rectangular, circular, triangular, diamond
(H)	Basic color(s) with negative connotations:	black
(I)	Traditional greeting methods include:	handshake, kiss
(J)	Safe topics for discussion include:	weather, fashion, travel, art, family, religion, domestic politics, food, sports, international politics, social conditions, money and personal wealth, sex.
(K)	Best time for conversations (before, during, after meals?):	up to you.
(L)	Forms of legal punishment:	jailing
(M)	Approximately length of time one could be detained by law and order authorities before being charged in court:	48 hours
(N)	January 15, 1999, for example, will normally be written as:	15/1/99
(O)	Emergency code number:	130
(P)	Ambulance code Number:	130
(Q)	Police code number:	132
(R)	Telephone (country) code:	238
(S)	Telex (country) code:	238
(T)	Electricity requirements:	220v
(U)	Legal drinking age:	18
(V)	Systems of weights and measures:	kilogram and meter
(W)	Legal age of incarceration:	18
(X)	Driving side of the road:	right
(Y)	Minimum expenditure expected of foreign visitors? $	$1,500.000 USD
(Z)	Name of currency:	escudos
(Za)	Some places off-limits to foreign visitors:	n/a
(Zb)	Some places, structures and items prohibited from being photographed:	no restrictions

CHAD	Is customary Is allowed Is permissible Is used. Is OK	Is not customary Is frowned upon	Is disallowed Is forbidden Is a crime	(See last page for comments on items referenced here)
Smoking in public	✓			
Eating in public	✓			
Not flushing public toilet	✓			
Spitting in public	✓			
Feeding animals & birds in public		✓		
Whistling in public		✓		
Drinking alcohol in public	✓			
Kissing in public			✓	
Breast feeding in public	✓			
Drunkenness (in public)			✓	
Cursing in public		✓		
Religious preaching in public			✓	
Begging (panhandling) in public	✓			
Giving money to beggars/panhandlers	✓			
Giving food/drink to beggars/panhandlers	✓			
Brushing teeth in public (other than in restrooms)		✓		
Strolling with pets in major public roads/streets		✓		
Chewing gum in public		✓		
Chewing gum in government offices		✓		
Combing hair in public (other than in toilets/restrooms)		✓		
Undressing/dressing in public		✓		
Wearing of dark glasses indoors in public places		✓		
Public display of wealth		✓		
Praying openly in public in non-designated areas	✓			
Walking bare feet in public	✓			
Chewing tobacco in public	✓			
Trimming one's finger or toe nails in public		✓		
Laughing aloud in public	✓			
Mingling of the sexes in public		✓		
Mixed bathing in public swimming pools		✓		
Distributing religious pamphlets (literature) in public/side streets	✓			

CHAD

	Is customary Is allowed Is permissible Is used. Is OK	Is not customary Is frowned upon	Is disallowed Is forbidden Is a crime	(See last page for comments on items referenced here)
Dancing on side street	✓			
Nude bathing			✓	
Littering			✓	
Binge Drinking			✓	
Hitchhiking			✓	
Jaywalking	✓			
Drunk driving			✓	
Speeding			✓	
Skating on side streets (side-walk)			✓	
Graffiti painting		✓		
Pilfering		✓		
Prostitution		✓		
Haggling in the market place		✓		
Consumption of alcoholic beverages in bars and restaurants	✓			
Gambling		✓		
Possession of pornographic materials			✓	
Possession of the Christian Bible	✓			
Possession of the Moslem Koran	✓			
Possession of bullet-proof vest			✓	
Possession of toy gun		✓		
Possession of fire crackers and fireworks			✓	
Possession of prescription drugs (without doctor's note)	✓			
Possession of regulated drugs (narcotics)			✓	
Possession of firearms (by foreigners)			✓	
Possession of pocket knife in public		✓		
Using walkie talkies			✓	
Using of "boom boxes"(loud sounding stereo system)			✓	
Using "walkman" (very small radio/cassettes with ear plugs) in public places		✓		
Using "walkman" (very small radio/cassettes with ear plugs) while driving or riding			✓	✓

CHAD

	Is customary Is allowed Is permissible Is used Is OK	Is not customary Is frowned upon	Is disallowed Is forbidden Is a crime	(See last page for comments on items referenced here)
Use of cellular phone	✓			
Use of binoculars/periscopes other than in sports arena	✓			
Taking photographs of people (without their permission)		✓		
Taking photographs at airports, train and bus stations			✓	
Taking photographs of airports			✓	
Taking photographs of churches and synagogues	✓			
Taking photographs of religious statues	✓			
Taking photographs of public buildings		✓		
Taking photographs of bridges		✓		
Tipping (gratuity)	✓			
Tipping (when service is rendered)	✓			
Tipping (when service is not rendered)	✓			
Tipping waiters/waitresses at restaurants and hotels	✓			
Tipping taxi/cab drivers	✓	✓		
Tipping baggage handlers, porters, door persons	✓			
Tipping of hair dressers/barbers			✓	
Overtipping	✓			
Undertipping	✓			
Spilling cigarette butt (ash) on side streets/on the floor	✓			
Men wearing lipstick			✓	
Wearing visible tattoo marks			✓	
Men painting/coloring their finger or toe nails			✓	
Cross dressing (men dressed like women & vice versa)			✓	
Walking in public without a shirt (i.e., with the upper half of the body naked)		✓		
Men wearing braided hair		✓		
Men wearing earrings			✓	
Men wearing dreadlock hair style		✓		
Homosexuality			✓	
Lesbianism			✓	

67

CHAD

	Is customary Is allowed Is permissible Is used Is OK	Is not customary Is frowned upon	Is disallowed Is forbidden Is a crime	(See last page for comments on items referenced here)
Females covering their hair (wearing headgear) in public	✓			
Females exposing their full face in public	✓			
Females driving automobiles	✓			
Females riding motorcycles	✓			
Females riding bicycles		✓		
Females smoking in public		✓		
Women wearing bras (braziers) in public			✓	
Use of lipstick by women		✓		
A woman extending her hands first when introduced	✓			
Female bashing	✓			
Females wearing trousers		✓		
Females wearing minis (short dresses)		✓		
Females wearing bikinis		✓		
Females wearing shorts		✓		
Persons of opposite sex holding hands in public	✓			
Persons of same sex holding hands in public	✓			
Handshake between opposite sex	✓			
Hugging in public by same sex			✓	
Hugging in public by opposite sex			✓	
Men and women walking side by side in public		✓		
Man walking ahead (in public), with the woman following	✓			
Woman walking ahead (in public), with the man following	✓			
Men opening doors for women		✓		
Sitting with legs crossed in the presence of elders			✓	
Talking to an elderly person with one's hat/cap on			✓	
Talking to an elderly person with hands positioned on both sides of one's waist			✓	
Blowing one's nose in public	✓			
Blowing one's nose in the presence of others	✓			
Addressing people by their title	✓			

68

	Is customary Is allowed Is permissible Is used. Is OK	Is not customary Is frowned upon	Is disallowed Is forbidden Is a crime	(See last page for comments on items referenced here)
Addressing people by their family name/surname/last name/given name		✓		
Addressing people by their first name/ given name	✓			
Women going through doors first	✓			
Men helping women with their coats		✓		
Men extending their hands to women first during greetings		✓		
Taking off one's hat when entering a private home		✓		
Removing one's shoes when entering a private home	✓			
Invited guests bringing food at social gatherings		✓		
Guests bringing drinks at social gatherings		✓		
Shaking hands when leaving a small group	✓			
Shaking hands with everyone present, upon arrival at a social gathering	✓			
Eating with the right hand	✓			
Eating with the left hand		✓		
Eating with both hands			✓	
Presenting a gift or passing on an object with the left hand		✓		
Asking a man about his wife	✓			
Asking a woman about her husband	✓			
Making prior appointments before a meeting or visit		✓		
Addressing an audience with one or both hands in the pocket		✓		
Carrying on conversation during meals	✓			
Females sitting with legs crossed	✓			
People discussing their wealth		✓		
Asking someone his or her age, or how old the person is		✓		
Complementing someone on his/her physical looks		✓		
Complementing someone on his/her attire		✓		
Use of both hands in handshake	✓			
In greeting, a handshake accompanied by a slight bow	✓			

69

	Is customary Is allowed Is permissible Is used. Is OK	Is not customary Is frowned upon	Is disallowed Is forbidden Is a crime	(See last page for comments on items referenced here)
Salutations such as "Good morning", "good afternoon", "Good evening"	✓			
The completion of a business deal with a handshake	✓			
Starting a negotiation session with a handshake	✓			
A gift for the host/hostess		✓		
Giving a business gift		✓		
A gift of money (use of money as gift)		✓		
Use of flowers as a gift		✓		
Use of business cards		✓		
Accepting/presenting gifts with both hands	✓			
Burning of the country's flag			✓	
Mutilation of the national currency			✓	
Casual wearing of clothings made with colors & marks of the national flag		✓		
Wearing of look-alike military (camouflage) fatigues (attire)			✓	
Sitting on the floor (on floor mats)	✓			
Discussion of religion	✓			
Discussion of politics	✓			
Discussion of sex		✓		
Patting/slapping someone on the buttocks		✓		
Patting/slapping someone on the back	✓			
Touching or patting someone's head/hair		✓		
Casual touching of any part of someone's body		✓		
Drinking directly out of a bottle/can		✓		
Placing one's leg(s) on the table or chair		✓		

70

CHAD

	Is customary Is allowed Is permissible Is used. Is OK	Is not customary Is frowned upon	Is disallowed Is forbidden Is a crime	(See last page for comments on items referenced here)
Showing the sole of one's foot (feet)		✓		
People standing very close when talking	✓			
Maintaining steady eye contact (direct gaze) when talking to someone		✓		
Kissing or exchange of kisses on the cheek			✓	
Counting money (change) in someone's palm	✓			
Finger pointing in public (in a daring manner)	✓			
Seeking attention by winking the eyes				n/a
Tapping the head to indicate someone is crazy				n/a
Twirling the head to indicate someone is crazy				n/a
Whistling as a way of requesting something/seeking attention				n/a
Using "thumbs-up" sign to mean OK		✓		
Forming a circle with the thumb and index finger (forefinger) to mean OK		✓		
Using the fingers to make a "V" sign for victory		✓		
Beckoning to someone with the index finger (forefinger)				n/a
The left to right waving of the hand with open palms facing outward to indicate "Good bye"	✓			
The use of a nod to show acknowledgement	✓			
Stopping/beckoning a taxi using a stretched hand with the thumb pointing upward	✓			
Using the thumb finger pointed to a direction, to request a ride or a hike				n/a
Raising one's hand/waving with an open fist to summon a taxi	✓			
Tapping one's foot/feet on the floor in a public gathering	✓			
Wiggling one's leg(s) when in a sitting position	✓			
Use of the hand (by motorists and cyclists) to signal direction of traffic	✓			

71

CHAD

		(See last page for comments on items referenced here)
Foreign tourists are welcome in the country.	yes	
The use of seat belt is mandatory.	no	
International driving license is accepted.	yes	
Foreign drivers license is accepted.	no	
It is considered impolite to yawn in public.	no	n/a
Death penalty for drug trafficking is the law.	no	
Life imprisonment for drug trafficking is the law.		n/a
Guilty until proven innocent in court is the law.	no	
Innocent until proven guilty in court is the law.	yes	
Pedestrians always have right of way.	yes	
Exit visas are required of visitors.	yes	
Crash helmet is mandatory for motor cyclist.	no	
Hanging is used as a form of legal punishment.	no	
Decapitation of a limb is used as a form of punishment.	no	
Caning is used as a form of legal punishment.	no	
Electric shock is used as a form of legal punishment.	no	
One is expected to stand up during the playing of the national anthem.	yes	
Crash helmet is mandatory for bicyclists.	no	
Guests are expected to eat every thing on their plates.	yes	
Table manners are very informal.	no	
One is expected to cover one's mouth when laughing.	no	
A vertical nod of the head means YES (OK).	yes	
A horizontal shaking of the head means NO (Not OK).	yes	
Prostitution is allowed only in designated areas.	no	
One is expected to take off one's hat during playing of national anthem.	yes	
Separate seating arrangements (between sexes) are maintained at movies.	no	
Separate seating arrangements (between sexes) are maintained at churches.	yes	
Uninvited visitors or guests may not be welcome, even among acquaintances.	yes	
Pets (e.g. cats, dog) are allowed in some hotels and restaurants.	no	
Couples invited for a meal may be separated during meals according to their sex.	yes	
Punctuality is the order of business.	no	
Automobiles are driven with headlights always turned on.	no	
Motorcycles are driven with headlights always turned on.	no	
Visitors with expired visa face mandatory jail time.	no	
Visitors without exit visa face jail time.	no	
Visitors without entry visa face mandatory (automatic) jail time.	no	

ADDITIONAL COUNTRY INFORMATION

(A)	The types of gifts to avoid:	n/a
(B)	Appropriate gifts for a foreigner to give:	perfume, jewelry, watches, cosmetics, African Fabrics, money
(C)	Best time to present gifts (at the beginning or at the end of a visit?):	at the beginning of visit
(D)	Best time to present gifts (on initial or later visits?):	on initial visit or on later visits
(E)	Best place to present gifts (in private or in public?):	in private
(F)	Number(s) with certain connotations and/or myths attached to them:	n/a
(G)	Basic shape(s) with negative connotations:	n/a
(H)	Basic color(s) with negative connotations:	n/a
(I)	Traditional greeting methods include:	a handshake, a hug
(J)	Safe topics for discussion include:	weather, fashion, travel, art, family, domestic politics, food, sports, international politics
(K)	Best time for conversations (before, during, after meals?):	anytime (before meal, during meal or after meals)
(L)	Forms of legal punishment:	jailing
(M)	Approximately length of time one could be detained by law and order authorities before being charged in court:	2 days
(N)	January 15, 1999, for example, will normally be written as:	15/1/99
(O)	Emergency code number:	17 police, 18 fire
(P)	Ambulance code Number:	51 77 26
(Q)	Police code number:	17
(R)	Telephone (country) code:	235
(S)	Telex (country) code:	984
(T)	Electricity requirements:	220 volt
(U)	Legal drinking age:	18 years
(V)	Systems of weights and measures:	metric
(W)	Legal age of incarceration:	18
(X)	Driving side of the road:	right
(Y)	Minimum expenditure expected of foreign visitors? $	n/a
(Z)	Name of currency:	CFA Franc
(Za)	Some places off-limits to foreign visitors:	military installations
(Zb)	Some places, structures and items prohibited from being photographed:	military installations

COMOROS ISLANDS	Is customary Is allowed Is permissible Is used. Is OK	Is not customary Is frowned upon	Is disallowed Is forbidden Is a crime	(See last page for comments on items referenced here)
Smoking in public	✓			
Eating in public		✓		
Not flushing public toilet	✓			
Spitting in public	✓			
Feeding animals & birds in public	✓			
Whistling in public	✓			
Drinking alcohol in public			✓	
Kissing in public			✓	
Breast feeding in public	✓			
Drunkenness (in public)			✓	
Cursing in public	✓			
Religious preaching in public	✓			
Begging (panhandling) in public		✓		
Giving money to beggars/panhandlers	✓			
Giving food/drink to beggars/panhandlers	✓			
Brushing teeth in public (other than in restrooms)			✓	
Strolling with pets in major public roads/streets	✓			
Chewing gum in public	✓			
Chewing gum in government offices	✓			
Combing hair in public (other than in toilets/restrooms)	✓			
Undressing/dressing in public			✓	
Wearing of dark glasses indoors in public places	✓			
Public display of wealth	✓			
Praying openly in public in non-designated areas	✓			
Walking bare feet in public	✓			
Chewing tobacco in public	✓			
Trimming one's finger or toe nails in public	✓			
Laughing aloud in public		✓		
Mingling of the sexes in public				n/a
Mixed bathing in public swimming pools				n/a
Distributing religious pamphlets (literature) in public/side streets				n/a

COMOROS ISLAND

	Is customary Is allowed Is permissible Is used. Is OK	Is not customary Is frowned upon	Is disallowed Is forbidden Is a crime	(See last page for comments on items referenced here)
Dancing on side street			✓	
Nude bathing			✓	
Littering			✓	
Binge Drinking	✓			
Hitchhiking	✓			
Jaywalking	✓			
Drunk driving			✓	
Speeding		✓		
Skating on side streets (side-walk)	✓			
Graffiti painting			✓	
Pilfering	✓			
Prostitution			✓	
Haggling in the market place				n/a
Consumption of alcoholic beverages in bars and restaurants				n/a
Gambling	✓			
Possession of pornographic materials			✓	
Possession of the Christian Bible	✓			
Possession of the Moslem Koran	✓			
Possession of bullet-proof vest	✓			
Possession of toy gun	✓			
Possession of fire crackers and fireworks	✓			
Possession of prescription drugs (without doctor's note)	✓			
Possession of regulated drugs (narcotics)			✓	
Possession of firearms (by foreigners)			✓	
Possession of pocket knife in public	✓			
Using walkie talkies	✓			
Using of "boom boxes"(loud sounding stereo system)	✓			
Using "walkman" (very small radio/cassettes with ear plugs) in public places	✓			
Using "walkman" (very small radio/cassettes with ear plugs) while driving or riding				n/a

COMOROS ISLAND

	Is customary Is allowed Is permissible Is used Is OK	Is not customary Is frowned upon	Is disallowed Is forbidden Is a crime	(See last page for comments on items referenced here)
Use of cellular phone	✓			
Use of binoculars/periscopes other than in sports arena	✓			
Taking photographs of people (without their permission)		✓		
Taking photographs at airports, train and bus stations		✓		
Taking photographs of airports		✓		
Taking photographs of churches and synagogues	✓			
Taking photographs of religious statues	✓			
Taking photographs of public buildings				n/a
Taking photographs of bridges				n/a
Tipping (gratuity)	✓			
Tipping (when service is rendered)	✓			
Tipping (when service is not rendered)	✓			
Tipping waiters/waitresses at restaurants and hotels				n/a
Tipping taxi/cab drivers				n/a
Tipping baggage handlers, porters, door persons				n/a
Tipping of hair dressers/barbers	✓			
Overtipping	✓			
Undertipping	✓			
Spilling cigarette butt (ash) on side streets/on the floor	✓			
Men wearing lipstick		✓		
Wearing visible tattoo marks	✓			
Men painting/coloring their finger or toe nails			✓	
Cross dressing (men dressed like women & vice versa)			✓	
Walking in public without a shirt (i.e., with the upper half of the body naked)				n/a
Men wearing braided hair	✓			
Men wearing earrings	✓			
Men wearing dreadlock hair style	✓			
Homosexuality			✓	
Lesbianism			✓	

76

COMOROS ISLAND

	Is customary Is allowed Is permissible Is used Is OK	Is not customary Is frowned upon	Is disallowed Is forbidden Is a crime	(See last page for comments on items referenced here)
Females covering their hair (wearing headgear) in public	✓			
Females exposing their full face in public	✓			
Females driving automobiles	✓			
Females riding motorcycles	✓			
Females riding bicycles	✓			
Females smoking in public	✓			
Women wearing bras (braziers) in public	✓			
Use of lipstick by women		✓		
A woman extending her hands first when introduced	✓			
Female bashing			✓	
Females wearing trousers			✓	
Females wearing minis (short dresses)	✓			
Females wearing bikinis			✓	
Females wearing shorts			✓	
Persons of opposite sex holding hands in public			✓	
Persons of same sex holding hands in public	✓			
Handshake between opposite sex	✓			
Hugging in public by same sex	✓			
Hugging in public by opposite sex				n/a
Men and women walking side by side in public				n/a
Man walking ahead (in public), with the woman following				n/a
Woman walking ahead (in public), with the man following		✓		
Men opening doors for women				n/a
Sitting with legs crossed in the presence of elders				n/a
Talking to an elderly person with one's hat/cap on			✓	
Talking to an elderly person with hands positioned on both sides of one's waist	✓			
Blowing one's nose in public	✓			
Blowing one's nose in the presence of others	✓			
Addressing people by their title	✓			

COMOROS ISLAND

	Is customary Is allowed Is permissible Is used. Is OK	Is not customary Is frowned upon	Is disallowed Is forbidden Is a crime	(See last page for comments on items referenced here)
Addressing people by their family name/surname/last name/given name	✓			
Addressing people by their first name/ given name	✓			
Women going through doors first	✓			
Men helping women with their coats	✓			
Men extending their hands to women first during greetings	✓			
Taking off one's hat when entering a private home		✓		
Removing one's shoes when entering a private home				n/a
Invited guests bringing food at social gatherings		✓		
Guests bringing drinks at social gatherings		✓		
Shaking hands when leaving a small group	✓			
Shaking hands with everyone present, upon arrival at a social gathering	✓			
Eating with the right hand	✓			
Eating with the left hand		✓		
Eating with both hands		✓		
Presenting a gift or passing on an object with the left hand		✓		
Asking a man about his wife	✓			
Asking a woman about her husband	✓			
Making prior appointments before a meeting or visit		✓		
Addressing an audience with one or both hands in the pocket				n/a
Carrying on conversation during meals	✓			
Females sitting with legs crossed	✓			
People discussing their wealth				n/a
Asking someone his or her age, or how old the person is				n/a
Complementing someone on his/her physical looks				n/a
Complementing someone on his/her attire	✓			
Use of both hands in handshake	✓			
In greeting, a handshake accompanied by a slight bow	✓			

COMOROS ISLAND

	Is customary Is allowed Is permissible Is used. Is OK	Is not customary Is frowned upon	Is disallowed Is forbidden Is a crime	(See last page for comments on items referenced here)
Salutations such as "Good morning", "good afternoon", "Good evening"	✓			
The completion of a business deal with a handshake				n/a
Starting a negotiation session with a handshake				n/a
A gift for the host/hostess	✓			
Giving a business gift	✓			
A gift of money (use of money as gift)	✓			
Use of flowers as a gift	✓			
Use of business cards		✓		
Accepting/presenting gifts with both hands	✓			
Burning of the country's flag	✓			
Mutilation of the national currency	✓			
Casual wearing of clothings made with colors & marks of the national flag		✓		
Wearing of look-alike military (camouflage) fatigues (attire)				n/a
Sitting on the floor (on floor mats)	✓			
Discussion of religion	✓			
Discussion of politics	✓			
Discussion of sex	✓			
Patting/slapping someone on the buttocks	✓			
Patting/slapping someone on the back	✓			
Touching or patting someone's head/hair	✓			
Casual touching of any part of someone's body				n/a
Drinking directly out of a bottle/can	✓			
Placing one's leg(s) on the table or chair		✓		

COMOROS ISLAND

	Is customary Is allowed Is permissible Is used. Is OK	Is not customary Is frowned upon	Is disallowed Is forbidden Is a crime	(See last page for comments on items referenced here)
Showing the sole of one's foot (feet)		✓		
People standing very close when talking				n/a
Maintaining steady eye contact (direct gaze) when talking to someone		✓		
Kissing or exchange of kisses on the cheek				n/a
Counting money (change) in someone's palm				n/a
Finger pointing in public (in a daring manner)				n/a
Seeking attention by winking the eyes				n/a
Tapping the head to indicate someone is crazy				n/a
Twirling the head to indicate someone is crazy				n/a
Whistling as a way of requesting something/seeking attention				n/a
Using "thumbs-up" sign to mean OK				n/a
Forming a circle with the thumb and index finger (forefinger) to mean OK				n/a
Using the fingers to make a "V" sign for victory				n/a
Beckoning to someone with the index finger (forefinger)				n/a
The left to right waving of the hand with open palms facing outward to indicate "Good bye"				n/a
The use of a nod to show acknowledgement				n/a
Stopping/beckoning a taxi using a stretched hand with the thumb pointing upward				n/a
Using the thumb finger pointed to a direction, to request a ride or a hike				n/a
Raising one's hand/waving with an open fist to summon a taxi				n/a
Tapping one's foot/feet on the floor in a public gathering				n/a
Wiggling one's leg(s) when in a sitting position				n/a
Use of the hand (by motorists and cyclists) to signal direction of traffic				n/a

COMOROS ISLAND

		(See last page for comments on items referenced here)
Foreign tourists are welcome in the country.	yes	
The use of seat belt is mandatory.		n/a
International driving license is accepted.	yes	
Foreign drivers license is accepted.	yes	
It is considered impolite to yawn in public.	yes	
Death penalty for drug trafficking is the law.	yes	
Life imprisonment for drug trafficking is the law.	yes	
Guilty until proven innocent in court is the law.	yes	
Innocent until proven guilty in court is the law.	yes	
Pedestrians always have right of way.	yes	
Exit visas are required of visitors.	yes	
Crash helmet is mandatory for motor cyclist.		n/a
Hanging is used as a form of legal punishment.		n/a
Decapitation of a limb is used as a form of punishment.	no	
Caning is used as a form of legal punishment.		n/a
Electric shock is used as a form of legal punishment.	yes	
One is expected to stand up during the playing of the national anthem.		n/a
Crash helmet is mandatory for bicyclists.	no	
Guests are expected to eat every thing on their plates.	no	
Table manners are very informal.		n/a
One is expected to cover one's mouth when laughing.	yes	
A vertical nod of the head means YES (OK).	yes	
A horizontal shaking of the head means NO (Not OK).	no	
Prostitution is allowed only in designated areas.	no	
One is expected to take off one's hat during playing of national anthem.	no	
Separate seating arrangements (between sexes) are maintained at movies.		n/a
Separate seating arrangements (between sexes) are maintained at churches.	no	
Uninvited visitors or guests may not be welcome, even among acquaintances.	no	
Pets (e.g. cats, dog) are allowed in some hotels and restaurants.	no	
Couples invited for a meal may be separated during meals according to their sex.	no	
Punctuality is the order of business.		n/a
Automobiles are driven with headlights always turned on.		n/a
Motorcycles are driven with headlights always turned on.		n/a
Visitors with expired visa face mandatory jail time.		n/a
Visitors without exit visa face jail time.		n/a
Visitors without entry visa face mandatory (automatic) jail time.		n/a

ADDITIONAL COUNTRY INFORMATION

(A)	The types of gifts to avoid:	n/a
(B)	Appropriate gifts for a foreigner to give:	any
(C)	Best time to present gifts (at the beginning or at the end of a visit?):	at the beginning
(D)	Best time to present gifts (on initial or later visits?):	n/a
(E)	Best place to present gifts (in private or in public?):	n/a
(F)	Number(s) with certain connotations and/or myths attached to them:	n/a
(G)	Basic shape(s) with negative connotations:	n/a
(H)	Basic color(s) with negative connotations:	n/a
(I)	Traditional greeting methods include:	n/a
(J)	Safe topics for discussion include:	weather, fashion, travel, art, family, religion, domestic politics, food, sports, international politics, social conditions, money and personal wealth, sex
(K)	Best time for conversations (before, during, after meals?):	n/a
(L)	Forms of legal punishment:	public humiliation and jailing
(M)	Approximately length of time one could be detained by law and order authorities before being charged in court:	n/a
(N)	January 15, 1999, for example, will normally be written as:	15/1/99
(O)	Emergency code number:	n/a
(P)	Ambulance code Number:	n/a
(Q)	Police code number:	n/a
(R)	Telephone (country) code:	n/a
(S)	Telex (country) code:	n/a
(T)	Electricity requirements:	n/a
(U)	Legal drinking age:	10 years
(V)	Systems of weights and measures:	n/a
(W)	Legal age of incarceration:	18 years
(X)	Driving side of the road:	left
(Y)	Minimum expenditure expected of foreign visitors? $	n/a
(Z)	Name of currency:	Comorion Franc/Riyal
(Za)	Some places off-limits to foreign visitors:	n/a
(Zb)	Some places, structures and items prohibited from being photographed:	n/a

DEM. REP. OF CONGO	Is customary Is allowed Is permissible Is used. Is OK	Is not customary Is frowned upon	Is disallowed Is forbidden Is a crime	(See last page for comments on items referenced here)
Smoking in public	✓			
Eating in public			✓	
Not flushing public toilet			✓	
Spitting in public	✓			
Feeding animals & birds in public			✓	
Whistling in public		✓		
Drinking alcohol in public			✓	
Kissing in public			✓	
Breast feeding in public	✓			
Drunkenness (in public)		✓		
Cursing in public		✓		
Religious preaching in public	✓			
Begging (panhandling) in public		✓		
Giving money to beggars/panhandlers	✓			
Giving food/drink to beggars/panhandlers	✓			
Brushing teeth in public (other than in restrooms)			✓	
Strolling with pets in major public roads/streets	✓			
Chewing gum in public	✓			
Chewing gum in government offices	✓			
Combing hair in public (other than in toilets/restrooms)		✓		
Undressing/dressing in public			✓	
Wearing of dark glasses indoors in public places	✓			
Public display of wealth		✓		
Praying openly in public in non-designated areas		✓		
Walking bare feet in public		✓		
Chewing tobacco in public		✓		
Trimming one's finger or toe nails in public		✓		
Laughing aloud in public	✓			
Mingling of the sexes in public	✓			
Mixed bathing in public swimming pools			✓	
Distributing religious pamphlets (literature) in public/side streets	✓			

DEMOCRATIC REP. OF CONGO

	Is customary Is allowed Is permissible Is used. Is OK	Is not customary Is frowned upon	Is disallowed Is forbidden Is a crime	(See last page for comments on items referenced here)
Dancing on side street			✓	
Nude bathing			✓	
Littering			✓	
Binge Drinking		✓		
Hitchhiking		✓		
Jaywalking			✓	
Drunk driving			✓	
Speeding			✓	
Skating on side streets (side-walk)	✓			
Graffiti painting			✓	
Pilfering			✓	
Prostitution			✓	
Haggling in the market place	✓			
Consumption of alcoholic beverages in bars and restaurants		✓		
Gambling			✓	
Possession of pornographic materials		✓		
Possession of the Christian Bible	✓			
Possession of the Moslem Koran	✓			
Possession of bullet-proof vest				1
Possession of toy gun	✓			
Possession of fire crackers and fireworks				2
Possession of prescription drugs (without doctor's note)			✓	
Possession of regulated drugs (narcotics)			✓	
Possession of firearms (by foreigners)		✓		
Possession of pocket knife in public			✓	
Using walkie talkies	✓			
Using of "boom boxes"(loud sounding stereo system)			✓	
Using "walkman" (very small radio/cassettes with ear plugs) in public places	✓			
Using "walkman" (very small radio/cassettes with ear plugs) while driving or riding				n/a

DEMOCRATIC REP. OF CONGO

	Is customary Is allowed Is permissible Is used Is OK	Is not customary Is frowned upon	Is disallowed Is forbidden Is a crime	(See last page for comments on items referenced here)
Use of cellular phone	✓			
Use of binoculars/periscopes other than in sports arena	✓			
Taking photographs of people (without their permission)			✓	
Taking photographs at airports, train and bus stations				3
Taking photographs of airports			✓	
Taking photographs of churches and synagogues	✓			
Taking photographs of religious statues			✓	
Taking photographs of public buildings				n/a
Taking photographs of bridges				n/a
Tipping (gratuity)	✓			
Tipping (when service is rendered)	✓			
Tipping (when service is not rendered)			✓	
Tipping waiters/waitresses at restaurants and hotels				n/a
Tipping taxi/cab drivers				n/a
Tipping baggage handlers, porters, door persons				n/a
Tipping of hair dressers/barbers				n/a
Overtipping		✓		
Undertipping		✓		
Spilling cigarette butt (ash) on side streets/on the floor			✓	
Men wearing lipstick			✓	
Wearing visible tattoo marks		✓		
Men painting/coloring their finger or toe nails			✓	
Cross dressing (men dressed like women & vice versa)			✓	
Walking in public without a shirt (i.e., with the upper half of the body naked)				n/a
Men wearing braided hair			✓	
Men wearing earrings			✓	
Men wearing dreadlock hair style			✓	
Homosexuality			✓	
Lesbianism			✓	

DEMOCRATIC REP. OF CONGO

	Is customary Is allowed Is permissible Is used Is OK	Is not customary Is frowned upon	Is disallowed Is forbidden Is a crime	(See last page for comments on items referenced here)
Females covering their hair (wearing headgear) in public	✓			
Females exposing their full face in public	✓			
Females driving automobiles	✓			
Females riding motorcycles	✓			
Females riding bicycles	✓			
Females smoking in public			✓	
Women wearing bras (braziers) in public	✓			
Use of lipstick by women	✓			
A woman extending her hands first when introduced			✓	
Female bashing	✓			
Females wearing trousers		✓		
Females wearing minis (short dresses)		✓		
Females wearing bikinis		✓		
Females wearing shorts		✓		
Persons of opposite sex holding hands in public			✓	
Persons of same sex holding hands in public	✓			
Handshake between opposite sex			✓	
Hugging in public by same sex	✓			
Hugging in public by opposite sex		✓		
Men and women walking side by side in public	✓			
Man walking ahead (in public), with the woman following	✓			
Woman walking ahead (in public), with the man following				n/a
Men opening doors for women	✓			
Sitting with legs crossed in the presence of elders		✓		
Talking to an elderly person with one's hat/cap on			✓	
Talking to an elderly person with hands positioned on both sides of one's waist		✓		
Blowing one's nose in public	✓			
Blowing one's nose in the presence of others	✓			
Addressing people by their title	✓			

DEMOCRATIC REP. OF CONGO

	Is customary Is allowed Is permissible Is used. Is OK	Is not customary Is frowned upon	Is disallowed Is forbidden Is a crime	(See last page for comments on items referenced here)
Addressing people by their family name/surname/last name/given name	✓			
Addressing people by their first name/ given name	✓			
Women going through doors first	✓			
Men helping women with their coats	✓			
Men extending their hands to women first during greetings	✓			
Taking off one's hat when entering a private home	✓			
Removing one's shoes when entering a private home				n/a
Invited guests bringing food at social gatherings	✓			
Guests bringing drinks at social gatherings	✓			
Shaking hands when leaving a small group	✓			
Shaking hands with everyone present, upon arrival at a social gathering	✓			
Eating with the right hand	✓			
Eating with the left hand	✓			
Eating with both hands	✓			
Presenting a gift or passing on an object with the left hand	✓			
Asking a man about his wife	✓			
Asking a woman about her husband	✓			
Making prior appointments before a meeting or visit	✓			
Addressing an audience with one or both hands in the pocket	✓			
Carrying on conversation during meals	✓			
Females sitting with legs crossed		✓		
People discussing their wealth	✓			
Asking someone his or her age, or how old the person is				n/a
Complementing someone on his/her physical looks	✓			
Complementing someone on his/her attire	✓			
Use of both hands in handshake	✓			
In greeting, a handshake accompanied by a slight bow	✓			

87

DEMOCRATIC REP. OF CONGO

	Is customary Is allowed Is permissible Is used. Is OK	Is not customary Is frowned upon	Is disallowed Is forbidden Is a crime	(See last page for comments on items referenced here)
Salutations such as "Good morning", "good afternoon", "Good evening"	✓			
The completion of a business deal with a handshake				n/a
Starting a negotiation session with a handshake				n/a
A gift for the host/hostess	✓			
Giving a business gift	✓			
A gift of money (use of money as gift)	✓			
Use of flowers as a gift				n/a
Use of business cards	✓			
Accepting/presenting gifts with both hands	✓			
Burning of the country's flag			✓	
Mutilation of the national currency			✓	
Casual wearing of clothings made with colors & marks of the national flag				n/a
Wearing of look-alike military (camouflage) fatigues (attire)			✓	
Sitting on the floor (on floor mats)	✓			
Discussion of religion	✓			
Discussion of politics	✓			
Discussion of sex	✓			
Patting/slapping someone on the buttocks			✓	
Patting/slapping someone on the back	✓			
Touching or patting someone's head/hair	✓			
Casual touching of any part of someone's body				n/a
Drinking directly out of a bottle/can		✓		
Placing one's leg(s) on the table or chair		✓		

DEMOCRATIC REP. OF CONGO

	Is customary Is allowed Is permissible Is used. Is OK	Is not customary Is frowned upon	Is disallowed Is forbidden Is a crime	(See last page for comments on items referenced here)
Showing the sole of one's foot (feet)				n/a
People standing very close when talking		✓		
Maintaining steady eye contact (direct gaze) when talking to someone		✓		
Kissing or exchange of kisses on the cheek	✓			
Counting money (change) in someone's palm			✓	
Finger pointing in public (in a daring manner)			✓	
Seeking attention by winking the eyes				n/a
Tapping the head to indicate someone is crazy				n/a
Twirling the head to indicate someone is crazy				n/a
Whistling as a way of requesting something/seeking attention				n/a
Using "thumbs-up" sign to mean OK				n/a
Forming a circle with the thumb and index finger (forefinger) to mean OK				n/a
Using the fingers to make a "V" sign for victory				n/a
Beckoning to someone with the index finger (forefinger)				n/a
The left to right waving of the hand with open palms facing outward to indicate "Good bye"				n/a
The use of a nod to show acknowledgement				n/a
Stopping/beckoning a taxi using a stretched hand with the thumb pointing upward				n/a
Using the thumb finger pointed to a direction, to request a ride or a hike				n/a
Raising one's hand/waving with an open fist to summon a taxi				n/a
Tapping one's foot/feet on the floor in a public gathering				n/a
Wiggling one's leg(s) when in a sitting position				n/a
Use of the hand (by motorists and cyclists) to signal direction of traffic				n/a

89

DEMOCRATIC REP. OF CONGO

		(See last page for comments on items referenced here)
Foreign tourists are welcome in the country.	yes	
The use of seat belt is mandatory.	no	
International driving license is accepted.	yes	
Foreign drivers license is accepted.	no	
It is considered impolite to yawn in public.	yes	
Death penalty for drug trafficking is the law.	no	
Life imprisonment for drug trafficking is the law.	yes	
Guilty until proven innocent in court is the law.	no	
Innocent until proven guilty in court is the law.	yes	
Pedestrians always have right of way.	no	
Exit visas are required of visitors.	yes	
Crash helmet is mandatory for motor cyclist.	no	
Hanging is used as a form of legal punishment.	no	
Decapitation of a limb is used as a form of punishment.	no	
Caning is used as a form of legal punishment.	no	
Electric shock is used as a form of legal punishment.	no	
One is expected to stand up during the playing of the national anthem.	yes	
Crash helmet is mandatory for bicyclists.	no	
Guests are expected to eat every thing on their plates.	no	
Table manners are very informal.	yes	
One is expected to cover one's mouth when laughing.	yes	
A vertical nod of the head means YES (OK).	yes	
A horizontal shaking of the head means NO (Not OK).	yes	
Prostitution is allowed only in designated areas.	yes	
One is expected to take off one's hat during playing of national anthem.	yes	
Separate seating arrangements (between sexes) are maintained at movies.	no	
Separate seating arrangements (between sexes) are maintained at churches.	no	
Uninvited visitors or guests may not be welcome, even among acquaintances.	no	
Pets (e.g. cats, dog) are allowed in some hotels and restaurants.	no	
Couples invited for a meal may be separated during meals according to their sex.	yes	
Punctuality is the order of business.	no	
Automobiles are driven with headlights always turned on.	yes	
Motorcycles are driven with headlights always turned on.		n/a
Visitors with expired visa face mandatory jail time.	no	
Visitors without exit visa face jail time.	no	

| Visitors without entry visa face mandatory (automatic) jail time. | | no | |

ADDITIONAL COUNTRY INFORMATION

(A)	The types of gifts to avoid:	white sheets
(B)	Appropriate gifts for a foreigner to give:	handicraft
(C)	Best time to present gifts (at the beginning or at the end of a visit?):	beginning
(D)	Best time to present gifts (on initial or later visits?):	n/a
(E)	Best place to present gifts (in private or in public?):	n/a
(F)	Number(s) with certain connotations and/or myths attached to them:	n/a
(G)	Basic shape(s) with negative connotations:	n/a
(H)	Basic color(s) with negative connotations:	n/a
(I)	Traditional greeting methods include:	n/a
(J)	Safe topics for discussion include:	weather, fashion, travel, art, family, religion, food, sports, social conditions, money personal wealth
(K)	Best time for conversations (before, during, after meals?):	n/a
(L)	Forms of legal punishment:	jailing
(M)	Approximately length of time one could be detained by law and order authorities before being charged in court:	can't tell
(N)	January 15, 1999, for example, will normally be written as:	15/1/99
(O)	Emergency code number:	17
(P)	Ambulance code Number:	18
(Q)	Police code number:	17
(R)	Telephone (country) code:	n/a
(S)	Telex (country) code:	n/a
(T)	Electricity requirements:	n/a
(U)	Legal drinking age:	21
(V)	Systems of weights and measures:	n/a
(W)	Legal age of incarceration:	20
(X)	Driving side of the road:	right
(Y)	Minimum expenditure expected of foreign visitors? $	no
(Z)	Name of currency:	CFA Franc
(Za)	Some places off-limits to foreign visitors:	n/a
(Zb)	Some places, structures and items prohibited from being photographed:	n/a

ENDNOTES

Item Number: *COMMENTS/EXPLANATIONS*

n/a: *Not applicable/Not available/No response*

(1)   for police only

(2)   only during official events

(3)   with permission from authorities

COTE D'IVOIRE (IVORY COAST)	Is customary Is allowed Is permissible Is used. Is OK	Is not customary Is frowned upon	Is disallowed Is forbidden Is a crime	(See last page for comments on items referenced here)
Smoking in public	✓			
Eating in public	✓			
Not flushing public toilet				n/a
Spitting in public	✓			
Feeding animals & birds in public	✓			
Whistling in public	✓			
Drinking alcohol in public	✓			
Kissing in public		✓		
Breast feeding in public	✓			
Drunkenness (in public)		✓		
Cursing in public		✓		
Religious preaching in public	✓			
Begging (panhandling) in public	✓			
Giving money to beggars/panhandlers	✓			
Giving food/drink to beggars/panhandlers	✓			
Brushing teeth in public (other than in restrooms)		✓		
Strolling with pets in major public roads/streets	✓			
Chewing gum in public	✓			
Chewing gum in government offices	✓			
Combing hair in public (other than in toilets/restrooms)		✓		
Undressing/dressing in public		✓		
Wearing of dark glasses indoors in public places		✓		
Public display of wealth	✓			
Praying openly in public in non-designated areas	✓			
Walking bare feet in public	✓			
Chewing tobacco in public	✓			
Trimming one's finger or toe nails in public	✓			
Laughing aloud in public	✓			
Mingling of the sexes in public	✓			
Mixed bathing in public swimming pools	✓			
Distributing religious pamphlets (literature) in public/side streets	✓			

93

COTE D'IVOIRE (IVORY COAST)

	Is customary Is allowed Is permissible Is used. Is OK	Is not customary Is frowned upon	Is disallowed Is forbidden Is a crime	(See last page for comments on items referenced here)
Dancing on side street	✓			
Nude bathing			✓	
Littering	✓			
Binge Drinking		✓		
Hitchhiking	✓			
Jaywalking			✓	
Drunk driving			✓	
Speeding			✓	
Skating on side streets (side-walk)	✓			
Graffiti painting				n/a
Pilfering			✓	
Prostitution			✓	
Haggling in the market place	✓			
Consumption of alcoholic beverages in bars and restaurants	✓			
Gambling			✓	
Possession of pornographic materials			✓	
Possession of the Christian Bible	✓			
Possession of the Moslem Koran	✓			
Possession of bullet-proof vest	✓			
Possession of toy gun	✓			
Possession of fire crackers and fireworks				n/a
Possession of prescription drugs (without doctor's note)	✓			
Possession of regulated drugs (narcotics)			✓	
Possession of firearms (by foreigners)			✓	
Possession of pocket knife in public				n/a
Using walkie talkies	✓			
Using of "boom boxes"(loud sounding stereo system)	✓			
Using "walkman" (very small radio/cassettes with ear plugs) in public places	✓			
Using "walkman" (very small radio/cassettes with ear plugs) while driving or riding				n/a

COTE D'IVOIRE (IVORY COAST)

	Is customary Is allowed Is permissible Is used Is OK	Is not customary Is frowned upon	Is disallowed Is forbidden Is a crime	(See last page for comments on items referenced here)
Use of cellular phone	✓			
Use of binoculars/periscopes other than in sports arena				n/a
Taking photographs of people (without their permission)		✓		
Taking photographs at airports, train and bus stations	✓			
Taking photographs of airports			✓	
Taking photographs of churches and synagogues	✓			
Taking photographs of religious statues	✓			
Taking photographs of public buildings			✓	
Taking photographs of bridges	✓			
Tipping (gratuity)	✓			
Tipping (when service is rendered)	✓			
Tipping (when service is not rendered)	✓			
Tipping waiters/waitresses at restaurants and hotels	✓			
Tipping taxi/cab drivers	✓			
Tipping baggage handlers, porters, door persons	✓			
Tipping of hair dressers/barbers	✓			
Overtipping				n/a
Undertipping		✓		
Spilling cigarette butt (ash) on side streets/on the floor	✓			
Men wearing lipstick		✓		
Wearing visible tattoo marks	✓			
Men painting/coloring their finger or toe nails		✓		
Cross dressing (men dressed like women & vice versa)		✓		
Walking in public without a shirt (i.e., with the upper half of the body naked)	✓			
Men wearing braided hair		✓		
Men wearing earrings		✓		
Men wearing dreadlock hair style	✓			
Homosexuality		✓		
Lesbianism		✓		

95

DO'S AND DON'TS AROUND THE WORLD: A COUNTRY GUIDE TO CULTURAL AND SOCIAL TABOOS AND ETIQUETTE
COTE D'IVOIRE (IVORY COAST)

	Is customary / Is allowed / Is permissible / Is used / Is OK	Is not customary / Is frowned upon	Is disallowed / Is forbidden / Is a crime	(See last page for comments on items referenced here)
Females covering their hair (wearing headgear) in public	✓			
Females exposing their full face in public	✓			
Females driving automobiles	✓			
Females riding motorcycles	✓			
Females riding bicycles	✓			
Females smoking in public	✓			
Women wearing bras (braziers) in public	✓			
Use of lipstick by women	✓			
A woman extending her hands first when introduced	✓			
Female bashing	✓			
Females wearing trousers	✓			
Females wearing minis (short dresses)	✓			
Females wearing bikinis	✓			
Females wearing shorts	✓			
Persons of opposite sex holding hands in public	✓			
Persons of same sex holding hands in public		✓		
Handshake between opposite sex	✓			
Hugging in public by same sex	✓			
Hugging in public by opposite sex	✓			
Men and women walking side by side in public	✓			
Man walking ahead (in public), with the woman following	✓			
Woman walking ahead (in public), with the man following	✓			
Men opening doors for women	✓			
Sitting with legs crossed in the presence of elders	✓			
Talking to an elderly person with one's hat/cap on		✓		
Talking to an elderly person with hands positioned on both sides of one's waist		✓		
Blowing one's nose in public	✓			
Blowing one's nose in the presence of others	✓			
Addressing people by their title	✓			

COTE D'IVOIRE (IVORY COAST)

	Is customary Is allowed Is permissible Is used. Is OK	Is not customary Is frowned upon	Is disallowed Is forbidden Is a crime	(See last page for comments on items referenced here)
Addressing people by their family name/surname/last name/given name	✓			
Addressing people by their first name/ given name	✓			
Women going through doors first	✓			
Men helping women with their coats	✓			
Men extending their hands to women first during greetings	✓			
Taking off one's hat when entering a private home	✓			
Removing one's shoes when entering a private home	✓			
Invited guests bringing food at social gatherings		✓		
Guests bringing drinks at social gatherings	✓			
Shaking hands when leaving a small group	✓			
Shaking hands with everyone present, upon arrival at a social gathering	✓			
Eating with the right hand	✓			
Eating with the left hand		✓		
Eating with both hands		✓		
Presenting a gift or passing on an object with the left hand		✓		
Asking a man about his wife	✓			
Asking a woman about her husband	✓			
Making prior appointments before a meeting or visit	✓			
Addressing an audience with one or both hands in the pocket		✓		
Carrying on conversation during meals	✓			
Females sitting with legs crossed	✓			
People discussing their wealth		✓		
Asking someone his or her age, or how old the person is		✓		
Complementing someone on his/her physical looks	✓			
Complementing someone on his/her attire	✓			
Use of both hands in handshake	✓			
In greeting, a handshake accompanied by a slight bow				n/a

COTE D'IVOIRE (IVORY COAST)

	Is customary Is allowed Is permissible Is used. Is OK	Is not customary Is frowned upon	Is disallowed Is forbidden Is a crime	(See last page for comments on items referenced here)
Salutations such as "Good morning", "good afternoon", "Good evening"	✓			
The completion of a business deal with a handshake	✓			
Starting a negotiation session with a handshake	✓			
A gift for the host/hostess	✓			
Giving a business gift	✓			
A gift of money (use of money as gift)	✓			
Use of flowers as a gift	✓			
Use of business cards	✓			
Accepting/presenting gifts with both hands	✓			
Burning of the country's flag			✓	
Mutilation of the national currency			✓	
Casual wearing of clothings made with colors & marks of the national flag	✓			
Wearing of look-alike military (camouflage) fatigues (attire)				n/a
Sitting on the floor (on floor mats)	✓			
Discussion of religion	✓			
Discussion of politics	✓			
Discussion of sex	✓			
Patting/slapping someone on the buttocks		✓		
Patting/slapping someone on the back	✓			
Touching or patting someone's head/hair		✓		
Casual touching of any part of someone's body		✓		
Drinking directly out of a bottle/can	✓			
Placing one's leg(s) on the table or chair		✓		

COTE D'IVOIRE (IVORY COAST)

	Is customary Is allowed Is permissible Is used. Is OK	Is not customary Is frowned upon	Is disallowed Is forbidden Is a crime	(See last page for comments on items referenced here)
Showing the sole of one's foot (feet)		✓		
People standing very close when talking		✓		
Maintaining steady eye contact (direct gaze) when talking to someone		✓		
Kissing or exchange of kisses on the cheek	✓			
Counting money (change) in someone's palm		✓		
Finger pointing in public (in a daring manner)		✓		
Seeking attention by winking the eyes	✓			
Tapping the head to indicate someone is crazy	✓			
Twirling the head to indicate someone is crazy	✓			
Whistling as a way of requesting something/seeking attention	✓			
Using "thumbs-up" sign to mean OK	✓			
Forming a circle with the thumb and index finger (forefinger) to mean OK		✓		
Using the fingers to make a "V" sign for victory	✓			
Beckoning to someone with the index finger (forefinger)		✓		
The left to right waving of the hand with open palms facing outward to indicate "Good bye"	✓			
The use of a nod to show acknowledgement	✓			
Stopping/beckoning a taxi using a stretched hand with the thumb pointing upward	✓			
Using the thumb finger pointed to a direction, to request a ride or a hike	✓			
Raising one's hand/waving with an open fist to summon a taxi	✓			
Tapping one's foot/feet on the floor in a public gathering		✓		
Wiggling one's leg(s) when in a sitting position	✓			
Use of the hand (by motorists and cyclists) to signal direction of traffic	✓			

99

COTE D'IVOIRE (IVORY COAST)

		(See last page for comments on items referenced here)
Foreign tourists are welcome in the country.	yes	
The use of seat belt is mandatory.	yes	
International driving license is accepted.	yes	
Foreign drivers license is accepted.	no	
It is considered impolite to yawn in public.	yes	
Death penalty for drug trafficking is the law.	no	
Life imprisonment for drug trafficking is the law.	no	
Guilty until proven innocent in court is the law.	yes	
Innocent until proven guilty in court is the law.	no	
Pedestrians always have right of way.	no	
Exit visas are required of visitors.	no	
Crash helmet is mandatory for motor cyclist.	yes	
Hanging is used as a form of legal punishment.	no	
Decapitation of a limb is used as a form of punishment.	no	
Caning is used as a form of legal punishment.	no	
Electric shock is used as a form of legal punishment.	no	
One is expected to stand up during the playing of the national anthem.	ues	
Crash helmet is mandatory for bicyclists.	no	
Guests are expected to eat every thing on their plates.	no	
Table manners are very informal.	yes	
One is expected to cover one's mouth when laughing.	no	
A vertical nod of the head means YES (OK).	yes	
A horizontal shaking of the head means NO (Not OK).	yes	
Prostitution is allowed only in designated areas.	no	
One is expected to take off one's hat during playing of national anthem.	yes	
Separate seating arrangements (between sexes) are maintained at movies.	no	
Separate seating arrangements (between sexes) are maintained at churches.	no	
Uninvited visitors or guests may not be welcome, even among acquaintances.	no	
Pets (e.g. cats, dog) are allowed in some hotels and restaurants.	no	
Couples invited for a meal may be separated during meals according to their sex.	no	
Punctuality is the order of business.	no	
Automobiles are driven with headlights always turned on.	no	
Motorcycles are driven with headlights always turned on.	yes	
Visitors with expired visa face mandatory jail time.	no	
Visitors without exit visa face jail time.	no	
Visitors without entry visa face mandatory (automatic) jail time.	no	

ADDITIONAL COUNTRY INFORMATION

(A)	The types of gifts to avoid:	n/a
(B)	Appropriate gifts for a foreigner to give:	liquor, wine, perfume
(C)	Best time to present gifts (at the beginning or at the end of a visit?):	beginning
(D)	Best time to present gifts (on initial or later visits?):	initial
(E)	Best place to present gifts (in private or in public?):	private
(F)	Number(s) with certain connotations and/or myths attached to them:	n/a
(G)	Basic shape(s) with negative connotations:	n/a
(H)	Basic color(s) with negative connotations:	black
(I)	Traditional greeting methods include:	handshake, hug
(J)	Safe topics for discussion include:	weather fashion, travel, art, family, religion, domestic politics, food, sports, international politics, social conditions, money and personal wealth, sex.
(K)	Best time for conversations (before, during, after meals?):	after meals
(L)	Forms of legal punishment:	Jailing
(M)	Approximately length of time one could be detained by law and order authorities before being charged in court:	n/a
(N)	January 15, 1999, for example, will normally be written as:	15/1/99
(O)	Emergency code number:	180
(P)	Ambulance code Number:	185/44-34-45
(Q)	Police code number:	111 or 170
(R)	Telephone (country) code:	225
(S)	Telex (country) code:	969
(T)	Electricity requirements:	220 volt
(U)	Legal drinking age:	21
(V)	Systems of weights and measures:	metric
(W)	Legal age of incarceration:	n/a
(X)	Driving side of the road:	right
(Y)	Minimum expenditure expected of foreign visitors? $	none
(Z)	Name of currency:	CFA France
(Za)	Some places off-limits to foreign visitors:	n/a
(Zb)	Some places, structures and items prohibited from being photographed:	n/a

REP. OF DJIBOUTI	Is customary Is allowed Is permissible Is used. Is OK	Is not customary Is frowned upon	Is disallowed Is forbidden Is a crime	(See last page for comments on items referenced here)
Smoking in public	✓			
Eating in public		✓		
Not flushing public toilet		✓		
Spitting in public		✓		
Feeding animals & birds in public		✓		
Whistling in public		✓		
Drinking alcohol in public		✓		
Kissing in public		✓		
Breast feeding in public	✓			
Drunkenness (in public)			✓	
Cursing in public		✓		
Religious preaching in public	✓			
Begging (panhandling) in public	✓			
Giving money to beggars/panhandlers	✓			
Giving food/drink to beggars/panhandlers	✓			
Brushing teeth in public (other than in restrooms)	✓			
Strolling with pets in major public roads/streets		✓		
Chewing gum in public	✓			
Chewing gum in government offices	✓			
Combing hair in public (other than in toilets/restrooms)		✓		
Undressing/dressing in public			✓	
Wearing of dark glasses indoors in public places		✓		
Public display of wealth	✓			
Praying openly in public in non-designated areas	✓			
Walking bare feet in public	✓			
Chewing tobacco in public	✓			
Trimming one's finger or toe nails in public	✓			
Laughing aloud in public	✓			
Mingling of the sexes in public	✓			
Mixed bathing in public swimming pools	✓			
Distributing religious pamphlets (literature) in public/side streets	✓			

✓

DJIBOUTI

	Is customary Is allowed Is permissible Is used. Is OK	Is not customary Is frowned upon	Is disallowed Is forbidden Is a crime	(See last page for comments on items referenced here)
Dancing on side street			✓	
Nude bathing			✓	
Littering			✓	
Binge Drinking	✓			
Hitchhiking		✓		
Jaywalking			✓	
Drunk driving			✓	
Speeding			✓	
Skating on side streets (side-walk)		✓		
Graffiti painting			✓	
Pilfering			✓	
Prostitution	✓			
Haggling in the market place			✓	
Consumption of alcoholic beverages in bars and restaurants	✓			
Gambling	✓			
Possession of pornographic materials			✓	
Possession of the Christian Bible	✓			
Possession of the Moslem Koran	✓			
Possession of bullet-proof vest	✓			
Possession of toy gun	✓			
Possession of fire crackers and fireworks		✓		
Possession of prescription drugs (without doctor's note)			✓	
Possession of regulated drugs (narcotics)			✓	
Possession of firearms (by foreigners)			✓	
Possession of pocket knife in public		✓		
Using walkie talkies	✓			
Using of "boom boxes"(loud sounding stereo system)		✓		
Using "walkman" (very small radio/cassettes with ear plugs) in public places	✓			
Using "walkman" (very small radio/cassettes with ear plugs) while driving or riding		✓		

103

	Is customary Is allowed Is permissible Is used Is OK	Is not customary Is frowned upon	Is disallowed Is forbidden Is a crime	(See last page for comments on items referenced here)
Use of cellular phone	✓			
Use of binoculars/periscopes other than in sports arena		✓		
Taking photographs of people (without their permission)		✓		
Taking photographs at airports, train and bus stations	✓			
Taking photographs of airports	✓			
Taking photographs of churches and synagogues	✓			
Taking photographs of religious statues	✓			
Taking photographs of public buildings	✓			
Taking photographs of bridges	✓			
Tipping (gratuity)	✓			
Tipping (when service is rendered)	✓			
Tipping (when service is not rendered)		✓		
Tipping waiters/waitresses at restaurants and hotels	✓			
Tipping taxi/cab drivers	✓			
Tipping baggage handlers, porters, door persons	✓			
Tipping of hair dressers/barbers	✓			
Overtipping	✓			
Undertipping	✓			
Spilling cigarette butt (ash) on side streets/on the floor				n/a
Men wearing lipstick			✓	
Wearing visible tattoo marks		✓		
Men painting/coloring their finger or toe nails		✓		
Cross dressing (men dressed like women & vice versa)			✓	
Walking in public without a shirt (i.e., with the upper half of the body naked)	✓			
Men wearing braided hair			✓	
Men wearing earrings			✓	
Men wearing dreadlock hair style		✓		
Homosexuality			✓	
Lesbianism			✓	

DJIBOUTI

	Is customary Is allowed Is permissible Is used Is OK	Is not customary Is frowned upon	Is disallowed Is forbidden Is a crime	(See last page for comments on items referenced here)
Females covering their hair (wearing headgear) in public	✓			
Females exposing their full face in public	✓			
Females driving automobiles	✓			
Females riding motorcycles	✓			
Females riding bicycles	✓			
Females smoking in public		✓		
Women wearing bras (braziers) in public			✓	
Use of lipstick by women	✓			
A woman extending her hands first when introduced		✓		
Female bashing			✓	
Females wearing trousers	✓			
Females wearing minis (short dresses)		✓		
Females wearing bikinis			✓	
Females wearing shorts		✓		
Persons of opposite sex holding hands in public		✓		
Persons of same sex holding hands in public	✓			
Handshake between opposite sex	✓			
Hugging in public by same sex	✓			
Hugging in public by opposite sex		✓		
Men and women walking side by side in public	✓			
Man walking ahead (in public), with the woman following	✓			
Woman walking ahead (in public), with the man following		✓		
Men opening doors for women	✓			
Sitting with legs crossed in the presence of elders	✓			
Talking to an elderly person with one's hat/cap on	✓			
Talking to an elderly person with hands positioned on both sides of one's waist	✓			
Blowing one's nose in public		✓		
Blowing one's nose in the presence of others	✓			
Addressing people by their title	✓			

105

	Is customary Is allowed Is permissible Is used. Is OK	Is not customary Is frowned upon	Is disallowed Is forbidden Is a crime	(See last page for comments on items referenced here)
Addressing people by their family name/surname/last name/given name	✓			
Addressing people by their first name/ given name	✓			
Women going through doors first		✓		
Men helping women with their coats		✓		
Men extending their hands to women first during greetings	✓			
Taking off one's hat when entering a private home	✓			
Removing one's shoes when entering a private home	✓			
Invited guests bringing food at social gatherings			✓	
Guests bringing drinks at social gatherings			✓	
Shaking hands when leaving a small group	✓			
Shaking hands with everyone present, upon arrival at a social gathering	✓			
Eating with the right hand	✓			
Eating with the left hand		✓		
Eating with both hands		✓		
Presenting a gift or passing on an object with the left hand		✓		
Asking a man about his wife	✓			
Asking a woman about her husband				n/a
Making prior appointments before a meeting or visit	✓			
Addressing an audience with one or both hands in the pocket		✓		
Carrying on conversation during meals	✓			
Females sitting with legs crossed	✓			
People discussing their wealth	✓			
Asking someone his or her age, or how old the person is	✓			
Complementing someone on his/her physical looks	✓			
Complementing someone on his/her attire	✓			
Use of both hands in handshake		✓		
In greeting, a handshake accompanied by a slight bow		✓		

DJIBOUTI

	Is customary Is allowed Is permissible Is used. Is OK	Is not customary Is frowned upon	Is disallowed Is forbidden Is a crime	(See last page for comments on items referenced here)
Salutations such as "Good morning", "good afternoon", "Good evening"	✓			
The completion of a business deal with a handshake	✓			
Starting a negotiation session with a handshake		✓		
A gift for the host/hostess	✓			
Giving a business gift	✓			
A gift of money (use of money as gift)	✓			
Use of flowers as a gift		✓		
Use of business cards	✓			
Accepting/presenting gifts with both hands	✓			
Burning of the country's flag			✓	
Mutilation of the national currency			✓	
Casual wearing of clothings made with colors & marks of the national flag			✓	
Wearing of look-alike military (camouflage) fatigues (attire)			✓	
Sitting on the floor (on floor mats)	✓			
Discussion of religion	✓			
Discussion of politics	✓			
Discussion of sex		✓		
Patting/slapping someone on the buttocks		✓		
Patting/slapping someone on the back	✓			
Touching or patting someone's head/hair	✓			
Casual touching of any part of someone's body		✓		
Drinking directly out of a bottle/can	✓			
Placing one's leg(s) on the table or chair		✓		

107

	Is customary Is allowed Is permissible Is used. Is OK	Is not customary Is frowned upon	Is disallowed Is forbidden Is a crime	(See last page for comments on items referenced here)
Showing the sole of one's foot (feet)	✓			
People standing very close when talking	✓			
Maintaining steady eye contact (direct gaze) when talking to someone	✓			
Kissing or exchange of kisses on the cheek		✓		
Counting money (change) in someone's palm	✓			
Finger pointing in public (in a daring manner)	✓	✓		
Seeking attention by winking the eyes	✓			
Tapping the head to indicate someone is crazy		✓		
Twirling the head to indicate someone is crazy		✓		
Whistling as a way of requesting something/seeking attention				n/a
Using "thumbs-up" sign to mean OK	✓			
Forming a circle with the thumb and index finger (forefinger) to mean OK		✓		
Using the fingers to make a "V" sign for victory	✓			
Beckoning to someone with the index finger (forefinger)		✓		
The left to right waving of the hand with open palms facing outward to indicate "Good bye"	✓			
The use of a nod to show acknowledgement	✓			
Stopping/beckoning a taxi using a stretched hand with the thumb pointing upward	✓			
Using the thumb finger pointed to a direction, to request a ride or a hike	✓			
Raising one's hand/waving with an open fist to summon a taxi	✓			
Tapping one's foot/feet on the floor in a public gathering		✓		
Wiggling one's leg(s) when in a sitting position		✓		
Use of the hand (by motorists and cyclists) to signal direction of traffic	✓			

108

DJIBOUTI

		(See last page for comments on items referenced here)
Foreign tourists are welcome in the country.	yes	
The use of seat belt is mandatory.	yes	
International driving license is accepted.	yes	
Foreign drivers license is accepted.	yes	
It is considered impolite to yawn in public.	no	
Death penalty for drug trafficking is the law.	no	
Life imprisonment for drug trafficking is the law.	yes	
Guilty until proven innocent in court is the law.	no	
Innocent until proven guilty in court is the law.	yes	
Pedestrians always have right of way.	yes	
Exit visas are required of visitors.	yes	
Crash helmet is mandatory for motor cyclist.	yes	
Hanging is used as a form of legal punishment.	no	
Decapitation of a limb is used as a form of punishment.	no	
Caning is used as a form of legal punishment.	no	
Electric shock is used as a form of legal punishment.	no	
One is expected to stand up during the playing of the national anthem.	yes	
Crash helmet is mandatory for bicyclists.	yes	
Guests are expected to eat every thing on their plates.	no	
Table manners are very informal.	yes	
One is expected to cover one's mouth when laughing.	no	
A vertical nod of the head means YES (OK).	yes	
A horizontal shaking of the head means NO (Not OK).	yes	
Prostitution is allowed only in designated areas.	no	
One is expected to take off one's hat during playing of national anthem.	yes	
Separate seating arrangements (between sexes) are maintained at movies.	no	
Separate seating arrangements (between sexes) are maintained at churches.	no	
Uninvited visitors or guests may not be welcome, even among acquaintances.	no	
Pets (e.g. cats, dog) are allowed in some hotels and restaurants.	no	
Couples invited for a meal may be separated during meals according to their sex.	no	
Punctuality is the order of business.	yes	
Automobiles are driven with headlights always turned on.	no	
Motorcycles are driven with headlights always turned on.	no	
Visitors with expired visa face mandatory jail time.	no	
Visitors without exit visa face jail time.	no	
Visitors without entry visa face mandatory (automatic) jail time.	no	

ADDITIONAL COUNTRY INFORMATION

(A)	The types of gifts to avoid:	drugs, guns
(B)	Appropriate gifts for a foreigner to give:	perfumes, cloth, gold rings
(C)	Best time to present gifts (at the beginning or at the end of a visit?):	beginning
(D)	Best time to present gifts (on initial or later visits?):	initial
(E)	Best place to present gifts (in private or in public?):	private
(F)	Number(s) with certain connotations and/or myths attached to them:	none
(G)	Basic shape(s) with negative connotations:	none
(H)	Basic color(s) with negative connotations:	none
(I)	Traditional greeting methods include:	handshake
(J)	Safe topics for discussion include:	weather, fashion, travel, art, family, religion, domestic politics, food, sports, international politics, social conditions, money and personal wealth
(K)	Best time for conversations (before, during, after meals?):	before, after
(L)	Forms of legal punishment:	jailing
(M)	Approximately length of time one could be detained by law and order authorities before being charged in court:	24 hrs.
(N)	January 15, 1999, for example, will normally be written as:	15/1/99
(O)	Emergency code number:	17
(P)	Ambulance code Number:	fire department 18
(Q)	Police code number:	35.01.03
(R)	Telephone (country) code:	253
(S)	Telex (country) code:	253
(T)	Electricity requirements:	220
(U)	Legal drinking age:	moslem country no legal drinking age
(V)	Systems of weights and measures:	metric
(W)	Legal age of incarceration:	18 yrs.
(X)	Driving side of the road:	left
(Y)	Minimum expenditure expected of foreign visitors? $	none
(Z)	Name of currency:	DT France
(Za)	Some places off-limits to foreign visitors:	military bases
(Zb)	Some places, structures and items prohibited from being photographed:	military bases

EGYPT	Is customary Is allowed Is permissible Is used. Is OK	Is not customary Is frowned upon	Is disallowed Is forbidden Is a crime	(See last page for comments on items referenced here)
Smoking in public	✓			
Eating in public	✓			
Not flushing public toilet		✓		
Spitting in public		✓		
Feeding animals & birds in public	✓			
Whistling in public	✓			
Drinking alcohol in public		✓		
Kissing in public	✓			
Breast feeding in public	✓			
Drunkenness (in public)	✓			
Cursing in public		✓		
Religious preaching in public		✓		
Begging (panhandling) in public		✓		
Giving money to beggars/panhandlers	✓			
Giving food/drink to beggars/panhandlers	✓			
Brushing teeth in public (other than in restrooms)		✓		
Strolling with pets in major public roads/streets		✓		
Chewing gum in public		✓		
Chewing gum in government offices			✓	
Combing hair in public (other than in toilets/restrooms)			✓	
Undressing/dressing in public		✓		
Wearing of dark glasses indoors in public places		✓		
Public display of wealth		✓		
Praying openly in public in non-designated areas	✓			
Walking bare feet in public	✓			
Chewing tobacco in public	✓			
Trimming one's finger or toe nails in public		✓		
Laughing aloud in public		✓		
Mingling of the sexes in public		✓		
Mixed bathing in public swimming pools		✓		
Distributing religious pamphlets (literature) in public/side streets	✓			

EGYPT

	Is customary Is allowed Is permissible Is used. Is OK	Is not customary Is frowned upon	Is disallowed Is forbidden Is a crime	(See last page for comments on items referenced here)
Dancing on side street	✓			
Nude bathing		✓		
Littering	✓			
Binge Drinking		✓		
Hitchhiking		✓		
Jaywalking		✓		
Drunk driving		✓		
Speeding	✓			
Skating on side streets (side-walk)		✓		
Graffiti painting	✓			
Pilfering	✓			
Prostitution		✓		
Haggling in the market place	✓			
Consumption of alcoholic beverages in bars and restaurants	✓			
Gambling	✓			
Possession of pornographic materials		✓		
Possession of the Christian Bible	✓			
Possession of the Moslem Koran	✓			
Possession of bullet-proof vest		✓		
Possession of toy gun		✓		
Possession of fire crackers and fireworks		✓		
Possession of prescription drugs (without doctor's note)	✓			
Possession of regulated drugs (narcotics)		✓		
Possession of firearms (by foreigners)			✓	
Possession of pocket knife in public			✓	
Using walkie talkies		✓		
Using of "boom boxes"(loud sounding stereo system)	✓			
Using "walkman" (very small radio/cassettes with ear plugs) in public places	✓			
Using "walkman" (very small radio/cassettes with ear plugs) while driving or riding		✓		

112

EGYPT

	Is customary Is allowed Is permissible Is used Is OK	Is not customary Is frowned upon	Is disallowed Is forbidden Is a crime	(See last page for comments on items referenced here)
Use of cellular phone	✓			
Use of binoculars/periscopes other than in sports arena	✓			
Taking photographs of people (without their permission)	✓			
Taking photographs at airports, train and bus stations	✓			
Taking photographs of airports	✓			
Taking photographs of churches and synagogues	✓			
Taking photographs of religious statues	✓			
Taking photographs of public buildings	✓			
Taking photographs of bridges	✓			
Tipping (gratuity)	✓			
Tipping (when service is rendered)	✓			
Tipping (when service is not rendered)		✓		
Tipping waiters/waitresses at restaurants and hotels	✓			
Tipping taxi/cab drivers	✓			
Tipping baggage handlers, porters, door persons	✓			
Tipping of hair dressers/barbers		✓		
Overtipping	✓			
Undertipping		✓		
Spilling cigarette butt (ash) on side streets/on the floor	✓			
Men wearing lipstick		✓		
Wearing visible tattoo marks	✓			
Men painting/coloring their finger or toe nails		✓		
Cross dressing (men dressed like women & vice versa)			✓	
Walking in public without a shirt (i.e., with the upper half of the body naked)			✓	
Men wearing braided hair			✓	
Men wearing earrings			✓	
Men wearing dreadlock hair style			✓	
Homosexuality			✓	
Lesbianism			✓	

EGYPT

	Is customary Is allowed Is permissible Is used Is OK	Is not customary Is frowned upon	Is disallowed Is forbidden Is a crime	(See last page for comments on items referenced here)
Females covering their hair (wearing headgear) in public	✓			
Females exposing their full face in public	✓			
Females driving automobiles	✓			
Females riding motorcycles		✓		
Females riding bicycles	✓			
Females smoking in public	✓			
Women wearing bras (braziers) in public		✓		
Use of lipstick by women	✓			
A woman extending her hands first when introduced		✓		
Female bashing		✓		
Females wearing trousers		✓		
Females wearing minis (short dresses)		✓		
Females wearing bikinis		✓		
Females wearing shorts		✓		
Persons of opposite sex holding hands in public	✓			
Persons of same sex holding hands in public	✓			
Handshake between opposite sex	✓			
Hugging in public by same sex	✓			
Hugging in public by opposite sex	✓			
Men and women walking side by side in public	✓			
Man walking ahead (in public), with the woman following	✓			
Woman walking ahead (in public), with the man following	✓			
Men opening doors for women	✓			
Sitting with legs crossed in the presence of elders		✓		
Talking to an elderly person with one's hat/cap on		✓		
Talking to an elderly person with hands positioned on both sides of one's waist	✓			
Blowing one's nose in public	✓			
Blowing one's nose in the presence of others	✓			
Addressing people by their title	✓			

DO'S AND DON'TS AROUND THE WORLD: A COUNTRY GUIDE TO CULTURAL AND SOCIAL TABOOS AND ETIQUETTE
EGYPT

	Is customary Is allowed Is permissible Is used. Is OK	Is not customary Is frowned upon	Is disallowed Is forbidden Is a crime	(See last page for comments on items referenced here)
Addressing people by their family name/surname/last name/given name	✓			
Addressing people by their first name/ given name	✓			
Women going through doors first	✓			
Men helping women with their coats	✓			
Men extending their hands to women first during greetings	✓			
Taking off one's hat when entering a private home		✓		
Removing one's shoes when entering a private home		✓		
Invited guests bringing food at social gatherings	✓			
Guests bringing drinks at social gatherings	✓			
Shaking hands when leaving a small group	✓			
Shaking hands with everyone present, upon arrival at a social gathering	✓			
Eating with the right hand	✓			
Eating with the left hand		✓		
Eating with both hands		✓		
Presenting a gift or passing on an object with the left hand		✓		
Asking a man about his wife		✓		
Asking a woman about her husband	✓			
Making prior appointments before a meeting or visit	✓			
Addressing an audience with one or both hands in the pocket		✓		
Carrying on conversation during meals	✓			
Females sitting with legs crossed	✓			
People discussing their wealth	✓			
Asking someone his or her age, or how old the person is	✓			
Complementing someone on his/her physical looks	✓			
Complementing someone on his/her attire	✓			
Use of both hands in handshake	✓			
In greeting, a handshake accompanied by a slight bow		✓		

115

EGYPT

	Is customary Is allowed Is permissible Is used. Is OK	Is not customary Is frowned upon	Is disallowed Is forbidden Is a crime	(See last page for comments on items referenced here)
Salutations such as "Good morning", "good afternoon", "Good evening"	✓			
The completion of a business deal with a handshake	✓			
Starting a negotiation session with a handshake	✓			
A gift for the host/hostess	✓			
Giving a business gift	✓			
A gift of money (use of money as gift)		✓		
Use of flowers as a gift	✓			
Use of business cards	✓			
Accepting/presenting gifts with both hands	✓			
Burning of the country's flag			✓	
Mutilation of the national currency			✓	
Casual wearing of clothings made with colors & marks of the national flag	✓			
Wearing of look-alike military (camouflage) fatigues (attire)	✓			
Sitting on the floor (on floor mats)	✓			
Discussion of religion	✓			
Discussion of politics	✓			
Discussion of sex		✓		
Patting/slapping someone on the buttocks		✓		
Patting/slapping someone on the back		✓		
Touching or patting someone's head/hair	✓			
Casual touching of any part of someone's body		✓		
Drinking directly out of a bottle/can		✓		
Placing one's leg(s) on the table or chair			✓	

116

EGYPT

	Is customary Is allowed Is permissible Is used. Is OK	Is not customary Is frowned upon	Is disallowed Is forbidden Is a crime	(See last page for comments on items referenced here)
Showing the sole of one's foot (feet)		✓		
People standing very close when talking	✓			
Maintaining steady eye contact (direct gaze) when talking to someone	✓			
Kissing or exchange of kisses on the cheek	✓			1
Counting money (change) in someone's palm	✓			
Finger pointing in public (in a daring manner)	✓			
Seeking attention by winking the eyes	✓			
Tapping the head to indicate someone is crazy	✓			
Twirling the head to indicate someone is crazy				n/a
Whistling as a way of requesting something/seeking attention	✓			
Using "thumbs-up" sign to mean OK	✓			
Forming a circle with the thumb and index finger (forefinger) to mean OK	✓			
Using the fingers to make a "V" sign for victory		✓		
Beckoning to someone with the index finger (forefinger)			✓	
The left to right waving of the hand with open palms facing outward to indicate "Good bye"				n/a
The use of a nod to show acknowledgement	✓			
Stopping/beckoning a taxi using a stretched hand with the thumb pointing upward	✓			
Using the thumb finger pointed to a direction, to request a ride or a hike	✓			
Raising one's hand/waving with an open fist to summon a taxi	✓			
Tapping one's foot/feet on the floor in a public gathering			✓	
Wiggling one's leg(s) when in a sitting position	✓			
Use of the hand (by motorists and cyclists) to signal direction of traffic	✓			

117

EGYPT

		(See last page for comments on items referenced here)
Foreign tourists are welcome in the country.	yes	
The use of seat belt is mandatory.	yes	
International driving license is accepted.	yes	
Foreign drivers license is accepted.	no	
It is considered impolite to yawn in public.	yes	
Death penalty for drug trafficking is the law.	yes	
Life imprisonment for drug trafficking is the law.	no	
Guilty until proven innocent in court is the law.	no	
Innocent until proven guilty in court is the law.	yes	
Pedestrians always have right of way.	yes	
Exit visas are required of visitors.	no	
Crash helmet is mandatory for motor cyclist.	yes	
Hanging is used as a form of legal punishment.	yes	
Decapitation of a limb is used as a form of punishment.	no	
Caning is used as a form of legal punishment.	no	
Electric shock is used as a form of legal punishment.	no	
One is expected to stand up during the playing of the national anthem.	yes	
Crash helmet is mandatory for bicyclists.	yes	
Guests are expected to eat every thing on their plates.	yes	
Table manners are very informal.	yes	
One is expected to cover one's mouth when laughing.	no	
A vertical nod of the head means YES (OK).	yes	
A horizontal shaking of the head means NO (Not OK).	yes	
Prostitution is allowed only in designated areas.	no	
One is expected to take off one's hat during playing of national anthem.	no	
Separate seating arrangements (between sexes) are maintained at movies.	no	
Separate seating arrangements (between sexes) are maintained at churches.	yes	
Uninvited visitors or guests may not be welcome, even among acquaintances.	no	
Pets (e.g. cats, dog) are allowed in some hotels and restaurants.	no	
Couples invited for a meal may be separated during meals according to their sex.	no	
Punctuality is the order of business.	yes	
Automobiles are driven with headlights always turned on.	no	
Motorcycles are driven with headlights always turned on.	no	
Visitors with expired visa face mandatory jail time.	no	
Visitors without exit visa face jail time.	no	
Visitors without entry visa face mandatory (automatic) jail time.	no	

EGYPT

ADDITIONAL COUNTRY INFORMATION

(A)	The types of gifts to avoid:	liquor
(B)	Appropriate gifts for a foreigner to give:	chocolate, perfumes
(C)	Best time to present gifts (at the beginning or at the end of a visit?):	n/a
(D)	Best time to present gifts (on initial or later visits?):	n/a
(E)	Best place to present gifts (in private or in public?):	n/a
(F)	Number(s) with certain connotations and/or myths attached to them:	n/a
(G)	Basic shape(s) with negative connotations:	n/a
(H)	Basic color(s) with negative connotations:	Black
(I)	Traditional greeting methods include:	n/a
(J)	Safe topics for discussion include:	weather, fashion, travel, art, family, religion, domestic politics, food, sports, international politics, social conditions, money
(K)	Best time for conversations (before, during, after meals?):	n/a
(L)	Forms of legal punishment:	jailing, hanging
(M)	Approximately length of time one could be detained by law and order authorities before being charged in court:	n/a
(N)	January 15, 1999, for example, will normally be written as:	15 January 1999
(O)	Emergency code number:	n/a (Also see endnote "O")
(P)	Ambulance code Number:	n/a
(Q)	Police code number:	122,126,390,6207
(R)	Telephone (country) code:	011 (202)
(S)	Telex (country) code:	n/a
(T)	Electricity requirements:	220
(U)	Legal drinking age:	21
(V)	Systems of weights and measures:	metric
(W)	Legal age of incarceration:	n/a
(X)	Driving side of the road:	right
(Y)	Minimum expenditure expected of foreign visitors? $	no
(Z)	Name of currency:	Egyptian Pound
(Za)	Some places off-limits to foreign visitors:	n/a
(Zb)	Some places, structures and items prohibited from being photographed:	n/a

ENDNOTES

Item Number: COMMENTS/EXPLANATIONS

n/a: Not applicable/Not available/No response

(1) Kissing is customary among the same sex. A male may kiss his finance, sister, mother or cousin on checks in public. Lips kissing is frowned upon in public.

(0) In case of emergency, major hotels can recommend a doctor, clinic or hospital, and may even have a doctor on call. City hospitals are modern and staffed by excellent professionals.

ERITREA	Is customary Is allowed Is permissible Is used. Is OK	Is not customary Is frowned upon	Is disallowed Is forbidden Is a crime	(See last page for comments on items referenced here)
Smoking in public	✓			1
Eating in public		✓		
Not flushing public toilet		✓		
Spitting in public		✓		
Feeding animals & birds in public	✓			
Whistling in public		✓		
Drinking alcohol in public	✓			2
Kissing in public		✓		3
Breast feeding in public	✓			
Drunkenness (in public)			✓	
Cursing in public		✓		
Religious preaching in public		✓		
Begging (panhandling) in public		✓		
Giving money to beggars/panhandlers	✓			
Giving food/drink to beggars/panhandlers	✓			
Brushing teeth in public (other than in restrooms)		✓		
Strolling with pets in major public roads/streets		✓		
Chewing gum in public	✓			
Chewing gum in government offices	✓			
Combing hair in public (other than in toilets/restrooms)		✓		
Undressing/dressing in public			✓	
Wearing of dark glasses indoors in public places	✓			
Public display of wealth		✓		
Praying openly in public in non-designated areas		✓		
Walking bare feet in public		✓		
Chewing tobacco in public		✓		
Trimming one's finger or toe nails in public		✓		
Laughing aloud in public		✓		
Mingling of the sexes in public	✓			
Mixed bathing in public swimming pools	✓			
Distributing religious pamphlets (literature) in public/side streets	✓			

	Is customary Is allowed Is permissible Is used. Is OK	Is not customary Is frowned upon	Is disallowed Is forbidden Is a crime	(See last page for comments on items referenced here)
Dancing on side street	✓			4
Nude bathing		✓		
Littering			✓	
Binge Drinking			✓	
Hitchhiking		✓		
Jaywalking		✓		
Drunk driving			✓	
Speeding			✓	
Skating on side streets (side-walk)			✓	
Graffiti painting		✓		
Pilfering			✓	
Prostitution			✓	
Haggling in the market place			✓	
Consumption of alcoholic beverages in bars and restaurants	✓			
Gambling	✓			
Possession of pornographic materials			✓	
Possession of the Christian Bible			✓	
Possession of the Moslem Koran	✓			
Possession of bullet-proof vest	✓			
Possession of toy gun		✓		
Possession of fire crackers and fireworks	✓			
Possession of prescription drugs (without doctor's note)			✓	
Possession of regulated drugs (narcotics)			✓	
Possession of firearms (by foreigners)	✓			
Possession of pocket knife in public		✓		
Using walkie talkies		✓		
Using of "boom boxes"(loud sounding stereo system)			✓	5
Using "walkman" (very small radio/cassettes with ear plugs) in public places		✓		
Using "walkman" (very small radio/cassettes with ear plugs) while driving or riding		✓		

122

ERITREA

	Is customary Is allowed Is permissible Is used Is OK	Is not customary Is frowned upon	Is disallowed Is forbidden Is a crime	(See last page for comments on items referenced here)
Use of cellular phone	✓			6
Use of binoculars/periscopes other than in sports arena		✓		
Taking photographs of people (without their permission)		✓		
Taking photographs at airports, train and bus stations	✓			7
Taking photographs of airports	✓			7
Taking photographs of churches and synagogues	✓			
Taking photographs of religious statues	✓			
Taking photographs of public buildings	✓			
Taking photographs of bridges	✓			
Tipping (gratuity)	✓			
Tipping (when service is rendered)	✓			
Tipping (when service is not rendered)		✓		
Tipping waiters/waitresses at restaurants and hotels	✓			
Tipping taxi/cab drivers	✓			
Tipping baggage handlers, porters, door persons	✓			
Tipping of hair dressers/barbers	✓			
Overtipping	✓			
Undertipping	✓			
Spilling cigarette butt (ash) on side streets/on the floor	✓			
Men wearing lipstick		✓		
Wearing visible tattoo marks		✓		
Men painting/coloring their finger or toe nails	✓			8
Cross dressing (men dressed like women & vice versa)		✓		
Walking in public without a shirt (i.e., with the upper half of the body naked)	✓			
Men wearing braided hair		✓		
Men wearing earrings		✓		
Men wearing dreadlock hair style		✓		
Homosexuality			✓	
Lesbianism			✓	

123

ERITREA

	Is customary Is allowed Is permissible Is used Is OK	Is not customary Is frowned upon	Is disallowed Is forbidden Is a crime	(See last page for comments on items referenced here)
Females covering their hair (wearing headgear) in public	✓			
Females exposing their full face in public	✓			
Females driving automobiles	✓			9
Females riding motorcycles	✓			9
Females riding bicycles	✓			9
Females smoking in public	✓			
Women wearing bras (braziers) in public		✓		10
Use of lipstick by women	✓			
A woman extending her hands first when introduced		✓		
Female bashing			✓	
Females wearing trousers	✓			
Females wearing minis (short dresses)		✓		
Females wearing bikinis		✓		11
Females wearing shorts	✓			
Persons of opposite sex holding hands in public	✓			
Persons of same sex holding hands in public	✓			
Handshake between opposite sex	✓			
Hugging in public by same sex	✓			
Hugging in public by opposite sex		✓		
Men and women walking side by side in public	✓			
Man walking ahead (in public), with the woman following	✓			
Woman walking ahead (in public), with the man following	✓			
Men opening doors for women		✓		
Sitting with legs crossed in the presence of elders	✓			
Talking to an elderly person with one's hat/cap on	✓			
Talking to an elderly person with hands positioned on both sides of one's waist	✓			
Blowing one's nose in public		✓		
Blowing one's nose in the presence of others	✓			
Addressing people by their title	✓			

ERITREA

	Is customary Is allowed Is permissible Is used. Is OK	Is not customary Is frowned upon	Is disallowed Is forbidden Is a crime	(See last page for comments on items referenced here)
Addressing people by their family name/surname/last name/given name		✓		
Addressing people by their first name/ given name	✓			
Women going through doors first		✓		
Men helping women with their coats		✓		
Men extending their hands to women first during greetings		✓		
Taking off one's hat when entering a private home	✓			
Removing one's shoes when entering a private home	✓			
Invited guests bringing food at social gatherings		✓		
Guests bringing drinks at social gatherings	✓			
Shaking hands when leaving a small group	✓			12
Shaking hands with everyone present, upon arrival at a social gathering	✓			
Eating with the right hand	✓			
Eating with the left hand		✓		
Eating with both hands		✓		
Presenting a gift or passing on an object with the left hand		✓		
Asking a man about his wife	✓			
Asking a woman about her husband	✓			
Making prior appointments before a meeting or visit		✓		13
Addressing an audience with one or both hands in the pocket		✓		
Carrying on conversation during meals	✓			
Females sitting with legs crossed	✓			
People discussing their wealth		✓		
Asking someone his or her age, or how old the person is	✓			
Complementing someone on his/her physical looks	✓			
Complementing someone on his/her attire	✓			
Use of both hands in handshake	✓			
In greeting, a handshake accompanied by a slight bow		✓		

125

ERITREA

	Is customary Is allowed Is permissible Is used. Is OK	Is not customary Is frowned upon	Is disallowed Is forbidden Is a crime	(See last page for comments on items referenced here)
Salutations such as "Good morning", "good afternoon", "Good evening"	✓			
The completion of a business deal with a handshake	✓			
Starting a negotiation session with a handshake	✓			
A gift for the host/hostess	✓			
Giving a business gift		✓		
A gift of money (use of money as gift)		✓		
Use of flowers as a gift	✓			
Use of business cards		✓		
Accepting/presenting gifts with both hands	✓			
Burning of the country's flag			✓	
Mutilation of the national currency			✓	
Casual wearing of clothings made with colors & marks of the national flag	✓			
Wearing of look-alike military (camouflage) fatigues (attire)	✓			
Sitting on the floor (on floor mats)	✓			14
Discussion of religion	✓			
Discussion of politics	✓			
Discussion of sex		✓		
Patting/slapping someone on the buttocks		✓		
Patting/slapping someone on the back	✓			
Touching or patting someone's head/hair	✓			
Casual touching of any part of someone's body	✓			
Drinking directly out of a bottle/can	✓			
Placing one's leg(s) on the table or chair	✓			

126

ERITREA

	Is customary Is allowed Is permissible Is used. Is OK	Is not customary Is frowned upon	Is disallowed Is forbidden Is a crime	(See last page for comments on items referenced here)
Showing the sole of one's foot (feet)	✓			
People standing very close when talking	✓			
Maintaining steady eye contact (direct gaze) when talking to someone	✓			15
Kissing or exchange of kisses on the cheek	✓			
Counting money (change) in someone's palm	✓			
Finger pointing in public (in a daring manner)		✓		
Seeking attention by winking the eyes	✓			
Tapping the head to indicate someone is crazy	✓			
Twirling the head to indicate someone is crazy	✓			
Whistling as a way of requesting something/seeking attention	✓			
Using "thumbs-up" sign to mean OK	✓			
Forming a circle with the thumb and index finger (forefinger) to mean OK	✓			
Using the fingers to make a "V" sign for victory	✓			
Beckoning to someone with the index finger (forefinger)	✓			
The left to right waving of the hand with open palms facing outward to indicate "Good bye"	✓			
The use of a nod to show acknowledgement	✓			
Stopping/beckoning a taxi using a stretched hand with the thumb pointing upward	✓			
Using the thumb finger pointed to a direction, to request a ride or a hike	✓			
Raising one's hand/waving with an open fist to summon a taxi	✓			
Tapping one's foot/feet on the floor in a public gathering	✓			
Wiggling one's leg(s) when in a sitting position	✓			
Use of the hand (by motorists and cyclists) to signal direction of traffic	✓			

127

ERITREA

		(See last page for comments on items referenced here)
Foreign tourists are welcome in the country.	yes	
The use of seat belt is mandatory.	no	
International driving license is accepted.	yes	
Foreign drivers license is accepted.	no	
It is considered impolite to yawn in public.	no	16
Death penalty for drug trafficking is the law.	no	
Life imprisonment for drug trafficking is the law.	no	
Guilty until proven innocent in court is the law.	no	
Innocent until proven guilty in court is the law.	yes	
Pedestrians always have right of way.	no	
Exit visas are required of visitors.	yes	
Crash helmet is mandatory for motor cyclist.	no	
Hanging is used as a form of legal punishment.	no	
Decapitation of a limb is used as a form of punishment.	no	
Caning is used as a form of legal punishment.	no	
Electric shock is used as a form of legal punishment.	no	
One is expected to stand up during the playing of the national anthem.	yes	
Crash helmet is mandatory for bicyclists.	yes	
Guests are expected to eat every thing on their plates.	no	
Table manners are very informal.	yes	
One is expected to cover one's mouth when laughing.	no	
A vertical nod of the head means YES (OK).	yes	17
A horizontal shaking of the head means NO (Not OK).	yes	
Prostitution is allowed only in designated areas.	no	
One is expected to take off one's hat during playing of national anthem.	yes	
Separate seating arrangements (between sexes) are maintained at movies.	no	
Separate seating arrangements (between sexes) are maintained at churches.	yes	
Uninvited visitors or guests may not be welcome, even among acquaintances.	no	
Pets (e.g. cats, dog) are allowed in some hotels and restaurants.	yes	
Couples invited for a meal may be separated during meals according to their sex.	yes	
Punctuality is the order of business.	no	
Automobiles are driven with headlights always turned on.	no	
Motorcycles are driven with headlights always turned on.	no	
Visitors with expired visa face mandatory jail time.	no	
Visitors without exit visa face jail time.	no	18
Visitors without entry visa face mandatory (automatic) jail time.	no	

ADDITIONAL COUNTRY INFORMATION

(A)	The types of gifts to avoid:	anything very expensive, as the receiver has an obligation to return something of equivalent value
(B)	Appropriate gifts for a foreigner to give:	stationery and books, calendars, watches, ties, jewelry
(C)	Best time to present gifts (at the beginning or at the end of a visit?):	beginning
(D)	Best time to present gifts (on initial or later visits?):	n/a
(E)	Best place to present gifts (in private or in public?):	n/a
(F)	Number(s) with certain connotations and/or myths attached to them:	n/a
(G)	Basic shape(s) with negative connotations:	n/a
(H)	Basic color(s) with negative connotations:	n/a
(I)	Traditional greeting methods include:	n/a
(J)	Safe topics for discussion include:	weather, fashion, travel, art, family, domestic politics, food, sports, international politics, social conditions
(K)	Best time for conversations (before, during, after meals?):	n/a
(L)	Forms of legal punishment:	jailing, execution by firing squad
(M)	Approximately length of time one could be detained by law and order authorities before being charged in court:	48 hours
(N)	January 15, 1999, for example, will normally be written as:	15/1/99
(O)	Emergency code number:	n/a
(P)	Ambulance code Number:	1222244 in the capital
(Q)	Police code number:	116219 in the capital
(R)	Telephone (country) code:	291
(S)	Telex (country) code:	291
(T)	Electricity requirements:	110 and 220 volts
(U)	Legal drinking age:	18 years
(V)	Systems of weights and measures:	metric
(W)	Legal age of incarceration:	16 years
(X)	Driving side of the road:	right
(Y)	Minimum expenditure expected of foreign visitors? $	no
(Z)	Name of currency:	Birr
(Za)	Some places off-limits to foreign visitors:	n/a
(Zb)	Some places, structures and items prohibited from being photographed:	n/a

ENDNOTES

Item Number: *COMMENTS/EXPLANATIONS*

n/a: Not applicable/Not available/No response

(1)   There is a trend to discourage smoking

(2)   In bars

(3)   Sexual kissing in public is frowned in some cultures. Kiss friends on the cheek when greeting

(4)   Except on public holidays

(5)   At loud volume in public

(6)   No cellular phone service on the country

(7)   Taking photographs in areas designated 'restricted' is illegal

(8)   Except as part of marriage ceremony in some places

(9)   Most people don't own, but it is okay

(10)   In the capital

(11)   Except at beaches

(12)   Can be done but not necessary

(13)   Except for some government offices

(14)   In some areas of the country; not in the capital

(15)   Regular eye contact, yes; staring, no.

(16)   If you cover your mouth

(17)   Yes in capital, in some areas, no.

(18)   No, but do not leave the country.

GABON	Is customary Is allowed Is permissible Is used. Is OK	Is not customary Is frowned upon	Is disallowed Is forbidden Is a crime	(See last page for comments on items referenced here)
Smoking in public		✓		
Eating in public		✓		
Not flushing public toilet			✓	
Spitting in public			✓	
Feeding animals & birds in public		✓		
Whistling in public		✓		
Drinking alcohol in public			✓	
Kissing in public			✓	
Breast feeding in public	✓			
Drunkenness (in public)			✓	
Cursing in public			✓	
Religious preaching in public			✓	
Begging (panhandling) in public			✓	
Giving money to beggars/panhandlers			✓	
Giving food/drink to beggars/panhandlers			✓	
Brushing teeth in public (other than in restrooms)		✓		
Strolling with pets in major public roads/streets		✓		
Chewing gum in public	✓			
Chewing gum in government offices	✓			
Combing hair in public (other than in toilets/restrooms)		✓		
Undressing/dressing in public		✓		
Wearing of dark glasses indoors in public places	✓			
Public display of wealth		✓		
Praying openly in public in non-designated areas		✓		
Walking bare feet in public	✓			
Chewing tobacco in public	✓			
Trimming one's finger or toe nails in public		✓		
Laughing aloud in public	✓			
Mingling of the sexes in public		✓		
Mixed bathing in public swimming pools		✓		
Distributing religious pamphlets (literature) in public/side streets		✓		

GABON

	Is customary Is allowed Is permissible Is used. Is OK	Is not customary Is frowned upon	Is disallowed Is forbidden Is a crime	(See last page for comments on items referenced here)
Dancing on side street		✓		
Nude bathing		✓		
Littering			✓	
Binge Drinking			✓	
Hitchhiking			✓	
Jaywalking			✓	
Drunk driving			✓	
Speeding			✓	
Skating on side streets (side-walk)	✓			
Graffiti painting		✓		
Pilfering		✓		
Prostitution			✓	
Haggling in the market place		✓		
Consumption of alcoholic beverages in bars and restaurants		✓		
Gambling	✓			
Possession of pornographic materials		✓		
Possession of the Christian Bible		✓		
Possession of the Moslem Koran	✓			
Possession of bullet-proof vest	✓			
Possession of toy gun	✓			
Possession of fire crackers and fireworks		✓		
Possession of prescription drugs (without doctor's note)			✓	
Possession of regulated drugs (narcotics)			✓	
Possession of firearms (by foreigners)			✓	
Possession of pocket knife in public		✓		
Using walkie talkies		✓		
Using of "boom boxes"(loud sounding stereo system)	✓			
Using "walkman" (very small radio/cassettes with ear plugs) in public places	✓			
Using "walkman" (very small radio/cassettes with ear plugs) while driving or riding			✓	

132

GABON

	Is customary Is allowed Is permissible Is used Is OK	Is not customary Is frowned upon	Is disallowed Is forbidden Is a crime	(See last page for comments on items referenced here)
Use of cellular phone	✓			
Use of binoculars/periscopes other than in sports arena		✓		
Taking photographs of people (without their permission)		✓		
Taking photographs at airports, train and bus stations	✓			
Taking photographs of airports	✓			
Taking photographs of churches and synagogues	✓			
Taking photographs of religious statues		✓		
Taking photographs of public buildings	✓			
Taking photographs of bridges	✓			
Tipping (gratuity)	✓			
Tipping (when service is rendered)	✓			
Tipping (when service is not rendered)			✓	
Tipping waiters/waitresses at restaurants and hotels	✓			
Tipping taxi/cab drivers		✓		
Tipping baggage handlers, porters, door persons	✓			
Tipping of hair dressers/barbers	✓			
Overtipping	✓			
Undertipping	✓			
Spilling cigarette butt (ash) on side streets/on the floor	✓			
Men wearing lipstick			✓	
Wearing visible tattoo marks		✓		
Men painting/coloring their finger or toe nails			✓	
Cross dressing (men dressed like women & vice versa)			✓	
Walking in public without a shirt (i.e., with the upper half of the body naked)		✓		
Men wearing braided hair		✓		
Men wearing earrings			✓	
Men wearing dreadlock hair style		✓		
Homosexuality			✓	
Lesbianism			✓	

133

		Is customary Is allowed Is permissible Is used Is OK	Is not customary Is frowned upon	Is disallowed Is forbidden Is a crime(See last page for comments on items referenced here)
Females covering their hair (wearing headgear) in public		✓		
Females exposing their full face in public	✓			
Females driving automobiles	✓			
Females riding motorcycles	✓			
Females riding bicycles	✓			
Females smoking in public	✓			
Women wearing bras (braziers) in public			✓	
Use of lipstick by women	✓			
A woman extending her hands first when introduced	✓			
Female bashing	✓			
Females wearing trousers	✓			
Females wearing minis (short dresses)	✓			
Females wearing bikinis		✓		
Females wearing shorts	✓			
Persons of opposite sex holding hands in public		✓		
Persons of same sex holding hands in public	✓			
Handshake between opposite sex	✓			
Hugging in public by same sex	✓			
Hugging in public by opposite sex	✓			
Men and women walking side by side in public	✓			
Man walking ahead (in public), with the woman following		✓		
Woman walking ahead (in public), with the man following		✓		
Men opening doors for women		✓		
Sitting with legs crossed in the presence of elders	✓			
Talking to an elderly person with one's hat/cap on		✓		
Talking to an elderly person with hands positioned on both sides of one's waist		✓		
Blowing one's nose in public			✓	
Blowing one's nose in the presence of others			✓	
Addressing people by their title	✓			

GABON

	Is customary Is allowed Is permissible Is used. Is OK	Is not customary Is frowned upon	Is disallowed Is forbidden Is a crime	(See last page for comments on items referenced here)
Addressing people by their family name/surname/last name/given name	✓			
Addressing people by their first name/ given name		✓		
Women going through doors first		✓		
Men helping women with their coats		✓		
Men extending their hands to women first during greetings	✓			
Taking off one's hat when entering a private home	✓			
Removing one's shoes when entering a private home		✓		
Invited guests bringing food at social gatherings	✓			
Guests bringing drinks at social gatherings	✓			
Shaking hands when leaving a small group	✓			
Shaking hands with everyone present, upon arrival at a social gathering	✓			
Eating with the right hand	✓			
Eating with the left hand	✓			
Eating with both hands		✓		
Presenting a gift or passing on an object with the left hand	✓			
Asking a man about his wife	✓			
Asking a woman about her husband	✓			
Making prior appointments before a meeting or visit	✓			
Addressing an audience with one or both hands in the pocket		✓		
Carrying on conversation during meals	✓			
Females sitting with legs crossed	✓			
People discussing their wealth	✓			
Asking someone his or her age, or how old the person is	✓			
Complementing someone on his/her physical looks	✓			
Complementing someone on his/her attire	✓			
Use of both hands in handshake	✓			
In greeting, a handshake accompanied by a slight bow		✓		

135

GABON

	Is customary Is allowed Is permissible Is used. Is OK	Is not customary Is frowned upon	Is disallowed Is forbidden Is a crime	(See last page for comments on items referenced here)
Salutations such as "Good morning", "good afternoon", "Good evening"	✓			
The completion of a business deal with a handshake	✓			
Starting a negotiation session with a handshake		✓		
A gift for the host/hostess		✓		
Giving a business gift		✓		
A gift of money (use of money as gift)		✓		
Use of flowers as a gift	✓			
Use of business cards	✓			
Accepting/presenting gifts with both hands	✓			
Burning of the country's flag			✓	
Mutilation of the national currency			✓	
Casual wearing of clothings made with colors & marks of the national flag	✓			
Wearing of look-alike military (camouflage) fatigues (attire)			✓	
Sitting on the floor (on floor mats)	✓			
Discussion of religion	✓			
Discussion of politics	✓			
Discussion of sex	✓			
Patting/slapping someone on the buttocks		✓		
Patting/slapping someone on the back		✓		
Touching or patting someone's head/hair		✓		
Casual touching of any part of someone's body		✓		
Drinking directly out of a bottle/can		✓		
Placing one's leg(s) on the table or chair		✓		

136

GABON

	Is customary Is allowed Is permissible Is used. Is OK	Is not customary Is frowned upon	Is disallowed Is forbidden Is a crime	(See last page for comments on items referenced here)
Showing the sole of one's foot (feet)		✓		
People standing very close when talking		✓		
Maintaining steady eye contact (direct gaze) when talking to someone	✓			
Kissing or exchange of kisses on the cheek	✓		✓	
Counting money (change) in someone's palm		✓		
Finger pointing in public (in a daring manner)			✓	
Seeking attention by winking the eyes	✓			
Tapping the head to indicate someone is crazy		✓		
Twirling the head to indicate someone is crazy		✓		
Whistling as a way of requesting something/seeking attention		✓		
Using "thumbs-up" sign to mean OK		✓		
Forming a circle with the thumb and index finger (forefinger) to mean OK		✓		
Using the fingers to make a "V" sign for victory		✓		
Beckoning to someone with the index finger (forefinger)				n/a
The left to right waving of the hand with open palms facing outward to indicate "Good bye"	✓			
The use of a nod to show acknowledgement	✓			
Stopping/beckoning a taxi using a stretched hand with the thumb pointing upward	✓			
Using the thumb finger pointed to a direction, to request a ride or a hike				n/a
Raising one's hand/waving with an open fist to summon a taxi	✓			
Tapping one's foot/feet on the floor in a public gathering				n/a
Wiggling one's leg(s) when in a sitting position				n/a
Use of the hand (by motorists and cyclists) to signal direction of traffic	✓			

137

GABON

		(See last page for comments on items referenced here)
Foreign tourists are welcome in the country.	yes	
The use of seat belt is mandatory.	yes	
International driving license is accepted.	yes	
Foreign drivers license is accepted.	yes	
It is considered impolite to yawn in public.	n/a	
Death penalty for drug trafficking is the law.	no	
Life imprisonment for drug trafficking is the law.	yes	
Guilty until proven innocent in court is the law.	no	
Innocent until proven guilty in court is the law.	yes	
Pedestrians always have right of way.	yes	
Exit visas are required of visitors.	no	
Crash helmet is mandatory for motor cyclist.	yes	
Hanging is used as a form of legal punishment.	no	
Decapitation of a limb is used as a form of punishment.	no	
Caning is used as a form of legal punishment.	no	
Electric shock is used as a form of legal punishment.	no	
One is expected to stand up during the playing of the national anthem.	yes	
Crash helmet is mandatory for bicyclists.	no	
Guests are expected to eat every thing on their plates.	no	
Table manners are very informal.	no	
One is expected to cover one's mouth when laughing.	yes	
A vertical nod of the head means YES (OK).	yes	
A horizontal shaking of the head means NO (Not OK).	yes	
Prostitution is allowed only in designated areas.	no	
One is expected to take off one's hat during playing of national anthem.	yes	
Separate seating arrangements (between sexes) are maintained at movies.	no	
Separate seating arrangements (between sexes) are maintained at churches.	no	
Uninvited visitors or guests may not be welcome, even among acquaintances.	no	
Pets (e.g. cats, dog) are allowed in some hotels and restaurants.	no	
Couples invited for a meal may be separated during meals according to their sex.	no	
Punctuality is the order of business.	yes	
Automobiles are driven with headlights always turned on.	yes	
Motorcycles are driven with headlights always turned on.	yes	
Visitors with expired visa face mandatory jail time.	no	
Visitors without exit visa face jail time.	no	
Visitors without entry visa face mandatory (automatic) jail time.	no	

ADDITIONAL COUNTRY INFORMATION

(A)	The types of gifts to avoid:	n/a
(B)	Appropriate gifts for a foreigner to give:	perfume, jewelry, watches, cosmetics, clothes, shoes, money
(C)	Best time to present gifts (at the beginning or at the end of a visit?):	at the beginning of visit or at the end
(D)	Best time to present gifts (on initial or later visits?):	on initial visit
(E)	Best place to present gifts (in private or in public?):	in private
(F)	Number(s) with certain connotations and/or myths attached to them:	n/a
(G)	Basic shape(s) with negative connotations:	n/a
(H)	Basic color(s) with negative connotations:	n/a
(I)	Traditional greeting methods include:	a handshake, a hug, kiss
(J)	Safe topics for discussion include:	weather, fashion, travel, art, family, domestic politics, food, sports, international politics
(K)	Best time for conversations (before, during, after meals?):	anytime (before meal, during meal or after meals)
(L)	Forms of legal punishment:	jailing
(M)	Approximately length of time one could be detained by law and order authorities before being charged in court:	n/a
(N)	January 15, 1999, for example, will normally be written as:	15/1/99
(O)	Emergency code number:	13
(P)	Ambulance code Number:	16
(Q)	Police code number:	16
(R)	Telephone (country) code:	241
(S)	Telex (country) code:	981
(T)	Electricity requirements:	220 volt
(U)	Legal drinking age:	21
(V)	Systems of weights and measures:	metric
(W)	Legal age of incarceration:	21
(X)	Driving side of the road:	right
(Y)	Minimum expenditure expected of foreign visitors? $	n/a
(Z)	Name of currency:	C/F Franc
(Za)	Some places off-limits to foreign visitors:	n/a
(Zb)	Some places, structures and items prohibited from being photographed:	military installations

GAMBIA	Is customary Is allowed Is permissible Is used. Is OK	Is not customary Is frowned upon	Is disallowed Is forbidden Is a crime	(See last page for comments on items referenced here)
Smoking in public	✓			
Eating in public	✓			
Not flushing public toilet		✓		
Spitting in public		✓		
Feeding animals & birds in public				n/a
Whistling in public				n/a
Drinking alcohol in public	✓			
Kissing in public		✓		
Breast feeding in public	✓			
Drunkenness (in public)		✓		
Cursing in public		✓		
Religious preaching in public	✓			
Begging (panhandling) in public		✓		
Giving money to beggars/panhandlers	✓			
Giving food/drink to beggars/panhandlers	✓			
Brushing teeth in public (other than in restrooms)		✓		
Strolling with pets in major public roads/streets	✓			
Chewing gum in public	✓			
Chewing gum in government offices				n/a
Combing hair in public (other than in toilets/restrooms)	✓			
Undressing/dressing in public		✓		
Wearing of dark glasses indoors in public places	✓			
Public display of wealth		✓		
Praying openly in public in non-designated areas	✓			
Walking bare feet in public	✓			
Chewing tobacco in public	✓			
Trimming one's finger or toe nails in public				n/a
Laughing aloud in public	✓			
Mingling of the sexes in public	✓			
Mixed bathing in public swimming pools	✓			
Distributing religious pamphlets (literature) in public/side streets	✓			

GAMBIA

	Is customary Is allowed Is permissible Is used. Is OK	Is not customary Is frowned upon	Is disallowed Is forbidden Is a crime	(See last page for comments on items referenced here)
Dancing on side street	✓			
Nude bathing			✓	
Littering			✓	
Binge Drinking		✓		
Hitchhiking	✓			
Jaywalking			✓	
Drunk driving			✓	
Speeding			✓	
Skating on side streets (side-walk)	✓			
Graffiti painting		✓		
Pilfering			✓	
Prostitution			✓	
Haggling in the market place	✓			
Consumption of alcoholic beverages in bars and restaurants	✓			
Gambling	✓			
Possession of pornographic materials		✓		
Possession of the Christian Bible	✓			
Possession of the Moslem Koran	✓			
Possession of bullet-proof vest				n/a
Possession of toy gun	✓			
Possession of fire crackers and fireworks				n/a
Possession of prescription drugs (without doctor's note)	✓			
Possession of regulated drugs (narcotics)			✓	
Possession of firearms (by foreigners)			✓	
Possession of pocket knife in public	✓			
Using walkie talkies	✓			
Using of "boom boxes"(loud sounding stereo system)	✓			
Using "walkman" (very small radio/cassettes with ear plugs) in public places	✓			
Using "walkman" (very small radio/cassettes with ear plugs) while driving or riding	✓			

GAMBIA

	Is customary Is allowed Is permissible Is used Is OK	Is not customary Is frowned upon	Is disallowed Is forbidden Is a crime	(See last page for comments on items referenced here)
Use of cellular phone	✓			
Use of binoculars/periscopes other than in sports arena				n/a
Taking photographs of people (without their permission)		✓		
Taking photographs at airports, train and bus stations				n/a
Taking photographs of airports				n/a
Taking photographs of churches and synagogues				n/a
Taking photographs of religious statues				n/a
Taking photographs of public buildings				n/a
Taking photographs of bridges				n/a
Tipping (gratuity)	✓			
Tipping (when service is rendered)	✓			
Tipping (when service is not rendered)		✓		
Tipping waiters/waitresses at restaurants and hotels	✓			
Tipping taxi/cab drivers	✓			
Tipping baggage handlers, porters, door persons	✓			
Tipping of hair dressers/barbers	✓			
Overtipping				n/a
Undertipping				n/a
Spilling cigarette butt (ash) on side streets/on the floor			✓	
Men wearing lipstick			✓	
Wearing visible tattoo marks			✓	
Men painting/coloring their finger or toe nails			✓	
Cross dressing (men dressed like women & vice versa)			✓	
Walking in public without a shirt (i.e., with the upper half of the body naked)		✓		
Men wearing braided hair	✓			
Men wearing earrings	✓			
Men wearing dreadlock hair style	✓			
Homosexuality		✓		
Lesbianism		✓		

GAMBIA

	Is customary Is allowed Is permissible Is used Is OK	Is not customary Is frowned upon	Is disallowed Is forbidden Is a crime	(See last page for comments on items referenced here)
Females covering their hair (wearing headgear) in public	✓			
Females exposing their full face in public	✓			
Females driving automobiles	✓			
Females riding motorcycles	✓			
Females riding bicycles	✓			
Females smoking in public		✓		
Women wearing bras (braziers) in public				n/a
Use of lipstick by women	✓			
A woman extending her hands first when introduced	✓			
Female bashing				n/a
Females wearing trousers	✓			
Females wearing minis (short dresses)	✓			
Females wearing bikinis	✓			
Females wearing shorts	✓			
Persons of opposite sex holding hands in public		✓		
Persons of same sex holding hands in public		✓		
Handshake between opposite sex	✓			
Hugging in public by same sex	✓			
Hugging in public by opposite sex	✓			
Men and women walking side by side in public	✓			
Man walking ahead (in public), with the woman following	✓			
Woman walking ahead (in public), with the man following	✓			
Men opening doors for women	✓			
Sitting with legs crossed in the presence of elders	✓			
Talking to an elderly person with one's hat/cap on		✓		
Talking to an elderly person with hands positioned on both sides of one's waist	✓			
Blowing one's nose in public		✓		
Blowing one's nose in the presence of others	✓			
Addressing people by their title	✓			

143

	Is customary Is allowed Is permissible Is used. Is OK	Is not customary Is frowned upon	Is disallowed Is forbidden Is a crime	(See last page for comments on items referenced here)
Addressing people by their family name/surname/last name/given name	✓			
Addressing people by their first name/ given name	✓			
Women going through doors first	✓			
Men helping women with their coats	✓			
Men extending their hands to women first during greetings	✓			
Taking off one's hat when entering a private home	✓			
Removing one's shoes when entering a private home	✓			
Invited guests bringing food at social gatherings	✓			
Guests bringing drinks at social gatherings	✓			
Shaking hands when leaving a small group	✓			
Shaking hands with everyone present, upon arrival at a social gathering	✓			
Eating with the right hand	✓			
Eating with the left hand		✓		
Eating with both hands		✓		
Presenting a gift or passing on an object with the left hand		✓		
Asking a man about his wife	✓			
Asking a woman about her husband	✓			
Making prior appointments before a meeting or visit	✓			
Addressing an audience with one or both hands in the pocket		✓		
Carrying on conversation during meals	✓			
Females sitting with legs crossed	✓			
People discussing their wealth	✓			
Asking someone his or her age, or how old the person is	✓			
Complementing someone on his/her physical looks	✓			
Complementing someone on his/her attire	✓			
Use of both hands in handshake	✓			
In greeting, a handshake accompanied by a slight bow		✓		

GAMBIA

	Is customary Is allowed Is permissible Is used. Is OK	Is not customary Is frowned upon	Is disallowed Is forbidden Is a crime	(See last page for comments on items referenced here)
Salutations such as "Good morning", "good afternoon", "Good evening"	✓			
The completion of a business deal with a handshake	✓			
Starting a negotiation session with a handshake	✓			
A gift for the host/hostess	✓			
Giving a business gift				n/a
A gift of money (use of money as gift)				
Use of flowers as a gift	✓			
Use of business cards	✓			
Accepting/presenting gifts with both hands			✓	
Burning of the country's flag			✓	
Mutilation of the national currency				n/a
Casual wearing of clothings made with colors & marks of the national flag	✓			
Wearing of look-alike military (camouflage) fatigues (attire)	✓			
Sitting on the floor (on floor mats)	✓			
Discussion of religion	✓			
Discussion of politics		✓		
Discussion of sex		✓		
Patting/slapping someone on the buttocks		✓		
Patting/slapping someone on the back		✓		
Touching or patting someone's head/hair		✓		
Casual touching of any part of someone's body		✓		
Drinking directly out of a bottle/can	✓			
Placing one's leg(s) on the table or chair		✓		

145

GAMBIA

	Is customary Is allowed Is permissible Is used. Is OK	Is not customary Is frowned upon	Is disallowed Is forbidden Is a crime	(See last page for comments on items referenced here)
Showing the sole of one's foot (feet)	✓			
People standing very close when talking		✓		
Maintaining steady eye contact (direct gaze) when talking to someone	✓			
Kissing or exchange of kisses on the cheek	✓			
Counting money (change) in someone's palm	✓			
Finger pointing in public (in a daring manner)		✓		
Seeking attention by winking the eyes		✓		
Tapping the head to indicate someone is crazy		✓		
Twirling the head to indicate someone is crazy		✓		
Whistling as a way of requesting something/seeking attention		✓		
Using "thumbs-up" sign to mean OK	✓			
Forming a circle with the thumb and index finger (forefinger) to mean OK				n/a
Using the fingers to make a "V" sign for victory	✓			
Beckoning to someone with the index finger (forefinger)	✓			
The left to right waving of the hand with open palms facing outward to indicate "Good bye"	✓			
The use of a nod to show acknowledgement	✓			
Stopping/beckoning a taxi using a stretched hand with the thumb pointing upward	✓			
Using the thumb finger pointed to a direction, to request a ride or a hike	✓			
Raising one's hand/waving with an open fist to summon a taxi	✓			
Tapping one's foot/feet on the floor in a public gathering		✓		
Wiggling one's leg(s) when in a sitting position				n/a
Use of the hand (by motorists and cyclists) to signal direction of traffic	✓			

146

GAMBIA

		(See last page for comments on items referenced here)
Foreign tourists are welcome in the country.	yes	
The use of seat belt is mandatory.	yes	
International driving license is accepted.	yes	
Foreign drivers license is accepted.	yes	
It is considered impolite to yawn in public.	yes	
Death penalty for drug trafficking is the law.	no	
Life imprisonment for drug trafficking is the law.	no	
Guilty until proven innocent in court is the law.	yes	
Innocent until proven guilty in court is the law.	no	
Pedestrians always have right of way.	yws	
Exit visas are required of visitors.	no	
Crash helmet is mandatory for motor cyclist.	yes	
Hanging is used as a form of legal punishment.	yes	
Decapitation of a limb is used as a form of punishment.	no	
Caning is used as a form of legal punishment.	no	
Electric shock is used as a form of legal punishment.	no	
One is expected to stand up during the playing of the national anthem.	yes	
Crash helmet is mandatory for bicyclists.	no	
Guests are expected to eat every thing on their plates.	no	
Table manners are very informal.	yes	
One is expected to cover one's mouth when laughing.	no	
A vertical nod of the head means YES (OK).	yes	
A horizontal shaking of the head means NO (Not OK).	yes	
Prostitution is allowed only in designated areas.	no	
One is expected to take off one's hat during playing of national anthem.	yes	
Separate seating arrangements (between sexes) are maintained at movies.	no	
Separate seating arrangements (between sexes) are maintained at churches.	no	
Uninvited visitors or guests may not be welcome, even among acquaintances.	no	
Pets (e.g. cats, dog) are allowed in some hotels and restaurants.	yes	
Couples invited for a meal may be separated during meals according to their sex.	no	
Punctuality is the order of business.	yes	
Automobiles are driven with headlights always turned on.	yes	
Motorcycles are driven with headlights always turned on.	yes	
Visitors with expired visa face mandatory jail time.	no	
Visitors without exit visa face jail time.	no	
Visitors without entry visa face mandatory (automatic) jail time.	no	

ADDITIONAL COUNTRY INFORMATION

(A)	The types of gifts to avoid:	n/a
(B)	Appropriate gifts for a foreigner to give:	n/a
(C)	Best time to present gifts (at the beginning or at the end of a visit?):	beginning
(D)	Best time to present gifts (on initial or later visits?):	initial
(E)	Best place to present gifts (in private or in public?):	optional
(F)	Number(s) with certain connotations and/or myths attached to them:	n/a
(G)	Basic shape(s) with negative connotations:	n/a
(H)	Basic color(s) with negative connotations:	n/a
(I)	Traditional greeting methods include:	handshake
(J)	Safe topics for discussion include:	weather, fashion, travel, art, family, religion, domestic politics, food, sports, international politics, social condition
(K)	Best time for conversations (before, during, after meals?):	n/a
(L)	Forms of legal punishment:	n/a
(M)	Approximately length of time one could be detained by law and order authorities before being charged in court:	n/a
(N)	January 15, 1999, for example, will normally be written as:	n/a
(O)	Emergency code number:	n/a
(P)	Ambulance code Number:	16
(Q)	Police code number:	17
(R)	Telephone (country) code:	220
(S)	Telex (country) code:	0996
(T)	Electricity requirements:	220 volts
(U)	Legal drinking age:	n/a
(V)	Systems of weights and measures:	metric
(W)	Legal age of incarceration:	n/a
(X)	Driving side of the road:	right
(Y)	Minimum expenditure expected of foreign visitors? $	n/a
(Z)	Name of currency:	Dalasi
(Za)	Some places off-limits to foreign visitors:	n/a
(Zb)	Some places, structures and items prohibited from being photographed:	n/a

GHANA	Is customary Is allowed Is permissible Is used. Is OK	Is not customary Is frowned upon	Is disallowed Is forbidden Is a crime	(See last page for comments on items referenced here)
Smoking in public	✓			
Eating in public	✓			
Not flushing public toilet		✓		
Spitting in public		✓		
Feeding animals & birds in public	✓			
Whistling in public		✓		
Drinking alcohol in public	✓			
Kissing in public		✓		
Breast feeding in public	✓			
Drunkenness (in public)		✓		
Cursing in public		✓		
Religious preaching in public	✓			
Begging (panhandling) in public			✓	
Giving money to beggars/panhandlers			✓	
Giving food/drink to beggars/panhandlers	✓			
Brushing teeth in public (other than in restrooms)		✓		
Strolling with pets in major public roads/streets	✓			
Chewing gum in public	✓			
Chewing gum in government offices		✓		
Combing hair in public (other than in toilets/restrooms)		✓		
Undressing/dressing in public		✓		
Wearing of dark glasses indoors in public places	✓			
Public display of wealth		✓		
Praying openly in public in non-designated areas	✓			
Walking bare feet in public	✓			
Chewing tobacco in public	✓			
Trimming one's finger or toe nails in public		✓		
Laughing aloud in public		✓		
Mingling of the sexes in public	✓			
Mixed bathing in public swimming pools	✓			
Distributing religious pamphlets (literature) in public/side streets	✓			

149

GHANA

	Is customary Is allowed Is permissible Is used. Is OK	Is not customary Is frowned upon	Is disallowed Is forbidden Is a crime	(See last page for comments on items referenced here)
Dancing on side street			✓	
Nude bathing			✓	
Littering			✓	
Binge Drinking	✓			
Hitchhiking	✓			
Jaywalking			✓	
Drunk driving			✓	
Speeding			✓	
Skating on side streets (side-walk)		✓		
Graffiti painting			✓	
Pilfering			✓	
Prostitution			✓	
Haggling in the market place	✓			
Consumption of alcoholic beverages in bars and restaurants	✓			
Gambling	✓			
Possession of pornographic materials			✓	
Possession of the Christian Bible	✓			
Possession of the Moslem Koran	✓			
Possession of bullet-proof vest	✓			
Possession of toy gun	✓			
Possession of fire crackers and fireworks	✓			
Possession of prescription drugs (without doctor's note)			✓	
Possession of regulated drugs (narcotics)			✓	
Possession of firearms (by foreigners)			✓	
Possession of pocket knife in public	✓			
Using walkie talkies	✓			
Using of "boom boxes"(loud sounding stereo system)	✓			
Using "walkman" (very small radio/cassettes with ear plugs) in public places	✓			
Using "walkman" (very small radio/cassettes with ear plugs) while driving or riding			✓	

150

GHANA

	Is customary Is allowed Is permissible Is used Is OK	Is not customary Is frowned upon	Is disallowed Is forbidden Is a crime	(See last page for comments on items referenced here)
Use of cellular phone	✓			
Use of binoculars/periscopes other than in sports arena	✓			
Taking photographs of people (without their permission)		✓		
Taking photographs at airports, train and bus stations			✓	
Taking photographs of airports			✓	
Taking photographs of churches and synagogues	✓			
Taking photographs of religious statues	✓			
Taking photographs of public buildings	✓			
Taking photographs of bridges			✓	
Tipping (gratuity)	✓			
Tipping (when service is rendered)	✓			
Tipping (when service is not rendered)		✓		
Tipping waiters/waitresses at restaurants and hotels	✓			
Tipping taxi/cab drivers	✓			
Tipping baggage handlers, porters, door persons	✓			
Tipping of hair dressers/barbers	✓			
Overtipping	✓			
Undertipping		✓		
Spilling cigarette butt (ash) on side streets/on the floor		✓		
Men wearing lipstick		✓		
Wearing visible tattoo marks	✓			1
Men painting/coloring their finger or toe nails		✓		
Cross dressing (men dressed like women & vice versa)			✓	
Walking in public without a shirt (i.e., with the upper half of the body naked)		✓		
Men wearing braided hair		✓		
Men wearing earrings		✓		
Men wearing dreadlock hair style	✓			
Homosexuality		✓		
Lesbianism		✓		

GHANA

	Is customary Is allowed Is permissible Is used Is OK	Is not customary Is frowned upon	Is disallowed Is forbidden Is a crime	(See last page for comments on items referenced here)
Females covering their hair (wearing headgear) in public	✓			
Females exposing their full face in public	✓			
Females driving automobiles	✓			
Females riding motorcycles	✓			
Females riding bicycles	✓			
Females smoking in public		✓		
Women wearing bras (braziers) in public		✓		
Use of lipstick by women	✓			
A woman extending her hands first when introduced		✓		
Female bashing			✓	
Females wearing trousers	✓			
Females wearing minis (short dresses)		✓		
Females wearing bikinis		✓		
Females wearing shorts		✓		
Persons of opposite sex holding hands in public	✓			
Persons of same sex holding hands in public	✓			
Handshake between opposite sex	✓			
Hugging in public by same sex	✓			
Hugging in public by opposite sex	✓			
Men and women walking side by side in public	✓			
Man walking ahead (in public), with the woman following	✓			
Woman walking ahead (in public), with the man following		✓		
Men opening doors for women	✓			
Sitting with legs crossed in the presence of elders	✓			
Talking to an elderly person with one's hat/cap on		✓		
Talking to an elderly person with hands positioned on both sides of one's waist		✓		
Blowing one's nose in public		✓		
Blowing one's nose in the presence of others		✓		
Addressing people by their title	✓			

GHANA

	Is customary Is allowed Is permissible Is used. Is OK	Is not customary Is frowned upon	Is disallowed Is forbidden Is a crime	(See last page for comments on items referenced here)
Addressing people by their family name/surname/last name/given name	✓			
Addressing people by their first name/ given name	✓			
Women going through doors first	✓			
Men helping women with their coats	✓			
Men extending their hands to women first during greetings	✓			
Taking off one's hat when entering a private home	✓			
Removing one's shoes when entering a private home	✓			
Invited guests bringing food at social gatherings		✓		
Guests bringing drinks at social gatherings		✓		
Shaking hands when leaving a small group	✓			
Shaking hands with everyone present, upon arrival at a social gathering	✓			
Eating with the right hand	✓			
Eating with the left hand		✓		
Eating with both hands		✓		
Presenting a gift or passing on an object with the left hand		✓		
Asking a man about his wife	✓			
Asking a woman about her husband	✓			
Making prior appointments before a meeting or visit	✓			
Addressing an audience with one or both hands in the pocket		✓		
Carrying on conversation during meals	✓			
Females sitting with legs crossed	✓			
People discussing their wealth		✓		
Asking someone his or her age, or how old the person is	✓			
Complementing someone on his/her physical looks	✓			
Complementing someone on his/her attire	✓			
Use of both hands in handshake	✓			
In greeting, a handshake accompanied by a slight bow	✓			

153

GHANA

	Is customary Is allowed Is permissible Is used. Is OK	Is not customary Is frowned upon	Is disallowed Is forbidden Is a crime	(See last page for comments on items referenced here)
Salutations such as "Good morning", "good afternoon", "Good evening"	✓			
The completion of a business deal with a handshake	✓			
Starting a negotiation session with a handshake	✓			
A gift for the host/hostess	✓			
Giving a business gift	✓			
A gift of money (use of money as gift)	✓			
Use of flowers as a gift	✓			2
Use of business cards	✓			
Accepting/presenting gifts with both hands	✓			
Burning of the country's flag			✓	
Mutilation of the national currency			✓	
Casual wearing of clothings made with colors & marks of the national flag	✓			
Wearing of look-alike military (camouflage) fatigues (attire)			✓	
Sitting on the floor (on floor mats)	✓			
Discussion of religion	✓			
Discussion of politics	✓			
Discussion of sex	✓			
Patting/slapping someone on the buttocks		✓		
Patting/slapping someone on the back	✓			
Touching or patting someone's head/hair	.	✓		3
Casual touching of any part of someone's body		✓		
Drinking directly out of a bottle/can		✓		
Placing one's leg(s) on the table or chair		✓		

154

GHANA

	Is customary Is allowed Is permissible Is used. Is OK	Is not customary Is frowned upon	Is disallowed Is forbidden Is a crime	(See last page for comments on items referenced here)
Showing the sole of one's foot (feet)		✓		
People standing very close when talking		✓		
Maintaining steady eye contact (direct gaze) when talking to someone		✓		
Kissing or exchange of kisses on the cheek		✓		
Counting money (change) in someone's palm	✓			
Finger pointing in public (in a daring manner)		✓		
Seeking attention by winking the eyes	✓			
Tapping the head to indicate someone is crazy		✓		
Twirling the head to indicate someone is crazy		✓		
Whistling as a way of requesting something/seeking attention	✓			
Using "thumbs-up" sign to mean OK		✓		
Forming a circle with the thumb and index finger (forefinger) to mean OK		✓		
Using the fingers to make a "V" sign for victory	✓			
Beckoning to someone with the index finger (forefinger)		✓		
The left to right waving of the hand with open palms facing outward to indicate "Good bye"	✓			
The use of a nod to show acknowledgement	✓			
Stopping/beckoning a taxi using a stretched hand with the thumb pointing upward		✓		
Using the thumb finger pointed to a direction, to request a ride or a hike		✓		
Raising one's hand/waving with an open fist to summon a taxi	✓			
Tapping one's foot/feet on the floor in a public gathering		✓		
Wiggling one's leg(s) when in a sitting position		✓		
Use of the hand (by motorists and cyclists) to signal direction of traffic	✓			

155

		(See last page for comments on items referenced here)
Foreign tourists are welcome in the country.	yes	
The use of seat belt is mandatory.	no	
International driving license is accepted.	yes	
Foreign drivers license is accepted.	yes	
It is considered impolite to yawn in public.	yes	
Death penalty for drug trafficking is the law.	no	
Life imprisonment for drug trafficking is the law.	no	
Guilty until proven innocent in court is the law.	no	
Innocent until proven guilty in court is the law.	yes	
Pedestrians always have right of way.	yes	
Exit visas are required of visitors.	no	
Crash helmet is mandatory for motor cyclist.	yes	
Hanging is used as a form of legal punishment.	yes	
Decapitation of a limb is used as a form of punishment.	no	
Caning is used as a form of legal punishment.	no	
Electric shock is used as a form of legal punishment.	no	
One is expected to stand up during the playing of the national anthem.	yes	
Crash helmet is mandatory for bicyclists.	yes	
Guests are expected to eat every thing on their plates.	no	
Table manners are very informal.	no	
One is expected to cover one's mouth when laughing.	no	
A vertical nod of the head means YES (OK).	yes	
A horizontal shaking of the head means NO (Not OK).	yes	
Prostitution is allowed only in designated areas.	no	
One is expected to take off one's hat during playing of national anthem.	yes	
Separate seating arrangements (between sexes) are maintained at movies.	no	
Separate seating arrangements (between sexes) are maintained at churches.	no	
Uninvited visitors or guests may not be welcome, even among acquaintances.	no	
Pets (e.g. cats, dog) are allowed in some hotels and restaurants.	no	
Couples invited for a meal may be separated during meals according to their sex.	no	
Punctuality is the order of business.	no	
Automobiles are driven with headlights always turned on.	no	
Motorcycles are driven with headlights always turned on.	no	
Visitors with expired visa face mandatory jail time.	no	
Visitors without exit visa face jail time.	no	
Visitors without entry visa face mandatory (automatic) jail time.	no	

GHANA

ADDITIONAL COUNTRY INFORMATION

(A)	The types of gifts to avoid:	none
(B)	Appropriate gifts for a foreigner to give:	no particular preference
(C)	Best time to present gifts (at the beginning or at the end of a visit?):	at the beginning
(D)	Best time to present gifts (on initial or later visits?):	on initial visit
(E)	Best place to present gifts (in private or in public?):	either
(F)	Number(s) with certain connotations and/or myths attached to them:	none
(G)	Basic shape(s) with negative connotations:	none
(H)	Basic color(s) with negative connotations:	black, red
(I)	Traditional greeting methods include:	handshake, hi, bow
(J)	Safe topics for discussion include:	weather, fashion, travel, art, family, food, sport, international politics, money and personal wealth
(K)	Best time for conversations (before, during, after meals?):	after meals
(L)	Forms of legal punishment:	jailing, public execution, hanging
(M)	Approximately length of time one could be detained by law and order authorities before being charged in court:	24 hours
(N)	January 15, 1999, for example, will normally be written as:	15/1/99
(O)	Emergency code number:	999
(P)	Ambulance code Number:	999
(Q)	Police code number:	999
(R)	Telephone (country) code:	233
(S)	Telex (country) code:	GH
(T)	Electricity requirements:	220 volt-240v
(U)	Legal drinking age:	18 years
(V)	Systems of weights and measures:	metrics
(W)	Legal age of incarceration:	16
(X)	Driving side of the road:	right
(Y)	Minimum expenditure expected of foreign visitors? $	none
(Z)	Name of currency:	Cedi
(Za)	Some places off-limits to foreign visitors:	military installations
(Zb)	Some places, structures and items prohibited from being photographed:	military installations

ENDNOTES

Item Number: *COMMENTS/EXPLANATIONS*

n/a: Not applicable/Not available/No response

(1) Tatoos on men, other than pornographic ones, are not forbidden.

(2) It is customary to use flowers as a gift for women. It is also customary to use flowers as a gift for both men and women on their jubilee party - or present flowers to artists.

(3) Provided this someone is a child.

REPUBLIC OF GUINEA	Is customary Is allowed Is permissible Is used. Is OK	Is not customary Is frowned upon	Is disallowed Is forbidden Is a crime	(See last page for comments on items referenced here)
Smoking in public	✓			
Eating in public	✓			
Not flushing public toilet		✓		
Spitting in public			✓	
Feeding animals & birds in public		✓		
Whistling in public		✓		
Drinking alcohol in public		✓		
Kissing in public			✓	
Breast feeding in public			✓	
Drunkenness (in public)	✓			
Cursing in public	✓			
Religious preaching in public	✓			
Begging (panhandling) in public	✓			
Giving money to beggars/panhandlers		✓		
Giving food/drink to beggars/panhandlers		✓		
Brushing teeth in public (other than in restrooms)	✓			
Strolling with pets in major public roads/streets	✓			
Chewing gum in public		✓		
Chewing gum in government offices	✓			
Combing hair in public (other than in toilets/restrooms)		✓		
Undressing/dressing in public	✓			
Wearing of dark glasses indoors in public places		✓		
Public display of wealth		✓		
Praying openly in public in non-designated areas	✓			
Walking bare feet in public	✓			
Chewing tobacco in public		✓		
Trimming one's finger or toe nails in public		✓		
Laughing aloud in public		✓		
Mingling of the sexes in public		✓		
Mixed bathing in public swimming pools	✓			
Distributing religious pamphlets (literature) in public/side streets	✓			

GUINEA, REP. OF

	Is customary Is allowed Is permissible Is used. Is OK	Is not customary Is frowned upon	Is disallowed Is forbidden Is a crime	(See last page for comments on items referenced here)
Dancing on side street		✓	✓	
Nude bathing			✓	
Littering		✓		
Binge Drinking		✓		
Hitchhiking	✓	✓		
Jaywalking	✓			
Drunk driving	✓			
Speeding	✓			
Skating on side streets (side-walk)		✓		
Graffiti painting		✓		
Pilfering		✓		
Prostitution			✓	
Haggling in the market place			✓	
Consumption of alcoholic beverages in bars and restaurants	✓			
Gambling	✓			
Possession of pornographic materials	✓			
Possession of the Christian Bible	✓			
Possession of the Moslem Koran	✓			
Possession of bullet-proof vest			✓	
Possession of toy gun				
Possession of fire crackers and fireworks				✓
Possession of prescription drugs (without doctor's note)			✓	
Possession of regulated drugs (narcotics)				✓
Possession of firearms (by foreigners)			✓	
Possession of pocket knife in public			✓	
Using walkie talkies			✓	
Using of "boom boxes"(loud sounding stereo system)			✓	
Using "walkman" (very small radio/cassettes with ear plugs) in public places				
Using "walkman" (very small radio/cassettes with ear plugs) while driving or riding				

160

GUINEA, REP. OF

	Is customary Is allowed Is permissible Is used Is OK	Is not customary Is frowned upon	Is disallowed Is forbidden Is a crime	(See last page for comments on items referenced here)
Use of cellular phone	✓			
Use of binoculars/periscopes other than in sports arena	✓			
Taking photographs of people (without their permission)	✓			
Taking photographs at airports, train and bus stations	✓			
Taking photographs of airports	✓			
Taking photographs of churches and synagogues	✓			
Taking photographs of religious statues	✓			
Taking photographs of public buildings	✓			
Taking photographs of bridges		✓		
Tipping (gratuity)		✓		
Tipping (when service is rendered)		✓		
Tipping (when service is not rendered)			✓	
Tipping waiters/waitresses at restaurants and hotels			✓	
Tipping taxi/cab drivers		✓		
Tipping baggage handlers, porters, door persons		✓		
Tipping of hair dressers/barbers		✓		
Overtipping	✓			
Undertipping	✓			
Spilling cigarette butt (ash) on side streets/on the floor		✓		
Men wearing lipstick	✓			
Wearing visible tattoo marks	✓			
Men painting/coloring their finger or toe nails	✓			
Cross dressing (men dressed like women & vice versa)	✓			
Walking in public without a shirt (i.e., with the upper half of the body naked)	✓			
Men wearing braided hair		✓		
Men wearing earrings		✓		
Men wearing dreadlock hair style		✓		
Homosexuality		✓		
Lesbianism		✓		

GUINEA, REP. OF

	Is customary Is allowed Is permissible Is used Is OK	Is not customary Is frowned upon	Is disallowed Is forbidden Is a crime	(See last page for comments on items referenced here)
Females covering their hair (wearing headgear) in public	✓			
Females exposing their full face in public	✓			
Females driving automobiles	✓			
Females riding motorcycles	✓			
Females riding bicycles	✓			
Females smoking in public	✓			
Women wearing bras (braziers) in public	✓			
Use of lipstick by women	✓			
A woman extending her hands first when introduced	✓			
Female bashing		✓		
Females wearing trousers		✓		
Females wearing minis (short dresses)	✓			
Females wearing bikinis	✓			
Females wearing shorts	✓			
Persons of opposite sex holding hands in public	✓			
Persons of same sex holding hands in public	✓			
Handshake between opposite sex	✓			
Hugging in public by same sex	✓			
Hugging in public by opposite sex	✓			
Men and women walking side by side in public		✓		
Man walking ahead (in public), with the woman following		✓		
Woman walking ahead (in public), with the man following		✓		
Men opening doors for women		✓		
Sitting with legs crossed in the presence of elders			✓	
Talking to an elderly person with one's hat/cap on			✓	
Talking to an elderly person with hands positioned on both sides of one's waist		✓		
Blowing one's nose in public	✓			
Blowing one's nose in the presence of others	✓			
Addressing people by their title	✓			

GUINEA, REP. OF

	Is customary Is allowed Is permissible Is used. Is OK	Is not customary Is frowned upon	Is disallowed Is forbidden Is a crime	(See last page for comments on items referenced here)
Addressing people by their family name/surname/last name/given name	✓			
Addressing people by their first name/ given name	✓			
Women going through doors first	✓			
Men helping women with their coats	✓			
Men extending their hands to women first during greetings	✓			
Taking off one's hat when entering a private home	✓			
Removing one's shoes when entering a private home	✓			
Invited guests bringing food at social gatherings	✓			
Guests bringing drinks at social gatherings	✓			
Shaking hands when leaving a small group	✓			
Shaking hands with everyone present, upon arrival at a social gathering	✓			
Eating with the right hand	✓			
Eating with the left hand	✓			
Eating with both hands	✓			
Presenting a gift or passing on an object with the left hand	✓			
Asking a man about his wife	✓			
Asking a woman about her husband	✓			
Making prior appointments before a meeting or visit	✓			
Addressing an audience with one or both hands in the pocket	✓			
Carrying on conversation during meals	✓			
Females sitting with legs crossed	✓			
People discussing their wealth	✓			
Asking someone his or her age, or how old the person is	✓			
Complementing someone on his/her physical looks	✓			
Complementing someone on his/her attire	✓			
Use of both hands in handshake	✓			
In greeting, a handshake accompanied by a slight bow	✓			

GUINEA, REP. OF

	Is customary Is allowed Is permissible Is used. Is OK	Is not customary Is frowned upon	Is disallowed Is forbidden Is a crime	(See last page for comments on items referenced here)
Salutations such as "Good morning", "good afternoon", "Good evening"	✓			
The completion of a business deal with a handshake	✓			
Starting a negotiation session with a handshake	✓			
A gift for the host/hostess	✓			
Giving a business gift	✓			
A gift of money (use of money as gift)	✓			
Use of flowers as a gift	✓			
Use of business cards	✓			
Accepting/presenting gifts with both hands	✓			
Burning of the country's flag	✓			
Mutilation of the national currency		✓		
Casual wearing of clothings made with colors & marks of the national flag			✓	
Wearing of look-alike military (camouflage) fatigues (attire)			✓	
Sitting on the floor (on floor mats)		✓		
Discussion of religion	✓			
Discussion of politics	✓			
Discussion of sex	✓			
Patting/slapping someone on the buttocks	✓			
Patting/slapping someone on the back	✓			
Touching or patting someone's head/hair	✓			
Casual touching of any part of someone's body	✓			
Drinking directly out of a bottle/can	✓			
Placing one's leg(s) on the table or chair	✓			

164

GUINEA, REP. OF

	Is customary Is allowed Is permissible Is used. Is OK	Is not customary Is frowned upon	Is disallowed Is forbidden Is a crime	(See last page for comments on items referenced here)
Showing the sole of one's foot (feet)	✓			
People standing very close when talking	✓			
Maintaining steady eye contact (direct gaze) when talking to someone				n/a
Kissing or exchange of kisses on the cheek				n/a
Counting money (change) in someone's palm				n/a
Finger pointing in public (in a daring manner)				n/a
Seeking attention by winking the eyes				n/a
Tapping the head to indicate someone is crazy				n/a
Twirling the head to indicate someone is crazy				n/a
Whistling as a way of requesting something/seeking attention				n/a
Using "thumbs-up" sign to mean OK				n/a
Forming a circle with the thumb and index finger (forefinger) to mean OK				n/a
Using the fingers to make a "V" sign for victory				n/a
Beckoning to someone with the index finger (forefinger)				n/a
The left to right waving of the hand with open palms facing outward to indicate "Good bye"				n/a
The use of a nod to show acknowledgement				n/a
Stopping/beckoning a taxi using a stretched hand with the thumb pointing upward				n/a
Using the thumb finger pointed to a direction, to request a ride or a hike				n/a
Raising one's hand/waving with an open fist to summon a taxi				n/a
Tapping one's foot/feet on the floor in a public gathering				n/a
Wiggling one's leg(s) when in a sitting position				n/a
Use of the hand (by motorists and cyclists) to signal direction of traffic				n/a

GUINEA, REP. OF

		(See last page for comments on items referenced here)
Foreign tourists are welcome in the country.	yes	
The use of seat belt is mandatory.	no	
International driving license is accepted.	yes	
Foreign drivers license is accepted.	no	
It is considered impolite to yawn in public.	no	
Death penalty for drug trafficking is the law.	no	
Life imprisonment for drug trafficking is the law.	no	
Guilty until proven innocent in court is the law.	no	
Innocent until proven guilty in court is the law.	yes	
Pedestrians always have right of way.	yes	
Exit visas are required of visitors.	yes	
Crash helmet is mandatory for motor cyclist.	yes	
Hanging is used as a form of legal punishment.	yes	
Decapitation of a limb is used as a form of punishment.	no	
Caning is used as a form of legal punishment.	no	
Electric shock is used as a form of legal punishment.	no	
One is expected to stand up during the playing of the national anthem.	no	
Crash helmet is mandatory for bicyclists.	yes	
Guests are expected to eat every thing on their plates.	yes	
Table manners are very informal.	yes	
One is expected to cover one's mouth when laughing.	yes	
A vertical nod of the head means YES (OK).	yes	
A horizontal shaking of the head means NO (Not OK).	yes	
Prostitution is allowed only in designated areas.	no	
One is expected to take off one's hat during playing of national anthem.	no	
Separate seating arrangements (between sexes) are maintained at movies.	no	
Separate seating arrangements (between sexes) are maintained at churches.	no	
Uninvited visitors or guests may not be welcome, even among acquaintances.	no	
Pets (e.g. cats, dog) are allowed in some hotels and restaurants.	yes	
Couples invited for a meal may be separated during meals according to their sex.	no	
Punctuality is the order of business.	no	
Automobiles are driven with headlights always turned on.		n/a
Motorcycles are driven with headlights always turned on.		n/a
Visitors with expired visa face mandatory jail time.	no	
Visitors without exit visa face jail time.	no	
Visitors without entry visa face mandatory (automatic) jail time.	no	

166

ADDITIONAL COUNTRY INFORMATION

(A)	The types of gifts to avoid:	n/a
(B)	Appropriate gifts for a foreigner to give:	perfume, dresses, money, toys, tapes, camera
(C)	Best time to present gifts (at the beginning or at the end of a visit?):	at the end
(D)	Best time to present gifts (on initial or later visits?):	n/a
(E)	Best place to present gifts (in private or in public?):	n/a
(F)	Number(s) with certain connotations and/or myths attached to them:	n/a
(G)	Basic shape(s) with negative connotations:	n/a
(H)	Basic color(s) with negative connotations:	n/a
(I)	Traditional greeting methods include:	n/a
(J)	Safe topics for discussion include:	weather, fashion, travel, art, family, religion, domestic politics, food, sports, international politics, social conditions, money personal wealth
(K)	Best time for conversations (before, during, after meals?):	n/a
(L)	Forms of legal punishment:	jailing
(M)	Approximately length of time one could be detained by law and order authorities before being charged in court:	48 hours
(N)	January 15, 1999, for example, will normally be written as:	15/1/99
(O)	Emergency code number:	17-18
(P)	Ambulance code Number:	46-48-74
(Q)	Police code number:	17-18
(R)	Telephone (country) code:	n/a
(S)	Telex (country) code:	n/a
(T)	Electricity requirements:	n/a
(U)	Legal drinking age:	none
(V)	Systems of weights and measures:	n/a
(W)	Legal age of incarceration:	18 years
(X)	Driving side of the road:	right
(Y)	Minimum expenditure expected of foreign visitors? $	no
(Z)	Name of currency:	Franc Guinean
(Za)	Some places off-limits to foreign visitors:	n/a
(Zb)	Some places, structures and items prohibited from being photographed:	n/a

KENYA	Is customary Is allowed Is permissible Is used. Is OK	Is not customary Is frowned upon	Is disallowed Is forbidden Is a crime	(See last page for comments on items referenced here)
Smoking in public	✓			
Eating in public	✓			
Not flushing public toilet		✓		
Spitting in public		✓		
Feeding animals & birds in public	✓			
Whistling in public		✓		
Drinking alcohol in public		✓		
Kissing in public		✓		
Breast feeding in public	✓			
Drunkenness (in public)		✓		
Cursing in public		✓		
Religious preaching in public	✓			
Begging (panhandling) in public		✓		
Giving money to beggars/panhandlers	✓			
Giving food/drink to beggars/panhandlers	✓			
Brushing teeth in public (other than in restrooms)	✓			
Strolling with pets in major public roads/streets		✓		
Chewing gum in public	✓			
Chewing gum in government offices		✓		
Combing hair in public (other than in toilets/restrooms)		✓		
Undressing/dressing in public			✓	
Wearing of dark glasses indoors in public places		✓		
Public display of wealth		✓		
Praying openly in public in non-designated areas	✓			
Walking bare feet in public		✓		
Chewing tobacco in public	✓			
Trimming one's finger or toe nails in public		✓		
Laughing aloud in public		✓		
Mingling of the sexes in public	✓			
Mixed bathing in public swimming pools	✓			
Distributing religious pamphlets (literature) in public/side streets	✓			

KENYA

	Is customary Is allowed Is permissible Is used. Is OK	Is not customary Is frowned upon	Is disallowed Is forbidden Is a crime	(See last page for comments on items referenced here)
Dancing on side street	✓			
Nude bathing	✓			
Littering		✓		
Binge Drinking	✓			
Hitchhiking	✓			
Jaywalking		✓		
Drunk driving			✓	
Speeding			✓	
Skating on side streets (side-walk)		✓		
Graffiti painting			✓	
Pilfering			✓	
Prostitution			✓	
Haggling in the market place		✓		
Consumption of alcoholic beverages in bars and restaurants	✓			
Gambling	✓			
Possession of pornographic materials			✓	
Possession of the Christian Bible	✓			
Possession of the Moslem Koran	✓			
Possession of bullet-proof vest	✓			
Possession of toy gun			✓	
Possession of fire crackers and fireworks	✓			
Possession of prescription drugs (without doctor's note)			✓	
Possession of regulated drugs (narcotics)			✓	
Possession of firearms (by foreigners)			✓	
Possession of pocket knife in public	✓			
Using walkie talkies	✓			
Using of "boom boxes"(loud sounding stereo system)		✓		
Using "walkman" (very small radio/cassettes with ear plugs) in public places	✓			
Using "walkman" (very small radio/cassettes with ear plugs) while driving or riding	✓			

169

KENYA

	Is customary Is allowed Is permissible Is used Is OK	Is not customary Is frowned upon	Is disallowed Is forbidden Is a crime	(See last page for comments on items referenced here)
Use of cellular phone	✓			
Use of binoculars/periscopes other than in sports arena	✓			
Taking photographs of people (without their permission)				✓
Taking photographs at airports, train and bus stations	✓			
Taking photographs of airports	✓			
Taking photographs of churches and synagogues	✓			
Taking photographs of religious statues	✓			
Taking photographs of public buildings	✓			
Taking photographs of bridges	✓			
Tipping (gratuity)	✓			
Tipping (when service is rendered)	✓			
Tipping (when service is not rendered)	✓			
Tipping waiters/waitresses at restaurants and hotels	✓			
Tipping taxi/cab drivers	✓			
Tipping baggage handlers, porters, door persons	✓			
Tipping of hair dressers/barbers	✓			
Overtipping	✓			
Undertipping	✓			
Spilling cigarette butt (ash) on side streets/on the floor		✓		
Men wearing lipstick		✓		
Wearing visible tattoo marks	✓			
Men painting/coloring their finger or toe nails		✓		
Cross dressing (men dressed like women & vice versa)		✓		
Walking in public without a shirt (i.e., with the upper half of the body naked)		✓		
Men wearing braided hair		✓		
Men wearing earrings		✓		
Men wearing dreadlock hair style	✓			
Homosexuality			✓	
Lesbianism			✓	

KENYA

	Is customary Is allowed Is permissible Is used Is OK	Is not customary Is frowned upon	Is disallowed Is forbidden Is a crime	(See last page for comments on items referenced here)
Females covering their hair (wearing headgear) in public	✓			
Females exposing their full face in public	✓			
Females driving automobiles	✓			
Females riding motorcycles	✓			
Females riding bicycles	✓			
Females smoking in public		✓		
Women wearing bras (braziers) in public		✓		
Use of lipstick by women	✓			
A woman extending her hands first when introduced	✓			
Female bashing			✓	
Females wearing trousers	✓			
Females wearing minis (short dresses)	✓			
Females wearing bikinis	✓			
Females wearing shorts	✓			
Persons of opposite sex holding hands in public	✓			
Persons of same sex holding hands in public		✓		
Handshake between opposite sex	✓			
Hugging in public by same sex		✓		
Hugging in public by opposite sex	✓			
Men and women walking side by side in public	✓			
Man walking ahead (in public), with the woman following	✓			
Woman walking ahead (in public), with the man following	✓			
Men opening doors for women	✓			
Sitting with legs crossed in the presence of elders	✓			
Talking to an elderly person with one's hat/cap on		✓		
Talking to an elderly person with hands positioned on both sides of one's waist		✓		
Blowing one's nose in public		✓		
Blowing one's nose in the presence of others		✓		
Addressing people by their title	✓			

171

KENYA

	Is customary Is allowed Is permissible Is used. Is OK	Is not customary Is frowned upon	Is disallowed Is forbidden Is a crime	(See last page for comments on items referenced here)
Addressing people by their family name/surname/last name/given name	✓			
Addressing people by their first name/ given name	✓			
Women going through doors first	✓			
Men helping women with their coats	✓			
Men extending their hands to women first during greetings	✓			
Taking off one's hat when entering a private home	✓			
Removing one's shoes when entering a private home	✓			
Invited guests bringing food at social gatherings	✓			
Guests bringing drinks at social gatherings	✓			
Shaking hands when leaving a small group	✓			
Shaking hands with everyone present, upon arrival at a social gathering	✓			
Eating with the right hand	✓			
Eating with the left hand	✓			
Eating with both hands		✓		
Presenting a gift or passing on an object with the left hand		✓		
Asking a man about his wife	✓			
Asking a woman about her husband	✓			
Making prior appointments before a meeting or visit	✓			
Addressing an audience with one or both hands in the pocket		✓		
Carrying on conversation during meals	✓			
Females sitting with legs crossed	✓			
People discussing their wealth	✓			
Asking someone his or her age, or how old the person is	✓			
Complementing someone on his/her physical looks	✓			
Complementing someone on his/her attire	✓			
Use of both hands in handshake	✓			
In greeting, a handshake accompanied by a slight bow	✓			

172

KENYA

	Is customary Is allowed Is permissible Is used. Is OK	Is not customary Is frowned upon	Is disallowed Is forbidden Is a crime	(See last page for comments on items referenced here)
Salutations such as "Good morning", "good afternoon", "Good evening"	✓			
The completion of a business deal with a handshake	✓			
Starting a negotiation session with a handshake	✓			
A gift for the host/hostess	✓			
Giving a business gift	✓			
A gift of money (use of money as gift)	✓			
Use of flowers as a gift	✓			
Use of business cards	✓			
Accepting/presenting gifts with both hands	✓			
Burning of the country's flag			✓	
Mutilation of the national currency			✓	
Casual wearing of clothings made with colors & marks of the national flag		✓		
Wearing of look-alike military (camouflage) fatigues (attire)			✓	
Sitting on the floor (on floor mats)	✓			
Discussion of religion	✓			
Discussion of politics	✓			
Discussion of sex	✓			
Patting/slapping someone on the buttocks		✓		
Patting/slapping someone on the back	✓			
Touching or patting someone's head/hair	✓			
Casual touching of any part of someone's body	✓			
Drinking directly out of a bottle/can	✓			
Placing one's leg(s) on the table or chair		✓		

173

KENYA

	Is customary Is allowed Is permissible Is used. Is OK	Is not customary Is frowned upon	Is disallowed Is forbidden Is a crime	(See last page for comments on items referenced here)
Showing the sole of one's foot (feet)	✓			
People standing very close when talking	✓			
Maintaining steady eye contact (direct gaze) when talking to someone	✓			
Kissing or exchange of kisses on the cheek	✓			
Counting money (change) in someone's palm	✓			
Finger pointing in public (in a daring manner)			✓	
Seeking attention by winking the eyes	✓			
Tapping the head to indicate someone is crazy		✓		
Twirling the head to indicate someone is crazy		✓		
Whistling as a way of requesting something/seeking attention	✓			
Using "thumbs-up" sign to mean OK	✓			
Forming a circle with the thumb and index finger (forefinger) to mean OK	✓			
Using the fingers to make a "V" sign for victory	✓			
Beckoning to someone with the index finger (forefinger)		✓		
The left to right waving of the hand with open palms facing outward to indicate "Good bye"	✓			
The use of a nod to show acknowledgement	✓			
Stopping/beckoning a taxi using a stretched hand with the thumb pointing upward	✓			
Using the thumb finger pointed to a direction, to request a ride or a hike		✓		
Raising one's hand/waving with an open fist to summon a taxi	✓			
Tapping one's foot/feet on the floor in a public gathering	✓			
Wiggling one's leg(s) when in a sitting position	✓			
Use of the hand (by motorists and cyclists) to signal direction of traffic	✓			

174

KENYA

		(See last page for comments on items referenced here)
Foreign tourists are welcome in the country.	yes	
The use of seat belt is mandatory.	no	
International driving license is accepted.	yes	
Foreign drivers license is accepted.	yes	
It is considered impolite to yawn in public.	yes	
Death penalty for drug trafficking is the law.	yes	
Life imprisonment for drug trafficking is the law.	no	
Guilty until proven innocent in court is the law.	no	
Innocent until proven guilty in court is the law.	yes	
Pedestrians always have right of way.	yes	
Exit visas are required of visitors.	yes	
Crash helmet is mandatory for motor cyclist.	yes	
Hanging is used as a form of legal punishment.	yes	
Decapitation of a limb is used as a form of punishment.	no	
Caning is used as a form of legal punishment.	yes	
Electric shock is used as a form of legal punishment.	no	
One is expected to stand up during the playing of the national anthem.	yes	
Crash helmet is mandatory for bicyclists.	no	
Guests are expected to eat every thing on their plates.	no	
Table manners are very informal.	yes	
One is expected to cover one's mouth when laughing.	no	
A vertical nod of the head means YES (OK).	yes	
A horizontal shaking of the head means NO (Not OK).	yes	
Prostitution is allowed only in designated areas.	no	
One is expected to take off one's hat during playing of national anthem.	yes	
Separate seating arrangements (between sexes) are maintained at movies.	no	
Separate seating arrangements (between sexes) are maintained at churches.	no	
Uninvited visitors or guests may not be welcome, even among acquaintances.	no	
Pets (e.g. cats, dog) are allowed in some hotels and restaurants.	no	
Couples invited for a meal may be separated during meals according to their sex.	no	
Punctuality is the order of business.	yes	
Automobiles are driven with headlights always turned on.	no	
Motorcycles are driven with headlights always turned on.	yes	
Visitors with expired visa face mandatory jail time.	yes	
Visitors without exit visa face jail time.	no	
Visitors without entry visa face mandatory (automatic) jail time.	no	

ADDITIONAL COUNTRY INFORMATION

(A)	The types of gifts to avoid:	n/a
(B)	Appropriate gifts for a foreigner to give:	watches, radio, clothes,shoes, etc.
(C)	Best time to present gifts (at the beginning or at the end of a visit?):	at the beginning
(D)	Best time to present gifts (on initial or later visits?):	on initial
(E)	Best place to present gifts (in private or in public?):	private
(F)	Number(s) with certain connotations and/or myths attached to them:	none
(G)	Basic shape(s) with negative connotations:	none
(H)	Basic color(s) with negative connotations:	none
(I)	Traditional greeting methods include:	a handshake, a hug, a nod, a bow
(J)	Safe topics for discussion include:	weather, fashion, travel, art, family, religion, domestic politics, food, sports, international politics, social conditions, money and personal wealth, sex.
(K)	Best time for conversations (before, during, after meals?):	after meals
(L)	Forms of legal punishment:	jailing, flogging, hanging
(M)	Approximately length of time one could be detained by law and order authorities before being charged in court:	24 hours
(N)	January 15, 1999, for example, will normally be written as:	1/15/99
(O)	Emergency code number:	999
(P)	Ambulance code Number:	999
(Q)	Police code number:	999
(R)	Telephone (country) code:	011-254
(S)	Telex (country) code:	n/a
(T)	Electricity requirements:	220 volts
(U)	Legal drinking age:	21 years
(V)	Systems of weights and measures:	metric
(W)	Legal age of incarceration:	21 years
(X)	Driving side of the road:	left
(Y)	Minimum expenditure expected of foreign visitors? $	no limit
(Z)	Name of currency:	Kenya Shilling
(Za)	Some places off-limits to foreign visitors:	security areas
(Zb)	Some places, structures and items prohibited from being photographed:	military installations

LESOTHO	Is customary Is allowed Is permissible Is used. Is OK	Is not customary Is frowned upon	Is disallowed Is forbidden Is a crime	(See last page for comments on items referenced here)
Smoking in public		✓		
Eating in public		✓		
Not flushing public toilet			✓	
Spitting in public			✓	
Feeding animals & birds in public		✓		
Whistling in public		✓		
Drinking alcohol in public			✓	
Kissing in public			✓	
Breast feeding in public	✓			
Drunkenness (in public)			✓	
Cursing in public		✓		
Religious preaching in public			✓	
Begging (panhandling) in public	✓			1
Giving money to beggars/panhandlers	✓			1
Giving food/drink to beggars/panhandlers	✓			1
Brushing teeth in public (other than in restrooms)		✓		
Strolling with pets in major public roads/streets		✓		
Chewing gum in public		✓		
Chewing gum in government offices		✓		
Combing hair in public (other than in toilets/restrooms)		✓		
Undressing/dressing in public		✓		
Wearing of dark glasses indoors in public places		✓		
Public display of wealth		✓		2
Praying openly in public in non-designated areas		✓		
Walking bare feet in public	✓			
Chewing tobacco in public		✓		
Trimming one's finger or toe nails in public		✓		
Laughing aloud in public		✓		
Mingling of the sexes in public		✓		
Mixed bathing in public swimming pools	✓			
Distributing religious pamphlets (literature) in public/side streets	✓			

LESOTHO

	Is customary Is allowed Is permissible Is used. Is OK	Is not customary Is frowned upon	Is disallowed Is forbidden Is a crime	(See last page for comments on items referenced here)
Dancing on side street		✓		
Nude bathing			✓	3
Littering			✓	4
Binge Drinking			✓	
Hitchhiking			✓	
Jaywalking			✓	
Drunk driving			✓	
Speeding			✓	
Skating on side streets (side-walk)			✓	
Graffiti painting		✓		
Pilfering		✓		
Prostitution		✓		
Haggling in the market place		✓		
Consumption of alcoholic beverages in bars and restaurants	✓			
Gambling		✓		
Possession of pornographic materials			✓	
Possession of the Christian Bible	✓			
Possession of the Moslem Koran	✓			
Possession of bullet-proof vest			✓	
Possession of toy gun			✓	
Possession of fire crackers and fireworks			✓	
Possession of prescription drugs (without doctor's note)			✓	5
Possession of regulated drugs (narcotics)			✓	
Possession of firearms (by foreigners)			✓	
Possession of pocket knife in public		✓		
Using walkie talkies			✓	
Using of "boom boxes"(loud sounding stereo system)			✓	
Using "walkman" (very small radio/cassettes with ear plugs) in public places		✓		
Using "walkman" (very small radio/cassettes with ear plugs) while driving or riding		✓		✓

LESOTHO

	Is customary Is allowed Is permissible Is used Is OK	Is not customary Is frowned upon	Is disallowed Is forbidden Is a crime	(See last page for comments on items referenced here)
Use of cellular phone	✓			
Use of binoculars/periscopes other than in sports arena	✓			
Taking photographs of people (without their permission)	✓			
Taking photographs at airports, train and bus stations	✓			
Taking photographs of airports	✓			
Taking photographs of churches and synagogues	✓			
Taking photographs of religious statues	✓			
Taking photographs of public buildings		✓		
Taking photographs of bridges		✓		
Tipping (gratuity)	✓			
Tipping (when service is rendered)	✓			
Tipping (when service is not rendered)	✓			
Tipping waiters/waitresses at restaurants and hotels	✓			
Tipping taxi/cab drivers	✓	✓		
Tipping baggage handlers, porters, door persons	✓			
Tipping of hair dressers/barbers			✓	
Overtipping	✓			
Undertipping	✓			
Spilling cigarette butt (ash) on side streets/on the floor	✓			
Men wearing lipstick			✓	6
Wearing visible tattoo marks			✓	
Men painting/coloring their finger or toe nails			✓	6
Cross dressing (men dressed like women & vice versa)			✓	6
Walking in public without a shirt (i.e., with the upper half of the body naked)	✓			
Men wearing braided hair	✓			
Men wearing earrings	✓			
Men wearing dreadlock hair style		✓		
Homosexuality			✓	
Lesbianism			✓	

	Is customary Is allowed Is permissible Is used Is OK	Is not customary Is frowned upon	Is disallowed Is forbidden Is a crime	(See last page for comments on items referenced here)
Females covering their hair (wearing headgear) in public	✓			
Females exposing their full face in public	✓			
Females driving automobiles	✓			
Females riding motorcycles	✓			
Females riding bicycles		✓		
Females smoking in public		✓		
Women wearing bras (braziers) in public			✓	
Use of lipstick by women		✓		
A woman extending her hands first when introduced	✓			
Female bashing	✓			
Females wearing trousers		✓		
Females wearing minis (short dresses)		✓		
Females wearing bikinis		✓		
Females wearing shorts		✓		
Persons of opposite sex holding hands in public			✓	
Persons of same sex holding hands in public			✓	
Handshake between opposite sex		✓		
Hugging in public by same sex			✓	
Hugging in public by opposite sex			✓	
Men and women walking side by side in public		✓		
Man walking ahead (in public), with the woman following		✓		
Woman walking ahead (in public), with the man following	✓			
Men opening doors for women		✓		
Sitting with legs crossed in the presence of elders			✓	
Talking to an elderly person with one's hat/cap on			✓	
Talking to an elderly person with hands positioned on both sides of one's waist			✓	
Blowing one's nose in public	✓			
Blowing one's nose in the presence of others	✓			
Addressing people by their title		✓		

180

LESOTHO

	Is customary Is allowed Is permissible Is used. Is OK	Is not customary Is frowned upon	Is disallowed Is forbidden Is a crime	(See last page for comments on items referenced here)
Addressing people by their family name/surname/last name/given name		✓		
Addressing people by their first name/ given name	✓			
Women going through doors first		✓		
Men helping women with their coats		✓		
Men extending their hands to women first during greetings		✓		
Taking off one's hat when entering a private home		✓		
Removing one's shoes when entering a private home	✓			
Invited guests bringing food at social gatherings		✓		
Guests bringing drinks at social gatherings		✓		
Shaking hands when leaving a small group	✓			
Shaking hands with everyone present, upon arrival at a social gathering	✓			
Eating with the right hand	✓			
Eating with the left hand		✓		
Eating with both hands			✓	
Presenting a gift or passing on an object with the left hand		✓		
Asking a man about his wife		✓		
Asking a woman about her husband	✓			
Making prior appointments before a meeting or visit		✓		
Addressing an audience with one or both hands in the pocket		✓		
Carrying on conversation during meals	✓			
Females sitting with legs crossed	✓			
People discussing their wealth		✓		
Asking someone his or her age, or how old the person is		✓		
Complementing someone on his/her physical looks		✓		
Complementing someone on his/her attire		✓		
Use of both hands in handshake	✓			
In greeting, a handshake accompanied by a slight bow	✓			

181

LESOTHO

	Is customary Is allowed Is permissible Is used. Is OK	Is not customary Is frowned upon	Is disallowed Is forbidden Is a crime	(See last page for comments on items referenced here)
Salutations such as "Good morning", "good afternoon", "Good evening"	✓			
The completion of a business deal with a handshake	✓			
Starting a negotiation session with a handshake	✓			
A gift for the host/hostess		✓		
Giving a business gift		✓		
A gift of money (use of money as gift)		✓		
Use of flowers as a gift		✓		
Use of business cards		✓		
Accepting/presenting gifts with both hands		✓		
Burning of the country's flag			✓	
Mutilation of the national currency			✓	
Casual wearing of clothings made with colors & marks of the national flag		✓		
Wearing of look-alike military (camouflage) fatigues (attire)			✓	
Sitting on the floor (on floor mats)	✓			
Discussion of religion	✓			
Discussion of politics	✓			
Discussion of sex		✓		
Patting/slapping someone on the buttocks	✓			
Patting/slapping someone on the back	✓			
Touching or patting someone's head/hair		✓		
Casual touching of any part of someone's body		✓		
Drinking directly out of a bottle/can		✓		
Placing one's leg(s) on the table or chair		✓		

182

	Is customary Is allowed Is permissible Is used. Is OK	Is not customary Is frowned upon	Is disallowed Is forbidden Is a crime	(See last page for comments on items referenced here)
Showing the sole of one's foot (feet)		✓		
People standing very close when talking	✓			
Maintaining steady eye contact (direct gaze) when talking to someone		✓		
Kissing or exchange of kisses on the cheek			✓	
Counting money (change) in someone's palm	✓			
Finger pointing in public (in a daring manner)		✓		
Seeking attention by winking the eyes				n/a
Tapping the head to indicate someone is crazy				n/a
Twirling the head to indicate someone is crazy				n/a
Whistling as a way of requesting something/seeking attention				n/a
Using "thumbs-up" sign to mean OK		✓		
Forming a circle with the thumb and index finger (forefinger) to mean OK		✓		
Using the fingers to make a "V" sign for victory		✓		
Beckoning to someone with the index finger (forefinger)				n/a
The left to right waving of the hand with open palms facing outward to indicate "Good bye"				n/a
The use of a nod to show acknowledgement				n/a
Stopping/beckoning a taxi using a stretched hand with the thumb pointing upward				n/a
Using the thumb finger pointed to a direction, to request a ride or a hike				n/a
Raising one's hand/waving with an open fist to summon a taxi	✓			
Tapping one's foot/feet on the floor in a public gathering				n/a
Wiggling one's leg(s) when in a sitting position				n/a
Use of the hand (by motorists and cyclists) to signal direction of traffic	✓			

LESOTHO

		(See last page for comments on items referenced here)
Foreign tourists are welcome in the country.	yes	
The use of seat belt is mandatory.	yes	
International driving license is accepted.	yes	
Foreign drivers license is accepted.	yes	
It is considered impolite to yawn in public.	no	
Death penalty for drug trafficking is the law.	no	
Life imprisonment for drug trafficking is the law.	no	
Guilty until proven innocent in court is the law.	no	
Innocent until proven guilty in court is the law.	yes	
Pedestrians always have right of way.	no	
Exit visas are required of visitors.	no	
Crash helmet is mandatory for motor cyclist.	yes	
Hanging is used as a form of legal punishment.	yes	
Decapitation of a limb is used as a form of punishment.	no	
Caning is used as a form of legal punishment.	yes	
Electric shock is used as a form of legal punishment.	no	
One is expected to stand up during the playing of the national anthem.	yes	
Crash helmet is mandatory for bicyclists.	no	
Guests are expected to eat every thing on their plates.	yes	
Table manners are very informal.	no	
One is expected to cover one's mouth when laughing.	no	
A vertical nod of the head means YES (OK).	yes	
A horizontal shaking of the head means NO (Not OK).	yes	
Prostitution is allowed only in designated areas.	no	
One is expected to take off one's hat during playing of national anthem.	yes	
Separate seating arrangements (between sexes) are maintained at movies.	no	
Separate seating arrangements (between sexes) are maintained at churches.	no	
Uninvited visitors or guests may not be welcome, even among acquaintances.	no	
Pets (e.g. cats, dog) are allowed in some hotels and restaurants.	yes	
Couples invited for a meal may be separated during meals according to their sex.	no	
Punctuality is the order of business.	yes	
Automobiles are driven with headlights always turned on.	no	
Motorcycles are driven with headlights always turned on.	no	
Visitors with expired visa face mandatory jail time.	no	
Visitors without exit visa face jail time.	no	
Visitors without entry visa face mandatory (automatic) jail time.	no	

ADDITIONAL COUNTRY INFORMATION

(A)	The types of gifts to avoid:	money, food, sweets
(B)	Appropriate gifts for a foreigner to give:	souvenirs from visitors countries.
(C)	Best time to present gifts (at the beginning or at the end of a visit?):	at the beginning of visit
(D)	Best time to present gifts (on initial or later visits?):	on initial visit or on later visits
(E)	Best place to present gifts (in private or in public?):	in public
(F)	Number(s) with certain connotations and/or myths attached to them:	n/a
(G)	Basic shape(s) with negative connotations:	n/a
(H)	Basic color(s) with negative connotations:	n/a
(I)	Traditional greeting methods include:	a handshake, a kiss
(J)	Safe topics for discussion include:	weather, fashion, travel, art, family, domestic politics, food, sports, international politics
(K)	Best time for conversations (before, during, after meals?):	anytime (before meal, during meal or after meals)
(L)	Forms of legal punishment:	jailing, flogging, hanging
(M)	Approximately length of time one could be detained by law and order authorities before being charged in court:	48 hours
(N)	January 15, 1999, for example, will normally be written as:	15/1/99
(O)	Emergency code number:	n/a
(P)	Ambulance code Number:	121
(Q)	Police code number:	123 and 124
(R)	Telephone (country) code:	226
(S)	Telex (country) code:	n/a
(T)	Electricity requirements:	220 - 240 volts Ac
(U)	Legal drinking age:	18 years
(V)	Systems of weights and measures:	metric system
(W)	Legal age of incarceration:	21
(X)	Driving side of the road:	left
(Y)	Minimum expenditure expected of foreign visitors? $	n/a
(Z)	Name of currency:	Maloti
(Za)	Some places off-limits to foreign visitors:	initiation schools
(Zb)	Some places, structures and items prohibited from being photographed:	palace, banks and all government buildings

ENDNOTES

Item Number: COMMENTS/EXPLANATIONS

n/a: Not applicable/Not available/No response

(1)   Begging is discouraged and therefore visitors are strongly advised against giving money to beggars.

(2)   Public display of wealth by visitor is strongly discouraged because it can attract unpleasant company e.g. mugger, robbers etc.

(3)   Lesotho has no coast (it is landlocked), therefore nude bathing in rivers, dams or ponds by adu is very unusual and more or less unacceptable, it is however common only to small children.

(4)   Littering is strictly forbidden by an Act of parliament; and measures are being taken to enforce t act, as there was widespread littering which destroyed some indigenous plants and the unnatura beauty of the country.

(5)   Possession of prescription drugs without a doctor's note should have very good reason, it is however not encouraged.

(6)   It is rather unusual to see a man wearing lipstick, painting nails or dressed like women in Lesoth these might attract unpleasant attention from everyone who sees such a person.

LIBERIA	Is customary Is allowed Is permissible Is used. Is OK	Is not customary Is frowned upon	Is disallowed Is forbidden Is a crime	(See last page for comments on items referenced here)
Smoking in public	✓			
Eating in public	✓	✓		
Not flushing public toilet		✓		
Spitting in public	✓			
Feeding animals & birds in public	✓			
Whistling in public	✓			
Drinking alcohol in public			✓	
Kissing in public			✓	
Breast feeding in public		✓		
Drunkenness (in public)				n/a
Cursing in public	✓			
Religious preaching in public	✓			
Begging (panhandling) in public	n/a			
Giving money to beggars/panhandlers	✓			
Giving food/drink to beggars/panhandlers	✓			
Brushing teeth in public (other than in restrooms)		✓		
Strolling with pets in major public roads/streets	✓			
Chewing gum in public	✓			
Chewing gum in government offices		✓		
Combing hair in public (other than in toilets/restrooms)		✓		
Undressing/dressing in public		✓		
Wearing of dark glasses indoors in public places		✓		
Public display of wealth		✓		
Praying openly in public in non-designated areas	✓			
Walking bare feet in public		✓		
Chewing tobacco in public		✓		
Trimming one's finger or toe nails in public		✓		
Laughing aloud in public	✓			
Mingling of the sexes in public	✓			
Mixed bathing in public swimming pools	✓			
Distributing religious pamphlets (literature) in public/side streets	✓			

187

LIBERIA

	Is customary Is allowed Is permissible Is used. Is OK	Is not customary Is frowned upon	Is disallowed Is forbidden Is a crime	(See last page for comments on items referenced here)
Dancing on side street		✓		
Nude bathing			✓	
Littering			✓	
Binge Drinking			✓	
Hitchhiking	✓			
Jaywalking	✓			
Drunk driving			✓	
Speeding			✓	
Skating on side streets (side-walk)			✓	
Graffiti painting			✓	
Pilfering			✓	
Prostitution	✓			
Haggling in the market place	✓			
Consumption of alcoholic beverages in bars and restaurants	✓			
Gambling			✓	
Possession of pornographic materials			✓	
Possession of the Christian Bible	✓			
Possession of the Moslem Koran	✓			
Possession of bullet-proof vest		✓		
Possession of toy gun		✓		
Possession of fire crackers and fireworks			✓	
Possession of prescription drugs (without doctor's note)	✓			
Possession of regulated drugs (narcotics)			✓	
Possession of firearms (by foreigners)			✓	
Possession of pocket knife in public		✓		
Using walkie talkies	✓			
Using of "boom boxes"(loud sounding stereo system)		✓		
Using "walkman" (very small radio/cassettes with ear plugs) in public places	✓			
Using "walkman" (very small radio/cassettes with ear plugs) while driving or riding	✓			

LIBERIA

	Is customary Is allowed Is permissible Is used Is OK	Is not customary Is frowned upon	Is disallowed Is forbidden Is a crime	(See last page for comments on items referenced here)
Use of cellular phone	✓			
Use of binoculars/periscopes other than in sports arena			✓	
Taking photographs of people (without their permission)		✓		
Taking photographs at airports, train and bus stations		✓		
Taking photographs of airports			✓	
Taking photographs of churches and synagogues	✓			
Taking photographs of religious statues	✓			
Taking photographs of public buildings		✓		
Taking photographs of bridges			✓	
Tipping (gratuity)	✓			
Tipping (when service is rendered)	✓			
Tipping (when service is not rendered)	✓			
Tipping waiters/waitresses at restaurants and hotels	✓			
Tipping taxi/cab drivers	✓			
Tipping baggage handlers, porters, door persons	✓			
Tipping of hair dressers/barbers	✓			
Overtipping	✓			
Undertipping		✓		
Spilling cigarette butt (ash) on side streets/on the floor		✓		
Men wearing lipstick		✓		
Wearing visible tattoo marks		✓		
Men painting/coloring their finger or toe nails		✓		
Cross dressing (men dressed like women & vice versa)				n/a
Walking in public without a shirt (i.e., with the upper half of the body naked)		✓		
Men wearing braided hair	✓			
Men wearing earrings	✓			
Men wearing dreadlock hair style	✓			
Homosexuality		✓		
Lesbianism		✓		

LIBERIA

	Is customary Is allowed Is permissible Is used Is OK	Is not customary Is frowned upon	Is disallowed Is forbidden Is a crime	(See last page for comments on items referenced here)
Females covering their hair (wearing headgear) in public	✓			
Females exposing their full face in public	✓			
Females driving automobiles	✓			
Females riding motorcycles	✓			
Females riding bicycles	✓			
Females smoking in public	✓			
Women wearing bras (braziers) in public	✓			
Use of lipstick by women	✓			
A woman extending her hands first when introduced	✓			
Female bashing		✓		
Females wearing trousers	✓			
Females wearing minis (short dresses)	✓			
Females wearing bikinis	✓			
Females wearing shorts	✓			
Persons of opposite sex holding hands in public	✓			
Persons of same sex holding hands in public	✓			
Handshake between opposite sex	✓			
Hugging in public by same sex	✓			
Hugging in public by opposite sex	✓			
Men and women walking side by side in public	✓			
Man walking ahead (in public), with the woman following	✓			
Woman walking ahead (in public), with the man following	✓			
Men opening doors for women	✓			
Sitting with legs crossed in the presence of elders		✓		
Talking to an elderly person with one's hat/cap on	✓			
Talking to an elderly person with hands positioned on both sides of one's waist	✓			
Blowing one's nose in public		✓		
Blowing one's nose in the presence of others		✓		
Addressing people by their title	✓			

LIBERIA

	Is customary Is allowed Is permissible Is used. Is OK	Is not customary Is frowned upon	Is disallowed Is forbidden Is a crime	(See last page for comments on items referenced here)
Addressing people by their family name/surname/last name/given name	✓			
Addressing people by their first name/ given name	✓			
Women going through doors first	✓			
Men helping women with their coats	✓			
Men extending their hands to women first during greetings	✓			
Taking off one's hat when entering a private home	✓			
Removing one's shoes when entering a private home	✓			
Invited guests bringing food at social gatherings	✓			
Guests bringing drinks at social gatherings	✓			
Shaking hands when leaving a small group	✓			
Shaking hands with everyone present, upon arrival at a social gathering	✓			
Eating with the right hand	✓			
Eating with the left hand		✓		
Eating with both hands		✓		
Presenting a gift or passing on an object with the left hand		✓		
Asking a man about his wife	✓			
Asking a woman about her husband	✓			
Making prior appointments before a meeting or visit	✓			
Addressing an audience with one or both hands in the pocket		✓		
Carrying on conversation during meals	✓			
Females sitting with legs crossed	✓			
People discussing their wealth		✓		
Asking someone his or her age, or how old the person is		✓		
Complementing someone on his/her physical looks	✓			
Complementing someone on his/her attire	✓			
Use of both hands in handshake	✓			
In greeting, a handshake accompanied by a slight bow		✓		

191

LIBERIA

	Is customary Is allowed Is permissible Is used. Is OK	Is not customary Is frowned upon	Is disallowed Is forbidden Is a crime	(See last page for comments on items referenced here)
Salutations such as "Good morning", "good afternoon", "Good evening"	✓			
The completion of a business deal with a handshake	✓			
Starting a negotiation session with a handshake	✓			
A gift for the host/hostess	✓			
Giving a business gift	✓			
A gift of money (use of money as gift)				
Use of flowers as a gift	✓			
Use of business cards	✓			
Accepting/presenting gifts with both hands	✓			
Burning of the country's flag			✓	
Mutilation of the national currency			✓	
Casual wearing of clothings made with colors & marks of the national flag	✓			
Wearing of look-alike military (camouflage) fatigues (attire)		✓		
Sitting on the floor (on floor mats)	✓			
Discussion of religion	✓			
Discussion of politics	✓			
Discussion of sex	✓			
Patting/slapping someone on the buttocks		✓		
Patting/slapping someone on the back	✓			
Touching or patting someone's head/hair		✓		
Casual touching of any part of someone's body	✓			
Drinking directly out of a bottle/can		✓		
Placing one's leg(s) on the table or chair		✓		

192

LIBERIA

	Is customary Is allowed Is permissible Is used. Is OK	Is not customary Is frowned upon	Is disallowed Is forbidden Is a crime	(See last page for comments on items referenced here)
Showing the sole of one's foot (feet)		✓		
People standing very close when talking	✓			
Maintaining steady eye contact (direct gaze) when talking to someone	✓			
Kissing or exchange of kisses on the cheek	✓			
Counting money (change) in someone's palm		✓		
Finger pointing in public (in a daring manner)		✓		
Seeking attention by winking the eyes		✓		
Tapping the head to indicate someone is crazy		✓		
Twirling the head to indicate someone is crazy		✓		
Whistling as a way of requesting something/seeking attention		✓		
Using "thumbs-up" sign to mean OK	✓			
Forming a circle with the thumb and index finger (forefinger) to mean OK	✓			
Using the fingers to make a "V" sign for victory	✓			
Beckoning to someone with the index finger (forefinger)	✓			
The left to right waving of the hand with open palms facing outward to indicate "Good bye"	✓			
The use of a nod to show acknowledgement	✓			
Stopping/beckoning a taxi using a stretched hand with the thumb pointing upward	✓			
Using the thumb finger pointed to a direction, to request a ride or a hike	✓			
Raising one's hand/waving with an open fist to summon a taxi	✓			
Tapping one's foot/feet on the floor in a public gathering		✓		
Wiggling one's leg(s) when in a sitting position		✓		
Use of the hand (by motorists and cyclists) to signal direction of traffic		✓		

LIBERIA

		(See last page for comments on items referenced here)
Foreign tourists are welcome in the country.	yes	
The use of seat belt is mandatory.	yes	
International driving license is accepted.	yes	
Foreign drivers license is accepted.	yes	
It is considered impolite to yawn in public.	no	
Death penalty for drug trafficking is the law.	no	
Life imprisonment for drug trafficking is the law.	no	
Guilty until proven innocent in court is the law.	no	
Innocent until proven guilty in court is the law.	yes	
Pedestrians always have right of way.	no	
Exit visas are required of visitors.	no	
Crash helmet is mandatory for motor cyclist.	no	
Hanging is used as a form of legal punishment.	yes	
Decapitation of a limb is used as a form of punishment.	no	
Caning is used as a form of legal punishment.	no	
Electric shock is used as a form of legal punishment.	no	
One is expected to stand up during the playing of the national anthem.	no	
Crash helmet is mandatory for bicyclists.	no	
Guests are expected to eat every thing on their plates.	no	
Table manners are very informal.	yes	
One is expected to cover one's mouth when laughing.	no	
A vertical nod of the head means YES (OK).	yes	
A horizontal shaking of the head means NO (Not OK).	yes	
Prostitution is allowed only in designated areas.	no	
One is expected to take off one's hat during playing of national anthem.	no	
Separate seating arrangements (between sexes) are maintained at movies.	no	
Separate seating arrangements (between sexes) are maintained at churches.	no	
Uninvited visitors or guests may not be welcome, even among acquaintances.	no	
Pets (e.g. cats, dog) are allowed in some hotels and restaurants.	yes	
Couples invited for a meal may be separated during meals according to their sex.	no	
Punctuality is the order of business.		n/a
Automobiles are driven with headlights always turned on.		n/a
Motorcycles are driven with headlights always turned on.		n/a
Visitors with expired visa face mandatory jail time.		n/a
Visitors without exit visa face jail time.		n/a
Visitors without entry visa face mandatory (automatic) jail time.		n/a

ADDITIONAL COUNTRY INFORMATION

(A)	The types of gifts to avoid:	n/a
(B)	Appropriate gifts for a foreigner to give:	n/a
(C)	Best time to present gifts (at the beginning or at the end of a visit?):	end
(D)	Best time to present gifts (on initial or later visits?):	initial
(E)	Best place to present gifts (in private or in public?):	private
(F)	Number(s) with certain connotations and/or myths attached to them:	n/a
(G)	Basic shape(s) with negative connotations:	n/a
(H)	Basic color(s) with negative connotations:	n/a
(I)	Traditional greeting methods include:	handshake
(J)	Safe topics for discussion include:	weather, fashion, travel, family, religion, sport, international politics
(K)	Best time for conversations (before, during, after meals?):	before meals, during meals
(L)	Forms of legal punishment:	jailing
(M)	Approximately length of time one could be detained by law and order authorities before being charged in court:	24
(N)	January 15, 1999, for example, will normally be written as:	1/15/99
(O)	Emergency code number:	none
(P)	Ambulance code Number:	none
(Q)	Police code number:	none
(R)	Telephone (country) code:	231
(S)	Telex (country) code:	n/a
(T)	Electricity requirements:	110
(U)	Legal drinking age:	none
(V)	Systems of weights and measures:	imperial
(W)	Legal age of incarceration:	n/a
(X)	Driving side of the road:	right
(Y)	Minimum expenditure expected of foreign visitors? $	none
(Z)	Name of currency:	dollars
(Za)	Some places off-limits to foreign visitors:	none
(Zb)	Some places, structures and items prohibited from being photographed:	military

MADAGASCAR	Is customary Is allowed Is permissible Is used. Is OK	Is not customary Is frowned upon	Is disallowed Is forbidden Is a crime	(See last page for comments on items referenced here)
Smoking in public	✓			
Eating in public				3
Not flushing public toilet		✓		
Spitting in public		✓		
Feeding animals & birds in public	✓			
Whistling in public	✓			
Drinking alcohol in public		✓		
Kissing in public		✓		
Breast feeding in public	✓			
Drunkenness (in public)		✓		
Cursing in public		✓		
Religious preaching in public	✓			
Begging (panhandling) in public	✓			
Giving money to beggars/panhandlers	✓			
Giving food/drink to beggars/panhandlers	✓			
Brushing teeth in public (other than in restrooms)		✓		
Strolling with pets in major public roads/streets	✓			
Chewing gum in public	✓			
Chewing gum in government offices		✓		
Combing hair in public (other than in toilets/restrooms)		✓		
Undressing/dressing in public		✓		
Wearing of dark glasses indoors in public places	✓			
Public display of wealth	✓			
Praying openly in public in non-designated areas	✓			
Walking bare feet in public	✓			
Chewing tobacco in public	✓			
Trimming one's finger or toe nails in public		✓		
Laughing aloud in public	✓			
Mingling of the sexes in public	✓			
Mixed bathing in public swimming pools	✓			
Distributing religious pamphlets (literature) in public/side streets	✓			

MADAGASCA

	Is customary Is allowed Is permissible Is used. Is OK	Is not customary Is frowned upon	Is disallowed Is forbidden Is a crime	(See last page for comments on items referenced here)
Dancing on side street	✓			
Nude bathing			✓	
Littering		✓		
Binge Drinking		✓		
Hitchhiking	✓			
Jaywalking	✓			
Drunk driving			✓	
Speeding		✓		
Skating on side streets (side-walk)		✓		
Graffiti painting		✓		
Pilfering			✓	
Prostitution		✓		
Haggling in the market place	✓			
Consumption of alcoholic beverages in bars and restaurants	✓			
Gambling		✓		
Possession of pornographic materials			✓	
Possession of the Christian Bible	✓			
Possession of the Moslem Koran	✓			
Possession of bullet-proof vest	✓			
Possession of toy gun		✓		
Possession of fire crackers and fireworks		✓		
Possession of prescription drugs (without doctor's note)		✓		
Possession of regulated drugs (narcotics)			✓	
Possession of firearms (by foreigners)			✓	
Possession of pocket knife in public			✓	
Using walkie talkies	✓			
Using of "boom boxes"(loud sounding stereo system)	✓			
Using "walkman" (very small radio/cassettes with ear plugs) in public places	✓			
Using "walkman" (very small radio/cassettes with ear plugs) while driving or riding		✓		

197

MADAGASCA

	Is customary Is allowed Is permissible Is used Is OK	Is not customary Is frowned upon	Is disallowed Is forbidden Is a crime	(See last page for comments on items referenced here)
Use of cellular phone	✓			
Use of binoculars/periscopes other than in sports arena	✓			
Taking photographs of people (without their permission)	✓			
Taking photographs at airports, train and bus stations	✓			
Taking photographs of airports	✓			
Taking photographs of churches and synagogues	✓			
Taking photographs of religious statues	✓			
Taking photographs of public buildings	✓			
Taking photographs of bridges	✓			
Tipping (gratuity)	✓			
Tipping (when service is rendered)	✓			
Tipping (when service is not rendered)	✓			
Tipping waiters/waitresses at restaurants and hotels	✓			
Tipping taxi/cab drivers	✓			
Tipping baggage handlers, porters, door persons	✓			
Tipping of hair dressers/barbers	✓			
Overtipping	✓			
Undertipping	✓			
Spilling cigarette butt (ash) on side streets/on the floor		✓		
Men wearing lipstick		✓		
Wearing visible tattoo marks	✓			
Men painting/coloring their finger or toe nails		✓		
Cross dressing (men dressed like women & vice versa)	✓			
Walking in public without a shirt (i.e., with the upper half of the body naked)		✓		
Men wearing braided hair	✓			
Men wearing earrings	✓			
Men wearing dreadlock hair style	✓			
Homosexuality		✓		
Lesbianism		✓		

MADAGASCA

	Is customary Is allowed Is permissible Is used Is OK	Is not customary Is frowned upon	Is disallowed Is forbidden Is a crime	(See last page for comments on items referenced here)
Females covering their hair (wearing headgear) in public	✓			
Females exposing their full face in public	✓			
Females driving automobiles	✓			
Females riding motorcycles	✓			
Females riding bicycles	✓			
Females smoking in public	✓			
Women wearing bras (braziers) in public		✓		
Use of lipstick by women	✓			
A woman extending her hands first when introduced	✓			
Female bashing		✓		
Females wearing trousers	✓			
Females wearing minis (short dresses)	✓			
Females wearing bikinis	✓			
Females wearing shorts	✓			
Persons of opposite sex holding hands in public	✓			
Persons of same sex holding hands in public	✓			
Handshake between opposite sex	✓			
Hugging in public by same sex	✓			
Hugging in public by opposite sex		✓		
Men and women walking side by side in public	✓			
Man walking ahead (in public), with the woman following	✓			
Woman walking ahead (in public), with the man following	✓			
Men opening doors for women	✓			
Sitting with legs crossed in the presence of elders		✓		
Talking to an elderly person with one's hat/cap on		✓		
Talking to an elderly person with hands positioned on both sides of one's waist	✓			
Blowing one's nose in public	✓			
Blowing one's nose in the presence of others	✓			
Addressing people by their title	✓			

	Is customary Is allowed Is permissible Is used. Is OK	Is not customary Is frowned upon	Is disallowed Is forbidden Is a crime	(See last page for comments on items referenced here)
Addressing people by their family name/surname/last name/given name	✓			
Addressing people by their first name/ given name	✓			
Women going through doors first	✓			
Men helping women with their coats	✓			
Men extending their hands to women first during greetings	✓			
Taking off one's hat when entering a private home	✓			
Removing one's shoes when entering a private home		✓		
Invited guests bringing food at social gatherings	✓			
Guests bringing drinks at social gatherings	✓			
Shaking hands when leaving a small group	✓			
Shaking hands with everyone present, upon arrival at a social gathering	✓			
Eating with the right hand	✓			
Eating with the left hand	✓			
Eating with both hands	✓			
Presenting a gift or passing on an object with the left hand	✓			
Asking a man about his wife	✓			
Asking a woman about her husband	✓			
Making prior appointments before a meeting or visit	✓			
Addressing an audience with one or both hands in the pocket		✓		
Carrying on conversation during meals	✓			
Females sitting with legs crossed	✓			
People discussing their wealth	✓			
Asking someone his or her age, or how old the person is	✓			
Complementing someone on his/her physical looks	✓			
Complementing someone on his/her attire	✓			
Use of both hands in handshake	✓			
In greeting, a handshake accompanied by a slight bow	✓			

MADAGASCA

	Is customary Is allowed Is permissible Is used. Is OK	Is not customary Is frowned upon	Is disallowed Is forbidden Is a crime	(See last page for comments on items referenced here)
Salutations such as "Good morning", "good afternoon", "Good evening"	n/a			
The completion of a business deal with a handshake	✓			
Starting a negotiation session with a handshake	✓			
A gift for the host/hostess	✓			
Giving a business gift	✓			
A gift of money (use of money as gift)	✓			
Use of flowers as a gift	✓			
Use of business cards	✓			
Accepting/presenting gifts with both hands	✓			
Burning of the country's flag		✓		
Mutilation of the national currency		✓		
Casual wearing of clothings made with colors & marks of the national flag	✓			
Wearing of look-alike military (camouflage) fatigues (attire)		✓		
Sitting on the floor (on floor mats)	✓			
Discussion of religion	✓			
Discussion of politics	✓			
Discussion of sex	✓			
Patting/slapping someone on the buttocks		✓		
Patting/slapping someone on the back	✓			
Touching or patting someone's head/hair		✓		
Casual touching of any part of someone's body		✓		
Drinking directly out of a bottle/can	✓			
Placing one's leg(s) on the table or chair		✓		

MADAGASCA

	Is customary Is allowed Is permissible Is used. Is OK	Is not customary Is frowned upon	Is disallowed Is forbidden Is a crime	(See last page for comments on items referenced here)
Showing the sole of one's foot (feet)	✓			
People standing very close when talking		✓		
Maintaining steady eye contact (direct gaze) when talking to someone	✓			
Kissing or exchange of kisses on the cheek	✓			
Counting money (change) in someone's palm		✓		
Finger pointing in public (in a daring manner)		✓		
Seeking attention by winking the eyes		✓		
Tapping the head to indicate someone is crazy		✓		
Twirling the head to indicate someone is crazy		✓		
Whistling as a way of requesting something/seeking attention		✓		
Using "thumbs-up" sign to mean OK	✓			
Forming a circle with the thumb and index finger (forefinger) to mean OK		✓		
Using the fingers to make a "V" sign for victory	✓			
Beckoning to someone with the index finger (forefinger)		✓		
The left to right waving of the hand with open palms facing outward to indicate "Good bye"	✓			
The use of a nod to show acknowledgement	✓			
Stopping/beckoning a taxi using a stretched hand with the thumb pointing upward	✓			
Using the thumb finger pointed to a direction, to request a ride or a hike		✓		
Raising one's hand/waving with an open fist to summon a taxi	✓			
Tapping one's foot/feet on the floor in a public gathering		✓		
Wiggling one's leg(s) when in a sitting position	✓			
Use of the hand (by motorists and cyclists) to signal direction of traffic	✓			

202

MADAGASCA

		(See last page for comments on items referenced here)
Foreign tourists are welcome in the country.	yes	
The use of seat belt is mandatory.	no	
International driving license is accepted.	yes	
Foreign drivers license is accepted.	yes	
It is considered impolite to yawn in public.	no	
Death penalty for drug trafficking is the law.	no	
Life imprisonment for drug trafficking is the law.	no	
Guilty until proven innocent in court is the law.	yes	
Innocent until proven guilty in court is the law.	no	
Pedestrians always have right of way.	yes	
Exit visas are required of visitors.	yes	
Crash helmet is mandatory for motor cyclist.	no	
Hanging is used as a form of legal punishment.	no	
Decapitation of a limb is used as a form of punishment.	yes	
Caning is used as a form of legal punishment.	yes	
Electric shock is used as a form of legal punishment.	no	
One is expected to stand up during the playing of the national anthem.	yes	
Crash helmet is mandatory for bicyclists.	yes	
Guests are expected to eat every thing on their plates.	yes	
Table manners are very informal.	yes	
One is expected to cover one's mouth when laughing.	yes	
A vertical nod of the head means YES (OK).	yes	
A horizontal shaking of the head means NO (Not OK).	yes	
Prostitution is allowed only in designated areas.	yes	
One is expected to take off one's hat during playing of national anthem.	yes	
Separate seating arrangements (between sexes) are maintained at movies.	no	
Separate seating arrangements (between sexes) are maintained at churches.	no	
Uninvited visitors or guests may not be welcome, even among acquaintances.	no	
Pets (e.g. cats, dog) are allowed in some hotels and restaurants.	yes	
Couples invited for a meal may be separated during meals according to their sex.	no	
Punctuality is the order of business.	yes	
Automobiles are driven with headlights always turned on.	yes	
Motorcycles are driven with headlights always turned on.	yes	
Visitors with expired visa face mandatory jail time.	no	
Visitors without exit visa face jail time.	no	
Visitors without entry visa face mandatory (automatic) jail time.	no	

ADDITIONAL COUNTRY INFORMATION

(A)	The types of gifts to avoid:	n/a
(B)	Appropriate gifts for a foreigner to give:	typical foreign items
(C)	Best time to present gifts (at the beginning or at the end of a visit?):	at the beginning
(D)	Best time to present gifts (on initial or later visits?):	on initial visit
(E)	Best place to present gifts (in private or in public?):	in private
(F)	Number(s) with certain connotations and/or myths attached to them:	n/a
(G)	Basic shape(s) with negative connotations:	none
(H)	Basic color(s) with negative connotations:	none
(I)	Traditional greeting methods include:	handshake, nod
(J)	Safe topics for discussion include:	travel, family, personal wealth
(K)	Best time for conversations (before, during, after meals?):	optional
(L)	Forms of legal punishment:	jailing
(M)	Approximately length of time one could be detained by law and order authorities before being charged in court:	48 hours
(N)	January 15, 1999, for example, will normally be written as:	15/1/99
(O)	Emergency code number:	18
(P)	Ambulance code Number:	n/a
(Q)	Police code number:	17
(R)	Telephone (country) code:	261
(S)	Telex (country) code:	n/a
(T)	Electricity requirements:	n/a
(U)	Legal drinking age:	18 years old
(V)	Systems of weights and measures:	M.K.S.A.
(W)	Legal age of incarceration:	18 year old
(X)	Driving side of the road:	right
(Y)	Minimum expenditure expected of foreign visitors? $	minimum of 2000 Ff (about 370 USD) per stay
(Z)	Name of currency:	Malagasy Franc (Fmg)
(Za)	Some places off-limits to foreign visitors:	n/a (See endnote "za")
(Zb)	Some places, structures and items prohibited from being photographed:	n/a (See endnote "zb")

ENDNOTES

Item Number: COMMENTS/EXPLANATIONS

n/a: Not applicable/Not available/No response

(Za)   Protected areas, natural reserves, monuments, tombs

(Zb)   military camps, presidentialpalace, inside of museum, airport

MALAWI	Is customary Is allowed Is permissible Is used. Is OK	Is not customary Is frowned upon	Is disallowed Is forbidden Is a crime	(See last page for comments on items referenced here)
Smoking in public		✓		
Eating in public	✓			
Not flushing public toilet			✓	
Spitting in public			✓	
Feeding animals & birds in public		✓		
Whistling in public		✓		
Drinking alcohol in public			✓	
Kissing in public		✓		
Breast feeding in public	✓			
Drunkenness (in public)			✓	
Cursing in public		✓		
Religious preaching in public	✓			
Begging (panhandling) in public			✓	
Giving money to beggars/panhandlers	✓			
Giving food/drink to beggars/panhandlers	✓			
Brushing teeth in public (other than in restrooms)			✓	
Strolling with pets in major public roads/streets	✓			
Chewing gum in public	✓			
Chewing gum in government offices	✓			
Combing hair in public (other than in toilets/restrooms)		✓		
Undressing/dressing in public	✓	✓		
Wearing of dark glasses indoors in public places	✓			
Public display of wealth	✓			
Praying openly in public in non-designated areas	✓			
Walking bare feet in public	✓			
Chewing tobacco in public	✓			
Trimming one's finger or toe nails in public	✓			
Laughing aloud in public	✓			
Mingling of the sexes in public	✓			
Mixed bathing in public swimming pools	✓			
Distributing religious pamphlets (literature) in public/side streets	✓			

MALAWI

	Is customary Is allowed Is permissible Is used. Is OK	Is not customary Is frowned upon	Is disallowed Is forbidden Is a crime	(See last page for comments on items referenced here)
Dancing on side street		✓		
Nude bathing		✓		
Littering		✓		
Binge Drinking	✓			
Hitchhiking	✓			
Jaywalking	✓			
Drunk driving			✓	
Speeding			✓	
Skating on side streets (side-walk)	✓			
Graffiti painting	✓			
Pilfering	✓			
Prostitution			✓	
Haggling in the market place			✓	
Consumption of alcoholic beverages in bars and restaurants	✓			
Gambling	✓			
Possession of pornographic materials		✓		
Possession of the Christian Bible	✓			
Possession of the Moslem Koran	✓			
Possession of bullet-proof vest	✓			
Possession of toy gun	✓			
Possession of fire crackers and fireworks	✓			
Possession of prescription drugs (without doctor's note)			✓	
Possession of regulated drugs (narcotics)			✓	
Possession of firearms (by foreigners)			✓	
Possession of pocket knife in public	✓			
Using walkie talkies	✓			
Using of "boom boxes"(loud sounding stereo system)	✓			
Using "walkman" (very small radio/cassettes with ear plugs) in public places	✓			
Using "walkman" (very small radio/cassettes with ear plugs) while driving or riding	✓			

	Is customary Is allowed Is permissible Is used Is OK ✓	Is not customary Is frowned upon	Is disallowed Is forbidden Is a crime	(See last page for comments on items referenced here)
Use of cellular phone	✓			
Use of binoculars/periscopes other than in sports arena			✓	
Taking photographs of people (without their permission)			✓	
Taking photographs at airports, train and bus stations			✓	
Taking photographs of airports	✓			
Taking photographs of churches and synagogues			✓	
Taking photographs of religious statues			✓	
Taking photographs of public buildings			✓	
Taking photographs of bridges			✓	
Tipping (gratuity)			✓	
Tipping (when service is rendered)			✓	
Tipping (when service is not rendered)			✓	
Tipping waiters/waitresses at restaurants and hotels			✓	
Tipping taxi/cab drivers	✓			
Tipping baggage handlers, porters, door persons	✓			
Tipping of hair dressers/barbers	✓			
Overtipping	✓			
Undertipping	✓			
Spilling cigarette butt (ash) on side streets/on the floor			✓	
Men wearing lipstick			✓	
Wearing visible tattoo marks			✓	
Men painting/coloring their finger or toe nails			✓	
Cross dressing (men dressed like women & vice versa)			✓	
Walking in public without a shirt (i.e., with the upper half of the body naked)		✓		
Men wearing braided hair		✓		
Men wearing earrings		✓		
Men wearing dreadlock hair style		✓		
Homosexuality		✓		
Lesbianism		✓		

MALAWI

	Is customary Is allowed Is permissible Is used Is OK	Is not customary Is frowned upon	Is disallowed Is forbidden Is a crime	(See last page for comments on items referenced here)
Females covering their hair (wearing headgear) in public	✓			
Females exposing their full face in public	✓			
Females driving automobiles	✓			
Females riding motorcycles	✓			
Females riding bicycles	✓			
Females smoking in public	✓			
Women wearing bras (braziers) in public		✓		
Use of lipstick by women	✓			
A woman extending her hands first when introduced	✓			
Female bashing		✓		
Females wearing trousers	✓			
Females wearing minis (short dresses)	✓			
Females wearing bikinis	✓			
Females wearing shorts	✓			
Persons of opposite sex holding hands in public	✓			
Persons of same sex holding hands in public	✓			
Handshake between opposite sex	✓			
Hugging in public by same sex	✓			
Hugging in public by opposite sex	✓			
Men and women walking side by side in public	✓			
Man walking ahead (in public), with the woman following	✓			
Woman walking ahead (in public), with the man following	✓			
Men opening doors for women	✓			
Sitting with legs crossed in the presence of elders		✓		
Talking to an elderly person with one's hat/cap on		✓		
Talking to an elderly person with hands positioned on both sides of one's waist		✓		
Blowing one's nose in public	✓			
Blowing one's nose in the presence of others	✓			
Addressing people by their title	✓			

MALAWI

	Is customary Is allowed Is permissible Is used. Is OK	Is not customary Is frowned upon	Is disallowed Is forbidden Is a crime	(See last page for comments on items referenced here)
Addressing people by their family name/surname/last name/given name	✓			
Addressing people by their first name/ given name	✓			
Women going through doors first	✓			
Men helping women with their coats	✓			
Men extending their hands to women first during greetings	✓			
Taking off one's hat when entering a private home	✓			
Removing one's shoes when entering a private home	✓			
Invited guests bringing food at social gatherings		✓		
Guests bringing drinks at social gatherings	✓			
Shaking hands when leaving a small group	✓			
Shaking hands with everyone present, upon arrival at a social gathering	✓			
Eating with the right hand	✓			
Eating with the left hand	✓			
Eating with both hands		✓		
Presenting a gift or passing on an object with the left hand		✓		
Asking a man about his wife	✓			
Asking a woman about her husband	✓			
Making prior appointments before a meeting or visit	✓			
Addressing an audience with one or both hands in the pocket		✓		
Carrying on conversation during meals	✓			
Females sitting with legs crossed		✓		
People discussing their wealth	✓			
Asking someone his or her age, or how old the person is	✓			
Complementing someone on his/her physical looks	✓			
Complementing someone on his/her attire	✓			
Use of both hands in handshake	✓			
In greeting, a handshake accompanied by a slight bow	✓			

MALAWI

	Is customary Is allowed Is permissible Is used. Is OK	Is not customary Is frowned upon	Is disallowed Is forbidden Is a crime	(See last page for comments on items referenced here)
Salutations such as "Good morning", "good afternoon", "Good evening"	✓			
The completion of a business deal with a handshake	✓			
Starting a negotiation session with a handshake		✓		
A gift for the host/hostess	✓			
Giving a business gift	✓			
A gift of money (use of money as gift)	✓			
Use of flowers as a gift		✓		
Use of business cards	✓			
Accepting/presenting gifts with both hands	✓			
Burning of the country's flag		✓		
Mutilation of the national currency		✓		
Casual wearing of clothings made with colors & marks of the national flag	✓			
Wearing of look-alike military (camouflage) fatigues (attire)	✓			
Sitting on the floor (on floor mats)	✓			
Discussion of religion	✓			
Discussion of politics	✓			
Discussion of sex	✓			
Patting/slapping someone on the buttocks		✓		
Patting/slapping someone on the back	✓			
Touching or patting someone's head/hair		✓		
Casual touching of any part of someone's body	✓			
Drinking directly out of a bottle/can		✓		
Placing one's leg(s) on the table or chair	✓			

211

MALAWI

	Is customary Is allowed Is permissible Is used. Is OK	Is not customary Is frowned upon	Is disallowed Is forbidden Is a crime	(See last page for comments on items referenced here)
Showing the sole of one's foot (feet)	✓			
People standing very close when talking	✓			
Maintaining steady eye contact (direct gaze) when talking to someone	✓			
Kissing or exchange of kisses on the cheek		✓		
Counting money (change) in someone's palm		✓		
Finger pointing in public (in a daring manner)		✓		
Seeking attention by winking the eyes		✓		
Tapping the head to indicate someone is crazy		✓		
Twirling the head to indicate someone is crazy	✓			
Whistling as a way of requesting something/seeking attention	✓			
Using "thumbs-up" sign to mean OK		✓		
Forming a circle with the thumb and index finger (forefinger) to mean OK		✓		
Using the fingers to make a "V" sign for victory		✓		
Beckoning to someone with the index finger (forefinger)	✓			
The left to right waving of the hand with open palms facing outward to indicate "Good bye"	✓			
The use of a nod to show acknowledgement	✓			
Stopping/beckoning a taxi using a stretched hand with the thumb pointing upward	✓			
Using the thumb finger pointed to a direction, to request a ride or a hike	✓			
Raising one's hand/waving with an open fist to summon a taxi	✓			
Tapping one's foot/feet on the floor in a public gathering		✓		
Wiggling one's leg(s) when in a sitting position		✓		
Use of the hand (by motorists and cyclists) to signal direction of traffic	✓			

212

MALAWI

		(See last page for comments on items referenced here)
Foreign tourists are welcome in the country.	yes	
The use of seat belt is mandatory.	yes	
International driving license is accepted.	yes	
Foreign drivers license is accepted.	yes	
It is considered impolite to yawn in public.	no	
Death penalty for drug trafficking is the law.	no	
Life imprisonment for drug trafficking is the law.	no	
Guilty until proven innocent in court is the law.	no	
Innocent until proven guilty in court is the law.	yes	
Pedestrians always have right of way.	yes	
Exit visas are required of visitors.	no	
Crash helmet is mandatory for motor cyclist.	yes	
Hanging is used as a form of legal punishment.	no	
Decapitation of a limb is used as a form of punishment.	no	
Caning is used as a form of legal punishment.	no	
Electric shock is used as a form of legal punishment.	no	
One is expected to stand up during the playing of the national anthem.	yes	
Crash helmet is mandatory for bicyclists.	no	
Guests are expected to eat every thing on their plates.	no	
Table manners are very informal.	no	
One is expected to cover one's mouth when laughing.	no	
A vertical nod of the head means YES (OK).	yes	
A horizontal shaking of the head means NO (Not OK).	yes	
Prostitution is allowed only in designated areas.	no	
One is expected to take off one's hat during playing of national anthem.	yes	
Separate seating arrangements (between sexes) are maintained at movies.	no	
Separate seating arrangements (between sexes) are maintained at churches.	no	
Uninvited visitors or guests may not be welcome, even among acquaintances.	no	
Pets (e.g. cats, dog) are allowed in some hotels and restaurants.	no	
Couples invited for a meal may be separated during meals according to their sex.	no	
Punctuality is the order of business.	no	
Automobiles are driven with headlights always turned on.	no	
Motorcycles are driven with headlights always turned on.	yes	
Visitors with expired visa face mandatory jail time.	no	
Visitors without exit visa face jail time.	no	
Visitors without entry visa face mandatory (automatic) jail time.	no	

ADDITIONAL COUNTRY INFORMATION

(A)	The types of gifts to avoid:	n/a
(B)	Appropriate gifts for a foreigner to give:	jewelry, cash, clothes
(C)	Best time to present gifts (at the beginning or at the end of a visit?):	beginning or end
(D)	Best time to present gifts (on initial or later visits?):	initial or afterwards
(E)	Best place to present gifts (in private or in public?):	private
(F)	Number(s) with certain connotations and/or myths attached to them:	13
(G)	Basic shape(s) with negative connotations:	nothing
(H)	Basic color(s) with negative connotations:	no
(I)	Traditional greeting methods include:	handshake, kneeling
(J)	Safe topics for discussion include:	weather, fashion, travel, art, family, religion, domestic politics, food, sports, international politics, social conditions, money and personal wealth
(K)	Best time for conversations (before, during, after meals?):	before meal and after meals
(L)	Forms of legal punishment:	jailing
(M)	Approximately length of time one could be detained by law and order authorities before being charged in court:	it depends on the crime/charge
(N)	January 15, 1999, for example, will normally be written as:	15/1/99
(O)	Emergency code number:	199
(P)	Ambulance code Number:	199
(Q)	Police code number:	199
(R)	Telephone (country) code:	265
(S)	Telex (country) code:	265
(T)	Electricity requirements:	220/240 volt
(U)	Legal drinking age:	18 +
(V)	Systems of weights and measures:	metric
(W)	Legal age of incarceration:	18
(X)	Driving side of the road:	right
(Y)	Minimum expenditure expected of foreign visitors? $	no
(Z)	Name of currency:	Kwacha
(Za)	Some places off-limits to foreign visitors:	palaces, military installations
(Zb)	Some places, structures and items prohibited from being photographed:	palaces, bridge, military installations

MALI	Is customary Is allowed Is permissible Is used. Is OK	Is not customary Is frowned upon	Is disallowed Is forbidden Is a crime	(See last page for comments on items referenced here)
Smoking in public	✓			
Eating in public	✓			
Not flushing public toilet	✓			
Spitting in public	✓			
Feeding animals & birds in public	✓			
Whistling in public	✓			
Drinking alcohol in public	✓			
Kissing in public	✓			
Breast feeding in public	✓			
Drunkenness (in public)	✓			
Cursing in public	✓			
Religious preaching in public	✓			
Begging (panhandling) in public	✓			
Giving money to beggars/panhandlers	✓			
Giving food/drink to beggars/panhandlers	✓			
Brushing teeth in public (other than in restrooms)	✓			
Strolling with pets in major public roads/streets	✓			
Chewing gum in public	✓			
Chewing gum in government offices	✓			
Combing hair in public (other than in toilets/restrooms)	✓			
Undressing/dressing in public	✓			
Wearing of dark glasses indoors in public places	✓			
Public display of wealth	✓			
Praying openly in public in non-designated areas	✓			
Walking bare feet in public	✓			
Chewing tobacco in public	✓			
Trimming one's finger or toe nails in public	✓			
Laughing aloud in public	✓			
Mingling of the sexes in public	✓			
Mixed bathing in public swimming pools	✓			
Distributing religious pamphlets (literature) in public/side streets	✓			

215

MALI

	Is customary Is allowed Is permissible Is used. Is OK	Is not customary Is frowned upon	Is disallowed Is forbidden Is a crime	(See last page for comments on items referenced here)
Dancing on side street	✓			
Nude bathing	✓			
Littering		✓		
Binge Drinking	✓			
Hitchhiking	✓			
Jaywalking	✓			
Drunk driving		✓		
Speeding		✓		
Skating on side streets (side-walk)				✓
Graffiti painting		✓		
Pilfering			✓	
Prostitution			✓	
Haggling in the market place	✓			
Consumption of alcoholic beverages in bars and restaurants	✓			
Gambling	✓			
Possession of pornographic materials	✓			
Possession of the Christian Bible	✓			
Possession of the Moslem Koran	✓			
Possession of bullet-proof vest		✓		
Possession of toy gun	✓			
Possession of fire crackers and fireworks		✓		
Possession of prescription drugs (without doctor's note)			✓	
Possession of regulated drugs (narcotics)			✓	
Possession of firearms (by foreigners)			✓	
Possession of pocket knife in public	✓			
Using walkie talkies	✓			
Using of "boom boxes"(loud sounding stereo system)	✓			
Using "walkman" (very small radio/cassettes with ear plugs) in public places	✓			
Using "walkman" (very small radio/cassettes with ear plugs) while driving or riding	✓			

216

MALI

	Is customary Is allowed Is permissible Is used Is OK	Is not customary Is frowned upon	Is disallowed Is forbidden Is a crime	(See last page for comments on items referenced here)
Use of cellular phone	✓			
Use of binoculars/periscopes other than in sports arena	✓			
Taking photographs of people (without their permission)		✓		
Taking photographs at airports, train and bus stations	✓			1
Taking photographs of airports		✓		2
Taking photographs of churches and synagogues	✓			
Taking photographs of religious statues	✓			
Taking photographs of public buildings	✓			
Taking photographs of bridges	✓			
Tipping (gratuity)	✓			
Tipping (when service is rendered)	✓			
Tipping (when service is not rendered)		✓		
Tipping waiters/waitresses at restaurants and hotels	✓			
Tipping taxi/cab drivers	✓			
Tipping baggage handlers, porters, door persons	✓			
Tipping of hair dressers/barbers	✓			
Overtipping	✓			
Undertipping	✓			
Spilling cigarette butt (ash) on side streets/on the floor	✓			
Men wearing lipstick	✓			
Wearing visible tattoo marks	✓			
Men painting/coloring their finger or toe nails	✓			
Cross dressing (men dressed like women & vice versa)	✓			
Walking in public without a shirt (i.e., with the upper half of the body naked)	✓			
Men wearing braided hair	✓			
Men wearing earrings	✓			
Men wearing dreadlock hair style	✓			
Homosexuality	✓			
Lesbianism	✓			

MALI

	Is customary Is allowed Is permissible Is used Is OK	Is not customary Is frowned upon	Is disallowed Is forbidden Is a crime	(See last page for comments on items referenced here)
Females covering their hair (wearing headgear) in public	✓			
Females exposing their full face in public	✓			
Females driving automobiles	✓			
Females riding motorcycles	✓			
Females riding bicycles	✓			
Females smoking in public	✓			
Women wearing bras (braziers) in public	✓			
Use of lipstick by women	✓			
A woman extending her hands first when introduced	✓			
Female bashing		✓		
Females wearing trousers	✓			
Females wearing minis (short dresses)	✓			
Females wearing bikinis	✓			
Females wearing shorts	✓			
Persons of opposite sex holding hands in public	✓			
Persons of same sex holding hands in public	✓			
Handshake between opposite sex	✓			
Hugging in public by same sex		✓		
Hugging in public by opposite sex	✓			
Men and women walking side by side in public	✓			
Man walking ahead (in public), with the woman following	✓			
Woman walking ahead (in public), with the man following	✓			
Men opening doors for women	✓			
Sitting with legs crossed in the presence of elders	✓			
Talking to an elderly person with one's hat/cap on	✓			
Talking to an elderly person with hands positioned on both sides of one's waist	✓			
Blowing one's nose in public	✓			
Blowing one's nose in the presence of others	✓			
Addressing people by their title	✓			

MALI

	Is customary Is allowed Is permissible Is used. Is OK	Is not customary Is frowned upon	Is disallowed Is forbidden Is a crime	(See last page for comments on items referenced here)
Addressing people by their family name/surname/last name/given name	✓			
Addressing people by their first name/ given name	✓			
Women going through doors first	✓			
Men helping women with their coats	✓			
Men extending their hands to women first during greetings	✓			
Taking off one's hat when entering a private home	✓			
Removing one's shoes when entering a private home	✓			
Invited guests bringing food at social gatherings	✓			
Guests bringing drinks at social gatherings	✓			
Shaking hands when leaving a small group	✓			
Shaking hands with everyone present, upon arrival at a social gathering	✓			
Eating with the right hand	✓			
Eating with the left hand		✓		
Eating with both hands		✓		
Presenting a gift or passing on an object with the left hand		✓		
Asking a man about his wife	✓			
Asking a woman about her husband	✓			
Making prior appointments before a meeting or visit	✓			
Addressing an audience with one or both hands in the pocket		✓		
Carrying on conversation during meals	✓			
Females sitting with legs crossed	✓			
People discussing their wealth	✓			
Asking someone his or her age, or how old the person is	✓			
Complementing someone on his/her physical looks	✓			
Complementing someone on his/her attire	✓			
Use of both hands in handshake	✓			
In greeting, a handshake accompanied by a slight bow	✓			

MALI

	Is customary Is allowed Is permissible Is used. Is OK	Is not customary Is frowned upon	Is disallowed Is forbidden Is a crime	(See last page for comments on items referenced here)
Salutations such as "Good morning", "good afternoon", "Good evening"	✓			
The completion of a business deal with a handshake	✓			
Starting a negotiation session with a handshake	✓			
A gift for the host/hostess	✓			
Giving a business gift	✓			
A gift of money (use of money as gift)	✓			
Use of flowers as a gift		✓		
Use of business cards	✓			
Accepting/presenting gifts with both hands	✓			
Burning of the country's flag			✓	
Mutilation of the national currency			✓	
Casual wearing of clothings made with colors & marks of the national flag	✓			
Wearing of look-alike military (camouflage) fatigues (attire)		✓		
Sitting on the floor (on floor mats)		✓		
Discussion of religion	✓			
Discussion of politics	✓			
Discussion of sex	✓			
Patting/slapping someone on the buttocks	✓			
Patting/slapping someone on the back	✓			
Touching or patting someone's head/hair	✓			
Casual touching of any part of someone's body	✓			
Drinking directly out of a bottle/can	✓			
Placing one's leg(s) on the table or chair	✓			

220

MALI

	Is customary Is allowed Is permissible Is used. Is OK	Is not customary Is frowned upon	Is disallowed Is forbidden Is a crime	(See last page for comments on items referenced here)
Showing the sole of one's foot (feet)	✓			
People standing very close when talking	✓			
Maintaining steady eye contact (direct gaze) when talking to someone	✓			
Kissing or exchange of kisses on the cheek	✓			
Counting money (change) in someone's palm	✓			
Finger pointing in public (in a daring manner)	✓			
Seeking attention by winking the eyes	✓			
Tapping the head to indicate someone is crazy	✓			
Twirling the head to indicate someone is crazy	✓			
Whistling as a way of requesting something/seeking attention	✓			
Using "thumbs-up" sign to mean OK	✓			
Forming a circle with the thumb and index finger (forefinger) to mean OK	✓			
Using the fingers to make a "V" sign for victory	✓			
Beckoning to someone with the index finger (forefinger)	✓			
The left to right waving of the hand with open palms facing outward to indicate "Good bye"	✓			
The use of a nod to show acknowledgement	✓			
Stopping/beckoning a taxi using a stretched hand with the thumb pointing upward	✓			
Using the thumb finger pointed to a direction, to request a ride or a hike	✓			
Raising one's hand/waving with an open fist to summon a taxi	✓			
Tapping one's foot/feet on the floor in a public gathering		✓		
Wiggling one's leg(s) when in a sitting position	✓			
Use of the hand (by motorists and cyclists) to signal direction of traffic	✓			

221

MALI

		(See last page for comments on items referenced here)
Foreign tourists are welcome in the country.	yes	
The use of seat belt is mandatory.	no	
International driving license is accepted.	yes	
Foreign drivers license is accepted.	no	
It is considered impolite to yawn in public.	no	
Death penalty for drug trafficking is the law.	no	
Life imprisonment for drug trafficking is the law.	yes	
Guilty until proven innocent in court is the law.	no	
Innocent until proven guilty in court is the law.	yes	
Pedestrians always have right of way.	no	
Exit visas are required of visitors.	yes	
Crash helmet is mandatory for motor cyclist.	yes	
Hanging is used as a form of legal punishment.	no	
Decapitation of a limb is used as a form of punishment.	no	
Caning is used as a form of legal punishment.	no	
Electric shock is used as a form of legal punishment.	no	
One is expected to stand up during the playing of the national anthem.	no	
Crash helmet is mandatory for bicyclists.	no	
Guests are expected to eat every thing on their plates.	yes	
Table manners are very informal.	no	
One is expected to cover one's mouth when laughing.	no	
A vertical nod of the head means (OK).	yes	
A horizontal shaking of the head means NO (Not OK).	yes	
Prostitution is allowed only in designated areas.	yes	
One is expected to take off one's hat during playing of national anthem.	no	
Separate seating arrangements (between sexes) are maintained at movies.	no	
Separate seating arrangements (between sexes) are maintained at churches.	no	
Uninvited visitors or guests may not be welcome, even among acquaintances.	no	3
Pets (e.g. cats, dog) are allowed in some hotels and restaurants.	no	
Couples invited for a meal may be separated during meals according to their sex.	no	
Punctuality is the order of business.	no	
Automobiles are driven with headlights always turned on.	yes	
Motorcycles are driven with headlights always turned on.	no	
Visitors with expired visa face mandatory jail time.	no	
Visitors without exit visa face jail time.	no	
Visitors without entry visa face mandatory (automatic) jail time.	no	

ADDITIONAL COUNTRY INFORMATION

(A)	The types of gifts to avoid:	n/a
(B)	Appropriate gifts for a foreigner to give:	n/a
(C)	Best time to present gifts (at the beginning or at the end of a visit?):	at the beginning
(D)	Best time to present gifts (on initial or later visits?):	initial
(E)	Best place to present gifts (in private or in public?):	n/a
(F)	Number(s) with certain connotations and/or myths attached to them:	n/a
(G)	Basic shape(s) with negative connotations:	n/a
(H)	Basic color(s) with negative connotations:	n/a
(I)	Traditional greeting methods include:	handshake
(J)	Safe topics for discussion include:	weather, fashion, travel, art, family, religion domestic politics, food, sports, international politics, social conditions, money and personal wealth, sex
(K)	Best time for conversations (before, during, after meals?):	n/a
(L)	Forms of legal punishment:	jailing
(M)	Approximately length of time one could be detained by law and order authorities before being charged in court:	48 hours
(N)	January 15, 1999, for example, will normally be written as:	15/1/99
(O)	Emergency code number:	18
(P)	Ambulance code Number:	n/a
(Q)	Police code number:	17
(R)	Telephone (country) code:	223
(S)	Telex (country) code:	0985
(T)	Electricity requirements:	220v
(U)	Legal drinking age:	n/a
(V)	Systems of weights and measures:	meter, grams, c
(W)	Legal age of incarceration:	n/a
(X)	Driving side of the road:	right
(Y)	Minimum expenditure expected of foreign visitors? $	no
(Z)	Name of currency:	Franc CFA
(Za)	Some places off-limits to foreign visitors:	n/a
(Zb)	Some places, structures and items prohibited from being photographed:	n/a

ENDNOTES

Item Number: *COMMENTS/EXPLANATIONS*

n/a: Not applicable/Not available/No response

(1)   It is illegal to photograph military installations.

(2)   Military installations, border posts.

(3)   Depends on who arrives.

MAURITIUS	Is customary Is allowed Is permissible Is used. Is OK	Is not customary Is frowned upon	Is disallowed Is forbidden Is a crime	(See last page for comments on items referenced here)
Smoking in public			✓	
Eating in public	✓			
Not flushing public toilet		✓		
Spitting in public		✓		
Feeding animals & birds in public	✓			
Whistling in public		✓		
Drinking alcohol in public		✓		
Kissing in public		✓		
Breast feeding in public	✓			
Drunkenness (in public)		✓		
Cursing in public			✓	
Religious preaching in public	✓			
Begging (panhandling) in public	✓			
Giving money to beggars/panhandlers	✓			
Giving food/drink to beggars/panhandlers	✓			
Brushing teeth in public (other than in restrooms)		✓		
Strolling with pets in major public roads/streets	✓			
Chewing gum in public	✓			
Chewing gum in government offices		✓		
Combing hair in public (other than in toilets/restrooms)	✓			
Undressing/dressing in public			✓	
Wearing of dark glasses indoors in public places	✓			
Public display of wealth	✓			
Praying openly in public in non-designated areas	✓			
Walking bare feet in public	✓			
Chewing tobacco in public		✓		
Trimming one's finger or toe nails in public		✓		
Laughing aloud in public		✓		
Mingling of the sexes in public	✓			
Mixed bathing in public swimming pools	✓			
Distributing religious pamphlets (literature) in public/side streets	✓			

MAURITIUS

	Is customary Is allowed Is permissible Is used. Is OK	Is not customary Is frowned upon	Is disallowed Is forbidden Is a crime	(See last page for comments on items referenced here)
Dancing on side street				1
Nude bathing			✓	
Littering			✓	
Binge Drinking		✓		
Hitchhiking	✓			
Jaywalking		✓		
Drunk driving			✓	
Speeding			✓	
Skating on side streets (side-walk)			✓	2
Graffiti painting			✓	
Pilfering			✓	
Prostitution			✓	
Haggling in the market place	✓			
Consumption of alcoholic beverages in bars and restaurants	✓			
Gambling	✓			
Possession of pornographic materials			✓	
Possession of the Christian Bible	✓			
Possession of the Moslem Koran	✓			
Possession of bullet-proof vest	✓			
Possession of toy gun	✓			
Possession of fire crackers and fireworks	✓			
Possession of prescription drugs (without doctor's note)			✓	
Possession of regulated drugs (narcotics)			✓	
Possession of firearms (by foreigners)				3
Possession of pocket knife in public			✓	
Using walkie talkies	✓			
Using of "boom boxes"(loud sounding stereo system)	✓			
Using "walkman" (very small radio/cassettes with ear plugs) in public places	✓			
Using "walkman" (very small radio/cassettes with ear plugs) while driving or riding	✓			

MAURITIUS

	Is customary Is allowed Is permissible Is used Is OK	Is not customary Is frowned upon	Is disallowed Is forbidden Is a crime	(See last page for comments on items referenced here)
Use of cellular phone	✓			
Use of binoculars/periscopes other than in sports arena	✓			
Taking photographs of people (without their permission)		✓		
Taking photographs at airports, train and bus stations	✓			
Taking photographs of airports	✓			
Taking photographs of churches and synagogues	✓			
Taking photographs of religious statues	✓			
Taking photographs of public buildings	✓			
Taking photographs of bridges	✓			
Tipping (gratuity)		✓		
Tipping (when service is rendered)	✓			
Tipping (when service is not rendered)		✓		
Tipping waiters/waitresses at restaurants and hotels	✓			
Tipping taxi/cab drivers	✓			
Tipping baggage handlers, porters, door persons	✓			
Tipping of hair dressers/barbers	✓			
Overtipping	✓			
Undertipping	✓			
Spilling cigarette butt (ash) on side streets/on the floor		✓		
Men wearing lipstick		✓		
Wearing visible tattoo marks	✓			
Men painting/coloring their finger or toe nails		✓		
Cross dressing (men dressed like women & vice versa)	✓			
Walking in public without a shirt (i.e., with the upper half of the body naked)		✓		
Men wearing braided hair	✓			
Men wearing earrings		✓		
Men wearing dreadlock hair style	✓			
Homosexuality			✓	
Lesbianism			✓	

227

MAURITIUS

	Is customary Is allowed Is permissible Is used Is OK	Is not customary Is frowned upon	Is disallowed Is forbidden Is a crime	(See last page for comments on items referenced here)
Females covering their hair (wearing headgear) in public	✓			
Females exposing their full face in public	✓			
Females driving automobiles	✓			
Females riding motorcycles	✓			
Females riding bicycles	✓			
Females smoking in public	✓			
Women wearing bras (braziers) in public	✓			
Use of lipstick by women	✓			
A woman extending her hands first when introduced	✓			
Female bashing	✓			
Females wearing trousers	✓			
Females wearing minis (short dresses)	✓			
Females wearing bikinis	✓			4
Females wearing shorts	✓			
Persons of opposite sex holding hands in public	✓			
Persons of same sex holding hands in public	✓			
Handshake between opposite sex	✓			
Hugging in public by same sex	✓			
Hugging in public by opposite sex	✓			
Men and women walking side by side in public	✓			
Man walking ahead (in public), with the woman following	✓			
Woman walking ahead (in public), with the man following	✓			
Men opening doors for women	✓			
Sitting with legs crossed in the presence of elders	✓			
Talking to an elderly person with one's hat/cap on	✓			
Talking to an elderly person with hands positioned on both sides of one's waist	✓			
Blowing one's nose in public	✓			
Blowing one's nose in the presence of others	✓			
Addressing people by their title	✓			

228

MAURITIUS

	Is customary Is allowed Is permissible Is used. Is OK	Is not customary Is frowned upon	Is disallowed Is forbidden Is a crime	(See last page for comments on items referenced here)
Addressing people by their family name/surname/last name/given name	✓			
Addressing people by their first name/ given name	✓			
Women going through doors first		✓		
Men helping women with their coats	✓			
Men extending their hands to women first during greetings	✓			
Taking off one's hat when entering a private home	✓			
Removing one's shoes when entering a private home		✓		
Invited guests bringing food at social gatherings		✓		
Guests bringing drinks at social gatherings	✓			
Shaking hands when leaving a small group	✓			
Shaking hands with everyone present, upon arrival at a social gathering	✓			
Eating with the right hand	✓			
Eating with the left hand		✓		
Eating with both hands		✓		
Presenting a gift or passing on an object with the left hand		✓		
Asking a man about his wife		✓		5
Asking a woman about her husband		✓		
Making prior appointments before a meeting or visit	✓			
Addressing an audience with one or both hands in the pocket	✓			
Carrying on conversation during meals	✓			
Females sitting with legs crossed	✓			
People discussing their wealth		✓		
Asking someone his or her age, or how old the person is	✓			
Complementing someone on his/her physical looks	✓			
Complementing someone on his/her attire	✓			
Use of both hands in handshake	✓			
In greeting, a handshake accompanied by a slight bow		✓		

229

MAURITIUS

	Is customary Is allowed Is permissible Is used. Is OK	Is not customary Is frowned upon	Is disallowed Is forbidden Is a crime	(See last page for comments on items referenced here)
Salutations such as "Good morning", "good afternoon", "Good evening"	✓			
The completion of a business deal with a handshake	✓			
Starting a negotiation session with a handshake	✓			
A gift for the host/hostess	✓			
Giving a business gift		✓		
A gift of money (use of money as gift)		✓		
Use of flowers as a gift	✓			
Use of business cards	✓			
Accepting/presenting gifts with both hands		✓		
Burning of the country's flag			✓	
Mutilation of the national currency			✓	
Casual wearing of clothings made with colors & marks of the national flag		✓		
Wearing of look-alike military (camouflage) fatigues (attire)		✓		
Sitting on the floor (on floor mats)		✓		
Discussion of religion		✓		
Discussion of politics	✓			
Discussion of sex		✓		
Patting/slapping someone on the buttocks			✓	
Patting/slapping someone on the back		✓		
Touching or patting someone's head/hair	✓			
Casual touching of any part of someone's body		✓		
Drinking directly out of a bottle/can	✓			
Placing one's leg(s) on the table or chair		✓		

230

MAURITIUS

	Is customary Is allowed Is permissible Is used. Is OK	Is not customary Is frowned upon	Is disallowed Is forbidden Is a crime	(See last page for comments on items referenced here)
Showing the sole of one's foot (feet)	✓	✓		
People standing very close when talking		✓		
Maintaining steady eye contact (direct gaze) when talking to someone	✓			
Kissing or exchange of kisses on the cheek	✓			
Counting money (change) in someone's palm	✓			
Finger pointing in public (in a daring manner)		✓		
Seeking attention by winking the eyes	✓			
Tapping the head to indicate someone is crazy	✓			
Twirling the head to indicate someone is crazy	✓			
Whistling as a way of requesting something/seeking attention			✓	
Using "thumbs-up" sign to mean OK	✓			
Forming a circle with the thumb and index finger (forefinger) to mean OK	✓			
Using the fingers to make a "V" sign for victory	✓			
Beckoning to someone with the index finger (forefinger)		✓		
The left to right waving of the hand with open palms facing outward to indicate "Good bye"	✓			
The use of a nod to show acknowledgement	✓			
Stopping/beckoning a taxi using a stretched hand with the thumb pointing upward		✓		
Using the thumb finger pointed to a direction, to request a ride or a hike	✓			
Raising one's hand/waving with an open fist to summon a taxi	✓			
Tapping one's foot/feet on the floor in a public gathering		✓		
Wiggling one's leg(s) when in a sitting position		✓		
Use of the hand (by motorists and cyclists) to signal direction of traffic	✓			

231

MAURITIUS

		(See last page for comments on items referenced here)
Foreign tourists are welcome in the country.	yes	
The use of seat belt is mandatory.	yes	
International driving license is accepted.	yes	
Foreign drivers license is accepted.	yes	
It is considered impolite to yawn in public.	yes	
Death penalty for drug trafficking is the law.	no	
Life imprisonment for drug trafficking is the law.	yes	
Guilty until proven innocent in court is the law.	no	
Innocent until proven guilty in court is the law.	yes	
Pedestrians always have right of way.	no	
Exit visas are required of visitors.	no	
Crash helmet is mandatory for motor cyclist.	yes	
Hanging is used as a form of legal punishment.	no	
Decapitation of a limb is used as a form of punishment.	no	
Caning is used as a form of legal punishment.	no	
Electric shock is used as a form of legal punishment.	no	
One is expected to stand up during the playing of the national anthem.	yes	
Crash helmet is mandatory for bicyclists.	no	
Guests are expected to eat every thing on their plates.	no	
Table manners are very informal.	no	
One is expected to cover one's mouth when laughing.	no	
A vertical nod of the head means YES (OK).	yes	
A horizontal shaking of the head means NO (Not OK).	yes	
Prostitution is allowed only in designated areas.	no	
One is expected to take off one's hat during playing of national anthem.	yes	
Separate seating arrangements (between sexes) are maintained at movies.	no	
Separate seating arrangements (between sexes) are maintained at churches.	no	
Uninvited visitors or guests may not be welcome, even among acquaintances.	no	
Pets (e.g. cats, dog) are allowed in some hotels and restaurants.	yes	
Couples invited for a meal may be separated during meals according to their sex.	no	
Punctuality is the order of business.	yes	
Automobiles are driven with headlights always turned on.	no	
Motorcycles are driven with headlights always turned on.	no	
Visitors with expired visa face mandatory jail time.	no	
Visitors without exit visa face jail time.	no	
Visitors without entry visa face mandatory (automatic) jail time.	no	

ADDITIONAL COUNTRY INFORMATION

(A)	The types of gifts to avoid:	money
(B)	Appropriate gifts for a foreigner to give:	flowers, souvenirs
(C)	Best time to present gifts (at the beginning or at the end of a visit?):	beginning
(D)	Best time to present gifts (on initial or later visits?):	during parties, receptions
(E)	Best place to present gifts (in private or in public?):	n/a
(F)	Number(s) with certain connotations and/or myths attached to them:	n/a
(G)	Basic shape(s) with negative connotations:	n/a
(H)	Basic color(s) with negative connotations:	n/a
(I)	Traditional greeting methods include:	handshaking
(J)	Safe topics for discussion include:	weather, fashion, travel, art, family, religion, domestic politics, food, sports, international politics, social conditions
(K)	Best time for conversations (before, during, after meals?):	eating time
(L)	Forms of legal punishment:	jailing
(M)	Approximately length of time one could be detained by law and order authorities before being charged in court:	24 hours
(N)	January 15, 1999, for example, will normally be written as:	15.01.1999
(O)	Emergency code number:	999
(P)	Ambulance code Number:	999
(Q)	Police code number:	999
(R)	Telephone (country) code:	230
(S)	Telex (country) code:	n/a
(T)	Electricity requirements:	220 volts
(U)	Legal drinking age:	18 years
(V)	Systems of weights and measures:	S.I. unit
(W)	Legal age of incarceration:	18 years
(X)	Driving side of the road:	right
(Y)	Minimum expenditure expected of foreign visitors? $	no
(Z)	Name of currency:	Rupee
(Za)	Some places off-limits to foreign visitors:	n/a
(Zb)	Some places, structures and items prohibited from being photographed:	government buildings

ENDNOTES

Item Number: *COMMENTS/EXPLANATIONS*

n/a: Not applicable/Not available/No response

(1)   Acceptable under some circumstances, e.g. festivals.

(2)   Skating, though not prohibited, may be dangerous.

(3)   In some places travellers would make a declaration regarding firearms when entering the country

(4)   At beaches and seaside.

(5)   Depends on what is being asked.

MOROCCO	Is customary Is allowed Is permissible Is used. Is OK	Is not customary Is frowned upon	Is disallowed Is forbidden Is a crime	(See last page for comments on items referenced here)
Smoking in public	✓			
Eating in public	✓			
Not flushing public toilet		✓		
Spitting in public		✓		
Feeding animals & birds in public	✓			
Whistling in public	✓			
Drinking alcohol in public			✓	
Kissing in public		✓		
Breast feeding in public	✓			
Drunkenness (in public)			✓	
Cursing in public	✓			
Religious preaching in public	✓			
Begging (panhandling) in public	✓			
Giving money to beggars/panhandlers	✓			
Giving food/drink to beggars/panhandlers	✓			
Brushing teeth in public (other than in restrooms)		✓		
Strolling with pets in major public roads/streets	✓			
Chewing gum in public	✓			
Chewing gum in government offices		✓		
Combing hair in public (other than in toilets/restrooms)	✓			
Undressing/dressing in public		✓		
Wearing of dark glasses indoors in public places	✓			
Public display of wealth	✓			
Praying openly in public in non-designated areas	✓			
Walking bare feet in public		✓		
Chewing tobacco in public	✓			
Trimming one's finger or toe nails in public		✓		
Laughing aloud in public	✓			
Mingling of the sexes in public	✓			
Mixed bathing in public swimming pools	✓			
Distributing religious pamphlets (literature) in public/side streets	✓			

235

MOROCCO

	Is customary Is allowed Is permissible Is used. Is OK	Is not customary Is frowned upon	Is disallowed Is forbidden Is a crime	(See last page for comments on items referenced here)
Dancing on side street		✓		
Nude bathing			✓	
Littering	✓			
Binge Drinking	✓			
Hitchhiking	✓			
Jaywalking	✓			
Drunk driving			✓	
Speeding			✓	
Skating on side streets (side-walk)	✓			
Graffiti painting	✓			
Pilfering	✓			
Prostitution			✓	
Haggling in the market place	✓			
Consumption of alcoholic beverages in bars and restaurants	✓			
Gambling	✓			
Possession of pornographic materials			✓	
Possession of the Christian Bible	✓			
Possession of the Moslem Koran	✓			
Possession of bullet-proof vest	✓			
Possession of toy gun	✓			
Possession of fire crackers and fireworks	✓			
Possession of prescription drugs (without doctor's note)		✓		
Possession of regulated drugs (narcotics)			✓	
Possession of firearms (by foreigners)	✓			
Possession of pocket knife in public	✓			
Using walkie talkies	✓			
Using of "boom boxes"(loud sounding stereo system)	✓			
Using "walkman" (very small radio/cassettes with ear plugs) in public places	✓			
Using "walkman" (very small radio/cassettes with ear plugs) while driving or riding	n/a			

MOROCCO

	Is customary Is allowed Is permissible Is used Is OK	Is not customary Is frowned upon	Is disallowed Is forbidden Is a crime	(See last page for comments on items referenced here)
Use of cellular phone	✓			
Use of binoculars/periscopes other than in sports arena	✓			
Taking photographs of people (without their permission)	✓			
Taking photographs at airports, train and bus stations	✓			
Taking photographs of airports	✓			
Taking photographs of churches and synagogues	✓			
Taking photographs of religious statues	✓			
Taking photographs of public buildings	✓			
Taking photographs of bridges	✓			
Tipping (gratuity)	✓			
Tipping (when service is rendered)	✓			
Tipping (when service is not rendered)	✓			
Tipping waiters/waitresses at restaurants and hotels	✓			
Tipping taxi/cab drivers	✓			
Tipping baggage handlers, porters, door persons	✓			
Tipping of hair dressers/barbers				n/a
Overtipping	✓			
Undertipping	✓			
Spilling cigarette butt (ash) on side streets/on the floor		✓		
Men wearing lipstick		✓		
Wearing visible tattoo marks	✓			
Men painting/coloring their finger or toe nails		✓		
Cross dressing (men dressed like women & vice versa)		✓		
Walking in public without a shirt (i.e., with the upper half of the body naked)		✓		
Men wearing braided hair	✓			
Men wearing earrings	✓			
Men wearing dreadlock hair style	✓			
Homosexuality			✓	
Lesbianism			✓	

MOROCCO

	Is customary Is allowed Is permissible Is used Is OK	Is not customary Is frowned upon	Is disallowed Is forbidden Is a crime	(See last page for comments on items referenced here)
Females covering their hair (wearing headgear) in public	✓			
Females exposing their full face in public	✓			
Females driving automobiles	✓			
Females riding motorcycles	✓			
Females riding bicycles	✓			
Females smoking in public	✓			
Women wearing bras (braziers) in public		✓		
Use of lipstick by women	✓			
A woman extending her hands first when introduced	✓			
Female bashing	✓			
Females wearing trousers	✓			
Females wearing minis (short dresses)	✓			
Females wearing bikinis	✓			
Females wearing shorts	✓			
Persons of opposite sex holding hands in public	✓		.	
Persons of same sex holding hands in public	✓			
Handshake between opposite sex	✓			
Hugging in public by same sex	✓			
Hugging in public by opposite sex	✓			
Men and women walking side by side in public	✓			
Man walking ahead (in public), with the woman following	✓			
Woman walking ahead (in public), with the man following	✓			
Men opening doors for women	✓			
Sitting with legs crossed in the presence of elders	✓			
Talking to an elderly person with one's hat/cap on	✓	.		
Talking to an elderly person with hands positioned on both sides of one's waist	✓			
Blowing one's nose in public	✓			
Blowing one's nose in the presence of others	✓			
Addressing people by their title	✓			

238

MOROCCO

	Is customary Is allowed Is permissible Is used. Is OK	Is not customary Is frowned upon	Is disallowed Is forbidden Is a crime	(See last page for comments on items referenced here)
Addressing people by their family name/surname/last name/given name	✓			
Addressing people by their first name/ given name	✓			
Women going through doors first		✓		
Men helping women with their coats	✓			
Men extending their hands to women first during greetings	✓			
Taking off one's hat when entering a private home	✓			
Removing one's shoes when entering a private home	✓			
Invited guests bringing food at social gatherings	✓			
Guests bringing drinks at social gatherings	✓			
Shaking hands when leaving a small group	✓			
Shaking hands with everyone present, upon arrival at a social gathering	✓			
Eating with the right hand	✓			
Eating with the left hand	✓			
Eating with both hands	✓			
Presenting a gift or passing on an object with the left hand	✓			
Asking a man about his wife	✓			
Asking a woman about her husband	✓			
Making prior appointments before a meeting or visit	✓			
Addressing an audience with one or both hands in the pocket	✓			
Carrying on conversation during meals	✓			
Females sitting with legs crossed	✓			
People discussing their wealth	✓			
Asking someone his or her age, or how old the person is	✓			
Complementing someone on his/her physical looks	✓			
Complementing someone on his/her attire	✓			
Use of both hands in handshake	✓			
In greeting, a handshake accompanied by a slight bow	✓			

MOROCCO

	Is customary Is allowed Is permissible Is used. Is OK	Is not customary Is frowned upon	Is disallowed Is forbidden Is a crime	(See last page for comments on items referenced here)
Salutations such as "Good morning", "good afternoon", "Good evening"	✓			
The completion of a business deal with a handshake	✓			
Starting a negotiation session with a handshake	✓			
A gift for the host/hostess	✓			
Giving a business gift	✓			
A gift of money (use of money as gift)	✓			
Use of flowers as a gift	✓			
Use of business cards	✓			
Accepting/presenting gifts with both hands	✓			
Burning of the country's flag			✓	
Mutilation of the national currency			✓	
Casual wearing of clothings made with colors & marks of the national flag	✓			
Wearing of look-alike military (camouflage) fatigues (attire)	✓			
Sitting on the floor (on floor mats)	✓			
Discussion of religion	✓			
Discussion of politics	✓			
Discussion of sex	✓			
Patting/slapping someone on the buttocks		✓		
Patting/slapping someone on the back	✓			
Touching or patting someone's head/hair	✓			
Casual touching of any part of someone's body		✓		
Drinking directly out of a bottle/can	✓			
Placing one's leg(s) on the table or chair	✓			

MOROCCO

	Is customary Is allowed Is permissible Is used. Is OK	Is not customary Is frowned upon	Is disallowed Is forbidden Is a crime	(See last page for comments on items referenced here)
Showing the sole of one's foot (feet)		✓		
People standing very close when talking	✓			
Maintaining steady eye contact (direct gaze) when talking to someone	✓			
Kissing or exchange of kisses on the cheek	✓			
Counting money (change) in someone's palm	✓			
Finger pointing in public (in a daring manner)	✓			
Seeking attention by winking the eyes				n/a
Tapping the head to indicate someone is crazy	✓			
Twirling the head to indicate someone is crazy	✓			
Whistling as a way of requesting something/seeking attention		✓		
Using "thumbs-up" sign to mean OK	✓			
Forming a circle with the thumb and index finger (forefinger) to mean OK		✓		
Using the fingers to make a "V" sign for victory	✓			
Beckoning to someone with the index finger (forefinger)		✓		
The left to right waving of the hand with open palms facing outward to indicate "Good bye"	✓			
The use of a nod to show acknowledgement	✓			
Stopping/beckoning a taxi using a stretched hand with the thumb pointing upward	✓			
Using the thumb finger pointed to a direction, to request a ride or a hike	✓			
Raising one's hand/waving with an open fist to summon a taxi	✓			
Tapping one's foot/feet on the floor in a public gathering		✓		
Wiggling one's leg(s) when in a sitting position		✓		
Use of the hand (by motorists and cyclists) to signal direction of traffic	✓			

MOROCCO

		(See last page for comments on items referenced here)
Foreign tourists are welcome in the country.	yes	
The use of seat belt is mandatory.	yes	
International driving license is accepted.	yes	
Foreign drivers license is accepted.	yes	
It is considered impolite to yawn in public.	yes	
Death penalty for drug trafficking is the law.	no	
Life imprisonment for drug trafficking is the law.	yes	
Guilty until proven innocent in court is the law.	yes	
Innocent until proven guilty in court is the law.	yes	
Pedestrians always have right of way.	no	
Exit visas are required of visitors.	no	
Crash helmet is mandatory for motor cyclist.	yes	
Hanging is used as a form of legal punishment.	no	
Decapitation of a limb is used as a form of punishment.	no	
Caning is used as a form of legal punishment.	no	
Electric shock is used as a form of legal punishment.		n/a
One is expected to stand up during the playing of the national anthem.	yes	
Crash helmet is mandatory for bicyclists.	yes	
Guests are expected to eat every thing on their plates.	no	
Table manners are very informal.	no	
One is expected to cover one's mouth when laughing.	no	
A vertical nod of the head means YES (OK).	yes	
A horizontal shaking of the head means NO (Not OK).	no	
Prostitution is allowed only in designated areas.		n/a
One is expected to take off one's hat during playing of national anthem.	yes	
Separate seating arrangements (between sexes) are maintained at movies.	no	
Separate seating arrangements (between sexes) are maintained at churches.	yes	
Uninvited visitors or guests may not be welcome, even among acquaintances.	no	
Pets (e.g. cats, dog) are allowed in some hotels and restaurants.	yes	
Couples invited for a meal may be separated during meals according to their sex.	yes	
Punctuality is the order of business.	yes	
Automobiles are driven with headlights always turned on.	no	
Motorcycles are driven with headlights always turned on.	no	
Visitors with expired visa face mandatory jail time.	no	
Visitors without exit visa face jail time.	no	
Visitors without entry visa face mandatory (automatic) jail time.	noes	

ADDITIONAL COUNTRY INFORMATION

(A)	The types of gifts to avoid:	n/a
(B)	Appropriate gifts for a foreigner to give:	n/a
(C)	Best time to present gifts (at the beginning or at the end of a visit?):	n/a
(D)	Best time to present gifts (on initial or later visits?):	n/a
(E)	Best place to present gifts (in private or in public?):	n/a
(F)	Number(s) with certain connotations and/or myths attached to them:	n/a
(G)	Basic shape(s) with negative connotations:	n/a
(H)	Basic color(s) with negative connotations:	n/a
(I)	Traditional greeting methods include:	n/a
(J)	Safe topics for discussion include:	weather, fashion, travel, art, family, religion, domestic politics, food, sports, international politics, social conditions, money
(K)	Best time for conversations (before, during, after meals?):	n/a
(L)	Forms of legal punishment:	n/a
(M)	Approximately length of time one could be detained by law and order authorities before being charged in court:	n/a
(N)	January 15, 1999, for example, will normally be written as:	15/1/99
(O)	Emergency code number:	19
(P)	Ambulance code Number:	16
(Q)	Police code number:	19
(R)	Telephone (country) code:	212
(S)	Telex (country) code:	n/a
(T)	Electricity requirements:	110 and 220 volt
(U)	Legal drinking age:	n/a
(V)	Systems of weights and measures:	metric
(W)	Legal age of incarceration:	n/a
(X)	Driving side of the road:	right
(Y)	Minimum expenditure expected of foreign visitors? $	n/a
(Z)	Name of currency:	dirham
(Za)	Some places off-limits to foreign visitors:	n/a
(Zb)	Some places, structures and items prohibited from being photographed:	n/a

NAMIBIA	Is customary Is allowed Is permissible Is used. Is OK	Is not customary Is frowned upon	Is disallowed Is forbidden Is a crime	(See last page for comments on items referenced here)
Smoking in public	✓			
Eating in public	✓			
Not flushing public toilet		✓		
Spitting in public		✓		
Feeding animals & birds in public	✓			
Whistling in public	✓			
Drinking alcohol in public		✓		
Kissing in public	✓			
Breast feeding in public	✓			
Drunkenness (in public)		✓		
Cursing in public		✓		
Religious preaching in public	✓			
Begging (panhandling) in public		✓		
Giving money to beggars/panhandlers	✓			
Giving food/drink to beggars/panhandlers	✓			
Brushing teeth in public (other than in restrooms)		✓		
Strolling with pets in major public roads/streets	✓			
Chewing gum in public	✓			
Chewing gum in government offices	✓			
Combing hair in public (other than in toilets/restrooms)	✓			
Undressing/dressing in public			✓	
Wearing of dark glasses indoors in public places	✓			
Public display of wealth	✓			
Praying openly in public in non-designated areas		✓		
Walking bare feet in public	✓			
Chewing tobacco in public		✓		
Trimming one's finger or toe nails in public		✓		
Laughing aloud in public	✓			
Mingling of the sexes in public	✓			
Mixed bathing in public swimming pools	✓			
Distributing religious pamphlets (literature) in public/side streets	✓			

NAMIBIA

	Is customary Is allowed Is permissible Is used. Is OK	Is not customary Is frowned upon	Is disallowed Is forbidden Is a crime	(See last page for comments on items referenced here)
Dancing on side street	✓			
Nude bathing			✓	
Littering			✓	
Binge Drinking		✓		
Hitchhiking	✓			
Jaywalking			✓	
Drunk driving			✓	
Speeding			✓	
Skating on side streets (side-walk)		✓		
Graffiti painting		✓		
Pilfering			✓	
Prostitution			✓	
Haggling in the market place	✓			
Consumption of alcoholic beverages in bars and restaurants	✓			
Gambling	✓			1
Possession of pornographic materials			✓	✓
Possession of the Christian Bible	✓			
Possession of the Moslem Koran	✓			
Possession of bullet-proof vest	✓			
Possession of toy gun	✓			
Possession of fire crackers and fireworks	✓			
Possession of prescription drugs (without doctor's note)			✓	
Possession of regulated drugs (narcotics)			✓	
Possession of firearms (by foreigners)	✓			2
Possession of pocket knife in public	✓			
Using walkie talkies	✓			3
Using of "boom boxes"(loud sounding stereo system)	✓			
Using "walkman" (very small radio/cassettes with ear plugs) in public places	✓			
Using "walkman" (very small radio/cassettes with ear plugs) while driving or riding	✓			

NAMIBIA

	Is customary Is allowed Is permissible Is used Is OK	Is not customary Is frowned upon	Is disallowed Is forbidden Is a crime	(See last page for comments on items referenced here)
Use of cellular phone	✓			
Use of binoculars/periscopes other than in sports arena	✓			
Taking photographs of people (without their permission)	✓			✓
Taking photographs at airports, train and bus stations	✓			
Taking photographs of airports	✓			
Taking photographs of churches and synagogues	✓			
Taking photographs of religious statues	✓			
Taking photographs of public buildings	✓			
Taking photographs of bridges	✓			
Tipping (gratuity)	✓			
Tipping (when service is rendered)	✓			
Tipping (when service is not rendered)		✓		
Tipping waiters/waitresses at restaurants and hotels	✓			
Tipping taxi/cab drivers	✓			
Tipping baggage handlers, porters, door persons	✓			
Tipping of hair dressers/barbers		✓		
Overtipping		✓		
Undertipping		✓		
Spilling cigarette butt (ash) on side streets/on the floor	✓			
Men wearing lipstick		✓		
Wearing visible tattoo marks	✓			
Men painting/coloring their finger or toe nails		✓		
Cross dressing (men dressed like women & vice versa)		✓		
Walking in public without a shirt (i.e., with the upper half of the body naked)	✓			
Men wearing braided hair	✓			
Men wearing earrings	✓			
Men wearing dreadlock hair style	✓			
Homosexuality		✓		
Lesbianism		✓		

NAMIBIA

	Is customary Is allowed Is permissible Is used Is OK	Is not customary Is frowned upon	Is disallowed Is forbidden Is a crime	(See last page for comments on items referenced here)
Females covering their hair (wearing headgear) in public	✓			
Females exposing their full face in public	✓			
Females driving automobiles	✓			
Females riding motorcycles	✓			
Females riding bicycles	✓			
Females smoking in public	✓			
Women wearing bras (braziers) in public	✓			
Use of lipstick by women	✓			
A woman extending her hands first when introduced	✓			
Female bashing			✓	
Females wearing trousers	✓			
Females wearing minis (short dresses)	✓			
Females wearing bikinis	✓			
Females wearing shorts	✓			
Persons of opposite sex holding hands in public	✓			
Persons of same sex holding hands in public	✓			
Handshake between opposite sex	✓			
Hugging in public by same sex	✓			
Hugging in public by opposite sex	✓			
Men and women walking side by side in public	✓			
Man walking ahead (in public), with the woman following	✓			
Woman walking ahead (in public), with the man following	✓			
Men opening doors for women	✓			
Sitting with legs crossed in the presence of elders	✓			
Talking to an elderly person with one's hat/cap on		✓		
Talking to an elderly person with hands positioned on both sides of one's waist	✓			
Blowing one's nose in public	✓			
Blowing one's nose in the presence of others	✓			
Addressing people by their title	✓			

247

NAMIBIA

	Is customary Is allowed Is permissible Is used. Is OK	Is not customary Is frowned upon	Is disallowed Is forbidden Is a crime	(See last page for comments on items referenced here)
Addressing people by their family name/surname/last name/given name	✓			
Addressing people by their first name/ given name	✓			
Women going through doors first	✓			
Men helping women with their coats	✓			
Men extending their hands to women first during greetings	✓			
Taking off one's hat when entering a private home	✓			
Removing one's shoes when entering a private home		✓		
Invited guests bringing food at social gatherings	✓			
Guests bringing drinks at social gatherings	✓			
Shaking hands when leaving a small group	✓			
Shaking hands with everyone present, upon arrival at a social gathering	✓			
Eating with the right hand	✓			
Eating with the left hand	✓			
Eating with both hands	✓			
Presenting a gift or passing on an object with the left hand	✓			
Asking a man about his wife	✓			
Asking a woman about her husband	✓			
Making prior appointments before a meeting or visit	✓			
Addressing an audience with one or both hands in the pocket	✓			
Carrying on conversation during meals	✓			
Females sitting with legs crossed	✓			
People discussing their wealth		✓		
Asking someone his or her age, or how old the person is	✓			
Complementing someone on his/her physical looks	✓			
Complementing someone on his/her attire	✓			
Use of both hands in handshake	✓			
In greeting, a handshake accompanied by a slight bow	✓			

NAMIBIA

	Is customary Is allowed Is permissible Is used. Is OK	Is not customary Is frowned upon	Is disallowed Is forbidden Is a crime	(See last page for comments on items referenced here)
Salutations such as "Good morning", "good afternoon", "Good evening"	✓			
The completion of a business deal with a handshake	✓			
Starting a negotiation session with a handshake	✓			
A gift for the host/hostess	✓			
Giving a business gift	✓			4
A gift of money (use of money as gift)	✓			
Use of flowers as a gift	✓			
Use of business cards	✓			
Accepting/presenting gifts with both hands	✓			
Burning of the country's flag			✓	
Mutilation of the national currency			✓	
Casual wearing of clothings made with colors & marks of the national flag	✓			
Wearing of look-alike military (camouflage) fatigues (attire)		✓		
Sitting on the floor (on floor mats)		✓		
Discussion of religion	✓			
Discussion of politics	✓			
Discussion of sex	✓			
Patting/slapping someone on the buttocks		✓		
Patting/slapping someone on the back	✓			
Touching or patting someone's head/hair	✓			
Casual touching of any part of someone's body		✓		
Drinking directly out of a bottle/can	✓			
Placing one's leg(s) on the table or chair		✓		

249

NAMIBIA

	Is customary Is allowed Is permissible Is used. Is OK	Is not customary Is frowned upon	Is disallowed Is forbidden Is a crime	(See last page for comments on items referenced here)
Showing the sole of one's foot (feet)		✓		
People standing very close when talking	✓			
Maintaining steady eye contact (direct gaze) when talking to someone	✓			
Kissing or exchange of kisses on the cheek	✓			
Counting money (change) in someone's palm	✓			
Finger pointing in public (in a daring manner)		✓		
Seeking attention by winking the eyes		✓		
Tapping the head to indicate someone is crazy		✓		
Twirling the head to indicate someone is crazy		✓		
Whistling as a way of requesting something/seeking attention		✓		
Using "thumbs-up" sign to mean OK	✓			
Forming a circle with the thumb and index finger (forefinger) to mean OK		✓		
Using the fingers to make a "V" sign for victory	✓			
Beckoning to someone with the index finger (forefinger)	✓			
The left to right waving of the hand with open palms facing outward to indicate "Good bye"	✓			
The use of a nod to show acknowledgement	✓			
Stopping/beckoning a taxi using a stretched hand with the thumb pointing upward		✓		
Using the thumb finger pointed to a direction, to request a ride or a hike	✓			
Raising one's hand/waving with an open fist to summon a taxi	✓			
Tapping one's foot/feet on the floor in a public gathering		✓		
Wiggling one's leg(s) when in a sitting position	✓			
Use of the hand (by motorists and cyclists) to signal direction of traffic	✓			

		(See last page for comments on items referenced here)
Foreign tourists are welcome in the country.	yes	
The use of seat belt is mandatory.	yes	
International driving license is accepted.	yes	
Foreign drivers license is accepted.	no	
It is considered impolite to yawn in public.	yes	
Death penalty for drug trafficking is the law.	no	
Life imprisonment for drug trafficking is the law.	no	
Guilty until proven innocent in court is the law.	no	
Innocent until proven guilty in court is the law.	yes	
Pedestrians always have right of way.	no	5
Exit visas are required of visitors.	no	
Crash helmet is mandatory for motor cyclist.	yes	
Hanging is used as a form of legal punishment.	no	
Decapitation of a limb is used as a form of punishment.	no	
Caning is used as a form of legal punishment.	no	
Electric shock is used as a form of legal punishment.	no	
One is expected to stand up during the playing of the national anthem.	yes	
Crash helmet is mandatory for bicyclists.	no	
Guests are expected to eat every thing on their plates.	no	
Table manners are very informal.	yes	
One is expected to cover one's mouth when laughing.	no	
A vertical nod of the head means YES (OK).	yes	
A horizontal shaking of the head means NO (Not OK).	yes	
Prostitution is allowed only in designated areas.	no	
One is expected to take off one's hat during playing of national anthem.	yes	
Separate seating arrangements (between sexes) are maintained at movies.	no	
Separate seating arrangements (between sexes) are maintained at churches.	no	
Uninvited visitors or guests may not be welcome, even among acquaintances.	yes	
Pets (e.g. cats, dog) are allowed in some hotels and restaurants.	yes	
Couples invited for a meal may be separated during meals according to their sex.	no	
Punctuality is the order of business.	yes	6
Automobiles are driven with headlights always turned on.	no	
Motorcycles are driven with headlights always turned on.	no	
Visitors with expired visa face mandatory jail time.	no	7
Visitors without exit visa face jail time.	no	
Visitors without entry visa face mandatory (automatic) jail time.	no	8

ADDITIONAL COUNTRY INFORMATION

(A)	The types of gifts to avoid:	n/a
(B)	Appropriate gifts for a foreigner to give:	n/a
(C)	Best time to present gifts (at the beginning or at the end of a visit?):	beginning
(D)	Best time to present gifts (on initial or later visits?):	initial
(E)	Best place to present gifts (in private or in public?):	either in private or in public
(F)	Number(s) with certain connotations and/or myths attached to them:	13-bad luck
(G)	Basic shape(s) with negative connotations:	none
(H)	Basic color(s) with negative connotations:	none
(I)	Traditional greeting methods include:	handshake, hug, kiss
(J)	Safe topics for discussion include:	weather, fashion, travel, art, family religion, domestic politics, food, sports, international politics, social conditions, money and personal wealth, sex
(K)	Best time for conversations (before, during, after meals?):	anytime
(L)	Forms of legal punishment:	jailing
(M)	Approximately length of time one could be detained by law and order authorities before being charged in court:	48 hours
(N)	January 15, 1999, for example, will normally be written as:	15/1/99
(O)	Emergency code number:	0
(P)	Ambulance code Number:	p
(Q)	Police code number:	q
(R)	Telephone (country) code:	61
(S)	Telex (country) code:	61
(T)	Electricity requirements:	220v
(U)	Legal drinking age:	18 years
(V)	Systems of weights and measures:	metric
(W)	Legal age of incarceration:	18 years
(X)	Driving side of the road:	left
(Y)	Minimum expenditure expected of foreign visitors? $	no
(Z)	Name of currency:	namibian dollar
(Za)	Some places off-limits to foreign visitors:	jails, military bases
(Zb)	Some places, structures and items prohibited from being photographed:	none

ENDNOTES

Item Number: COMMENTS/EXPLANATIONS

n/a: Not applicable/Not available/No response

(1)   In legal establishments only.

(2)   Firearms must be licensed.

(3)   Walkie talkies must be licensed by post office.

(4)   Could be construed as bribery in public service.

(5)   Traffic regulation! pedestrian have right-of-way at crossing if they adhere to regulation don't.

(6)   Africans are nations known for always being late

(7)   Persons without entry visa will not be allowed in.

(8)   Alternatively, they'll be deported.

(O)   National number! every town has its own.

(P)   National number! every town has its own.

(Q)   National number! every town has its own.

NIGER REPUBLIC	Is customary Is allowed Is permissible Is used. Is OK	Is not customary Is frowned upon	Is disallowed Is forbidden Is a crime	(See last page for comments on items referenced here)
Smoking in public			✓	
Eating in public			✓	
Not flushing public toilet			✓	
Spitting in public			✓	
Feeding animals & birds in public		✓		
Whistling in public		✓		
Drinking alcohol in public		✓		
Kissing in public			✓	
Breast feeding in public			✓	
Drunkenness (in public)			✓	
Cursing in public		✓		
Religious preaching in public			✓	
Begging (panhandling) in public			✓	
Giving money to beggars/panhandlers			✓	
Giving food/drink to beggars/panhandlers			✓	
Brushing teeth in public (other than in restrooms)			✓	
Strolling with pets in major public roads/streets		✓		
Chewing gum in public		✓		
Chewing gum in government offices		✓		
Combing hair in public (other than in toilets/restrooms)			✓	
Undressing/dressing in public			✓	
Wearing of dark glasses indoors in public places			✓	
Public display of wealth			✓	
Praying openly in public in non-designated areas			✓	
Walking bare feet in public			✓	
Chewing tobacco in public			✓	
Trimming one's finger or toe nails in public		✓		
Laughing aloud in public		✓		
Mingling of the sexes in public		✓		
Mixed bathing in public swimming pools		✓		
Distributing religious pamphlets (literature) in public/side streets	✓			

NIGER REPUBLIC

	Is customary Is allowed Is permissible Is used. Is OK	Is not customary Is frowned upon	Is disallowed Is forbidden Is a crime	(See last page for comments on items referenced here)
Dancing on side street			✓	
Nude bathing			✓	
Littering			✓	
Binge Drinking			✓	
Hitchhiking			✓	
Jaywalking			✓	
Drunk driving			✓	
Speeding			✓	
Skating on side streets (side-walk)			✓	
Graffiti painting		✓		
Pilfering		✓		
Prostitution		✓		
Haggling in the market place		✓		
Consumption of alcoholic beverages in bars and restaurants		✓		
Gambling		✓		
Possession of pornographic materials		✓		
Possession of the Christian Bible			✓	
Possession of the Moslem Koran			✓	
Possession of bullet-proof vest			✓	
Possession of toy gun			✓	
Possession of fire crackers and fireworks			✓	
Possession of prescription drugs (without doctor's note)			✓	
Possession of regulated drugs (narcotics)			✓	
Possession of firearms (by foreigners)		✓		
Possession of pocket knife in public		✓		
Using walkie talkies	✓			
Using of "boom boxes"(loud sounding stereo system)	✓			
Using "walkman" (very small radio/cassettes with ear plugs) in public places		✓		
Using "walkman" (very small radio/cassettes with ear plugs) while driving or riding		✓		

255

NIGER REPUBLIC

	Is customary Is allowed Is permissible Is used Is OK	Is not customary Is frowned upon	Is disallowed Is forbidden Is a crime	(See last page for comments on items referenced here)
Use of cellular phone	✓			
Use of binoculars/periscopes other than in sports arena	✓			
Taking photographs of people (without their permission)	✓			
Taking photographs at airports, train and bus stations	✓			
Taking photographs of airports	✓			
Taking photographs of churches and synagogues	✓			
Taking photographs of religious statues	✓			
Taking photographs of public buildings		✓		
Taking photographs of bridges		✓		
Tipping (gratuity)		✓		
Tipping (when service is rendered)		✓		
Tipping (when service is not rendered)		✓		
Tipping waiters/waitresses at restaurants and hotels		✓		
Tipping taxi/cab drivers		✓	✓	
Tipping baggage handlers, porters, door persons			✓	
Tipping of hair dressers/barbers			✓	
Overtipping	✓			
Undertipping	✓			
Spilling cigarette butt (ash) on side streets/on the floor	✓			
Men wearing lipstick	✓			
Wearing visible tattoo marks		✓		
Men painting/coloring their finger or toe nails		✓		
Cross dressing (men dressed like women & vice versa)		✓		
Walking in public without a shirt (i.e., with the upper half of the body naked)		✓		
Men wearing braided hair		✓		
Men wearing earrings		✓		
Men wearing dreadlock hair style		✓		
Homosexuality		✓		
Lesbianism	✓			

256

NIGER REPUBLIC

	Is customary Is allowed Is permissible Is used Is OK	Is not customary Is frowned upon	Is disallowed Is forbidden Is a crime	(See last page for comments on items referenced here)
Females covering their hair (wearing headgear) in public			✓	
Females exposing their full face in public			✓	
Females driving automobiles			✓	
Females riding motorcycles			✓	
Females riding bicycles		✓		
Females smoking in public		✓		
Women wearing bras (braziers) in public			✓	
Use of lipstick by women			✓	
A woman extending her hands first when introduced	✓			
Female bashing	✓			
Females wearing trousers		✓		
Females wearing minis (short dresses)		✓		
Females wearing bikinis		✓		
Females wearing shorts		✓		
Persons of opposite sex holding hands in public		✓		
Persons of same sex holding hands in public		✓		
Handshake between opposite sex		✓		
Hugging in public by same sex		✓		
Hugging in public by opposite sex		✓		
Men and women walking side by side in public				
Man walking ahead (in public), with the woman following		✓		
Woman walking ahead (in public), with the man following		✓		
Men opening doors for women		✓		
Sitting with legs crossed in the presence of elders		✓		
Talking to an elderly person with one's hat/cap on	✓			
Talking to an elderly person with hands positioned on both sides of one's waist	✓			
Blowing one's nose in public	✓			
Blowing one's nose in the presence of others	✓			
Addressing people by their title		✓		

NIGER REPUBLIC

	Is customary Is allowed Is permissible Is used. Is OK	Is not customary Is frowned upon	Is disallowed Is forbidden Is a crime	(See last page for comments on items referenced here)
Addressing people by their family name/surname/last name/given name	✓			
Addressing people by their first name/ given name	✓			
Women going through doors first	✓			
Men helping women with their coats	✓			
Men extending their hands to women first during greetings		✓		
Taking off one's hat when entering a private home		✓		
Removing one's shoes when entering a private home		✓		
Invited guests bringing food at social gatherings		✓		
Guests bringing drinks at social gatherings		✓		
Shaking hands when leaving a small group	✓			
Shaking hands with everyone present, upon arrival at a social gathering	✓			
Eating with the right hand		✓		
Eating with the left hand		✓		
Eating with both hands			✓	
Presenting a gift or passing on an object with the left hand		✓		
Asking a man about his wife		✓		
Asking a woman about her husband	✓			
Making prior appointments before a meeting or visit	✓			
Addressing an audience with one or both hands in the pocket	✓			
Carrying on conversation during meals	✓			
Females sitting with legs crossed	✓			
People discussing their wealth		✓		
Asking someone his or her age, or how old the person is		✓		
Complementing someone on his/her physical looks		✓		
Complementing someone on his/her attire		✓		
Use of both hands in handshake			✓	
In greeting, a handshake accompanied by a slight bow			✓	

258

NIGER REPUBLIC

	Is customary Is allowed Is permissible Is used. Is OK	Is not customary Is frowned upon	Is disallowed Is forbidden Is a crime	(See last page for comments on items referenced here)
Salutations such as "Good morning", "good afternoon", "Good evening"	✓			
The completion of a business deal with a handshake	✓			
Starting a negotiation session with a handshake	✓			
A gift for the host/hostess		✓		
Giving a business gift		✓		
A gift of money (use of money as gift)		✓		
Use of flowers as a gift		✓		1
Use of business cards		✓		
Accepting/presenting gifts with both hands		✓		
Burning of the country's flag		✓		
Mutilation of the national currency		✓		
Casual wearing of clothings made with colors & marks of the national flag		✓		
Wearing of look-alike military (camouflage) fatigues (attire)		✓		
Sitting on the floor (on floor mats)	✓			
Discussion of religion	✓			
Discussion of politics	✓			
Discussion of sex	✓			
Patting/slapping someone on the buttocks	✓			
Patting/slapping someone on the back	✓			
Touching or patting someone's head/hair		✓		
Casual touching of any part of someone's body		✓		
Drinking directly out of a bottle/can		✓		
Placing one's leg(s) on the table or chair		✓		

NIGER REPUBLIC

	Is customary Is allowed Is permissible Is used. Is OK	Is not customary Is frowned upon	Is disallowed Is forbidden Is a crime	(See last page for comments on items referenced here)
Showing the sole of one's foot (feet)	✓			
People standing very close when talking	✓			
Maintaining steady eye contact (direct gaze) when talking to someone		✓		
Kissing or exchange of kisses on the cheek			✓	
Counting money (change) in someone's palm				n/a
Finger pointing in public (in a daring manner)				n/a
Seeking attention by winking the eyes				n/a
Tapping the head to indicate someone is crazy				n/a
Twirling the head to indicate someone is crazy				n/a
Whistling as a way of requesting something/seeking attention				n/a
Using "thumbs-up" sign to mean OK				n/a
Forming a circle with the thumb and index finger (forefinger) to mean OK				n/a
Using the fingers to make a "V" sign for victory				n/a
Beckoning to someone with the index finger (forefinger)				n/a
The left to right waving of the hand with open palms facing outward to indicate "Good bye"				n/a
The use of a nod to show acknowledgement				n/a
Stopping/beckoning a taxi using a stretched hand with the thumb pointing upward				n/a
Using the thumb finger pointed to a direction, to request a ride or a hike				n/a
Raising one's hand/waving with an open fist to summon a taxi				n/a
Tapping one's foot/feet on the floor in a public gathering				n/a
Wiggling one's leg(s) when in a sitting position				n/a
Use of the hand (by motorists and cyclists) to signal direction of traffic				n/a

260

NIGER REPUBLIC

		(See last page for comments on items referenced here)
Foreign tourists are welcome in the country.	yes	
The use of seat belt is mandatory.	no	
International driving license is accepted.	yes	
Foreign drivers license is accepted.	no	
It is considered impolite to yawn in public.		n/a
Death penalty for drug trafficking is the law.	no	
Life imprisonment for drug trafficking is the law.	no	
Guilty until proven innocent in court is the law.	no	
Innocent until proven guilty in court is the law.	yes	
Pedestrians always have right of way.	yes	
Exit visas are required of visitors.	yes	
Crash helmet is mandatory for motor cyclist.	yes	
Hanging is used as a form of legal punishment.	no	
Decapitation of a limb is used as a form of punishment.	no	
Caning is used as a form of legal punishment.	no	
Electric shock is used as a form of legal punishment.	no	
One is expected to stand up during the playing of the national anthem.	yes	
Crash helmet is mandatory for bicyclists.	no	
Guests are expected to eat every thing on their plates.	yes	
Table manners are very informal.	no	
One is expected to cover one's mouth when laughing.	no	
A vertical nod of the head means YES (OK).	yes	
A horizontal shaking of the head means NO (Not OK).	yes	
Prostitution is allowed only in designated areas.	no	
One is expected to take off one's hat during playing of national anthem.	yes	
Separate seating arrangements (between sexes) are maintained at movies.	no	
Separate seating arrangements (between sexes) are maintained at churches.	yes	
Uninvited visitors or guests may not be welcome, even among acquaintances.	yes	
Pets (e.g. cats, dog) are allowed in some hotels and restaurants.	no	
Couples invited for a meal may be separated during meals according to their sex.		n/a
Punctuality is the order of business.	no	
Automobiles are driven with headlights always turned on.	no	
Motorcycles are driven with headlights always turned on.	no	
Visitors with expired visa face mandatory jail time.	no	
Visitors without exit visa face jail time.		2
Visitors without entry visa face mandatory (automatic) jail time.		2

ADDITIONAL COUNTRY INFORMATION

(A)	The types of gifts to avoid:	n/a
(B)	Appropriate gifts for a foreigner to give:	perfume, jewelry, watches, cosmetics
(C)	Best time to present gifts (at the beginning or at the end of a visit?):	at the beginning
(D)	Best time to present gifts (on initial or later visits?):	n/a
(E)	Best place to present gifts (in private or in public?):	n/a
(F)	Number(s) with certain connotations and/or myths attached to them:	n/a
(G)	Basic shape(s) with negative connotations:	n/a
(H)	Basic color(s) with negative connotations:	n/a
(I)	Traditional greeting methods include:	n/a
(J)	Safe topics for discussion include:	weather, fashion, travel, art, family, domestic politics, food, sports, international politics
(K)	Best time for conversations (before, during, after meals?):	n/a
(L)	Forms of legal punishment:	n/a
(M)	Approximately length of time one could be detained by law and order authorities before being charged in court:	may take many months
(N)	January 15, 1999, for example, will normally be written as:	15/1/99
(O)	Emergency code number:	information 12
(P)	Ambulance code Number:	hospital 722521 or 734727 (CHU)
(Q)	Police code number:	17 or 7325533
(R)	Telephone (country) code:	n/a
(S)	Telex (country) code:	n/a
(T)	Electricity requirements:	n/a
(U)	Legal drinking age:	21
(V)	Systems of weights and measures:	n/a
(W)	Legal age of incarceration:	21
(X)	Driving side of the road:	right
(Y)	Minimum expenditure expected of foreign visitors? $	Yes, $500
(Z)	Name of currency:	(1 french Francs = 100 CFA) CFA
(Za)	Some places off-limits to foreign visitors:	n/a
(Zb)	Some places, structures and items prohibited from being photographed:	n/a

ENDNOTES

Item Number: *COMMENTS/EXPLANATIONS*

n/a: Not applicable/Not available/No response

(1)   Flowersn are not used

(2)   Visa is mandatory

NIGERIA	Is customary Is allowed Is permissible Is used. Is OK	Is not customary Is frowned upon	Is disallowed Is forbidden Is a crime	(See last page for comments on items referenced here)
Smoking in public			✓	
Eating in public	✓			
Not flushing public toilet		✓		
Spitting in public		✓		
Feeding animals & birds in public		✓		
Whistling in public				n/a
Drinking alcohol in public		✓		
Kissing in public	✓			
Breast feeding in public		✓		
Drunkenness (in public)		✓		
Cursing in public	✓			
Religious preaching in public	✓			
Begging (panhandling) in public	✓			
Giving money to beggars/panhandlers	✓			
Giving food/drink to beggars/panhandlers		✓		
Brushing teeth in public (other than in restrooms)		✓		
Strolling with pets in major public roads/streets		✓		
Chewing gum in public		✓		
Chewing gum in government offices		✓		
Combing hair in public (other than in toilets/restrooms)		✓		
Undressing/dressing in public			✓	
Wearing of dark glasses indoors in public places		✓		
Public display of wealth		✓		
Praying openly in public in non-designated areas	✓			
Walking bare feet in public	✓			
Chewing tobacco in public	✓			
Trimming one's finger or toe nails in public	✓			
Laughing aloud in public	✓			
Mingling of the sexes in public	✓			
Mixed bathing in public swimming pools		✓		
Distributing religious pamphlets (literature) in public/side streets	✓			

NIGERIA

	Is customary Is allowed Is permissible Is used. Is OK	Is not customary Is frowned upon	Is disallowed Is forbidden Is a crime	(See last page for comments on items referenced here)
Dancing on side street		✓		
Nude bathing	✓			
Littering		✓		
Binge Drinking				n/a
Hitchhiking				n/a
Jaywalking				n/a
Drunk driving		✓		
Speeding		✓		
Skating on side streets (side-walk)				n/a
Graffiti painting				n/a
Pilfering		✓		
Prostitution		✓		
Haggling in the market place	✓			
Consumption of alcoholic beverages in bars and restaurants	✓			
Gambling	✓			
Possession of pornographic materials		✓		
Possession of the Christian Bible	✓			
Possession of the Moslem Koran	✓			
Possession of bullet-proof vest		✓		
Possession of toy gun	✓			
Possession of fire crackers and fireworks		✓		
Possession of prescription drugs (without doctor's note)		✓		
Possession of regulated drugs (narcotics)			✓	
Possession of firearms (by foreigners)			✓	
Possession of pocket knife in public		✓		?
Using walkie talkies	✓			
Using of "boom boxes"(loud sounding stereo system)		✓		
Using "walkman" (very small radio/cassettes with ear plugs) in public places	✓			
Using "walkman" (very small radio/cassettes with ear plugs) while driving or riding		✓		

NIGERIA

	Is customary Is allowed Is permissible Is used Is OK	Is not customary Is frowned upon	Is disallowed Is forbidden Is a crime	(See last page for comments on items referenced here)
Use of cellular phone	✓			
Use of binoculars/periscopes other than in sports arena				n/a
Taking photographs of people (without their permission)			✓	
Taking photographs at airports, train and bus stations			✓	
Taking photographs of airports		✓		
Taking photographs of churches and synagogues	✓			
Taking photographs of religious statues	✓			
Taking photographs of public buildings	✓			
Taking photographs of bridges	✓			
Tipping (gratuity)		✓		
Tipping (when service is rendered)	✓			
Tipping (when service is not rendered)		✓		
Tipping waiters/waitresses at restaurants and hotels		✓		
Tipping taxi/cab drivers				n/a
Tipping baggage handlers, porters, door persons		✓		
Tipping of hair dressers/barbers		✓		
Overtipping		✓		
Undertipping				n/a
Spilling cigarette butt (ash) on side streets/on the floor		✓		
Men wearing lipstick		✓		
Wearing visible tattoo marks	✓			
Men painting/coloring their finger or toe nails		✓		
Cross dressing (men dressed like women & vice versa)			✓	
Walking in public without a shirt (i.e., with the upper half of the body naked)		✓		
Men wearing braided hair		✓		
Men wearing earrings		✓		
Men wearing dreadlock hair style		✓		
Homosexuality			✓	
Lesbianism			✓	

266

NIGERIA

	Is customary Is allowed Is permissible Is used Is OK	Is not customary Is frowned upon	Is disallowed Is forbidden Is a crime	(See last page for comments on items referenced here)
Females covering their hair (wearing headgear) in public	✓			
Females exposing their full face in public	✓			
Females driving automobiles	✓			
Females riding motorcycles	✓			
Females riding bicycles	✓			
Females smoking in public	✓			
Women wearing bras (braziers) in public	✓			
Use of lipstick by women	✓			
A woman extending her hands first when introduced		✓		
Female bashing				n/a
Females wearing trousers	✓			
Females wearing minis (short dresses)		✓		
Females wearing bikinis	✓			
Females wearing shorts	✓			
Persons of opposite sex holding hands in public		✓		
Persons of same sex holding hands in public	✓			
Handshake between opposite sex	✓			
Hugging in public by same sex	✓			
Hugging in public by opposite sex		✓		
Men and women walking side by side in public	✓			
Man walking ahead (in public), with the woman following	✓			
Woman walking ahead (in public), with the man following	✓			
Men opening doors for women		✓		
Sitting with legs crossed in the presence of elders		✓		
Talking to an elderly person with one's hat/cap on		✓		
Talking to an elderly person with hands positioned on both sides of one's waist				n/a
Blowing one's nose in public		✓		
Blowing one's nose in the presence of others		✓		
Addressing people by their title	✓			

NIGERIA

	Is customary Is allowed Is permissible Is used. Is OK	Is not customary Is frowned upon	Is disallowed Is forbidden Is a crime	(See last page for comments on items referenced here)
Addressing people by their family name/surname/last name/given name	✓			
Addressing people by their first name/ given name	✓			
Women going through doors first	✓			
Men helping women with their coats	✓			
Men extending their hands to women first during greetings	✓			
Taking off one's hat when entering a private home	✓			
Removing one's shoes when entering a private home	✓			
Invited guests bringing food at social gatherings	✓			
Guests bringing drinks at social gatherings	✓			
Shaking hands when leaving a small group	✓			
Shaking hands with everyone present, upon arrival at a social gathering	✓			
Eating with the right hand	✓			
Eating with the left hand		✓		
Eating with both hands		✓		
Presenting a gift or passing on an object with the left hand		✓		
Asking a man about his wife	✓			
Asking a woman about her husband	✓			
Making prior appointments before a meeting or visit	✓			
Addressing an audience with one or both hands in the pocket		✓		
Carrying on conversation during meals	✓			
Females sitting with legs crossed	✓			
People discussing their wealth		✓		
Asking someone his or her age, or how old the person is	✓			
Complementing someone on his/her physical looks	✓			
Complementing someone on his/her attire	✓			
Use of both hands in handshake	✓			
In greeting, a handshake accompanied by a slight bow	✓			

NIGERIA

	Is customary Is allowed Is permissible Is used. Is OK	Is not customary Is frowned upon	Is disallowed Is forbidden Is a crime	(See last page for comments on items referenced here)
Salutations such as "Good morning", "good afternoon", "Good evening"	✓			
The completion of a business deal with a handshake				n/a
Starting a negotiation session with a handshake	✓			
A gift for the host/hostess	✓			
Giving a business gift	✓			
A gift of money (use of money as gift)	✓			
Use of flowers as a gift				n/a
Use of business cards	✓			
Accepting/presenting gifts with both hands	✓			
Burning of the country's flag			✓	
Mutilation of the national currency			✓	
Casual wearing of clothings made with colors & marks of the national flag		✓		
Wearing of look-alike military (camouflage) fatigues (attire)			✓	
Sitting on the floor (on floor mats)	✓			
Discussion of religion	✓			
Discussion of politics	✓			
Discussion of sex		✓		
Patting/slapping someone on the buttocks			✓	
Patting/slapping someone on the back			✓	
Touching or patting someone's head/hair	✓			
Casual touching of any part of someone's body			✓	
Drinking directly out of a bottle/can	✓			
Placing one's leg(s) on the table or chair		✓		

269

NIGERIA

	Is customary Is allowed Is permissible Is used. Is OK	Is not customary Is frowned upon	Is disallowed Is forbidden Is a crime	(See last page for comments on items referenced here)
Showing the sole of one's foot (feet)		✓		
People standing very close when talking		✓		
Maintaining steady eye contact (direct gaze) when talking to someone	✓			
Kissing or exchange of kisses on the cheek	✓			
Counting money (change) in someone's palm		✓		
Finger pointing in public (in a daring manner)		✓		
Seeking attention by winking the eyes		✓		
Tapping the head to indicate someone is crazy		✓		
Twirling the head to indicate someone is crazy		✓		
Whistling as a way of requesting something/seeking attention	✓			
Using "thumbs-up" sign to mean OK	✓			
Forming a circle with the thumb and index finger (forefinger) to mean OK	✓			
Using the fingers to make a "V" sign for victory	✓			
Beckoning to someone with the index finger (forefinger)	✓			
The left to right waving of the hand with open palms facing outward to indicate "Good bye"	✓			
The use of a nod to show acknowledgement	✓			
Stopping/beckoning a taxi using a stretched hand with the thumb pointing upward				n/a
Using the thumb finger pointed to a direction, to request a ride or a hike				n/a
Raising one's hand/waving with an open fist to summon a taxi	✓			
Tapping one's foot/feet on the floor in a public gathering		✓		
Wiggling one's leg(s) when in a sitting position	✓			
Use of the hand (by motorists and cyclists) to signal direction of traffic		✓		

270

NIGERIA

		(See last page for comments on items referenced here)
Foreign tourists are welcome in the country.	yes	
The use of seat belt is mandatory.	no	
International driving license is accepted.	yes	
Foreign drivers license is accepted.	yes	
It is considered impolite to yawn in public.	no	
Death penalty for drug trafficking is the law.	no	
Life imprisonment for drug trafficking is the law.	no	
Guilty until proven innocent in court is the law.	yes	
Innocent until proven guilty in court is the law.	no	
Pedestrians always have right of way.	no	
Exit visas are required of visitors.	yes	
Crash helmet is mandatory for motor cyclist.	yes	
Hanging is used as a form of legal punishment.	yes	
Decapitation of a limb is used as a form of punishment.	no	
Caning is used as a form of legal punishment.	yes	
Electric shock is used as a form of legal punishment.	no	
One is expected to stand up during the playing of the national anthem.	yes	
Crash helmet is mandatory for bicyclists.	no	
Guests are expected to eat every thing on their plates.	no	
Table manners are very informal.	no	
One is expected to cover one's mouth when laughing.	no	
A vertical nod of the head means YES (OK).	yes	
A horizontal shaking of the head means NO (Not OK).	yes	
Prostitution is allowed only in designated areas.	no	
One is expected to take off one's hat during playing of national anthem.	yes	
Separate seating arrangements (between sexes) are maintained at movies.	no	
Separate seating arrangements (between sexes) are maintained at churches.	n/a	
Uninvited visitors or guests may not be welcome, even among acquaintances.	no	
Pets (e.g. cats, dog) are allowed in some hotels and restaurants.	no	
Couples invited for a meal may be separated during meals according to their sex.	no	
Punctuality is the order of business.	yes	
Automobiles are driven with headlights always turned on.	n/a	
Motorcycles are driven with headlights always turned on.	yes	
Visitors with expired visa face mandatory jail time.	n/a	
Visitors without exit visa face jail time.	n/a	
Visitors without entry visa face mandatory (automatic) jail time.	n/a	

ADDITIONAL COUNTRY INFORMATION

(A)	The types of gifts to avoid:	n/a
(B)	Appropriate gifts for a foreigner to give:	clothes
(C)	Best time to present gifts (at the beginning or at the end of a visit?):	at the beginning
(D)	Best time to present gifts (on initial or later visits?):	initial visit
(E)	Best place to present gifts (in private or in public?):	private
(F)	Number(s) with certain connotations and/or myths attached to them:	n/a
(G)	Basic shape(s) with negative connotations:	n/a
(H)	Basic color(s) with negative connotations:	black
(I)	Traditional greeting methods include:	handshake, hug, bow, kneeling
(J)	Safe topics for discussion include:	weather, fashion, travel, art, family, religion, domestic politics, food, sports, international politics, social conditions.
(K)	Best time for conversations (before, during, after meals?):	before or after meals
(L)	Forms of legal punishment:	jailing, public execution, firing sword, flogging, canning, hanging.
M)	Approximately length of time one could be detained by law and order authorities before being charged in court:	n/a
(N)	January 15, 1999, for example, will normally be written as:	15/1/99
(O)	Emergency code number:	n/a
)	Ambulance code Number:	n/a
(Q)	Police code number:	999
(R)	Telephone (country) code:	234
(S)	Telex (country) code:	961
(T)	Electricity requirements:	n/a
(U)	Legal drinking age:	12 years
(V)	Systems of weights and measures:	kg
(W)	Legal age of incarceration:	18 years
(X)	Driving side of the road:	right
(Y)	Minimum expenditure expected of foreign visitors? $	6000 naira per day
(Z)	Name of currency:	naira
(Za)	Some places off-limits to foreign visitors:	military istallations
(Zb)	Some places, structures and items prohibited from being photographed:	military istallations

RWANDA	Is customary Is allowed Is permissible Is used. Is OK	Is not customary Is frowned upon	Is disallowed Is forbidden Is a crime	(See last page for comments on items referenced here)
Smoking in public	✓			
Eating in public		✓	✓	
Not flushing public toilet	✓			
Spitting in public			✓	
Feeding animals & birds in public	✓			
Whistling in public		✓		
Drinking alcohol in public	✓			
Kissing in public			✓	
Breast feeding in public	✓			
Drunkenness (in public)			✓	
Cursing in public			✓	
Religious preaching in public	✓			
Begging (panhandling) in public		✓		
Giving money to beggars/panhandlers	✓			
Giving food/drink to beggars/panhandlers	✓			
Brushing teeth in public (other than in restrooms)			✓	
Strolling with pets in major public roads/streets	✓			
Chewing gum in public		✓		
Chewing gum in government offices			✓	
Combing hair in public (other than in toilets/restrooms)			✓	
Undressing/dressing in public			✓	
Wearing of dark glasses indoors in public places		✓		
Public display of wealth		✓		
Praying openly in public in non-designated areas		✓		
Walking bare feet in public	✓			
Chewing tobacco in public				n/a
Trimming one's finger or toe nails in public			✓	
Laughing aloud in public	✓			
Mingling of the sexes in public				n/a
Mixed bathing in public swimming pools				n/a
Distributing religious pamphlets (literature) in public/side streets				n/a

RWANDA

	Is customary Is allowed Is permissible Is used. Is OK	Is not customary Is frowned upon	Is disallowed Is forbidden Is a crime	(See last page for comments on items referenced here)
Dancing on side street		✓		
Nude bathing			✓	
Littering			✓	
Binge Drinking		✓		
Hitchhiking	✓			
Jaywalking	✓			
Drunk driving			✓	
Speeding			✓	
Skating on side streets (side-walk)				1
Graffiti painting			✓	
Pilfering	✓			
Prostitution			✓	
Haggling in the market place				n/a
Consumption of alcoholic beverages in bars and restaurants				n/a
Gambling	✓			
Possession of pornographic materials			✓	
Possession of the Christian Bible	✓			
Possession of the Moslem Koran	✓			
Possession of bullet-proof vest	✓			
Possession of toy gun				2
Possession of fire crackers and fireworks		✓		
Possession of prescription drugs (without doctor's note)			✓	
Possession of regulated drugs (narcotics)			✓	
Possession of firearms (by foreigners)			✓	
Possession of pocket knife in public	✓			
Using walkie talkies		✓		3
Using of "boom boxes"(loud sounding stereo system)	✓			
Using "walkman" (very small radio/cassettes with ear plugs) in public places		✓		
Using "walkman" (very small radio/cassettes with ear plugs) while driving or riding				n/a

RWANDA

	Is customary Is allowed Is permissible Is used Is OK	Is not customary Is frowned upon	Is disallowed Is forbidden Is a crime	(See last page for comments on items referenced here)
Use of cellular phone		✓		
Use of binoculars/periscopes other than in sports arena		✓		
Taking photographs of people (without their permission)		✓		
Taking photographs at airports, train and bus stations			✓	
Taking photographs of airports			✓	
Taking photographs of churches and synagogues	✓			
Taking photographs of religious statues	✓			
Taking photographs of public buildings				n/a
Taking photographs of bridges				n/a
Tipping (gratuity)		✓		
Tipping (when service is rendered)		✓		
Tipping (when service is not rendered)			✓	
Tipping waiters/waitresses at restaurants and hotels				n/a
Tipping taxi/cab drivers				n/a
Tipping baggage handlers, porters, door persons				n/a
Tipping of hair dressers/barbers				n/a
Overtipping		✓		
Undertipping		✓		
Spilling cigarette butt (ash) on side streets/on the floor			✓	
Men wearing lipstick			✓	
Wearing visible tattoo marks		✓		
Men painting/coloring their finger or toe nails			✓	
Cross dressing (men dressed like women & vice versa)		✓		
Walking in public without a shirt (i.e., with the upper half of the body naked)				n/a
Men wearing braided hair		✓		
Men wearing earrings		✓		
Men wearing dreadlock hair style		✓		
Homosexuality			✓	
Lesbianism			✓	

RWANDA

	Is customary Is allowed Is permissible Is used Is OK	Is not customary Is frowned upon	Is disallowed Is forbidden Is a crime	(See last page for comments on items referenced here)
Females covering their hair (wearing headgear) in public	✓			
Females exposing their full face in public	✓			
Females driving automobiles	✓			
Females riding motorcycles	✓			
Females riding bicycles	✓			
Females smoking in public	✓			
Women wearing bras (braziers) in public			✓	4
Use of lipstick by women		✓		
A woman extending her hands first when introduced	✓			
Female bashing	✓			
Females wearing trousers		✓		
Females wearing minis (short dresses)			✓	
Females wearing bikinis		✓		
Females wearing shorts				n/a
Persons of opposite sex holding hands in public		✓		
Persons of same sex holding hands in public	✓			
Handshake between opposite sex	✓			
Hugging in public by same sex	✓			
Hugging in public by opposite sex	✓			
Men and women walking side by side in public				n/a
Man walking ahead (in public), with the woman following				n/a
Woman walking ahead (in public), with the man following				n/a
Men opening doors for women	✓			
Sitting with legs crossed in the presence of elders			✓	
Talking to an elderly person with one's hat/cap on				n/a
Talking to an elderly person with hands positioned on both sides of one's waist				n/a
Blowing one's nose in public		✓		
Blowing one's nose in the presence of others		✓		
Addressing people by their title	✓			

276

DO'S AND DON'TS AROUND THE WORLD: A COUNTRY GUIDE TO CULTURAL AND SOCIAL TABOOS AND ETIQUETTE

RWANDA

	Is customary / Is allowed / Is permissible / Is used. / Is OK	Is not customary / Is frowned upon	Is disallowed / Is forbidden / Is a crime	(See last page for comments on items referenced here)
Addressing people by their family name/surname/last name/given name	✓			
Addressing people by their first name/ given name		✓		5
Women going through doors first	✓			6
Men helping women with their coats	✓			7
Men extending their hands to women first during greetings	✓			
Taking off one's hat when entering a private home	✓			
Removing one's shoes when entering a private home				n/a
Invited guests bringing food at social gatherings	✓			
Guests bringing drinks at social gatherings	✓			
Shaking hands when leaving a small group	✓			
Shaking hands with everyone present, upon arrival at a social gathering	✓			
Eating with the right hand	✓			
Eating with the left hand	✓			
Eating with both hands		✓		8
Presenting a gift or passing on an object with the left hand	✓			
Asking a man about his wife	✓			
Asking a woman about her husband	✓			
Making prior appointments before a meeting or visit	✓			
Addressing an audience with one or both hands in the pocket	✓			
Carrying on conversation during meals				n/a
Females sitting with legs crossed		✓		
People discussing their wealth				n/a
Asking someone his or her age, or how old the person is				n/a
Complementing someone on his/her physical looks				n/a
Complementing someone on his/her attire				n/a
Use of both hands in handshake	✓			
In greeting, a handshake accompanied by a slight bow	✓			

RWANDA

	Is customary Is allowed Is permissible Is used. Is OK	Is not customary Is frowned upon	Is disallowed Is forbidden Is a crime	(See last page for comments on items referenced here)
Salutations such as "Good morning", "good afternoon", "Good evening"	✓			
The completion of a business deal with a handshake				n/a
Starting a negotiation session with a handshake				n/a
A gift for the host/hostess	✓			
Giving a business gift	✓			
A gift of money (use of money as gift)	✓			9
Use of flowers as a gift	✓			
Use of business cards	✓			
Accepting/presenting gifts with both hands	✓			
Burning of the country's flag			✓	
Mutilation of the national currency			✓	
Casual wearing of clothings made with colors & marks of the national flag				n/a
Wearing of look-alike military (camouflage) fatigues (attire)			✓	
Sitting on the floor (on floor mats)	✓			
Discussion of religion	✓			10
Discussion of politics	✓			
Discussion of sex	✓			
Patting/slapping someone on the buttocks		✓		
Patting/slapping someone on the back		✓		
Touching or patting someone's head/hair		✓		
Casual touching of any part of someone's body				n/a
Drinking directly out of a bottle/can	✓			
Placing one's leg(s) on the table or chair	✓			

RWANDA

	Is customary Is allowed Is permissible Is used. Is OK	Is not customary Is frowned upon	Is disallowed Is forbidden Is a crime	(See last page for comments on items referenced here)
Showing the sole of one's foot (feet)				n/a
People standing very close when talking	✓			
Maintaining steady eye contact (direct gaze) when talking to someone	✓			11
Kissing or exchange of kisses on the cheek	✓			
Counting money (change) in someone's palm				n/a
Finger pointing in public (in a daring manner)	✓			
Seeking attention by winking the eyes				n/a
Tapping the head to indicate someone is crazy				n/a
Twirling the head to indicate someone is crazy				n/a
Whistling as a way of requesting something/seeking attention				n/a
Using "thumbs-up" sign to mean OK				n/a
Forming a circle with the thumb and index finger (forefinger) to mean OK				n/a
Using the fingers to make a "V" sign for victory				n/a
Beckoning to someone with the index finger (forefinger)				n/a
The left to right waving of the hand with open palms facing outward to indicate "Good bye"				n/a
The use of a nod to show acknowledgement				n/a
Stopping/beckoning a taxi using a stretched hand with the thumb pointing upward				n/a
Using the thumb finger pointed to a direction, to request a ride or a hike				n/a
Raising one's hand/waving with an open fist to summon a taxi				n/a
Tapping one's foot/feet on the floor in a public gathering				n/a
Wiggling one's leg(s) when in a sitting position				n/a
Use of the hand (by motorists and cyclists) to signal direction of traffic				n/a

RWANDA

		(See last page for comments on items referenced here)
Foreign tourists are welcome in the country.	yes	
The use of seat belt is mandatory.	no	
International driving license is accepted.	yes	
Foreign drivers license is accepted.	yes	
It is considered impolite to yawn in public.	yes	
Death penalty for drug trafficking is the law.	no	12
Life imprisonment for drug trafficking is the law.	no	12
Guilty until proven innocent in court is the law.	yes	
Innocent until proven guilty in court is the law.	no	
Pedestrians always have right of way.	no	
Exit visas are required of visitors.	yes	
Crash helmet is mandatory for motor cyclist.	yes	
Hanging is used as a form of legal punishment.	yes	
Decapitation of a limb is used as a form of punishment.	yes	
Caning is used as a form of legal punishment.	yes	
Electric shock is used as a form of legal punishment.	no	
One is expected to stand up during the playing of the national anthem.	yes	
Crash helmet is mandatory for bicyclists.	yes	
Guests are expected to eat every thing on their plates.	yes	
Table manners are very informal.	yes	
One is expected to cover one's mouth when laughing.	yes	
A vertical nod of the head means YES (OK).	yes	
A horizontal shaking of the head means NO (Not OK).	yes	
Prostitution is allowed only in designated areas.	no	
One is expected to take off one's hat during playing of national anthem.	yes	
Separate seating arrangements (between sexes) are maintained at movies.	no	
Separate seating arrangements (between sexes) are maintained at churches.	no	
Uninvited visitors or guests may not be welcome, even among acquaintances.	no	
Pets (e.g. cats, dog) are allowed in some hotels and restaurants.	no	
Couples invited for a meal may be separated during meals according to their sex.	no	
Punctuality is the order of business.	yes	
Automobiles are driven with headlights always turned on.		n/a
Motorcycles are driven with headlights always turned on.		n/a
Visitors with expired visa face mandatory jail time.	yes	
Visitors without exit visa face jail time.	no	
Visitors without entry visa face mandatory (automatic) jail time.	no	

ADDITIONAL COUNTRY INFORMATION

(A)	The types of gifts to avoid:	gifts that remind people of their various misfortunes
(B)	Appropriate gifts for a foreigner to give:	anything from wherever they come from
(C)	Best time to present gifts (at the beginning or at the end of a visit?):	at the beginning or end
(D)	Best time to present gifts (on initial or later visits?):	n/a
(E)	Best place to present gifts (in private or in public?):	n/a
(F)	Number(s) with certain connotations and/or myths attached to them:	n/a
(G)	Basic shape(s) with negative connotations:	n/a
(H)	Basic color(s) with negative connotations:	n/a
(I)	Traditional greeting methods include:	n/a
(J)	Safe topics for discussion include:	family
(K)	Best time for conversations (before, during, after meals?):	religion,food, international politics, social conditions.
(L)	Forms of legal punishment:	n/a
(M)	Approximately length of time one could be detained by law and order authorities before being charged in court:	firing squad for soldiers who kill innocent people.
(N)	January 15, 1999, for example, will normally be written as:	a week, but it can vary with case and investigations made.
(O)	Emergency code number:	15/1/99
(P)	Ambulance code Number:	n/a
(Q)	Police code number:	n/a
(R)	Telephone (country) code:	n/a
(S)	Telex (country) code:	n/a
(T)	Electricity requirements:	n/a
(U)	Legal drinking age:	21
(V)	Systems of weights and measures:	n/a
(W)	Legal age of incarceration:	14
(X)	Driving side of the road:	right
(Y)	Minimum expenditure expected of foreign visitors? $	no
(Z)	Name of currency:	France Rwandais
(Za)	Some places off-limits to foreign visitors:	n/a
(Zb)	Some places, structures and items prohibited from being photographed:	n/a

ENDNOTES

Item Number: COMMENTS/EXPLANATIONS

n/a: Not applicable/Not available/No response

(1)   No skating in Rwanda.

(2)   Toy guns in the hands of children are still toys, but in the hands of an adult they are suspicious.

(3)   At work or for officially recognized work.

(4)   No one would dare! On the beaches, yes.

(5)   Except among friends.

(6)   Not strictly.

(7)   They don't wear them (this is reversed).

(8)   It depends on what you are eating.

(9)   To poor families, yes.

(10)   Not much.

(11)   Although steady eye contact is not allowed in Rwandan/African culture, foreigners would be ver wrong interpreting it as shifty. It is a sign of respect especially when talking to an elderly perso or someone older or higher up than you.

(12)   Drug taking is prohibited.

SAO TOME & PRINCIPE	Is customary Is allowed Is permissible Is used. Is OK	Is not customary Is frowned upon	Is disallowed Is forbidden Is a crime	(See last page for comments on items referenced here)
Smoking in public		✓		
Eating in public		✓		
Not flushing public toilet			✓	
Spitting in public			✓	
Feeding animals & birds in public		✓		
Whistling in public		✓		
Drinking alcohol in public			✓	
Kissing in public			✓	
Breast feeding in public	✓			
Drunkenness (in public)			✓	
Cursing in public		✓		
Religious preaching in public			✓	
Begging (panhandling) in public		✓		
Giving money to beggars/panhandlers		✓		
Giving food/drink to beggars/panhandlers		✓		
Brushing teeth in public (other than in restrooms)		✓		
Strolling with pets in major public roads/streets		✓		
Chewing gum in public		✓		
Chewing gum in government offices		✓		
Combing hair in public (other than in toilets/restrooms)		✓		
Undressing/dressing in public		✓		
Wearing of dark glasses indoors in public places		✓		
Public display of wealth		✓		
Praying openly in public in non-designated areas		✓		
Walking bare feet in public	✓			
Chewing tobacco in public		✓		
Trimming one's finger or toe nails in public		✓		
Laughing aloud in public		✓		
Mingling of the sexes in public		✓		
Mixed bathing in public swimming pools		✓		
Distributing religious pamphlets (literature) in public/side streets	✓			

SAO TOME AND PRINCIPE

	Is customary Is allowed Is permissible Is used. Is OK	Is not customary Is frowned upon	Is disallowed Is forbidden Is a crime	(See last page for comments on items referenced here)
Dancing on side street			✓	
Nude bathing			✓	
Littering			✓	
Binge Drinking			✓	
Hitchhiking			✓	
Jaywalking			✓	
Drunk driving			✓	
Speeding			✓	
Skating on side streets (side-walk)			✓	
Graffiti painting		✓		
Pilfering		✓		
Prostitution			✓	
Haggling in the market place		✓		
Consumption of alcoholic beverages in bars and restaurants	✓			
Gambling			✓	
Possession of pornographic materials			✓	
Possession of the Christian Bible	✓			
Possession of the Moslem Koran		✓		
Possession of bullet-proof vest			✓	
Possession of toy gun			✓	
Possession of fire crackers and fireworks			✓	
Possession of prescription drugs (without doctor's note)			✓	
Possession of regulated drugs (narcotics)			✓	
Possession of firearms (by foreigners)			✓	
Possession of pocket knife in public		✓		
Using walkie talkies			✓	
Using of "boom boxes"(loud sounding stereo system)			✓	
Using "walkman" (very small radio/cassettes with ear plugs) in public places		✓		
Using "walkman" (very small radio/cassettes with ear plugs) while driving or riding			✓	

SAO TOME AND PRINCIPE

	Is customary Is allowed Is permissible Is used Is OK	Is not customary Is frowned upon	Is disallowed Is forbidden Is a crime	(See last page for comments on items referenced here)
Use of cellular phone	✓			
Use of binoculars/periscopes other than in sports arena	✓			
Taking photographs of people (without their permission)		✓		
Taking photographs at airports, train and bus stations	✓			
Taking photographs of airports	✓			
Taking photographs of churches and synagogues	✓			
Taking photographs of religious statues	✓			
Taking photographs of public buildings		✓		
Taking photographs of bridges		✓		
Tipping (gratuity)	✓			
Tipping (when service is rendered)	✓			
Tipping (when service is not rendered)	✓			
Tipping waiters/waitresses at restaurants and hotels	✓			
Tipping taxi/cab drivers	✓	✓		
Tipping baggage handlers, porters, door persons	✓			
Tipping of hair dressers/barbers	✓			
Overtipping	✓			
Undertipping	✓			
Spilling cigarette butt (ash) on side streets/on the floor	✓			
Men wearing lipstick			✓	
Wearing visible tattoo marks			✓	
Men painting/coloring their finger or toe nails			✓	
Cross dressing (men dressed like women & vice versa)			✓	
Walking in public without a shirt (i.e., with the upper half of the body naked)		✓		
Men wearing braided hair		✓		
Men wearing earrings			✓	
Men wearing dreadlock hair style		✓		
Homosexuality			✓	
Lesbianism			✓	

285

SAO TOME AND PRINCIPE

	Is customary Is allowed Is permissible Is used Is OK	Is not customary Is frowned upon	Is disallowed Is forbidden Is a crime	(See last page for comments on items referenced here)
Females covering their hair (wearing headgear) in public	✓			
Females exposing their full face in public	✓			
Females driving automobiles	✓			
Females riding motorcycles	✓			
Females riding bicycles		✓		
Females smoking in public		✓		
Women wearing bras (braziers) in public			✓	
Use of lipstick by women		✓		
A woman extending her hands first when introduced	✓			
Female bashing	✓			
Females wearing trousers		✓		
Females wearing minis (short dresses)		✓		
Females wearing bikinis		✓		
Females wearing shorts		✓		
Persons of opposite sex holding hands in public		✓		
Persons of same sex holding hands in public		✓		
Handshake between opposite sex		✓		
Hugging in public by same sex			✓	
Hugging in public by opposite sex			✓	
Men and women walking side by side in public	✓			
Man walking ahead (in public), with the woman following		✓		
Woman walking ahead (in public), with the man following	✓			
Men opening doors for women	✓			
Sitting with legs crossed in the presence of elders			✓	
Talking to an elderly person with one's hat/cap on			✓	
Talking to an elderly person with hands positioned on both sides of one's waist			✓	
Blowing one's nose in public		✓		
Blowing one's nose in the presence of others	✓			
Addressing people by their title		✓		

SAO TOME AND PRINCIPE

	Is customary Is allowed Is permissible Is used. Is OK	Is not customary Is frowned upon	Is disallowed Is forbidden Is a crime	(See last page for comments on items referenced here)
Addressing people by their family name/surname/last name/given name		✓		
Addressing people by their first name/ given name	✓			
Women going through doors first		✓		
Men helping women with their coats		✓		
Men extending their hands to women first during greetings		✓		
Taking off one's hat when entering a private home		✓		
Removing one's shoes when entering a private home	✓			
Invited guests bringing food at social gatherings		✓		
Guests bringing drinks at social gatherings		✓		
Shaking hands when leaving a small group	✓			
Shaking hands with everyone present, upon arrival at a social gathering	✓			
Eating with the right hand	✓			
Eating with the left hand		✓		
Eating with both hands			✓	
Presenting a gift or passing on an object with the left hand		✓		
Asking a man about his wife		✓		
Asking a woman about her husband	✓			
Making prior appointments before a meeting or visit		✓		
Addressing an audience with one or both hands in the pocket		✓		
Carrying on conversation during meals	✓			
Females sitting with legs crossed	✓			
People discussing their wealth		✓		
Asking someone his or her age, or how old the person is		✓		
Complementing someone on his/her physical looks		✓		
Complementing someone on his/her attire		✓		
Use of both hands in handshake	✓			
In greeting, a handshake accompanied by a slight bow	✓			

287

SAO TOME AND PRINCIPE

	Is customary Is allowed Is permissible Is used. Is OK	Is not customary Is frowned upon	Is disallowed Is forbidden Is a crime	(See last page for comments on items referenced here)
Salutations such as "Good morning", "good afternoon", "Good evening"	✓			
The completion of a business deal with a handshake	✓			
Starting a negotiation session with a handshake	✓			
A gift for the host/hostess		✓		
Giving a business gift		✓		
A gift of money (use of money as gift)		✓		
Use of flowers as a gift		✓		
Use of business cards		✓		
Accepting/presenting gifts with both hands		✓		
Burning of the country's flag			✓	
Mutilation of the national currency			✓	
Casual wearing of clothings made with colors & marks of the national flag		✓		
Wearing of look-alike military (camouflage) fatigues (attire)			✓	
Sitting on the floor (on floor mats)	✓			
Discussion of religion	✓			
Discussion of politics	✓			
Discussion of sex		✓		
Patting/slapping someone on the buttocks	✓			
Patting/slapping someone on the back	✓			
Touching or patting someone's head/hair		✓		
Casual touching of any part of someone's body		✓		
Drinking directly out of a bottle/can		✓		
Placing one's leg(s) on the table or chair		✓		

SAO TOME AND PRINCIPE

	Is customary Is allowed Is permissible Is used. Is OK	Is not customary Is frowned upon	Is disallowed Is forbidden Is a crime	(See last page for comments on items referenced here)
Showing the sole of one's foot (feet)		✓		
People standing very close when talking	✓			
Maintaining steady eye contact (direct gaze) when talking to someone		✓		
Kissing or exchange of kisses on the cheek			✓	
Counting money (change) in someone's palm	✓			
Finger pointing in public (in a daring manner)		✓		
Seeking attention by winking the eyes				n/a
Tapping the head to indicate someone is crazy				n/a
Twirling the head to indicate someone is crazy				n/a
Whistling as a way of requesting something/seeking attention				n/a
Using "thumbs-up" sign to mean OK		✓		
Forming a circle with the thumb and index finger (forefinger) to mean OK		✓		
Using the fingers to make a "V" sign for victory		✓		
Beckoning to someone with the index finger (forefinger)				n/a
The left to right waving of the hand with open palms facing outward to indicate "Good bye"				n/a
The use of a nod to show acknowledgement				n/a
Stopping/beckoning a taxi using a stretched hand with the thumb pointing upward				n/a
Using the thumb finger pointed to a direction, to request a ride or a hike				n/a
Raising one's hand/waving with an open fist to summon a taxi	✓			
Tapping one's foot/feet on the floor in a public gathering				n/a
Wiggling one's leg(s) when in a sitting position				n/a
Use of the hand (by motorists and cyclists) to signal direction of traffic	✓			

		(See last page for comments on items referenced here)
Foreign tourists are welcome in the country.	yes	
The use of seat belt is mandatory.	no	
International driving license is accepted.	yes	
Foreign drivers license is accepted.	no	
It is considered impolite to yawn in public.		n/a
Death penalty for drug trafficking is the law.		n/a
Life imprisonment for drug trafficking is the law.		n/a
Guilty until proven innocent in court is the law.	no	
Innocent until proven guilty in court is the law.	yes	
Pedestrians always have right of way.	yes	
Exit visas are required of visitors.	no	
Crash helmet is mandatory for motor cyclist.	yes	
Hanging is used as a form of legal punishment.	no	
Decapitation of a limb is used as a form of punishment.	no	
Caning is used as a form of legal punishment.	no	
Electric shock is used as a form of legal punishment.	no	
One is expected to stand up during the playing of the national anthem.	yes	
Crash helmet is mandatory for bicyclists.	no	
Guests are expected to eat every thing on their plates.	yes	
Table manners are very informal.	no	
One is expected to cover one's mouth when laughing.	yes	
A vertical nod of the head means YES (OK).	yes	
A horizontal shaking of the head means NO (Not OK).	no	
Prostitution is allowed only in designated areas.	no	
One is expected to take off one's hat during playing of national anthem.	yes	
Separate seating arrangements (between sexes) are maintained at movies.	no	
Separate seating arrangements (between sexes) are maintained at churches.	no	
Uninvited visitors or guests may not be welcome, even among acquaintances.	yes	
Pets (e.g. cats, dog) are allowed in some hotels and restaurants.	no	
Couples invited for a meal may be separated during meals according to their sex.	no	
Punctuality is the order of business.	yes	
Automobiles are driven with headlights always turned on.	no	
Motorcycles are driven with headlights always turned on.	no	
Visitors with expired visa face mandatory jail time.	no	
Visitors without exit visa face jail time.	no	
Visitors without entry visa face mandatory (automatic) jail time.	no	

ADDITIONAL COUNTRY INFORMATION

(A)	The types of gifts to avoid:	n/a
(B)	Appropriate gifts for a foreigner to give:	perfume, jewelry, watches, cosmetics
(C)	Best time to present gifts (at the beginning or at the end of a visit?):	at the beginning of visit
(D)	Best time to present gifts (on initial or later visits?):	on initial visit or on later visits
(E)	Best place to present gifts (in private or in public?):	in private
(F)	Number(s) with certain connotations and/or myths attached to them:	n/a
(G)	Basic shape(s) with negative connotations:	n/a
(H)	Basic color(s) with negative connotations:	n/a
(I)	Traditional greeting methods include:	a handshake, a hug
(J)	Safe topics for discussion include:	weather, fashion, travel, art, family, domestic politics, food, sports, international politics
(K)	Best time for conversations (before, during, after meals?):	anytime (before meal, during meal or after meals)
(L)	Forms of legal punishment:	jailing
(M)	Approximately length of time one could be detained by law and order authorities before being charged in court:	three days
(N)	January 15, 1999, for example, will normally be written as:	15/1/99
(O)	Emergency code number:	n/a
(P)	Ambulance code Number:	n/a
(Q)	Police code number:	n/a
(R)	Telephone (country) code:	239-12
(S)	Telex (country) code:	239-12
(T)	Electricity requirements:	220 volt
(U)	Legal drinking age:	18 years
(V)	Systems of weights and measures:	metric
(W)	Legal age of incarceration:	21
(X)	Driving side of the road:	right
(Y)	Minimum expenditure expected of foreign visitors? $	n/a
(Z)	Name of currency:	Dobras
(Za)	Some places off-limits to foreign visitors:	military installations
(Zb)	Some places, structures and items prohibited from being photographed:	military installations

SENEGAL	Is customary Is allowed Is permissible Is used. Is OK	Is not customary Is frowned upon	Is disallowed Is forbidden Is a crime	(See last page for comments on items referenced here)
Smoking in public	✓			
Eating in public	✓			
Not flushing public toilet		✓		
Spitting in public		✓		
Feeding animals & birds in public	✓			
Whistling in public		✓		
Drinking alcohol in public		✓		
Kissing in public		✓		
Breast feeding in public			✓	
Drunkenness (in public)		✓		
Cursing in public	✓			
Religious preaching in public	✓			
Begging (panhandling) in public	✓			
Giving money to beggars/panhandlers	✓			
Giving food/drink to beggars/panhandlers		✓		
Brushing teeth in public (other than in restrooms)	✓			
Strolling with pets in major public roads/streets	✓			
Chewing gum in public		✓		
Chewing gum in government offices	✓			
Combing hair in public (other than in toilets/restrooms)			✓	
Undressing/dressing in public	✓			
Wearing of dark glasses indoors in public places	✓			
Public display of wealth	✓			
Praying openly in public in non-designated areas		✓		
Walking bare feet in public	✓			
Chewing tobacco in public	✓			
Trimming one's finger or toe nails in public	✓			
Laughing aloud in public	✓			
Mingling of the sexes in public	✓			
Mixed bathing in public swimming pools	✓			
Distributing religious pamphlets (literature) in public/side streets		✓		

SENEGAL

	Is customary Is allowed Is permissible Is used. Is OK	Is not customary Is frowned upon	Is disallowed Is forbidden Is a crime	(See last page for comments on items referenced here)
Dancing on side street			✓	
Nude bathing		✓		
Littering				n/a
Binge Drinking				n/a
Hitchhiking	✓			
Jaywalking			✓	
Drunk driving			✓	
Speeding	✓			
Skating on side streets (side-walk)			✓	
Graffiti painting			✓	
Pilfering				n/a
Prostitution				n/a
Haggling in the market place	✓			
Consumption of alcoholic beverages in bars and restaurants			✓	
Gambling			✓	
Possession of pornographic materials	✓			
Possession of the Christian Bible	✓			
Possession of the Moslem Koran	✓			
Possession of bullet-proof vest	✓			
Possession of toy gun	✓			
Possession of fire crackers and fireworks	✓			
Possession of prescription drugs (without doctor's note)			✓	
Possession of regulated drugs (narcotics)			✓	
Possession of firearms (by foreigners)	✓			
Possession of pocket knife in public	✓			
Using walkie talkies	✓			
Using of "boom boxes"(loud sounding stereo system)	✓			
Using "walkman" (very small radio/cassettes with ear plugs) in public places			✓	
Using "walkman" (very small radio/cassettes with ear plugs) while driving or riding	✓			

SENEGAL

	Is customary Is allowed Is permissible Is used Is OK	Is not customary Is frowned upon	Is disallowed Is forbidden Is a crime	(See last page for comments on items referenced here)
Use of cellular phone	✓			
Use of binoculars/periscopes other than in sports arena	✓			
Taking photographs of people (without their permission)			✓	
Taking photographs at airports, train and bus stations	✓			
Taking photographs of airports	✓			
Taking photographs of churches and synagogues	✓			
Taking photographs of religious statues	✓			
Taking photographs of public buildings	✓			
Taking photographs of bridges	✓			
Tipping (gratuity)	✓			
Tipping (when service is rendered)	✓			
Tipping (when service is not rendered)	✓			
Tipping waiters/waitresses at restaurants and hotels	✓			
Tipping taxi/cab drivers	✓			
Tipping baggage handlers, porters, door persons	✓			
Tipping of hair dressers/barbers	✓			
Overtipping	✓			
Undertipping	✓			
Spilling cigarette butt (ash) on side streets/on the floor	✓			
Men wearing lipstick		✓		
Wearing visible tattoo marks	✓			
Men painting/coloring their finger or toe nails		✓		
Cross dressing (men dressed like women & vice versa)		✓		
Walking in public without a shirt (i.e., with the upper half of the body naked)		✓		
Men wearing braided hair	✓			
Men wearing earrings	✓			
Men wearing dreadlock hair style	✓			
Homosexuality		✓		
Lesbianism		✓		

SENEGAL

	Is customary Is allowed Is permissible Is used Is OK	Is not customary Is frowned upon	Is disallowed Is forbidden Is a crime	(See last page for comments on items referenced here)
Females covering their hair (wearing headgear) in public	✓			
Females exposing their full face in public	✓			
Females driving automobiles	✓			
Females riding motorcycles	✓			
Females riding bicycles	✓			
Females smoking in public		✓		
Women wearing bras (braziers) in public		✓		
Use of lipstick by women	✓			
A woman extending her hands first when introduced	✓			
Female bashing		✓		
Females wearing trousers	✓			
Females wearing minis (short dresses)	✓			
Females wearing bikinis	✓			
Females wearing shorts	✓			
Persons of opposite sex holding hands in public	✓			
Persons of same sex holding hands in public	✓			
Handshake between opposite sex	✓			
Hugging in public by same sex	✓			
Hugging in public by opposite sex	✓			
Men and women walking side by side in public	✓			
Man walking ahead (in public), with the woman following	✓			
Woman walking ahead (in public), with the man following	✓			
Men opening doors for women	✓			
Sitting with legs crossed in the presence of elders		✓		
Talking to an elderly person with one's hat/cap on		✓		
Talking to an elderly person with hands positioned on both sides of one's waist		✓		
Blowing one's nose in public		✓		
Blowing one's nose in the presence of others		✓		
Addressing people by their title	✓			

SENEGAL

	Is customary Is allowed Is permissible Is used. Is OK	Is not customary Is frowned upon	Is disallowed Is forbidden Is a crime	(See last page for comments on items referenced here)
Addressing people by their family name/surname/last name/given name	✓			
Addressing people by their first name/ given name	✓			
Women going through doors first	✓			
Men helping women with their coats	✓			
Men extending their hands to women first during greetings	✓			
Taking off one's hat when entering a private home	✓			
Removing one's shoes when entering a private home	✓			
Invited guests bringing food at social gatherings	✓			
Guests bringing drinks at social gatherings	✓			
Shaking hands when leaving a small group	✓			
Shaking hands with everyone present, upon arrival at a social gathering	✓			
Eating with the right hand	✓			
Eating with the left hand		✓		
Eating with both hands		✓		
Presenting a gift or passing on an object with the left hand		✓		
Asking a man about his wife	✓			
Asking a woman about her husband	✓			
Making prior appointments before a meeting or visit	✓			
Addressing an audience with one or both hands in the pocket		✓		
Carrying on conversation during meals	✓			
Females sitting with legs crossed		✓		
People discussing their wealth	✓			
Asking someone his or her age, or how old the person is	✓			
Complementing someone on his/her physical looks	✓			
Complementing someone on his/her attire	✓			
Use of both hands in handshake	✓			
In greeting, a handshake accompanied by a slight bow	✓			

SENEGAL

	Is customary Is allowed Is permissible Is used. Is OK	Is not customary Is frowned upon	Is disallowed Is forbidden Is a crime	(See last page for comments on items referenced here)
Salutations such as "Good morning", "good afternoon", "Good evening"	✓			
The completion of a business deal with a handshake	✓			
Starting a negotiation session with a handshake	✓			
A gift for the host/hostess	✓			
Giving a business gift	✓			
A gift of money (use of money as gift)	✓			
Use of flowers as a gift	✓			
Use of business cards	✓			
Accepting/presenting gifts with both hands	✓			
Burning of the country's flag			✓	
Mutilation of the national currency			✓	
Casual wearing of clothings made with colors & marks of the national flag	✓			
Wearing of look-alike military (camouflage) fatigues (attire)	✓			
Sitting on the floor (on floor mats)	✓			
Discussion of religion	✓			
Discussion of politics	✓			
Discussion of sex	✓			
Patting/slapping someone on the buttocks		✓		
Patting/slapping someone on the back	✓			
Touching or patting someone's head/hair	✓			
Casual touching of any part of someone's body		✓		
Drinking directly out of a bottle/can	✓			
Placing one's leg(s) on the table or chair		✓		

297

SENEGAL

	Is customary Is allowed Is permissible Is used. Is OK	Is not customary Is frowned upon	Is disallowed Is forbidden Is a crime	(See last page for comments on items referenced here)
Showing the sole of one's foot (feet)				n/a
People standing very close when talking	✓			
Maintaining steady eye contact (direct gaze) when talking to someone		✓		
Kissing or exchange of kisses on the cheek		✓		
Counting money (change) in someone's palm	✓			
Finger pointing in public (in a daring manner)	✓			
Seeking attention by winking the eyes		✓		
Tapping the head to indicate someone is crazy	✓			
Twirling the head to indicate someone is crazy	✓			
Whistling as a way of requesting something/seeking attention		✓		
Using "thumbs-up" sign to mean OK	✓			
Forming a circle with the thumb and index finger (forefinger) to mean OK	✓			
Using the fingers to make a "V" sign for victory	✓			
Beckoning to someone with the index finger (forefinger)	✓			
The left to right waving of the hand with open palms facing outward to indicate "Good bye"	✓			
The use of a nod to show acknowledgement	✓			
Stopping/beckoning a taxi using a stretched hand with the thumb pointing upward	✓			
Using the thumb finger pointed to a direction, to request a ride or a hike	✓			
Raising one's hand/waving with an open fist to summon a taxi	✓			
Tapping one's foot/feet on the floor in a public gathering	✓			
Wiggling one's leg(s) when in a sitting position	✓			
Use of the hand (by motorists and cyclists) to signal direction of traffic	✓			

298

		(See last page for comments on items referenced here)
Foreign tourists are welcome in the country.	yes	
The use of seat belt is mandatory.	yes	
International driving license is accepted.	yes	
Foreign drivers license is accepted.	no	
It is considered impolite to yawn in public.	yes	
Death penalty for drug trafficking is the law.	no	
Life imprisonment for drug trafficking is the law.	no	
Guilty until proven innocent in court is the law.	no	
Innocent until proven guilty in court is the law.	yes	
Pedestrians always have right of way.	yes	
Exit visas are required of visitors.	no	
Crash helmet is mandatory for motor cyclist.	no	
Hanging is used as a form of legal punishment.	no	
Decapitation of a limb is used as a form of punishment.	no	
Caning is used as a form of legal punishment.	no	
Electric shock is used as a form of legal punishment.	no	
One is expected to stand up during the playing of the national anthem.	yes	
Crash helmet is mandatory for bicyclists.	no	
Guests are expected to eat every thing on their plates.	no	
Table manners are very informal.	yes	
One is expected to cover one's mouth when laughing.	yes	
A vertical nod of the head means YES (OK).	yes	
A horizontal shaking of the head means NO (Not OK).	yes	
Prostitution is allowed only in designated areas.	no	
One is expected to take off one's hat during playing of national anthem.	no	
Separate seating arrangements (between sexes) are maintained at movies.	no	
Separate seating arrangements (between sexes) are maintained at churches.	no	
Uninvited visitors or guests may not be welcome, even among acquaintances.	no	
Pets (e.g. cats, dog) are allowed in some hotels and restaurants.	yes	
Couples invited for a meal may be separated during meals according to their sex.	no	
Punctuality is the order of business.	yes	
Automobiles are driven with headlights always turned on.	no	
Motorcycles are driven with headlights always turned on.	yes	
Visitors with expired visa face mandatory jail time.	no	
Visitors without exit visa face jail time.	no	
Visitors without entry visa face mandatory (automatic) jail time.	no	

ADDITIONAL COUNTRY INFORMATION

(A)	The types of gifts to avoid:	n/a
(B)	Appropriate gifts for a foreigner to give:	n/a
(C)	Best time to present gifts (at the beginning or at the end of a visit?):	n/a
(D)	Best time to present gifts (on initial or later visits?):	initial
(E)	Best place to present gifts (in private or in public?):	in private, if possible
(F)	Number(s) with certain connotations and/or myths attached to them:	n/a
(G)	Basic shape(s) with negative connotations:	n/a
(H)	Basic color(s) with negative connotations:	n/a
(I)	Traditional greeting methods include:	handshake, hug, genuflecting
(J)	Safe topics for discussion include:	no restrictions except discussion of sex in public.
(K)	Best time for conversations (before, during, after meals?):	jailing, private execution, firing squad
(L)	Forms of legal punishment:	48 hours monthly
(M)	Approximately length of time one could be detained by law and order authorities before being charged in court:	15/1/99
(N)	January 15, 1999, for example, will normally be written as:	12
(O)	Emergency code number:	12
(P)	Ambulance code Number:	12
(Q)	Police code number:	221
(R)	Telephone (country) code:	221
(S)	Telex (country) code:	221
(T)	Electricity requirements:	220v
(U)	Legal drinking age:	21
(V)	Systems of weights and measures:	kiles
(W)	Legal age of incarceration:	21
(X)	Driving side of the road:	right
(Y)	Minimum expenditure expected of foreign visitors? $	n/a
(Z)	Name of currency:	francs CFA
(Za)	Some places off-limits to foreign visitors:	military and security buildings.
(Zb)	Some places, structures and items prohibited from being photographed:	none

300

SEYCHELLES	Is customary Is allowed Is permissible Is used. Is OK	Is not customary Is frowned upon	Is disallowed Is forbidden Is a crime	(See last page for comments on items referenced here)
Smoking in public	✓			
Eating in public	✓			
Not flushing public toilet			✓	
Spitting in public		✓		
Feeding animals & birds in public	✓			
Whistling in public	✓			
Drinking alcohol in public			✓	
Kissing in public		✓		
Breast feeding in public	✓			
Drunkenness (in public)		✓		
Cursing in public		✓		
Religious preaching in public		✓		
Begging (panhandling) in public		✓		
Giving money to beggars/panhandlers		✓		
Giving food/drink to beggars/panhandlers				n/a
Brushing teeth in public (other than in restrooms)		✓		
Strolling with pets in major public roads/streets	✓			
Chewing gum in public	✓			
Chewing gum in government offices		✓		
Combing hair in public (other than in toilets/restrooms)		✓		
Undressing/dressing in public		✓		
Wearing of dark glasses indoors in public places	✓			
Public display of wealth	✓			
Praying openly in public in non-designated areas		✓		
Walking bare feet in public	✓			
Chewing tobacco in public	✓			
Trimming one's finger or toe nails in public		✓		
Laughing aloud in public	✓			
Mingling of the sexes in public	✓			
Mixed bathing in public swimming pools	✓			
Distributing religious pamphlets (literature) in public/side streets		✓		

301

SEYCHELLLES

	Is customary Is allowed Is permissible Is used. Is OK	Is not customary Is frowned upon	Is disallowed Is forbidden Is a crime	(See last page for comments on items referenced here)
Dancing on side street	✓			
Nude bathing			✓	
Littering		✓		
Binge Drinking		✓		
Hitchhiking		✓		
Jaywalking	✓			
Drunk driving			✓	
Speeding		✓		
Skating on side streets (side-walk)		✓		
Graffiti painting			✓	
Pilfering			✓	
Prostitution		✓		
Haggling in the market place	✓			
Consumption of alcoholic beverages in bars and restaurants	✓			
Gambling	✓			
Possession of pornographic materials		✓		
Possession of the Christian Bible	✓			
Possession of the Moslem Koran	✓			
Possession of bullet-proof vest		✓		
Possession of toy gun	✓			
Possession of fire crackers and fireworks	✓			
Possession of prescription drugs (without doctor's note)		✓		
Possession of regulated drugs (narcotics)			✓	
Possession of firearms (by foreigners)			✓	
Possession of pocket knife in public	✓			
Using walkie talkies	✓			
Using of "boom boxes"(loud sounding stereo system)	✓			
Using "walkman" (very small radio/cassettes with ear plugs) in public places	✓			
Using "walkman" (very small radio/cassettes with ear plugs) while driving or riding		✓		

SEYCHELLLES

	Is customary Is allowed Is permissible Is used Is OK	Is not customary Is frowned upon	Is disallowed Is forbidden Is a crime	(See last page for comments on items referenced here)
Use of cellular phone	✓			
Use of binoculars/periscopes other than in sports arena	✓			
Taking photographs of people (without their permission)	✓			
Taking photographs at airports, train and bus stations	✓			
Taking photographs of airports	✓			
Taking photographs of churches and synagogues	✓			
Taking photographs of religious statues	✓			
Taking photographs of public buildings	✓			
Taking photographs of bridges	✓			
Tipping (gratuity)	✓			
Tipping (when service is rendered)	✓			
Tipping (when service is not rendered)		✓		
Tipping waiters/waitresses at restaurants and hotels	✓			
Tipping taxi/cab drivers		✓		
Tipping baggage handlers, porters, door persons	✓			
Tipping of hair dressers/barbers		✓		
Overtipping		✓		
Undertipping		✓		
Spilling cigarette butt (ash) on side streets/on the floor		✓		
Men wearing lipstick		✓		
Wearing visible tattoo marks	✓			
Men painting/coloring their finger or toe nails		✓		
Cross dressing (men dressed like women & vice versa)		✓		
Walking in public without a shirt (i.e., with the upper half of the body naked)	✓			
Men wearing braided hair	✓			
Men wearing earrings	✓			
Men wearing dreadlock hair style	✓			
Homosexuality		✓		
Lesbianism		✓		

SEYCHELLLES

	Is customary Is allowed Is permissible Is used Is OK	Is not customary Is frowned upon	Is disallowed Is forbidden Is a crime	(See last page for comments on items referenced here)
Females covering their hair (wearing headgear) in public	✓			
Females exposing their full face in public	✓			
Females driving automobiles	✓			
Females riding motorcycles		✓		
Females riding bicycles	✓			
Females smoking in public	✓			
Women wearing bras (braziers) in public		✓		
Use of lipstick by women	✓			
A woman extending her hands first when introduced	✓			
Female bashing		✓		
Females wearing trousers	✓			
Females wearing minis (short dresses)	✓			
Females wearing bikinis	✓			
Females wearing shorts	✓			
Persons of opposite sex holding hands in public	✓			
Persons of same sex holding hands in public		✓		
Handshake between opposite sex	✓			
Hugging in public by same sex	✓			
Hugging in public by opposite sex		✓		
Men and women walking side by side in public	✓			
Man walking ahead (in public), with the woman following		✓		
Woman walking ahead (in public), with the man following		✓		
Men opening doors for women		✓		
Sitting with legs crossed in the presence of elders	✓			
Talking to an elderly person with one's hat/cap on	✓			
Talking to an elderly person with hands positioned on both sides of one's waist		✓		
Blowing one's nose in public		✓		
Blowing one's nose in the presence of others		✓		
Addressing people by their title	✓			

SEYCHELLLES

	Is customary Is allowed Is permissible Is used. Is OK	Is not customary Is frowned upon	Is disallowed Is forbidden Is a crime	(See last page for comments on items referenced here)
Addressing people by their family name/surname/last name/given name		✓		
Addressing people by their first name/ given name	✓			
Women going through doors first		✓		
Men helping women with their coats		✓		
Men extending their hands to women first during greetings	✓			
Taking off one's hat when entering a private home		✓		
Removing one's shoes when entering a private home		✓		
Invited guests bringing food at social gatherings	✓			
Guests bringing drinks at social gatherings	✓			
Shaking hands when leaving a small group	✓			
Shaking hands with everyone present, upon arrival at a social gathering	✓			
Eating with the right hand	✓			
Eating with the left hand	✓			
Eating with both hands	✓			
Presenting a gift or passing on an object with the left hand	✓			
Asking a man about his wife	✓			
Asking a woman about her husband	✓			
Making prior appointments before a meeting or visit		✓		
Addressing an audience with one or both hands in the pocket		✓		
Carrying on conversation during meals	✓			
Females sitting with legs crossed	✓			
People discussing their wealth		✓		
Asking someone his or her age, or how old the person is	✓			
Complementing someone on his/her physical looks	✓			
Complementing someone on his/her attire	✓			
Use of both hands in handshake		✓		
In greeting, a handshake accompanied by a slight bow		✓		

305

SEYCHELLLES

	Is customary Is allowed Is permissible Is used. Is OK	Is not customary Is frowned upon	Is disallowed Is forbidden Is a crime	(See last page for comments on items referenced here)
Salutations such as "Good morning", "good afternoon", "Good evening"	✓			
The completion of a business deal with a handshake	✓			
Starting a negotiation session with a handshake	✓			
A gift for the host/hostess	✓			
Giving a business gift	✓			
A gift of money (use of money as gift)	✓			
Use of flowers as a gift	✓			
Use of business cards	✓			
Accepting/presenting gifts with both hands		✓		
Burning of the country's flag			✓	
Mutilation of the national currency			✓	
Casual wearing of clothings made with colors & marks of the national flag		✓		
Wearing of look-alike military (camouflage) fatigues (attire)		✓		
Sitting on the floor (on floor mats)		✓		
Discussion of religion	✓			
Discussion of politics	✓			
Discussion of sex	✓			
Patting/slapping someone on the buttocks		✓		
Patting/slapping someone on the back	✓			
Touching or patting someone's head/hair	✓			
Casual touching of any part of someone's body	✓			
Drinking directly out of a bottle/can	✓			
Placing one's leg(s) on the table or chair		✓		

SEYCHELLLES

	Is customary Is allowed Is permissible Is used. Is OK	Is not customary Is frowned upon	Is disallowed Is forbidden Is a crime	(See last page for comments on items referenced here)
Showing the sole of one's foot (feet)	✓			
People standing very close when talking	✓			
Maintaining steady eye contact (direct gaze) when talking to someone	✓			
Kissing or exchange of kisses on the cheek	✓			
Counting money (change) in someone's palm		✓		
Finger pointing in public (in a daring manner)		✓		
Seeking attention by winking the eyes	✓			
Tapping the head to indicate someone is crazy	✓			
Twirling the head to indicate someone is crazy		✓		
Whistling as a way of requesting something/seeking attention		✓		
Using "thumbs-up" sign to mean OK	✓			
Forming a circle with the thumb and index finger (forefinger) to mean OK		✓		
Using the fingers to make a "V" sign for victory		✓		
Beckoning to someone with the index finger (forefinger)		✓		
The left to right waving of the hand with open palms facing outward to indicate "Good bye"	✓			
The use of a nod to show acknowledgement	✓			
Stopping/beckoning a taxi using a stretched hand with the thumb pointing upward		✓		
Using the thumb finger pointed to a direction, to request a ride or a hike	✓			
Raising one's hand/waving with an open fist to summon a taxi	✓			
Tapping one's foot/feet on the floor in a public gathering		✓		
Wiggling one's leg(s) when in a sitting position	✓			
Use of the hand (by motorists and cyclists) to signal direction of traffic	✓			

SEYCHELLLES

		(See last page for comments on items referenced here)
Foreign tourists are welcome in the country.	yes	
The use of seat belt is mandatory.	no	
International driving license is accepted.	yes	
Foreign drivers license is accepted.	yes	
It is considered impolite to yawn in public.	yes	
Death penalty for drug trafficking is the law.	no	
Life imprisonment for drug trafficking is the law.	no	
Guilty until proven innocent in court is the law.	no	
Innocent until proven guilty in court is the law.	no	
Pedestrians always have right of way.	yes	
Exit visas are required of visitors.	yes	
Crash helmet is mandatory for motor cyclist.	no	
Hanging is used as a form of legal punishment.	no	
Decapitation of a limb is used as a form of punishment.	no	
Caning is used as a form of legal punishment.	no	
Electric shock is used as a form of legal punishment.	no	
One is expected to stand up during the playing of the national anthem.	yes	
Crash helmet is mandatory for bicyclists.	no	
Guests are expected to eat every thing on their plates.	no	
Table manners are very informal.	yes	
One is expected to cover one's mouth when laughing.	mp	
A vertical nod of the head means YES (OK).	yes	
A horizontal shaking of the head means NO (Not OK).	yes	
Prostitution is allowed only in designated areas.	no	
One is expected to take off one's hat during playing of national anthem.	yes	
Separate seating arrangements (between sexes) are maintained at movies.	no	
Separate seating arrangements (between sexes) are maintained at churches.	no	
Uninvited visitors or guests may not be welcome, even among acquaintances.	no	
Pets (e.g. cats, dog) are allowed in some hotels and restaurants.	no	
Couples invited for a meal may be separated during meals according to their sex.	no	
Punctuality is the order of business.		usually
Automobiles are driven with headlights always turned on.	no	
Motorcycles are driven with headlights always turned on.	no	
Visitors with expired visa face mandatory jail time.	no	
Visitors without exit visa face jail time.	no	
Visitors without entry visa face mandatory (automatic) jail time.	no	

ADDITIONAL COUNTRY INFORMATION

(A)	The types of gifts to avoid:	n/a
(B)	Appropriate gifts for a foreigner to give:	anything useful
(C)	Best time to present gifts (at the beginning or at the end of a visit?):	beginning
(D)	Best time to present gifts (on initial or later visits?):	on initial visit
(E)	Best place to present gifts (in private or in public?):	private
(F)	Number(s) with certain connotations and/or myths attached to them:	13- bad luck
(G)	Basic shape(s) with negative connotations:	none
(H)	Basic color(s) with negative connotations:	none
(I)	Traditional greeting methods include:	handshake/kiss
(J)	Safe topics for discussion include:	weather, fashion, travel, art, family, religion, domestic politics, food, sports, international politics, social conditions, money and personal wealth, sex.
(K)	Best time for conversations (before, during, after meals?):	any
(L)	Forms of legal punishment:	jailing
(M)	Approximately length of time one could be detained by law and order authorities before being charged in court:	3 weeks
(N)	January 15, 1999, for example, will normally be written as:	15/1/99
(O)	Emergency code number:	999
(P)	Ambulance code Number:	999
(Q)	Police code number:	999
(R)	Telephone (country) code:	248
(S)	Telex (country) code:	248
(T)	Electricity requirements:	240 volts
(U)	Legal drinking age:	18 years
(V)	Systems of weights and measures:	metric
(W)	Legal age of incarceration:	18 years
(X)	Driving side of the road:	left
(Y)	Minimum expenditure expected of foreign visitors? $	none
(Z)	Name of currency:	Seychelles Rupees
(Za)	Some places off-limits to foreign visitors:	army camps
(Zb)	Some places, structures and items prohibited from being photographed:	military areas

SIERRA LEONE	Is customary Is allowed Is permissible Is used. Is OK	Is not customary Is frowned upon	Is disallowed Is forbidden Is a crime	(See last page for comments on items referenced here)
Smoking in public	✓			
Eating in public	✓			
Not flushing public toilet				n/a
Spitting in public		✓		
Feeding animals & birds in public	✓			
Whistling in public	✓			
Drinking alcohol in public	✓			
Kissing in public		✓		
Breast feeding in public	✓			
Drunkenness (in public)		✓		
Cursing in public	✓			
Religious preaching in public	✓			
Begging (panhandling) in public	✓			
Giving money to beggars/panhandlers	✓			
Giving food/drink to beggars/panhandlers		✓		
Brushing teeth in public (other than in restrooms)	✓			
Strolling with pets in major public roads/streets	✓			
Chewing gum in public	✓			
Chewing gum in government offices		✓		
Combing hair in public (other than in toilets/restrooms)		✓		
Undressing/dressing in public			✓	
Wearing of dark glasses indoors in public places	✓			
Public display of wealth		✓		
Praying openly in public in non-designated areas	✓			
Walking bare feet in public	✓			
Chewing tobacco in public		✓		
Trimming one's finger or toe nails in public		✓		
Laughing aloud in public		✓		
Mingling of the sexes in public	✓			
Mixed bathing in public swimming pools	✓			
Distributing religious pamphlets (literature) in public/side streets	✓			

310

SIERRA LEONE

	Is customary Is allowed Is permissible Is used. Is OK	Is not customary Is frowned upon	Is disallowed Is forbidden Is a crime	(See last page for comments on items referenced here)
Dancing on side street		✓		
Nude bathing		✓		
Littering		✓		
Binge Drinking		✓		
Hitchhiking	✓			
Jaywalking				n/a
Drunk driving	✓			
Speeding	✓			
Skating on side streets (side-walk)		✓		✓
Graffiti painting			✓	
Pilfering			✓	
Prostitution			✓	
Haggling in the market place	✓			
Consumption of alcoholic beverages in bars and restaurants	✓			
Gambling	✓			
Possession of pornographic materials		✓		
Possession of the Christian Bible	✓			
Possession of the Moslem Koran	✓			
Possession of bullet-proof vest	✓			
Possession of toy gun	✓			
Possession of fire crackers and fireworks			✓	
Possession of prescription drugs (without doctor's note)	✓			
Possession of regulated drugs (narcotics)			✓	
Possession of firearms (by foreigners)			✓	
Possession of pocket knife in public			✓	
Using walkie talkies	✓			
Using of "boom boxes"(loud sounding stereo system)	✓			
Using "walkman" (very small radio/cassettes with ear plugs) in public places	✓			
Using "walkman" (very small radio/cassettes with ear plugs) while driving or riding	✓			

311

SIERRA LEONE

	Is customary Is allowed Is permissible Is used Is OK	Is not customary Is frowned upon	Is disallowed Is forbidden Is a crime	(See last page for comments on items referenced here)
Use of cellular phone	✓			
Use of binoculars/periscopes other than in sports arena	✓			
Taking photographs of people (without their permission)			✓	
Taking photographs at airports, train and bus stations	✓			
Taking photographs of airports	✓			
Taking photographs of churches and synagogues	✓			
Taking photographs of religious statues	✓			
Taking photographs of public buildings	✓			
Taking photographs of bridges	✓			
Tipping (gratuity)	✓			
Tipping (when service is rendered)	✓			
Tipping (when service is not rendered)	✓			
Tipping waiters/waitresses at restaurants and hotels	✓			
Tipping taxi/cab drivers	✓			
Tipping baggage handlers, porters, door persons	✓			
Tipping of hair dressers/barbers	✓			
Overtipping	✓			
Undertipping	✓			
Spilling cigarette butt (ash) on side streets/on the floor		✓		
Men wearing lipstick		✓		
Wearing visible tattoo marks		✓		
Men painting/coloring their finger or toe nails		✓		
Cross dressing (men dressed like women & vice versa)		✓		
Walking in public without a shirt (i.e., with the upper half of the body naked)		✓		
Men wearing braided hair		✓		
Men wearing earrings		✓		
Men wearing dreadlock hair style	n/a			
Homosexuality			✓	
Lesbianism			✓	

SIERRA LEONE

	Is customary Is allowed Is permissible Is used Is OK	Is not customary Is frowned upon	Is disallowed Is forbidden Is a crime	(See last page for comments on items referenced here)
Females covering their hair (wearing headgear) in public	✓			
Females exposing their full face in public	✓			
Females driving automobiles	✓			
Females riding motorcycles	✓			
Females riding bicycles	✓			
Females smoking in public		✓		
Women wearing bras (braziers) in public		✓		
Use of lipstick by women	✓			
A woman extending her hands first when introduced	✓			
Female bashing	✓			
Females wearing trousers	✓			
Females wearing minis (short dresses)	✓			
Females wearing bikinis		✓		
Females wearing shorts	✓			
Persons of opposite sex holding hands in public	✓			
Persons of same sex holding hands in public		✓		
Handshake between opposite sex	✓			
Hugging in public by same sex	✓			
Hugging in public by opposite sex	✓			
Men and women walking side by side in public	✓			
Man walking ahead (in public), with the woman following	✓			
Woman walking ahead (in public), with the man following		✓		
Men opening doors for women	✓			
Sitting with legs crossed in the presence of elders		✓		
Talking to an elderly person with one's hat/cap on		✓		
Talking to an elderly person with hands positioned on both sides of one's waist		✓		
Blowing one's nose in public		✓		
Blowing one's nose in the presence of others		✓		
Addressing people by their title	✓			

SIERRA LEONE

	Is customary Is allowed Is permissible Is used. Is OK	Is not customary Is frowned upon	Is disallowed Is forbidden Is a crime	(See last page for comments on items referenced here)
Addressing people by their family name/surname/last name/given name	✓			
Addressing people by their first name/ given name	✓			
Women going through doors first	✓			
Men helping women with their coats	✓			
Men extending their hands to women first during greetings	✓			
Taking off one's hat when entering a private home	✓			
Removing one's shoes when entering a private home	✓			
Invited guests bringing food at social gatherings	✓			
Guests bringing drinks at social gatherings	✓			
Shaking hands when leaving a small group	✓			
Shaking hands with everyone present, upon arrival at a social gathering	✓			
Eating with the right hand	✓			
Eating with the left hand	✓			
Eating with both hands		✓		
Presenting a gift or passing on an object with the left hand		✓		
Asking a man about his wife	✓			
Asking a woman about her husband	✓			
Making prior appointments before a meeting or visit	✓			
Addressing an audience with one or both hands in the pocket		✓		
Carrying on conversation during meals	✓			
Females sitting with legs crossed	✓			
People discussing their wealth	✓			
Asking someone his or her age, or how old the person is	✓			
Complementing someone on his/her physical looks	✓			
Complementing someone on his/her attire	✓			
Use of both hands in handshake	✓			
In greeting, a handshake accompanied by a slight bow	✓			

SIERRA LEONE

	Is customary Is allowed Is permissible Is used. Is OK	Is not customary Is frowned upon	Is disallowed Is forbidden Is a crime	(See last page for comments on items referenced here)
Salutations such as "Good morning", "good afternoon", "Good evening"	✓			
The completion of a business deal with a handshake	✓			
Starting a negotiation session with a handshake	✓			
A gift for the host/hostess	✓			
Giving a business gift	✓			
A gift of money (use of money as gift)	✓			
Use of flowers as a gift	✓			
Use of business cards	✓			
Accepting/presenting gifts with both hands	✓			
Burning of the country's flag			✓	
Mutilation of the national currency			✓	
Casual wearing of clothings made with colors & marks of the national flag	✓			
Wearing of look-alike military (camouflage) fatigues (attire)		✓		
Sitting on the floor (on floor mats)	✓			
Discussion of religion	✓			
Discussion of politics	✓			
Discussion of sex	✓			
Patting/slapping someone on the buttocks	✓			
Patting/slapping someone on the back	✓			
Touching or patting someone's head/hair	✓			
Casual touching of any part of someone's body	✓			
Drinking directly out of a bottle/can	✓			
Placing one's leg(s) on the table or chair	✓			

315

SIERRA LEONE

	Is customary Is allowed Is permissible Is used. Is OK	Is not customary Is frowned upon	Is disallowed Is forbidden Is a crime	(See last page for comments on items referenced here)
Showing the sole of one's foot (feet)				n/a
People standing very close when talking	✓			
Maintaining steady eye contact (direct gaze) when talking to someone	✓			
Kissing or exchange of kisses on the cheek	✓			
Counting money (change) in someone's palm				n/a
Finger pointing in public (in a daring manner)		✓		
Seeking attention by winking the eyes		✓		
Tapping the head to indicate someone is crazy	✓			
Twirling the head to indicate someone is crazy	✓			
Whistling as a way of requesting something/seeking attention	✓			
Using "thumbs-up" sign to mean OK	✓			
Forming a circle with the thumb and index finger (forefinger) to mean OK		✓		
Using the fingers to make a "V" sign for victory	✓			
Beckoning to someone with the index finger (forefinger)				n/a
The left to right waving of the hand with open palms facing outward to indicate "Good bye"	✓			
The use of a nod to show acknowledgement	✓			
Stopping/beckoning a taxi using a stretched hand with the thumb pointing upward		✓		
Using the thumb finger pointed to a direction, to request a ride or a hike		✓		
Raising one's hand/waving with an open fist to summon a taxi	✓			
Tapping one's foot/feet on the floor in a public gathering		✓		
Wiggling one's leg(s) when in a sitting position	✓			
Use of the hand (by motorists and cyclists) to signal direction of traffic	✓			

316

SIERRA LEONE

		(See last page for comments on items referenced here)
Foreign tourists are welcome in the country.	yes	
The use of seat belt is mandatory.		n/a
International driving license is accepted.	yes	
Foreign drivers license is accepted.		n/a
It is considered impolite to yawn in public.	no	
Death penalty for drug trafficking is the law.	no	
Life imprisonment for drug trafficking is the law.	yes	
Guilty until proven innocent in court is the law.	yes	
Innocent until proven guilty in court is the law.	yes	
Pedestrians always have right of way.	no	
Exit visas are required of visitors.	no	
Crash helmet is mandatory for motor cyclist.	yes	
Hanging is used as a form of legal punishment.	yes	
Decapitation of a limb is used as a form of punishment.	yes	
Caning is used as a form of legal punishment.	no	
Electric shock is used as a form of legal punishment.	yes	
One is expected to stand up during the playing of the national anthem.	yes	
Crash helmet is mandatory for bicyclists.	no	
Guests are expected to eat every thing on their plates.	no	
Table manners are very informal.	no	
One is expected to cover one's mouth when laughing.	no	
A vertical nod of the head means YES (OK).	yes	
A horizontal shaking of the head means NO (Not OK).	no	
Prostitution is allowed only in designated areas.	no	
One is expected to take off one's hat during playing of national anthem.	yes	
Separate seating arrangements (between sexes) are maintained at movies.	no	
Separate seating arrangements (between sexes) are maintained at churches.	no	
Uninvited visitors or guests may not be welcome, even among acquaintances.	no	
Pets (e.g. cats, dog) are allowed in some hotels and restaurants.		n/a
Couples invited for a meal may be separated during meals according to their sex.	no	
Punctuality is the order of business.	yes	
Automobiles are driven with headlights always turned on.	no	
Motorcycles are driven with headlights always turned on.	no	
Visitors with expired visa face mandatory jail time.	no	
Visitors without exit visa face jail time.	no	
Visitors without entry visa face mandatory (automatic) jail time.	no	

ADDITIONAL COUNTRY INFORMATION

(A)	The types of gifts to avoid:	n/a
(B)	Appropriate gifts for a foreigner to give:	anything you find appropriate
(C)	Best time to present gifts (at the beginning or at the end of a visit?):	at the beginning or end
(D)	Best time to present gifts (on initial or later visits?):	depends on the occasion
(E)	Best place to present gifts (in private or in public?):	n/a
(F)	Number(s) with certain connotations and/or myths attached to them:	n/a
(G)	Basic shape(s) with negative connotations:	n/a
(H)	Basic color(s) with negative connotations:	red- danger! black (used for mourning and funeral)
(I)	Traditional greeting methods include:	handshake, hug, bow, kneeling, placing the hands in praying positions, patting the others back.
(J)	Safe topics for discussion include:	weather, fashion, travel, art, family, religion, food, sports, international politics, social conditions, money, personal wealth
(K)	Best time for conversations (before, during, after meals?):	anytime
(L)	Forms of legal punishment:	jailing, hanging
(M)	Approximately length of time one could be detained by law and order authorities before being charged in court:	n/a
(N)	January 15, 1999, for example, will normally be written as:	1/15/1999 or 15/1/1999
(O)	Emergency code number:	fire 019
(P)	Ambulance code Number:	099
(Q)	Police code number:	015
(R)	Telephone (country) code:	232 22
(S)	Telex (country) code:	n/a
)	Electricity requirements:	220 volts AC
(U)	Legal drinking age:	14 years
(V)	Systems of weights and measures:	metric and imperial
(W)	Legal age of incarceration:	18 years
(X)	Driving side of the road:	left
(Y)	Minimum expenditure expected of foreign visitors? $	for accommodation and extra spending at least $70
(Z)	Name of currency:	Leones
(Za)	Some places off-limits to foreign visitors:	n/a
(Zb)	Some places, structures and items prohibited from being photographed:	n/a

SOUTH AFRICA	Is customary Is allowed Is permissible Is used. Is OK	Is not customary Is frowned upon	Is disallowed Is forbidden Is a crime	(See last page for comments on items referenced here)
Smoking in public	✓			
Eating in public	✓			
Not flushing public toilet		✓		
Spitting in public		✓		
Feeding animals & birds in public		✓		
Whistling in public	✓			
Drinking alcohol in public		✓		
Kissing in public	✓			
Breast feeding in public	✓			
Drunkenness (in public)		✓		
Cursing in public		✓		
Religious preaching in public		✓		
Begging (panhandling) in public		✓		
Giving money to beggars/panhandlers	✓			
Giving food/drink to beggars/panhandlers	✓			
Brushing teeth in public (other than in restrooms)		✓		
Strolling with pets in major public roads/streets	✓			
Chewing gum in public	✓			
Chewing gum in government offices	✓			
Combing hair in public (other than in toilets/restrooms)	✓			
Undressing/dressing in public		✓		
Wearing of dark glasses indoors in public places	✓			
Public display of wealth	✓			
Praying openly in public in non-designated areas	✓			
Walking bare feet in public	✓			
Chewing tobacco in public	✓			
Trimming one's finger or toe nails in public		✓		
Laughing aloud in public	✓			
Mingling of the sexes in public	✓			
Mixed bathing in public swimming pools	✓			
Distributing religious pamphlets (literature) in public/side streets	✓			

SOUTH AFRICA

	Is customary Is allowed Is permissible Is used. Is OK	Is not customary Is frowned upon	Is disallowed Is forbidden Is a crime	(See last page for comments on items referenced here)
Dancing on side street	✓			
Nude bathing		✓		
Littering			✓	
Binge Drinking		✓		
Hitchhiking	✓			
Jaywalking		✓		
Drunk driving			✓	
Speeding			✓	
Skating on side streets (side-walk)		✓		
Graffiti painting			✓	
Pilfering				n/a
Prostitution			✓	
Haggling in the market place	✓			
Consumption of alcoholic beverages in bars and restaurants	✓			
Gambling	✓			
Possession of pornographic materials			✓	
Possession of the Christian Bible	✓			
Possession of the Moslem Koran	✓			
Possession of bullet-proof vest		✓		
Possession of toy gun			✓	
Possession of fire crackers and fireworks			✓	
Possession of prescription drugs (without doctor's note)	✓			
Possession of regulated drugs (narcotics)			✓	
Possession of firearms (by foreigners)			✓	
Possession of pocket knife in public		✓		
Using walkie talkies	✓			
Using of "boom boxes"(loud sounding stereo system)		✓		
Using "walkman" (very small radio/cassettes with ear plugs) in public places	✓			
Using "walkman" (very small radio/cassettes with ear plugs) while driving or riding			✓	

SOUTH AFRICA

	Is customary Is allowed Is permissible Is used Is OK	Is not customary Is frowned upon	Is disallowed Is forbidden Is a crime	(See last page for comments on items referenced here)
Use of cellular phone	✓			
Use of binoculars/periscopes other than in sports arena	✓			
Taking photographs of people (without their permission)		✓		
Taking photographs at airports, train and bus stations	✓			
Taking photographs of airports	✓			
Taking photographs of churches and synagogues	✓			
Taking photographs of religious statues	✓			
Taking photographs of public buildings	✓			
Taking photographs of bridges	✓			
Tipping (gratuity)	✓			
Tipping (when service is rendered)	✓			
Tipping (when service is not rendered)	✓			
Tipping waiters/waitresses at restaurants and hotels	✓			
Tipping taxi/cab drivers	✓			
Tipping baggage handlers, porters, door persons	✓			
Tipping of hair dressers/barbers		✓		
Overtipping	✓			
Undertipping		✓		
Spilling cigarette butt (ash) on side streets/on the floor		✓		
Men wearing lipstick		✓		
Wearing visible tattoo marks	✓			
Men painting/coloring their finger or toe nails		✓		
Cross dressing (men dressed like women & vice versa)		✓		
Walking in public without a shirt (i.e., with the upper half of the body naked)		✓		
Men wearing braided hair	✓			
Men wearing earrings	✓			
Men wearing dreadlock hair style	✓			
Homosexuality		✓		
Lesbianism		✓		

SOUTH AFRICA

	Is customary Is allowed Is permissible Is used Is OK	Is not customary Is frowned upon	Is disallowed Is forbidden Is a crime	(See last page for comments on items referenced here)
Females covering their hair (wearing headgear) in public	✓			
Females exposing their full face in public	✓			
Females driving automobiles	✓			
Females riding motorcycles	✓			
Females riding bicycles	✓			
Females smoking in public		✓		.
Women wearing bras (braziers) in public	✓			
Use of lipstick by women	✓			
A woman extending her hands first when introduced			✓	
Female bashing	✓			
Females wearing trousers	✓			
Females wearing minis (short dresses)	✓			
Females wearing bikinis	✓			
Females wearing shorts	✓			
Persons of opposite sex holding hands in public		✓		
Persons of same sex holding hands in public	✓			
Handshake between opposite sex		✓		
Hugging in public by same sex	✓			
Hugging in public by opposite sex	✓			
Men and women walking side by side in public		✓		
Man walking ahead (in public), with the woman following		✓		
Woman walking ahead (in public), with the man following	✓			
Men opening doors for women	✓			
Sitting with legs crossed in the presence of elders		✓		
Talking to an elderly person with one's hat/cap on		✓		
Talking to an elderly person with hands positioned on both sides of one's waist	✓			
Blowing one's nose in public	✓			
Blowing one's nose in the presence of others	✓			
Addressing people by their title	✓			

SOUTH AFRICA

	Is customary Is allowed Is permissible Is used. Is OK	Is not customary Is frowned upon	Is disallowed Is forbidden Is a crime	(See last page for comments on items referenced here)
Addressing people by their family name/surname/last name/given name	✓			
Addressing people by their first name/ given name	✓			
Women going through doors first	✓			
Men helping women with their coats	✓			
Men extending their hands to women first during greetings	✓			
Taking off one's hat when entering a private home	✓			
Removing one's shoes when entering a private home		✓		
Invited guests bringing food at social gatherings	✓			
Guests bringing drinks at social gatherings	✓			
Shaking hands when leaving a small group	✓			
Shaking hands with everyone present, upon arrival at a social gathering	✓			
Eating with the right hand	✓			
Eating with the left hand	✓			
Eating with both hands	✓			
Presenting a gift or passing on an object with the left hand	✓			
Asking a man about his wife	✓			
Asking a woman about her husband	✓			
Making prior appointments before a meeting or visit	✓			
Addressing an audience with one or both hands in the pocket		✓		
Carrying on conversation during meals	✓			
Females sitting with legs crossed	✓			
People discussing their wealth		✓		
Asking someone his or her age, or how old the person is		✓		
Complementing someone on his/her physical looks	✓			
Complementing someone on his/her attire	✓			
Use of both hands in handshake	✓			
In greeting, a handshake accompanied by a slight bow		✓		

323

SOUTH AFRICA

	Is customary Is allowed Is permissible Is used. Is OK	Is not customary Is frowned upon	Is disallowed Is forbidden Is a crime	(See last page for comments on items referenced here)
Salutations such as "Good morning", "good afternoon", "Good evening"	✓			
The completion of a business deal with a handshake	✓			
Starting a negotiation session with a handshake		✓		
A gift for the host/hostess	✓			
Giving a business gift	✓			
A gift of money (use of money as gift)	✓			
Use of flowers as a gift			✓	
Use of business cards			✓	
Accepting/presenting gifts with both hands	✓			
Burning of the country's flag			✓	
Mutilation of the national currency		✓		
Casual wearing of clothings made with colors & marks of the national flag	✓			
Wearing of look-alike military (camouflage) fatigues (attire)	✓			
Sitting on the floor (on floor mats)	✓			
Discussion of religion		✓		
Discussion of politics	✓			
Discussion of sex	✓			
Patting/slapping someone on the buttocks		✓		
Patting/slapping someone on the back	✓			
Touching or patting someone's head/hair		✓		
Casual touching of any part of someone's body	✓			
Drinking directly out of a bottle/can		✓		
Placing one's leg(s) on the table or chair	✓			

SOUTH AFRICA

	Is customary Is allowed Is permissible Is used. Is OK	Is not customary Is frowned upon	Is disallowed Is forbidden Is a crime	(See last page for comments on items referenced here)
Showing the sole of one's foot (feet)	✓			
People standing very close when talking		✓		
Maintaining steady eye contact (direct gaze) when talking to someone	✓			
Kissing or exchange of kisses on the cheek	✓			
Counting money (change) in someone's palm	✓			
Finger pointing in public (in a daring manner)		✓		
Seeking attention by winking the eyes		✓		
Tapping the head to indicate someone is crazy		✓		
Twirling the head to indicate someone is crazy		✓		
Whistling as a way of requesting something/seeking attention		✓		
Using "thumbs-up" sign to mean OK	✓			
Forming a circle with the thumb and index finger (forefinger) to mean OK	✓			
Using the fingers to make a "V" sign for victory	✓			
Beckoning to someone with the index finger (forefinger)	✓			
The left to right waving of the hand with open palms facing outward to indicate "Good bye"	✓			
The use of a nod to show acknowledgement	✓			
Stopping/beckoning a taxi using a stretched hand with the thumb pointing upward		✓		
Using the thumb finger pointed to a direction, to request a ride or a hike	✓			
Raising one's hand/waving with an open fist to summon a taxi		✓		
Tapping one's foot/feet on the floor in a public gathering		✓		
Wiggling one's leg(s) when in a sitting position		✓		
Use of the hand (by motorists and cyclists) to signal direction of traffic		✓		

		(See last page for comments on items referenced here)
Foreign tourists are welcome in the country.	yes	
The use of seat belt is mandatory.	yes	
International driving license is accepted.	yes	
Foreign drivers license is accepted.	yes	
It is considered impolite to yawn in public.	yes	
Death penalty for drug trafficking is the law.	no	
Life imprisonment for drug trafficking is the law.	no	
Guilty until proven innocent in court is the law.	no	
Innocent until proven guilty in court is the law.	yes	
Pedestrians always have right of way.	no/yes	
Exit visas are required of visitors.	no	
Crash helmet is mandatory for motor cyclist.	yes	
Hanging is used as a form of legal punishment.	no	
Decapitation of a limb is used as a form of punishment.	no	
Caning is used as a form of legal punishment.	no	
Electric shock is used as a form of legal punishment.	no	
One is expected to stand up during the playing of the national anthem.	yes	
Crash helmet is mandatory for bicyclists.	no	
Guests are expected to eat every thing on their plates.	no	
Table manners are very informal.	no	
One is expected to cover one's mouth when laughing.	no	
A vertical nod of the head means YES (OK).	yes	
A horizontal shaking of the head means NO (Not OK).	yes	
Prostitution is allowed only in designated areas.	no	
One is expected to take off one's hat during playing of national anthem.	yes	
Separate seating arrangements (between sexes) are maintained at movies.	no	
Separate seating arrangements (between sexes) are maintained at churches.	no	
Uninvited visitors or guests may not be welcome, even among acquaintances.	no	
Pets (e.g. cats, dog) are allowed in some hotels and restaurants.	yes	
Couples invited for a meal may be separated during meals according to their sex.	no	
Punctuality is the order of business.	yes	
Automobiles are driven with headlights always turned on.	no	
Motorcycles are driven with headlights always turned on.	no	
Visitors with expired visa face mandatory jail time.	no	
Visitors without exit visa face jail time.	no	
Visitors without entry visa face mandatory (automatic) jail time.	no	

ADDITIONAL COUNTRY INFORMATION

(A)	The types of gifts to avoid:	n/a
(B)	Appropriate gifts for a foreigner to give:	n/a
(C)	Best time to present gifts (at the beginning or at the end of a visit?):	beginning
(D)	Best time to present gifts (on initial or later visits?):	initial
(E)	Best place to present gifts (in private or in public?):	private
(F)	Number(s) with certain connotations and/or myths attached to them:	n/a
(G)	Basic shape(s) with negative connotations:	n/a
(H)	Basic color(s) with negative connotations:	n/a
(I)	Traditional greeting methods include:	handshake
(J)	Safe topics for discussion include:	weather, fashion, travel, art, family, religion, domestic politics, food, sports, international politics, social conditions.
(K)	Best time for conversations (before, during, after meals?):	before meals, during meals or after meals
(L)	Forms of legal punishment:	jailing
(M)	Approximately length of time one could be detained by law and order authorities before being charged in court:	n/a
(N)	January 15, 1999, for example, will normally be written as:	1/15/99
(O)	Emergency code number:	n/a
(P)	Ambulance code Number:	n/a
(Q)	Police code number:	n/a
(R)	Telephone (country) code:	27
(S)	Telex (country) code:	n/a
(T)	Electricity requirements:	220 volts
(U)	Legal drinking age:	18
(V)	Systems of weights and measures:	metric
(W)	Legal age of incarceration:	18
(X)	Driving side of the road:	left
(Y)	Minimum expenditure expected of foreign visitors? $	none
(Z)	Name of currency:	Rand
(Za)	Some places off-limits to foreign visitors:	army barracks and government installations and buildings
(Zb)	Some places, structures and items prohibited from being photographed:	military installations

SWAZILAND	Is customary Is allowed Is permissible Is used. Is OK	Is not customary Is frowned upon	Is disallowed Is forbidden Is a crime	(See last page for comments on items referenced here)
Smoking in public	✓			
Eating in public	✓			
Not flushing public toilet		✓		
Spitting in public		✓		
Feeding animals & birds in public	✓			
Whistling in public	✓			
Drinking alcohol in public			✓	
Kissing in public	✓			
Breast feeding in public	✓			
Drunkenness (in public)			✓	
Cursing in public			✓	
Religious preaching in public	✓			
Begging (panhandling) in public		✓		
Giving money to beggars/panhandlers	✓			
Giving food/drink to beggars/panhandlers	✓			
Brushing teeth in public (other than in restrooms)		✓		
Strolling with pets in major public roads/streets	✓			
Chewing gum in public	✓			
Chewing gum in government offices		✓		
Combing hair in public (other than in toilets/restrooms)		✓		
Undressing/dressing in public			✓	
Wearing of dark glasses indoors in public places		✓		
Public display of wealth		✓		
Praying openly in public in non-designated areas		✓		
Walking bare feet in public	✓			
Chewing tobacco in public	✓			
Trimming one's finger or toe nails in public		✓		
Laughing aloud in public		✓		
Mingling of the sexes in public	✓			
Mixed bathing in public swimming pools	✓			
Distributing religious pamphlets (literature) in public/side streets	✓			

328

SWAZILAND

	Is customary Is allowed Is permissible Is used. Is OK	Is not customary Is frowned upon	Is disallowed Is forbidden Is a crime	(See last page for comments on items referenced here)
Dancing on side street	✓			
Nude bathing		✓		
Littering			✓	
Binge Drinking			✓	
Hitchhiking	✓			
Jaywalking		✓		
Drunk driving			✓	
Speeding			✓	
Skating on side streets (side-walk)			✓	
Graffiti painting			✓	
Pilfering			✓	
Prostitution			✓	
Haggling in the market place	✓			
Consumption of alcoholic beverages in bars and restaurants	✓			
Gambling	✓			
Possession of pornographic materials			✓	
Possession of the Christian Bible	✓			
Possession of the Moslem Koran	✓			
Possession of bullet-proof vest	✓			
Possession of toy gun	✓			
Possession of fire crackers and fireworks	✓			
Possession of prescription drugs (without doctor's note)			✓	
Possession of regulated drugs (narcotics)			✓	
Possession of firearms (by foreigners)	✓			
Possession of pocket knife in public	✓			
Using walkie talkies	✓			
Using of "boom boxes"(loud sounding stereo system)		✓		
Using "walkman" (very small radio/cassettes with ear plugs) in public places	✓			
Using "walkman" (very small radio/cassettes with ear plugs) while driving or riding	✓			

SWAZILAND

	Is customary Is allowed Is permissible Is used Is OK	Is not customary Is frowned upon	Is disallowed Is forbidden Is a crime	(See last page for comments on items referenced here)
Use of cellular phone	✓			
Use of binoculars/periscopes other than in sports arena		✓		
Taking photographs of people (without their permission)		✓		
Taking photographs at airports, train and bus stations			✓	
Taking photographs of airports			✓	
Taking photographs of churches and synagogues	✓			
Taking photographs of religious statues	✓			
Taking photographs of public buildings			✓	
Taking photographs of bridges			✓	
Tipping (gratuity)	✓			
Tipping (when service is rendered)	✓			
Tipping (when service is not rendered)				
Tipping waiters/waitresses at restaurants and hotels	✓			
Tipping taxi/cab drivers	✓			
Tipping baggage handlers, porters, door persons	✓			
Tipping of hair dressers/barbers	✓			
Overtipping	✓			
Undertipping	✓			
Spilling cigarette butt (ash) on side streets/on the floor		✓		
Men wearing lipstick	✓			
Wearing visible tattoo marks	✓			
Men painting/coloring their finger or toe nails	✓			
Cross dressing (men dressed like women & vice versa)	✓			
Walking in public without a shirt (i.e., with the upper half of the body naked)		✓		
Men wearing braided hair	✓			
Men wearing earrings	✓			
Men wearing dreadlock hair style	✓			
Homosexuality		✓		
Lesbianism		✓		

SWAZILAND

	Is customary Is allowed Is permissible Is used Is OK	Is not customary Is frowned upon	Is disallowed Is forbidden Is a crime	(See last page for comments on items referenced here)
Females covering their hair (wearing headgear) in public	✓			
Females exposing their full face in public	✓			
Females driving automobiles	✓			
Females riding motorcycles	✓			
Females riding bicycles	✓			
Females smoking in public	✓			
Women wearing bras (braziers) in public	✓			
Use of lipstick by women	✓			
A woman extending her hands first when introduced	✓			
Female bashing			✓	
Females wearing trousers	✓			
Females wearing minis (short dresses)	✓			
Females wearing bikinis	✓			
Females wearing shorts	✓			
Persons of opposite sex holding hands in public	✓			
Persons of same sex holding hands in public	✓			
Handshake between opposite sex	✓			
Hugging in public by same sex	✓			
Hugging in public by opposite sex	✓			
Men and women walking side by side in public	✓			
Man walking ahead (in public), with the woman following	✓			
Woman walking ahead (in public), with the man following	✓			
Men opening doors for women	✓			
Sitting with legs crossed in the presence of elders	✓			
Talking to an elderly person with one's hat/cap on		✓		
Talking to an elderly person with hands positioned on both sides of one's waist	✓			
Blowing one's nose in public	✓			
Blowing one's nose in the presence of others	✓			
Addressing people by their title	✓			

SWAZILAND

	Is customary Is allowed Is permissible Is used. Is OK	Is not customary Is frowned upon	Is disallowed Is forbidden Is a crime	(See last page for comments on items referenced here)
Addressing people by their family name/surname/last name/given name	✓			
Addressing people by their first name/ given name	✓			
Women going through doors first	✓			
Men helping women with their coats	✓			
Men extending their hands to women first during greetings	✓			
Taking off one's hat when entering a private home	✓			
Removing one's shoes when entering a private home	✓			
Invited guests bringing food at social gatherings	✓			
Guests bringing drinks at social gatherings	✓			
Shaking hands when leaving a small group	✓			
Shaking hands with everyone present, upon arrival at a social gathering	✓			
Eating with the right hand	✓			
Eating with the left hand		✓		
Eating with both hands		✓		
Presenting a gift or passing on an object with the left hand		✓		
Asking a man about his wife	✓			
Asking a woman about her husband	✓			
Making prior appointments before a meeting or visit	✓			
Addressing an audience with one or both hands in the pocket		✓		
Carrying on conversation during meals	✓			
Females sitting with legs crossed	✓			
People discussing their wealth	✓			
Asking someone his or her age, or how old the person is		✓		
Complementing someone on his/her physical looks	✓			
Complementing someone on his/her attire	✓			
Use of both hands in handshake	✓			
In greeting, a handshake accompanied by a slight bow	✓			

SWAZILAND

	Is customary Is allowed Is permissible Is used. Is OK	Is not customary Is frowned upon	Is disallowed Is forbidden Is a crime	(See last page for comments on items referenced here)
Salutations such as "Good morning", "good afternoon", "Good evening"	✓			
The completion of a business deal with a handshake	✓			
Starting a negotiation session with a handshake	✓			
A gift for the host/hostess	✓			
Giving a business gift	✓			
A gift of money (use of money as gift)	✓			
Use of flowers as a gift	✓			
Use of business cards	✓			
Accepting/presenting gifts with both hands	✓			
Burning of the country's flag			✓	
Mutilation of the national currency		✓		
Casual wearing of clothings made with colors & marks of the national flag	✓			
Wearing of look-alike military (camouflage) fatigues (attire)			✓	
Sitting on the floor (on floor mats)	✓			
Discussion of religion	✓			
Discussion of politics	✓			
Discussion of sex	✓			
Patting/slapping someone on the buttocks			✓	
Patting/slapping someone on the back		✓		
Touching or patting someone's head/hair			✓	
Casual touching of any part of someone's body			✓	
Drinking directly out of a bottle/can			✓	
Placing one's leg(s) on the table or chair			✓	

333

SWAZILAND

	Is customary Is allowed Is permissible Is used. Is OK	Is not customary Is frowned upon	Is disallowed Is forbidden Is a crime	(See last page for comments on items referenced here)
Showing the sole of one's foot (feet)			✓	
People standing very close when talking		✓		
Maintaining steady eye contact (direct gaze) when talking to someone	✓			
Kissing or exchange of kisses on the cheek		✓		
Counting money (change) in someone's palm	✓			
Finger pointing in public (in a daring manner)		✓		
Seeking attention by winking the eyes		✓		
Tapping the head to indicate someone is crazy		✓		
Twirling the head to indicate someone is crazy		✓		
Whistling as a way of requesting something/seeking attention		✓		
Using "thumbs-up" sign to mean OK	✓			
Forming a circle with the thumb and index finger (forefinger) to mean OK		✓		
Using the fingers to make a "V" sign for victory	✓			
Beckoning to someone with the index finger (forefinger)		✓		
The left to right waving of the hand with open palms facing outward to indicate "Good bye"		✓		
The use of a nod to show acknowledgement	✓			
Stopping/beckoning a taxi using a stretched hand with the thumb pointing upward	✓			
Using the thumb finger pointed to a direction, to request a ride or a hike	✓			
Raising one's hand/waving with an open fist to summon a taxi	✓			
Tapping one's foot/feet on the floor in a public gathering		✓		
Wiggling one's leg(s) when in a sitting position		✓		
Use of the hand (by motorists and cyclists) to signal direction of traffic	✓			

334

SWAZILAND

		(See last page for comments on items referenced here)
Foreign tourists are welcome in the country.	yes	
The use of seat belt is mandatory.	yes	
International driving license is accepted.	yes	
Foreign drivers license is accepted.	yes	
It is considered impolite to yawn in public.	no	
Death penalty for drug trafficking is the law.	no	
Life imprisonment for drug trafficking is the law.	no	
Guilty until proven innocent in court is the law.	no	
Innocent until proven guilty in court is the law.	yes	
Pedestrians always have right of way.	no	
Exit visas are required of visitors.	yes	
Crash helmet is mandatory for motor cyclist.	no	
Hanging is used as a form of legal punishment.	no	
Decapitation of a limb is used as a form of punishment.	yes	
Caning is used as a form of legal punishment.	no	
Electric shock is used as a form of legal punishment.	yes	
One is expected to stand up during the playing of the national anthem.	yes	
Crash helmet is mandatory for bicyclists.	no	
Guests are expected to eat every thing on their plates.	no	
Table manners are very informal.	no	
One is expected to cover one's mouth when laughing.	no	
A vertical nod of the head means YES (OK).	yes	
A horizontal shaking of the head means NO (Not OK).	yes	
Prostitution is allowed only in designated areas.	no	
One is expected to take off one's hat during playing of national anthem.	no	
Separate seating arrangements (between sexes) are maintained at movies.	no	
Separate seating arrangements (between sexes) are maintained at churches.	no	
Uninvited visitors or guests may not be welcome, even among acquaintances.	no	
Pets (e.g. cats, dog) are allowed in some hotels and restaurants.	yes	
Couples invited for a meal may be separated during meals according to their sex.	no	
Punctuality is the order of business.	no	
Automobiles are driven with headlights always turned on.	yes	
Motorcycles are driven with headlights always turned on.	yes	
Visitors with expired visa face mandatory jail time.	no	
Visitors without exit visa face jail time.	yes	
Visitors without entry visa face mandatory (automatic) jail time.	no	

ADDITIONAL COUNTRY INFORMATION

(A)	The types of gifts to avoid:	n/a
(B)	Appropriate gifts for a foreigner to give:	n/a
(C)	Best time to present gifts (at the beginning or at the end of a visit?):	end
(D)	Best time to present gifts (on initial or later visits?):	initial
(E)	Best place to present gifts (in private or in public?):	private
(F)	Number(s) with certain connotations and/or myths attached to them:	none
(G)	Basic shape(s) with negative connotations:	none
(H)	Basic color(s) with negative connotations:	none
(I)	Traditional greeting methods include:	handshake, hugging (friends)
(J)	Safe topics for discussion include:	weather
(K)	Best time for conversations (before, during, after meals?):	anytime
(L)	Forms of legal punishment:	jailing, flogging, hanging
(M)	Approximately length of time one could be detained by law and order authorities before being charged in court:	24 hours
(N)	January 15, 1999, for example, will normally be written as:	15.1.99
(O)	Emergency code number:	n/a
(P)	Ambulance code Number:	n/a
(Q)	Police code number:	n/a
(R)	Telephone (country) code:	n/a
(S)	Telex (country) code:	n/a
(T)	Electricity requirements:	n/a
(U)	Legal drinking age:	18 yrs
(V)	Systems of weights and measures:	metric
(W)	Legal age of incarceration:	16 yrs.
(X)	Driving side of the road:	left
(Y)	Minimum expenditure expected of foreign visitors? $	n/a
(Z)	Name of currency:	emalangeni
(Za)	Some places off-limits to foreign visitors:	palaces; government buildings, bridges
(Zb)	Some places, structures and items prohibited from being photographed:	n/a

TANZANIA	Is customary Is allowed Is permissible Is used. Is OK	Is not customary Is frowned upon	Is disallowed Is forbidden Is a crime	(See last page for comments on items referenced here)
Smoking in public		✓		
Eating in public		✓		
Not flushing public toilet			✓	
Spitting in public			✓	
Feeding animals & birds in public	✓			
Whistling in public	✓			
Drinking alcohol in public		✓		
Kissing in public		✓		
Breast feeding in public	✓			
Drunkenness (in public)			✓	
Cursing in public			✓	
Religious preaching in public	✓			1
Begging (panhandling) in public		✓		
Giving money to beggars/panhandlers	✓			
Giving food/drink to beggars/panhandlers	✓			
Brushing teeth in public (other than in restrooms)		✓		
Strolling with pets in major public roads/streets		✓		
Chewing gum in public	✓			
Chewing gum in government offices	✓			
Combing hair in public (other than in toilets/restrooms)	✓			
Undressing/dressing in public			✓	
Wearing of dark glasses indoors in public places		✓		
Public display of wealth		✓		
Praying openly in public in non-designated areas	✓			
Walking bare feet in public	✓			
Chewing tobacco in public	✓			
Trimming one's finger or toe nails in public	✓			
Laughing aloud in public	✓			
Mingling of the sexes in public	✓			
Mixed bathing in public swimming pools	✓			
Distributing religious pamphlets (literature) in public/side streets	✓			

337

TANZANIA

	Is customary Is allowed Is permissible Is used. Is OK	Is not customary Is frowned upon	Is disallowed Is forbidden Is a crime	(See last page for comments on items referenced here)
Dancing on side street		✓		
Nude bathing			✓	
Littering		✓		
Binge Drinking		✓		
Hitchhiking	✓			
Jaywalking			✓	
Drunk driving			✓	
Speeding			✓	
Skating on side streets (side-walk)			✓	
Graffiti painting			✓	
Pilfering			✓	
Prostitution			✓	
Haggling in the market place			✓	
Consumption of alcoholic beverages in bars and restaurants	✓			
Gambling			✓	
Possession of pornographic materials			✓	
Possession of the Christian Bible	✓			
Possession of the Moslem Koran	✓			
Possession of bullet-proof vest	✓			
Possession of toy gun			✓	
Possession of fire crackers and fireworks			✓	
Possession of prescription drugs (without doctor's note)			✓	
Possession of regulated drugs (narcotics)			✓	
Possession of firearms (by foreigners)			✓	
Possession of pocket knife in public	✓			
Using walkie talkies	✓			
Using of "boom boxes"(loud sounding stereo system)		✓		
Using "walkman" (very small radio/cassettes with ear plugs) in public places	✓			
Using "walkman" (very small radio/cassettes with ear plugs) while driving or riding			✓	

338

TANZANIA

	Is customary Is allowed Is permissible Is used Is OK	Is not customary Is frowned upon	Is disallowed Is forbidden Is a crime	(See last page for comments on items referenced here)
Use of cellular phone	✓			
Use of binoculars/periscopes other than in sports arena	✓			
Taking photographs of people (without their permission)	✓			
Taking photographs at airports, train and bus stations	✓			2
Taking photographs of airports	✓			
Taking photographs of churches and synagogues	✓			
Taking photographs of religious statues	✓			
Taking photographs of public buildings	✓			
Taking photographs of bridges		✓		
Tipping (gratuity)	✓			
Tipping (when service is rendered)	✓			
Tipping (when service is not rendered)	✓			
Tipping waiters/waitresses at restaurants and hotels	✓			
Tipping taxi/cab drivers	✓			
Tipping baggage handlers, porters, door persons	✓			
Tipping of hair dressers/barbers	✓			
Overtipping	✓			
Undertipping	✓			
Spilling cigarette butt (ash) on side streets/on the floor		✓		
Men wearing lipstick		✓		
Wearing visible tattoo marks		✓		
Men painting/coloring their finger or toe nails		✓		
Cross dressing (men dressed like women & vice versa)		✓		
Walking in public without a shirt (i.e., with the upper half of the body naked)		✓		
Men wearing braided hair		✓		
Men wearing earrings		✓		
Men wearing dreadlock hair style		✓		
Homosexuality			✓	
Lesbianism			✓	

339

TANZANIA

	Is customary Is allowed Is permissible Is used Is OK	Is not customary Is frowned upon	Is disallowed Is forbidden Is a crime	(See last page for comments on items referenced here)
Females covering their hair (wearing headgear) in public	✓			
Females exposing their full face in public	✓			
Females driving automobiles	✓			
Females riding motorcycles	✓			
Females riding bicycles	✓			
Females smoking in public	✓			
Women wearing bras (braziers) in public			✓	
Use of lipstick by women	✓			
A woman extending her hands first when introduced	✓			
Female bashing	✓			
Females wearing trousers	✓			
Females wearing minis (short dresses)	✓			
Females wearing bikinis		✓		
Females wearing shorts		✓		
Persons of opposite sex holding hands in public			✓	
Persons of same sex holding hands in public		✓		
Handshake between opposite sex	✓			
Hugging in public by same sex	✓			
Hugging in public by opposite sex		✓		
Men and women walking side by side in public	✓			
Man walking ahead (in public), with the woman following	✓			
Woman walking ahead (in public), with the man following	✓			
Men opening doors for women	✓			
Sitting with legs crossed in the presence of elders	✓			
Talking to an elderly person with one's hat/cap on		✓		
Talking to an elderly person with hands positioned on both sides of one's waist		✓		
Blowing one's nose in public	✓			
Blowing one's nose in the presence of others	✓			
Addressing people by their title	✓			

TANZANIA

	Is customary Is allowed Is permissible Is used. Is OK	Is not customary Is frowned upon	Is disallowed Is forbidden Is a crime	(See last page for comments on items referenced here)
Addressing people by their family name/surname/last name/given name	✓			
Addressing people by their first name/ given name	✓			3
Women going through doors first	✓			
Men helping women with their coats	✓			
Men extending their hands to women first during greetings	✓			
Taking off one's hat when entering a private home	✓			
Removing one's shoes when entering a private home	✓			
Invited guests bringing food at social gatherings	✓			
Guests bringing drinks at social gatherings	✓			
Shaking hands when leaving a small group	✓			
Shaking hands with everyone present, upon arrival at a social gathering	✓			
Eating with the right hand	✓			
Eating with the left hand	✓			
Eating with both hands		✓		
Presenting a gift or passing on an object with the left hand		✓		
Asking a man about his wife	✓			
Asking a woman about her husband	✓			
Making prior appointments before a meeting or visit	✓			
Addressing an audience with one or both hands in the pocket	✓			
Carrying on conversation during meals	✓			
Females sitting with legs crossed	✓			
People discussing their wealth	✓			
Asking someone his or her age, or how old the person is	✓			
Complementing someone on his/her physical looks	✓			
Complementing someone on his/her attire	✓			
Use of both hands in handshake	✓			
In greeting, a handshake accompanied by a slight bow	✓			

341

TANZANIA

		Is customary Is allowed Is permissible Is used. Is OK	Is not customary Is frowned upon	Is disallowed Is forbidden Is a crime	(See last page for comments on items referenced here)
(146)	Salutations such as "Good morning", "good afternoon", "Good evening"	✓			
(147)	The completion of a business deal with a handshake	✓			
(148)	Starting a negotiation session with a handshake	✓			
(149)	A gift for the host/hostess	✓			
(150)	Giving a business gift	✓			
(151)	A gift of money (use of money as gift)		✓		
(152)	Use of flowers as a gift	✓			
(153)	Use of business cards	✓			
(154)	Accepting/presenting gifts with both hands	✓			
(155)	Burning of the country's flag			✓	
(156)	Mutilation of the national currency			✓	
(157)	Casual wearing of clothings made with colors & marks of the national flag		✓		
(158)	Wearing of look-alike military (camouflage) fatigues (attire)	✓			
(159)	Sitting on the floor (on floor mats)	✓			
(160)	Discussion of religion	✓			
(161)	Discussion of politics				
(162)	Discussion of sex		✓		
(163)	Patting/slapping someone on the buttocks		✓		
(164)	Patting/slapping someone on the back	✓			
(165)	Touching or patting someone's head/hair		✓		
(166)	Casual touching of any part of someone's body	✓			
(167)	Drinking directly out of a bottle/can	✓			
(168)	Placing one's leg(s) on the table or chair		✓		

342

TANZANIA

	Is customary Is allowed Is permissible Is used. Is OK	Is not customary Is frowned upon	Is disallowed Is forbidden Is a crime	(See last page for comments on items referenced here)
Showing the sole of one's foot (feet)		✓		
People standing very close when talking	✓			
Maintaining steady eye contact (direct gaze) when talking to someone	✓			
Kissing or exchange of kisses on the cheek	✓			
Counting money (change) in someone's palm	✓			
Finger pointing in public (in a daring manner)		✓		
Seeking attention by winking the eyes		✓		
Tapping the head to indicate someone is crazy		✓		
Twirling the head to indicate someone is crazy		✓		
Whistling as a way of requesting something/seeking attention	✓			
Using "thumbs-up" sign to mean OK	✓			
Forming a circle with the thumb and index finger (forefinger) to mean OK	✓			
Using the fingers to make a "V" sign for victory	✓			
Beckoning to someone with the index finger (forefinger)	✓			
The left to right waving of the hand with open palms facing outward to indicate "Good bye"	✓			
The use of a nod to show acknowledgement	✓			
Stopping/beckoning a taxi using a stretched hand with the thumb pointing upward	✓			
Using the thumb finger pointed to a direction, to request a ride or a hike	✓			
Raising one's hand/waving with an open fist to summon a taxi	✓			
Tapping one's foot/feet on the floor in a public gathering	✓			
Wiggling one's leg(s) when in a sitting position	✓			
Use of the hand (by motorists and cyclists) to signal direction of traffic	✓			

343

TANZANIA

		(See last page for comments on items referenced here)
Foreign tourists are welcome in the country.	yes	
The use of seat belt is mandatory.	yes	
International driving license is accepted.	yes	
Foreign drivers license is accepted.	no	
It is considered impolite to yawn in public.	no	
Death penalty for drug trafficking is the law.	no	
Life imprisonment for drug trafficking is the law.	no	
Guilty until proven innocent in court is the law.	no	
Innocent until proven guilty in court is the law.	yes	
Pedestrians always have right of way.	no	
Exit visas are required of visitors.	no	
Crash helmet is mandatory for motor cyclist.	yes	
Hanging is used as a form of legal punishment.	no	
Decapitation of a limb is used as a form of punishment.	no	
Caning is used as a form of legal punishment.	no	
Electric shock is used as a form of legal punishment.	no	
One is expected to stand up during the playing of the national anthem.	yes	
Crash helmet is mandatory for bicyclists.	yes	
Guests are expected to eat every thing on their plates.	no	
Table manners are very informal.	yes	
One is expected to cover one's mouth when laughing.	no	
A vertical nod of the head means YES (OK).	yes	
A horizontal shaking of the head means NO (Not OK).	yes	
Prostitution is allowed only in designated areas.	no	
One is expected to take off one's hat during playing of national anthem.	yes	
Separate seating arrangements (between sexes) are maintained at movies.	no	
Separate seating arrangements (between sexes) are maintained at churches.	no	
Uninvited visitors or guests may not be welcome, even among acquaintances.	yes	
Pets (e.g. cats, dog) are allowed in some hotels and restaurants.	no	
Couples invited for a meal may be separated during meals according to their sex.		n/a
Punctuality is the order of business.	yes	
Automobiles are driven with headlights always turned on.	no	
Motorcycles are driven with headlights always turned on.	no	4
Visitors with expired visa face mandatory jail time.	no	
Visitors without exit visa face jail time.	no	
Visitors without entry visa face mandatory (automatic) jail time.	no	

ADDITIONAL COUNTRY INFORMATION

(A)	The types of gifts to avoid:	weapons, unauthorized drugs
(B)	Appropriate gifts for a foreigner to give:	perfumes, jewelry, watches, cosmetics, flowers
(C)	Best time to present gifts (at the beginning or at the end of a visit?):	beginning
(D)	Best time to present gifts (on initial or later visits?):	anytime
(E)	Best place to present gifts (in private or in public?):	in private
(F)	Number(s) with certain connotations and/or myths attached to them:	n/a
(G)	Basic shape(s) with negative connotations:	n/a
(H)	Basic color(s) with negative connotations:	black
(I)	Traditional greeting methods include:	handshake, hugs
(J)	Safe topics for discussion include:	weather, travel, fashion, travel, art, family, religion, food, sports, international politics, economics
(K)	Best time for conversations (before, during, after meals?):	before and after
(L)	Forms of legal punishment:	jailing, hanging
(M)	Approximately length of time one could be detained by law and order authorities before being charged in court:	24 hours
(N)	January 15, 1999, for example, will normally be written as:	15-1-99
(O)	Emergency code number:	999
(P)	Ambulance code Number:	999
(Q)	Police code number:	999
(R)	Telephone (country) code:	255 - 51
(S)	Telex (country) code:	255 - 51
(T)	Electricity requirements:	220
(U)	Legal drinking age:	18 years
(V)	Systems of weights and measures:	metric
(W)	Legal age of incarceration:	18
(X)	Driving side of the road:	left
(Y)	Minimum expenditure expected of foreign visitors? $	U.S. $ 50 per day
(Z)	Name of currency:	Tanzania shilling
(Za)	Some places off-limits to foreign visitors:	military installations
(Zb)	Some places, structures and items prohibited from being photographed:	military installation

ENDNOTES

Item Number: ***COMMENTS/EXPLANATIONS***

n/a: Not applicable/Not available/No response

(1)   Religious preaching is allowed as long as the preacher does not use the occasion to criticize other religious.

(2)   Photograph taking is allowed in common areas and not in sensitive places.

(3)   You can address people by their first names if they are of your age or you are used to them.

(4)   Although it is not mandatory it is recommended that one turns headlights on when driving a motor cycle.

TOGO	Is customary Is allowed Is permissible Is used. Is OK	Is not customary Is frowned upon	Is disallowed Is forbidden Is a crime	(See last page for comments on items referenced here)
Smoking in public	✓			
Eating in public	✓			
Not flushing public toilet		✓		
Spitting in public			✓	
Feeding animals & birds in public	✓			
Whistling in public			✓	
Drinking alcohol in public			✓	
Kissing in public		✓		
Breast feeding in public	✓			
Drunkenness (in public)			✓	
Cursing in public			✓	
Religious preaching in public	✓			
Begging (panhandling) in public		✓		
Giving money to beggars/panhandlers	✓			
Giving food/drink to beggars/panhandlers	✓			
Brushing teeth in public (other than in restrooms)			✓	
Strolling with pets in major public roads/streets	✓			
Chewing gum in public			✓	
Chewing gum in government offices	✓			
Combing hair in public (other than in toilets/restrooms)	✓			
Undressing/dressing in public		✓		
Wearing of dark glasses indoors in public places	✓			
Public display of wealth	✓			
Praying openly in public in non-designated areas	✓			
Walking bare feet in public	✓			
Chewing tobacco in public	✓			
Trimming one's finger or toe nails in public	✓			
Laughing aloud in public	✓			
Mingling of the sexes in public				n/a
Mixed bathing in public swimming pools				n/a
Distributing religious pamphlets (literature) in public/side streets				n/a

347

	Is customary Is allowed Is permissible Is used. Is OK	Is not customary Is frowned upon	Is disallowed Is forbidden Is a crime	(See last page for comments on items referenced here)
Dancing on side street		✓		
Nude bathing			✓	
Littering			✓	
Binge Drinking	✓			
Hitchhiking	✓			
Jaywalking			✓	
Drunk driving			✓	
Speeding			✓	
Skating on side streets (side-walk)				n/a
Graffiti painting			✓	
Pilfering			✓	
Prostitution			✓	
Haggling in the market place				n/a
Consumption of alcoholic beverages in bars and restaurants				n/a
Gambling	✓			
Possession of pornographic materials		✓		
Possession of the Christian Bible	✓			
Possession of the Moslem Koran	✓			
Possession of bullet-proof vest	✓			
Possession of toy gun	✓			
Possession of fire crackers and fireworks	✓			
Possession of prescription drugs (without doctor's note)			✓	
Possession of regulated drugs (narcotics)			✓	
Possession of firearms (by foreigners)			✓	
Possession of pocket knife in public	✓			
Using walkie talkies	✓			
Using of "boom boxes"(loud sounding stereo system)	✓			
Using "walkman" (very small radio/cassettes with ear plugs) in public places	✓			
Using "walkman" (very small radio/cassettes with ear plugs) while driving or riding				n/a

348

	Is customary Is allowed Is permissible Is used Is OK	Is not customary Is frowned upon	Is disallowed Is forbidden Is a crime	(See last page for comments on items referenced here)
Use of cellular phone	✓			
Use of binoculars/periscopes other than in sports arena	✓			
Taking photographs of people (without their permission)			✓	
Taking photographs at airports, train and bus stations	✓			
Taking photographs of airports			✓	
Taking photographs of churches and synagogues	✓			
Taking photographs of religious statues	✓			
Taking photographs of public buildings				n/a
Taking photographs of bridges				n/a
Tipping (gratuity)	✓			
Tipping (when service is rendered)	✓			
Tipping (when service is not rendered)	✓			
Tipping waiters/waitresses at restaurants and hotels				n/a
Tipping taxi/cab drivers				n/a
Tipping baggage handlers, porters, door persons				n/a
Tipping of hair dressers/barbers				n/a
Overtipping	✓			
Undertipping	✓			
Spilling cigarette butt (ash) on side streets/on the floor			✓	
Men wearing lipstick		✓		
Wearing visible tattoo marks	✓			
Men painting/coloring their finger or toe nails		✓		
Cross dressing (men dressed like women & vice versa)	✓			
Walking in public without a shirt (i.e., with the upper half of the body naked)				n/a
Men wearing braided hair	✓			
Men wearing earrings	✓			
Men wearing dreadlock hair style	✓			
Homosexuality		✓		
Lesbianism		✓		

TOGO

	Is customary Is allowed Is permissible Is used Is OK	Is not customary Is frowned upon	Is disallowed Is forbidden Is a crime	(See last page for comments on items referenced here)
Females covering their hair (wearing headgear) in public	✓			
Females exposing their full face in public	✓			
Females driving automobiles	✓			
Females riding motorcycles	✓			
Females riding bicycles	✓			
Females smoking in public	✓			
Women wearing bras (braziers) in public	✓			
Use of lipstick by women	✓			
A woman extending her hands first when introduced	✓			
Female bashing			✓	
Females wearing trousers	✓			
Females wearing minis (short dresses)	✓			
Females wearing bikinis	✓			
Females wearing shorts			✓	
Persons of opposite sex holding hands in public	✓			
Persons of same sex holding hands in public	✓			
Handshake between opposite sex	✓			
Hugging in public by same sex	✓			
Hugging in public by opposite sex	✓			
Men and women walking side by side in public				n/a
Man walking ahead (in public), with the woman following				n/a
Woman walking ahead (in public), with the man following				n/a
Men opening doors for women	✓			
Sitting with legs crossed in the presence of elders		✓		
Talking to an elderly person with one's hat/cap on				n/a
Talking to an elderly person with hands positioned on both sides of one's waist				n/a
Blowing one's nose in public	✓			
Blowing one's nose in the presence of others		✓		
Addressing people by their title	✓			

TOGO

	Is customary Is allowed Is permissible Is used. Is OK	Is not customary Is frowned upon	Is disallowed Is forbidden Is a crime	(See last page for comments on items referenced here)
Addressing people by their family name/surname/last name/given name	✓			
Addressing people by their first name/ given name	✓			
Women going through doors first	✓			
Men helping women with their coats	✓			
Men extending their hands to women first during greetings	✓			
Taking off one's hat when entering a private home	✓			
Removing one's shoes when entering a private home				n/a
Invited guests bringing food at social gatherings	✓			
Guests bringing drinks at social gatherings	✓			
Shaking hands when leaving a small group	✓			
Shaking hands with everyone present, upon arrival at a social gathering	✓			
Eating with the right hand	✓			
Eating with the left hand		✓		
Eating with both hands		✓		
Presenting a gift or passing on an object with the left hand		✓		
Asking a man about his wife	✓			
Asking a woman about her husband	✓			
Making prior appointments before a meeting or visit	✓			
Addressing an audience with one or both hands in the pocket		✓		
Carrying on conversation during meals				n/a
Females sitting with legs crossed	✓			
People discussing their wealth	✓			
Asking someone his or her age, or how old the person is				n/a
Complementing someone on his/her physical looks				n/a
Complementing someone on his/her attire				n/a
Use of both hands in handshake		✓		
In greeting, a handshake accompanied by a slight bow	✓			

TOGO

	Is customary Is allowed Is permissible Is used. Is OK	Is not customary Is frowned upon	Is disallowed Is forbidden Is a crime	(See last page for comments on items referenced here)
Salutations such as "Good morning", "good afternoon", "good evening"	✓			
The completion of a business deal with a handshake				n/a
Starting a negotiation session with a handshake				n/a
A gift for the host/hostess	✓			
Giving a business gift	✓			
A gift of money (use of money as gift)	✓			
Use of flowers as a gift	✓			
Use of business cards	✓			
Accepting/presenting gifts with both hands	✓			
Burning of the country's flag			✓	
Mutilation of the national currency			✓	
Casual wearing of clothings made with colors & marks of the national flag				n/a
Wearing of look-alike military (camouflage) fatigues (attire)	✓			
Sitting on the floor (on floor mats)			✓	
Discussion of religion	✓			
Discussion of politics	✓			
Discussion of sex	✓			
Patting/slapping someone on the buttocks			✓	
Patting/slapping someone on the back	✓			
Touching or patting someone's head/hair	✓			
Casual touching of any part of someone's body				n/a
Drinking directly out of a bottle/can	✓			
Placing one's leg(s) on the table or chair		✓		

352

TOGO

	Is customary Is allowed Is permissible Is used. Is OK	Is not customary Is frowned upon	Is disallowed Is forbidden Is a crime	(See last page for comments on items referenced here)
Showing the sole of one's foot (feet)				n/a
People standing very close when talking	✓			
Maintaining steady eye contact (direct gaze) when talking to someone	✓			
Kissing or exchange of kisses on the cheek	✓			
Counting money (change) in someone's palm				n/a
Finger pointing in public (in a daring manner)			✓	
Seeking attention by winking the eyes				n/a
Tapping the head to indicate someone is crazy				n/a
Twirling the head to indicate someone is crazy				n/a
Whistling as a way of requesting something/seeking attention				n/a
Using "thumbs-up" sign to mean OK				n/a
Forming a circle with the thumb and index finger (forefinger) to mean OK				n/a
Using the fingers to make a "V" sign for victory				n/a
Beckoning to someone with the index finger (forefinger)				n/a
The left to right waving of the hand with open palms facing outward to indicate "Good bye"				n/a
The use of a nod to show acknowledgement				n/a
Stopping/beckoning a taxi using a stretched hand with the thumb pointing upward				n/a
Using the thumb finger pointed to a direction, to request a ride or a hike				n/a
Raising one's hand/waving with an open fist to summon a taxi				n/a
Tapping one's foot/feet on the floor in a public gathering				n/a
Wiggling one's leg(s) when in a sitting position				n/a
Use of the hand (by motorists and cyclists) to signal direction of traffic				n/a

353

		(See last page for comments on items referenced here)
Foreign tourists are welcome in the country.	yes	
The use of seat belt is mandatory.	no	
International driving license is accepted.	yes	
Foreign drivers license is accepted.	yes	
It is considered impolite to yawn in public.	yes	
Death penalty for drug trafficking is the law.	no	
Life imprisonment for drug trafficking is the law.	no	
Guilty until proven innocent in court is the law.	no	
Innocent until proven guilty in court is the law.	no	
Pedestrians always have right of way.	no	
Exit visas are required of visitors.	no	
Crash helmet is mandatory for motor cyclist.	yes	
Hanging is used as a form of legal punishment.	no	
Decapitation of a limb is used as a form of punishment.	no	
Caning is used as a form of legal punishment.	no	
Electric shock is used as a form of legal punishment.	yes	
One is expected to stand up during the playing of the national anthem.	yes	
Crash helmet is mandatory for bicyclists.	no	
Guests are expected to eat every thing on their plates.	no	
Table manners are very informal.	yes	
One is expected to cover one's mouth when laughing.	no	
A vertical nod of the head means YES (OK).	yes	
A horizontal shaking of the head means NO (Not OK).	yes	
Prostitution is allowed only in designated areas.	no	
One is expected to take off one's hat during playing of national anthem.	yes	
Separate seating arrangements (between sexes) are maintained at movies.	no	
Separate seating arrangements (between sexes) are maintained at churches.	no	
Uninvited visitors or guests may not be welcome, even among acquaintances.	yes	
Pets (e.g. cats, dog) are allowed in some hotels and restaurants.	no	
Couples invited for a meal may be separated during meals according to their sex.	no	
Punctuality is the order of business.	yes	
Automobiles are driven with headlights always turned on.		n/a
Motorcycles are driven with headlights always turned on.		n/a
Visitors with expired visa face mandatory jail time.	yes	
Visitors without exit visa face jail time.	yes	
Visitors without entry visa face mandatory (automatic) jail time.	yes	

ADDITIONAL COUNTRY INFORMATION

(A)	The types of gifts to avoid:	n/a
(B)	Appropriate gifts for a foreigner to give:	it depends on the title of the person to whom to offer gift
(C)	Best time to present gifts (at the beginning or at the end of a visit?):	at the beginning or at the end
(D)	Best time to present gifts (on initial or later visits?):	n/a
(E)	Best place to present gifts (in private or in public?):	n/a
(F)	Number(s) with certain connotations and/or myths attached to them:	n/a
(G)	Basic shape(s) with negative connotations:	n/a
(H)	Basic color(s) with negative connotations:	n/a
(I)	Traditional greeting methods include:	n/a
(J)	Safe topics for discussion include:	weather, fashion, travel, art, family, religion, domestic politics, food, sports, international politics, social conditions, money, personal wealth, sex.
(K)	Best time for conversations (before, during, after meals?):	n/a
(L)	Forms of legal punishment:	jailing
(M)	Approximately length of time one could be detained by law and order authorities before being charged in court:	n/a
(N)	January 15, 1999, for example, will normally be written as:	15/1/99
(O)	Emergency code number:	n/a
(P)	Ambulance code Number:	n/a
(Q)	Police code number:	n/a
(R)	Telephone (country) code:	n/a
(S)	Telex (country) code:	n/a
(T)	Electricity requirements:	n/a
(U)	Legal drinking age:	18
(V)	Systems of weights and measures:	n/a
(W)	Legal age of incarceration:	18
(X)	Driving side of the road:	right
(Y)	Minimum expenditure expected of foreign visitors? $	n/a
(Z)	Name of currency:	CFA
(Za)	Some places off-limits to foreign visitors:	n/a
(Zb)	Some places, structures and items prohibited from being photographed:	n/a

TUNISIA	Is customary Is allowed Is permissible Is used. Is OK	Is not customary Is frowned upon	Is disallowed Is forbidden Is a crime	(See last page for comments on items referenced here)
Smoking in public	✓			
Eating in public	✓			
Not flushing public toilet			✓	
Spitting in public			✓	
Feeding animals & birds in public	✓			
Whistling in public	✓			
Drinking alcohol in public			✓	
Kissing in public		✓		
Breast feeding in public			✓	
Drunkenness (in public)			✓	
Cursing in public			✓	
Religious preaching in public	✓			
Begging (panhandling) in public			✓	
Giving money to beggars/panhandlers	✓			
Giving food/drink to beggars/panhandlers	✓			
Brushing teeth in public (other than in restrooms)			✓	
Strolling with pets in major public roads/streets	✓			
Chewing gum in public	✓			
Chewing gum in government offices			✓	
Combing hair in public (other than in toilets/restrooms)	✓			
Undressing/dressing in public			✓	
Wearing of dark glasses indoors in public places	✓			
Public display of wealth	✓			
Praying openly in public in non-designated areas	✓			
Walking bare feet in public	✓			
Chewing tobacco in public			✓	
Trimming one's finger or toe nails in public			✓	
Laughing aloud in public	✓			
Mingling of the sexes in public	✓			
Mixed bathing in public swimming pools	✓			
Distributing religious pamphlets (literature) in public/side streets			✓	

TUNISIA

	Is customary Is allowed Is permissible Is used. Is OK	Is not customary Is frowned upon	Is disallowed Is forbidden Is a crime	(See last page for comments on items referenced here)
Dancing on side street	✓			
Nude bathing			✓	
Littering			✓	
Binge Drinking			✓	
Hitchhiking	✓			
Jaywalking			✓	
Drunk driving			✓	
Speeding			✓	
Skating on side streets (side-walk)			✓	
Graffiti painting			✓	
Pilfering			✓	
Prostitution			✓	
Haggling in the market place	✓			
Consumption of alcoholic beverages in bars and restaurants	✓			
Gambling			✓	
Possession of pornographic materials			✓	
Possession of the Christian Bible	✓			
Possession of the Moslem Koran	✓			
Possession of bullet-proof vest			✓	
Possession of toy gun	✓			
Possession of fire crackers and fireworks	✓			
Possession of prescription drugs (without doctor's note)			✓	
Possession of regulated drugs (narcotics)			✓	
Possession of firearms (by foreigners)			✓	
Possession of pocket knife in public			✓	
Using walkie talkies			✓	
Using of "boom boxes"(loud sounding stereo system)	✓			
Using "walkman" (very small radio/cassettes with ear plugs) in public places	✓			
Using "walkman" (very small radio/cassettes with ear plugs) while driving or riding	✓			

357

	Is customary Is allowed Is permissible Is used Is OK	Is not customary Is frowned upon	Is disallowed Is forbidden Is a crime	(See last page for comments on items referenced here)
Use of cellular phone	✓			
Use of binoculars/periscopes other than in sports arena	✓			
Taking photographs of people (without their permission)			✓	
Taking photographs at airports, train and bus stations	✓			
Taking photographs of airports	✓			
Taking photographs of churches and synagogues	✓			
Taking photographs of religious statues	✓			
Taking photographs of public buildings	✓			
Taking photographs of bridges	✓			
Tipping (gratuity)	✓			
Tipping (when service is rendered)	✓			
Tipping (when service is not rendered)	✓			
Tipping waiters/waitresses at restaurants and hotels	✓			
Tipping taxi/cab drivers	✓			
Tipping baggage handlers, porters, door persons	✓			
Tipping of hair dressers/barbers	✓			
Overtipping	✓			
Undertipping	✓			
Spilling cigarette butt (ash) on side streets/on the floor			✓	
Men wearing lipstick			✓	
Wearing visible tattoo marks	✓			
Men painting/coloring their finger or toe nails	✓			
Cross dressing (men dressed like women & vice versa)			✓	
Walking in public without a shirt (i.e., with the upper half of the body naked)			✓	
Men wearing braided hair	✓			
Men wearing earrings	✓			
Men wearing dreadlock hair style	✓			
Homosexuality			✓	
Lesbianism			✓	

358

TUNISIA

	Is customary / Is allowed / Is permissible / Is used / Is OK	Is not customary / Is frowned upon	Is disallowed / Is forbidden / Is a crime	(See last page for comments on items referenced here)
Females covering their hair (wearing headgear) in public	✓			
Females exposing their full face in public	✓			
Females driving automobiles	✓			
Females riding motorcycles	✓			
Females riding bicycles	✓			
Females smoking in public	✓			
Women wearing bras (braziers) in public			✓	
Use of lipstick by women	✓			
A woman extending her hands first when introduced	✓			
Female bashing			✓	
Females wearing trousers	✓			
Females wearing minis (short dresses)	✓			
Females wearing bikinis	✓			
Females wearing shorts	✓			
Persons of opposite sex holding hands in public	✓			
Persons of same sex holding hands in public	✓			
Handshake between opposite sex	✓			
Hugging in public by same sex	✓			
Hugging in public by opposite sex	✓			
Men and women walking side by side in public	✓			
Man walking ahead (in public), with the woman following			✓	
Woman walking ahead (in public), with the man following			✓	
Men opening doors for women	✓			
Sitting with legs crossed in the presence of elders			✓	
Talking to an elderly person with one's hat/cap on	✓			
Talking to an elderly person with hands positioned on both sides of one's waist			✓	
Blowing one's nose in public	✓			
Blowing one's nose in the presence of others	✓			
Addressing people by their title	✓			

TUNISIA

	Is customary Is allowed Is permissible Is used. Is OK	Is not customary Is frowned upon	Is disallowed Is forbidden Is a crime	(See last page for comments on items referenced here)
Addressing people by their family name/surname/last name/given name	✓			
Addressing people by their first name/ given name	✓			
Women going through doors first	✓			
Men helping women with their coats	✓			
Men extending their hands to women first during greetings	✓			
Taking off one's hat when entering a private home	✓			
Removing one's shoes when entering a private home	✓			
Invited guests bringing food at social gatherings	✓			
Guests bringing drinks at social gatherings	✓			
Shaking hands when leaving a small group	✓			
Shaking hands with everyone present, upon arrival at a social gathering	✓			
Eating with the right hand	✓			
Eating with the left hand	✓			
Eating with both hands	✓			
Presenting a gift or passing on an object with the left hand	✓			
Asking a man about his wife	✓			
Asking a woman about her husband	✓			
Making prior appointments before a meeting or visit	✓			
Addressing an audience with one or both hands in the pocket			✓	
Carrying on conversation during meals	✓			
Females sitting with legs crossed	✓			
People discussing their wealth	✓			
Asking someone his or her age, or how old the person is	✓			
Complementing someone on his/her physical looks	✓			
Complementing someone on his/her attire	✓			
Use of both hands in handshake	✓			
In greeting, a handshake accompanied by a slight bow	✓			

TUNISIA

	Is customary Is allowed Is permissible Is used. Is OK	Is not customary Is frowned upon	Is disallowed Is forbidden Is a crime	(See last page for comments on items referenced here)
Salutations such as "Good morning", "good afternoon", "Good evening"	✓			
The completion of a business deal with a handshake	✓			
Starting a negotiation session with a handshake	✓			
A gift for the host/hostess	✓			
Giving a business gift	✓			
A gift of money (use of money as gift)	✓			
Use of flowers as a gift	✓			
Use of business cards	✓			
Accepting/presenting gifts with both hands	✓			
Burning of the country's flag	✓			
Mutilation of the national currency			✓	
Casual wearing of clothings made with colors & marks of the national flag	✓			
Wearing of look-alike military (camouflage) fatigues (attire)			✓	
Sitting on the floor (on floor mats)		✓		
Discussion of religion	✓			
Discussion of politics	✓			
Discussion of sex	✓			
Patting/slapping someone on the buttocks			✓	
Patting/slapping someone on the back			✓	
Touching or patting someone's head/hair			✓	
Casual touching of any part of someone's body			✓	
Drinking directly out of a bottle/can			✓	
Placing one's leg(s) on the table or chair	✓			

361

TUNISIA

	Is customary Is allowed Is permissible Is used. Is OK	Is not customary Is frowned upon	Is disallowed Is forbidden Is a crime	(See last page for comments on items referenced here)
Showing the sole of one's foot (feet)			✓	n/a
People standing very close when talking		3		
Maintaining steady eye contact (direct gaze) when talking to someone	✓			
Kissing or exchange of kisses on the cheek	✓			
Counting money (change) in someone's palm	✓			n/a
Finger pointing in public (in a daring manner)			✓	
Seeking attention by winking the eyes	✓			
Tapping the head to indicate someone is crazy	✓			
Twirling the head to indicate someone is crazy	✓			
Whistling as a way of requesting something/seeking attention	✓			
Using "thumbs-up" sign to mean OK	✓			
Forming a circle with the thumb and index finger (forefinger) to mean OK	✓			
Using the fingers to make a "V" sign for victory	✓			
Beckoning to someone with the index finger (forefinger)			✓	
The left to right waving of the hand with open palms facing outward to indicate "Good bye"	✓			
The use of a nod to show acknowledgement	✓			
Stopping/beckoning a taxi using a stretched hand with the thumb pointing upward	✓			
Using the thumb finger pointed to a direction, to request a ride or a hike	✓			
Raising one's hand/waving with an open fist to summon a taxi	✓			
Tapping one's foot/feet on the floor in a public gathering			✓	
Wiggling one's leg(s) when in a sitting position			✓	
Use of the hand (by motorists and cyclists) to signal direction of traffic	✓			

362

TUNISIA

		(See last page for comments on items referenced here)
Foreign tourists are welcome in the country.	yes	
The use of seat belt is mandatory.	yes	
International driving license is accepted.	yes	
Foreign drivers license is accepted.	yes	
It is considered impolite to yawn in public.	yes	
Death penalty for drug trafficking is the law.	no	
Life imprisonment for drug trafficking is the law.	no	
Guilty until proven innocent in court is the law.	no	
Innocent until proven guilty in court is the law.	yes	
Pedestrians always have right of way.	yes	
Exit visas are required of visitors.	no	
Crash helmet is mandatory for motor cyclist.	yes	
Hanging is used as a form of legal punishment.	yes	
Decapitation of a limb is used as a form of punishment.	no	
Caning is used as a form of legal punishment.	no	
Electric shock is used as a form of legal punishment.	no	
One is expected to stand up during the playing of the national anthem.	yes	
Crash helmet is mandatory for bicyclists.	no	
Guests are expected to eat every thing on their plates.	yes	
Table manners are very informal.	yes	
One is expected to cover one's mouth when laughing.	no	
A vertical nod of the head means YES (OK).	yes	
A horizontal shaking of the head means NO (Not OK).	yes	
Prostitution is allowed only in designated areas.	yes	
One is expected to take off one's hat during playing of national anthem.	yes	
Separate seating arrangements (between sexes) are maintained at movies.	no	
Separate seating arrangements (between sexes) are maintained at churches.	no	
Uninvited visitors or guests may not be welcome, even among acquaintances.	no	
Pets (e.g. cats, dog) are allowed in some hotels and restaurants.	no	
Couples invited for a meal may be separated during meals according to their sex.	no	
Punctuality is the order of business.	yes	
Automobiles are driven with headlights always turned on.	no	n/a
Motorcycles are driven with headlights always turned on.	no	n/a
Visitors with expired visa face mandatory jail time.	no	
Visitors without exit visa face jail time.	no	
Visitors without entry visa face mandatory (automatic) jail time.	no	

ADDITIONAL COUNTRY INFORMATION

(A)	The types of gifts to avoid:	n/a
(B)	Appropriate gifts for a foreigner to give:	dress, books, handicrafts
(C)	Best time to present gifts (at the beginning or at the end of a visit?):	beginning
(D)	Best time to present gifts (on initial or later visits?):	n/a
(E)	Best place to present gifts (in private or in public?):	n/a
(F)	Number(s) with certain connotations and/or myths attached to them:	n/a
(G)	Basic shape(s) with negative connotations:	n/a
(H)	Basic color(s) with negative connotations:	n/a
(I)	Traditional greeting methods include:	n/a
(J)	Safe topics for discussion include:	weather, fashion, travel, art, family, religion, domestic politics, food, sports, international politics, social conditions, money and personal wealth, sex.
(K)	Best time for conversations (before, during, after meals?):	n/a
(L)	Forms of legal punishment:	jailing, hanging
(M)	Approximately length of time one could be detained by law and order authorities before being charged in court:	10 days
(N)	January 15, 1999, for example, will normally be written as:	15/1/1999
(O)	Emergency code number:	198
(P)	Ambulance code Number:	343.709-884826
(Q)	Police code number:	(505) 341.250 - 197 & 198
(R)	Telephone (country) code:	n/a
(S)	Telex (country) code:	n/a
(T)	Electricity requirements:	n/a
(U)	Legal drinking age:	20
(V)	Systems of weights and measures:	n/a
(W)	Legal age of incarceration:	20
(X)	Driving side of the road:	right
(Y)	Minimum expenditure expected of foreign visitors? $	n/a
(Z)	Name of currency:	Dinar
(Za)	Some places off-limits to foreign visitors:	n/a
(Zb)	Some places, structures and items prohibited from being photographed:	n/a

UGANDA	Is customary Is allowed Is permissible Is used. Is OK	Is not customary Is frowned upon	Is disallowed Is forbidden Is a crime	(See last page for comments on items referenced here)
Smoking in public	✓			
Eating in public		✓		
Not flushing public toilet	✓			
Spitting in public	✓			
Feeding animals & birds in public		✓		
Whistling in public	✓			
Drinking alcohol in public	✓			
Kissing in public		✓		
Breast feeding in public		✓		
Drunkenness (in public)			✓	
Cursing in public	✓			
Religious preaching in public	✓			
Begging (panhandling) in public	✓			
Giving money to beggars/panhandlers	✓			
Giving food/drink to beggars/panhandlers	✓			
Brushing teeth in public (other than in restrooms)		✓		
Strolling with pets in major public roads/streets	✓			
Chewing gum in public	✓			
Chewing gum in government offices		✓		
Combing hair in public (other than in toilets/restrooms)		✓		
Undressing/dressing in public	✓			
Wearing of dark glasses indoors in public places	✓			
Public display of wealth	✓			
Praying openly in public in non-designated areas	✓			
Walking bare feet in public	✓			
Chewing tobacco in public	✓			
Trimming one's finger or toe nails in public	✓			
Laughing aloud in public	✓			
Mingling of the sexes in public				n/a
Mixed bathing in public swimming pools				n/a
Distributing religious pamphlets (literature) in public/side streets				n/a

365

UGANDA

	Is customary Is allowed Is permissible Is used. Is OK	Is not customary Is frowned upon	Is disallowed Is forbidden Is a crime	(See last page for comments on items referenced here)
Dancing on side street		✓		
Nude bathing	✓			1
Littering		✓		
Binge Drinking	✓			
Hitchhiking	✓			
Jaywalking	✓			
Drunk driving			✓	
Speeding			✓	
Skating on side streets (side-walk)		✓		
Graffiti painting			✓	
Pilfering	✓			
Prostitution			✓	
Haggling in the market place				n/a
Consumption of alcoholic beverages in bars and restaurants				n/a
Gambling	✓			
Possession of pornographic materials	✓			
Possession of the Christian Bible	✓			
Possession of the Moslem Koran	✓			
Possession of bullet-proof vest		✓		
Possession of toy gun	✓			
Possession of fire crackers and fireworks	✓			2
Possession of prescription drugs (without doctor's note)	✓			3
Possession of regulated drugs (narcotics)			✓	
Possession of firearms (by foreigners)			✓	
Possession of pocket knife in public	✓			
Using walkie talkies	✓			
Using of "boom boxes"(loud sounding stereo system)	✓			
Using "walkman" (very small radio/cassettes with ear plugs) in public places	✓			
Using "walkman" (very small radio/cassettes with ear plugs) while driving or riding				n/a

UGANDA

	Is customary Is allowed Is permissible Is used Is OK	Is not customary Is frowned upon	Is disallowed Is forbidden Is a crime	(See last page for comments on items referenced here)
Use of cellular phone	✓			
Use of binoculars/periscopes other than in sports arena	✓			
Taking photographs of people (without their permission)		✓		
Taking photographs at airports, train and bus stations	✓			
Taking photographs of airports	✓			
Taking photographs of churches and synagogues	✓			
Taking photographs of religious statues	✓			
Taking photographs of public buildings				n/a
Taking photographs of bridges				n/a
Tipping (gratuity)	✓			
Tipping (when service is rendered)	✓			
Tipping (when service is not rendered)	✓			
Tipping waiters/waitresses at restaurants and hotels				n/a
Tipping taxi/cab drivers				n/a
Tipping baggage handlers, porters, door persons				n/a
Tipping of hair dressers/barbers				n/a
Overtipping	✓			
Undertipping	✓			
Spilling cigarette butt (ash) on side streets/on the floor	✓			
Men wearing lipstick		✓		
Wearing visible tattoo marks	✓			
Men painting/coloring their finger or toe nails		✓		
Cross dressing (men dressed like women & vice versa)		✓		
Walking in public without a shirt (i.e., with the upper half of the body naked)				n/a
Men wearing braided hair		✓		
Men wearing earrings		✓		
Men wearing dreadlock hair style		✓		
Homosexuality		✓		
Lesbianism		✓		

UGANDA

	Is customary Is allowed Is permissible Is used Is OK	Is not customary Is frowned upon	Is disallowed Is forbidden Is a crime	(See last page for comments on items referenced here)
Females covering their hair (wearing headgear) in public	✓			
Females exposing their full face in public	✓			
Females driving automobiles	✓			
Females riding motorcycles	✓			
Females riding bicycles	✓			
Females smoking in public	✓			
Women wearing bras (braziers) in public				4
Use of lipstick by women		✓		
A woman extending her hands first when introduced	✓			
Female bashing		✓		
Females wearing trousers	✓			
Females wearing minis (short dresses)	✓			
Females wearing bikinis		✓		
Females wearing shorts	✓			
Persons of opposite sex holding hands in public	✓			
Persons of same sex holding hands in public	✓			
Handshake between opposite sex	✓			
Hugging in public by same sex	✓			
Hugging in public by opposite sex	✓			
Men and women walking side by side in public				n/a
Man walking ahead (in public), with the woman following				n/a
Woman walking ahead (in public), with the man following				n/a
Men opening doors for women	✓			
Sitting with legs crossed in the presence of elders	✓			
Talking to an elderly person with one's hat/cap on				n/a
Talking to an elderly person with hands positioned on both sides of one's waist				n/a
Blowing one's nose in public	✓			
Blowing one's nose in the presence of others	✓			
Addressing people by their title	✓			

UGANDA

	Is customary Is allowed Is permissible Is used. Is OK	Is not customary Is frowned upon	Is disallowed Is forbidden Is a crime	(See last page for comments on items referenced here)
Addressing people by their family name/surname/last name/given name	✓			
Addressing people by their first name/ given name	✓			
Women going through doors first	✓			
Men helping women with their coats	✓			
Men extending their hands to women first during greetings		✓		
Taking off one's hat when entering a private home	✓			
Removing one's shoes when entering a private home				n/a
Invited guests bringing food at social gatherings	✓			
Guests bringing drinks at social gatherings	✓			
Shaking hands when leaving a small group	✓			
Shaking hands with everyone present, upon arrival at a social gathering	✓			
Eating with the right hand	✓			
Eating with the left hand	✓			
Eating with both hands	✓			
Presenting a gift or passing on an object with the left hand	✓			
Asking a man about his wife	✓			
Asking a woman about her husband	✓			
Making prior appointments before a meeting or visit	✓			
Addressing an audience with one or both hands in the pocket	✓			
Carrying on conversation during meals				n/a
Females sitting with legs crossed	✓			
People discussing their wealth	✓			
Asking someone his or her age, or how old the person is				n/a
Complementing someone on his/her physical looks				n/a
Complementing someone on his/her attire				n/a
Use of both hands in handshake	✓			
In greeting, a handshake accompanied by a slight bow	✓			

369

UGANDA

	Is customary Is allowed Is permissible Is used. Is OK	Is not customary Is frowned upon	Is disallowed Is forbidden Is a crime	(See last page for comments on items referenced here)
Salutations such as "Good morning", "good afternoon", "Good evening"	✓			
The completion of a business deal with a handshake				n/a
Starting a negotiation session with a handshake				n/a
A gift for the host/hostess	✓			
Giving a business gift	✓			
A gift of money (use of money as gift)	✓			
Use of flowers as a gift	✓			
Use of business cards	✓			
Accepting/presenting gifts with both hands	✓			
Burning of the country's flag	✓			
Mutilation of the national currency	✓			
Casual wearing of clothings made with colors & marks of the national flag				n/a
Wearing of look-alike military (camouflage) fatigues (attire)			✓	
Sitting on the floor (on floor mats)	✓			
Discussion of religion	✓			
Discussion of politics	✓			
Discussion of sex	✓			
Patting/slapping someone on the buttocks		✓		
Patting/slapping someone on the back	✓			
Touching or patting someone's head/hair	✓			
Casual touching of any part of someone's body				n/a
Drinking directly out of a bottle/can	✓			
Placing one's leg(s) on the table or chair	✓			

370

UGANDA

	Is customary Is allowed Is permissible Is used. Is OK	Is not customary Is frowned upon	Is disallowed Is forbidden Is a crime	(See last page for comments on items referenced here)
Showing the sole of one's foot (feet)				n/a
People standing very close when talking	✓			
Maintaining steady eye contact (direct gaze) when talking to someone	✓			
Kissing or exchange of kisses on the cheek	✓			
Counting money (change) in someone's palm				n/a
Finger pointing in public (in a daring manner)	✓			
Seeking attention by winking the eyes				n/a
Tapping the head to indicate someone is crazy				n/a
Twirling the head to indicate someone is crazy				n/a
Whistling as a way of requesting something/seeking attention				n/a
Using "thumbs-up" sign to mean OK				n/a
Forming a circle with the thumb and index finger (forefinger) to mean OK				n/a
Using the fingers to make a "V" sign for victory				n/a
Beckoning to someone with the index finger (forefinger)				n/a
The left to right waving of the hand with open palms facing outward to indicate "Good bye"				n/a
The use of a nod to show acknowledgement				n/a
Stopping/beckoning a taxi using a stretched hand with the thumb pointing upward				n/a
Using the thumb finger pointed to a direction, to request a ride or a hike				n/a
Raising one's hand/waving with an open fist to summon a taxi				n/a
Tapping one's foot/feet on the floor in a public gathering				n/a
Wiggling one's leg(s) when in a sitting position				n/a
Use of the hand (by motorists and cyclists) to signal direction of traffic				n/a

371

UGANDA

		(See last page for comments on items referenced here)
Foreign tourists are welcome in the country.	yes	
The use of seat belt is mandatory.	no	
International driving license is accepted.	yes	
Foreign drivers license is accepted.	yes	
It is considered impolite to yawn in public.	no	
Death penalty for drug trafficking is the law.	no	
Life imprisonment for drug trafficking is the law.	yes	
Guilty until proven innocent in court is the law.	no	
Innocent until proven guilty in court is the law.	yes	
Pedestrians always have right of way.	no	
Exit visas are required of visitors.	no	
Crash helmet is mandatory for motor cyclist.	no	
Hanging is used as a form of legal punishment.	yes	
Decapitation of a limb is used as a form of punishment.	no	
Caning is used as a form of legal punishment.	no	
Electric shock is used as a form of legal punishment.	no	
One is expected to stand up during the playing of the national anthem.	yes	
Crash helmet is mandatory for bicyclists.	no	
Guests are expected to eat every thing on their plates.	no	
Table manners are very informal.	yes	
One is expected to cover one's mouth when laughing.	no	
A vertical nod of the head means YES (OK).	yes	
A horizontal shaking of the head means NO (Not OK).	yes	
Prostitution is allowed only in designated areas.	no	
One is expected to take off one's hat during playing of national anthem.	no	
Separate seating arrangements (between sexes) are maintained at movies.	no	
Separate seating arrangements (between sexes) are maintained at churches.	no	
Uninvited visitors or guests may not be welcome, even among acquaintances.	no	
Pets (e.g. cats, dog) are allowed in some hotels and restaurants.	no	
Couples invited for a meal may be separated during meals according to their sex.	no	
Punctuality is the order of business.	yes	
Automobiles are driven with headlights always turned on.		n/a
Motorcycles are driven with headlights always turned on.		n/a
Visitors with expired visa face mandatory jail time.	no	
Visitors without exit visa face jail time.	no	
Visitors without entry visa face mandatory (automatic) jail time.	no	

ADDITIONAL COUNTRY INFORMATION

(A)	The types of gifts to avoid:	none
(B)	Appropriate gifts for a foreigner to give:	clothes and electronics
(C)	Best time to present gifts (at the beginning or at the end of a visit?):	end
(D)	Best time to present gifts (on initial or later visits?):	n/a
(E)	Best place to present gifts (in private or in public?):	n/a
(F)	Number(s) with certain connotations and/or myths attached to them:	n/a
(G)	Basic shape(s) with negative connotations:	n/a
(H)	Basic color(s) with negative connotations:	n/a
(I)	Traditional greeting methods include:	n/a
(J)	Safe topics for discussion include:	weather, fashion, travel, art, family, religion, domestic politics, food, sports, international politics, social conditions, money and personal wealth, sex.
(K)	Best time for conversations (before, during, after meals?):	n/a
(L)	Forms of legal punishment:	death by hanging & jailing
(M)	Approximately length of time one could be detained by law and order authorities before being charged in court:	24 hours
(N)	January 15, 1999, for example, will normally be written as:	15/1/99
(O)	Emergency code number:	999
(P)	Ambulance code Number:	999
(Q)	Police code number:	999
(R)	Telephone (country) code:	n/a
(S)	Telex (country) code:	n/a
(T)	Electricity requirements:	n/a
(U)	Legal drinking age:	16 (U)
(V)	Systems of weights and measures:	imperial
(W)	Legal age of incarceration:	16
(X)	Driving side of the road:	left
(Y)	Minimum expenditure expected of foreign visitors? $	no
(Z)	Name of currency:	shilling
Za)	Some places off-limits to foreign visitors:	n/a
Zb)	Some places, structures and items prohibited from being photographed:	n/a

ENDNOTES

Item Number:COMMENTS/EXPLANATIONS

N/A: Not applicable/Not available/No response

(1)   Okay in a private home and some lakes.

(2)   With police permission.

(3)   Depends on the type of regulated drugs.

(4)   Allowed on beaches and hotel swimming pools.

(U)   Not legally enforced.

ZAIRE	Is customary Is allowed Is permissible Is used. Is OK	Is not customary Is frowned upon	Is disallowed Is forbidden Is a crime	(See last page for comments on items referenced here)
Smoking in public	✓			
Eating in public	✓			
Not flushing public toilet		✓		
Spitting in public			✓	
Feeding animals & birds in public	✓			
Whistling in public		✓		
Drinking alcohol in public	✓			
Kissing in public		✓		
Breast feeding in public			✓	
Drunkenness (in public)			✓	
Cursing in public		✓		
Religious preaching in public		✓		
Begging (panhandling) in public	✓			
Giving money to beggars/panhandlers	✓			
Giving food/drink to beggars/panhandlers		✓		
Brushing teeth in public (other than in restrooms)	✓			
Strolling with pets in major public roads/streets		✓		
Chewing gum in public		✓		
Chewing gum in government offices		✓		
Combing hair in public (other than in toilets/restrooms)			✓	
Undressing/dressing in public	✓			
Wearing of dark glasses indoors in public places	✓			
Public display of wealth	✓			
Praying openly in public in non-designated areas		✓		
Walking bare feet in public	✓			
Chewing tobacco in public		✓		
Trimming one's finger or toe nails in public	✓			
Laughing aloud in public		✓		
Mingling of the sexes in public				n/a
Mixed bathing in public swimming pools				n/a
Distributing religious pamphlets (literature) in public/side streets				n/a

375

ZAIRE

	Is customary Is allowed Is permissible Is used. Is OK	Is not customary Is frowned upon	Is disallowed Is forbidden Is a crime	(See last page for comments on items referenced here)
Dancing on side street	✓			
Nude bathing			✓	
Littering		✓		
Binge Drinking		✓		
Hitchhiking		✓		
Jaywalking			✓	
Drunk driving			✓	
Speeding			✓	
Skating on side streets (side-walk)		✓		
Graffiti painting			✓	
Pilfering			✓	
Prostitution			✓	
Haggling in the market place				
Consumption of alcoholic beverages in bars and restaurants				n/a
Gambling		✓		
Possession of pornographic materials			✓	
Possession of the Christian Bible	✓			
Possession of the Moslem Koran	✓			
Possession of bullet-proof vest		✓		
Possession of toy gun		✓		
Possession of fire crackers and fireworks	✓			
Possession of prescription drugs (without doctor's note)	✓			
Possession of regulated drugs (narcotics)			✓	
Possession of firearms (by foreigners)			✓	
Possession of pocket knife in public		✓		
Using walkie talkies	✓			
Using of "boom boxes"(loud sounding stereo system)		✓		
Using "walkman" (very small radio/cassettes with ear plugs) in public places		✓		
Using "walkman" (very small radio/cassettes with ear plugs) while driving or riding				n/a

ZAIRE

	Is customary Is allowed Is permissible Is used Is OK	Is not customary Is frowned upon	Is disallowed Is forbidden Is a crime	(See last page for comments on items referenced here)
Use of cellular phone	✓			
Use of binoculars/periscopes other than in sports arena	✓			
Taking photographs of people (without their permission)			✓	
Taking photographs at airports, train and bus stations			✓	
Taking photographs of airports			✓	
Taking photographs of churches and synagogues	✓			
Taking photographs of religious statues	✓			
Taking photographs of public buildings				n/a
Taking photographs of bridges				n/a
Tipping (gratuity)	✓			
Tipping (when service is rendered)	✓			
Tipping (when service is not rendered)	✓			
Tipping waiters/waitresses at restaurants and hotels				n/a
Tipping taxi/cab drivers				n/a
Tipping baggage handlers, porters, door persons				n/a
Tipping of hair dressers/barbers				n/a
Overtipping		✓		
Undertipping		✓		
Spilling cigarette butt (ash) on side streets/on the floor	✓			
Men wearing lipstick		✓		
Wearing visible tattoo marks			✓	
Men painting/coloring their finger or toe nails		✓		
Cross dressing (men dressed like women & vice versa)			✓	
Walking in public without a shirt (i.e., with the upper half of the body naked)				n/a
Men wearing braided hair		✓		
Men wearing earrings		✓		
Men wearing dreadlock hair style		✓		
Homosexuality			✓	
Lesbianism			✓	

377

ZAIRE

	Is customary / Is allowed / Is permissible / Is used / Is OK	Is not customary / Is frowned upon	Is disallowed / Is forbidden / Is a crime	(See last page for comments on items referenced here)
Females covering their hair (wearing headgear) in public		✓		
Females exposing their full face in public		✓		
Females driving automobiles	✓			
Females riding motorcycles	✓			
Females riding bicycles	✓			
Females smoking in public	✓			
Women wearing bras (braziers) in public	✓			
Use of lipstick by women	✓			
A woman extending her hands first when introduced		✓		
Female bashing		✓		
Females wearing trousers		✓		
Females wearing minis (short dresses)		✓		
Females wearing bikinis			✓	
Females wearing shorts	✓			
Persons of opposite sex holding hands in public		✓		
Persons of same sex holding hands in public		✓		
Handshake between opposite sex	✓			
Hugging in public by same sex	✓			
Hugging in public by opposite sex	✓			
Men and women walking side by side in public				n/a
Man walking ahead (in public), with the woman following				n/a
Woman walking ahead (in public), with the man following				n/a
Men opening doors for women	✓			
Sitting with legs crossed in the presence of elders	✓			
Talking to an elderly person with one's hat/cap on				n/a
Talking to an elderly person with hands positioned on both sides of one's waist				n/a
Blowing one's nose in public	✓			
Blowing one's nose in the presence of others		✓		
Addressing people by their title	✓			

378

ZAIRE

	Is customary Is allowed Is permissible Is used. Is OK	Is not customary Is frowned upon	Is disallowed Is forbidden Is a crime	(See last page for comments on items referenced here)
Addressing people by their family name/surname/last name/given name	✓			
Addressing people by their first name/ given name	✓			
Women going through doors first	✓			
Men helping women with their coats	✓			
Men extending their hands to women first during greetings	✓			
Taking off one's hat when entering a private home	✓			
Removing one's shoes when entering a private home	✓			
Invited guests bringing food at social gatherings				n/a
Guests bringing drinks at social gatherings	✓			
Shaking hands when leaving a small group	✓			
Shaking hands with everyone present, upon arrival at a social gathering	✓			
Eating with the right hand	✓			
Eating with the left hand	✓			
Eating with both hands		✓		
Presenting a gift or passing on an object with the left hand		✓		
Asking a man about his wife		✓		
Asking a woman about her husband	✓			
Making prior appointments before a meeting or visit	✓			
Addressing an audience with one or both hands in the pocket		✓		
Carrying on conversation during meals				n/a
Females sitting with legs crossed	✓			
People discussing their wealth		✓		
Asking someone his or her age, or how old the person is				n/a
Complementing someone on his/her physical looks				n/a
Complementing someone on his/her attire				n/a
Use of both hands in handshake	✓			
In greeting, a handshake accompanied by a slight bow	✓			

379

	Is ✓ customary Is allowed Is permissible Is used. Is OK	Is not customary Is frowned upon	Is disallowed Is forbidden Is a crime	(See last page for comments on items referenced here)
Salutations such as "Good morning", "good afternoon", "Good evening"	✓			
The completion of a business deal with a handshake				n/a
Starting a negotiation session with a handshake				n/a
A gift for the host/hostess	✓			
Giving a business gift	✓			
A gift of money (use of money as gift)	✓			
Use of flowers as a gift	✓			
Use of business cards	✓			
Accepting/presenting gifts with both hands	✓			
Burning of the country's flag			✓	
Mutilation of the national currency	✓			
Casual wearing of clothings made with colors & marks of the national flag				n/a
Wearing of look-alike military (camouflage) fatigues (attire)			✓	
Sitting on the floor (on floor mats)		✓		
Discussion of religion	✓			
Discussion of politics	✓			
Discussion of sex		✓		
Patting/slapping someone on the buttocks	✓			
Patting/slapping someone on the back	✓			
Touching or patting someone's head/hair	✓			
Casual touching of any part of someone's body				n/a
Drinking directly out of a bottle/can	✓			
Placing one's leg(s) on the table or chair	✓			

ZAIRE

	Is customary Is allowed Is permissible Is used. Is OK	Is not customary Is frowned upon	Is disallowed Is forbidden Is a crime	(See last page for comments on items referenced here)
Showing the sole of one's foot (feet)				n/a
People standing very close when talking	✓			
Maintaining steady eye contact (direct gaze) when talking to someone	✓			
Kissing or exchange of kisses on the cheek		✓		
Counting money (change) in someone's palm				n/a
Finger pointing in public (in a daring manner)	✓			
Seeking attention by winking the eyes				n/a
Tapping the head to indicate someone is crazy				n/a
Twirling the head to indicate someone is crazy				n/a
Whistling as a way of requesting something/seeking attention				n/a
Using "thumbs-up" sign to mean OK				n/a
Forming a circle with the thumb and index finger (forefinger) to mean OK				n/a
Using the fingers to make a "V" sign for victory				n/a
Beckoning to someone with the index finger (forefinger)				n/a
The left to right waving of the hand with open palms facing outward to indicate "Good bye"				n/a
The use of a nod to show acknowledgement				n/a
Stopping/beckoning a taxi using a stretched hand with the thumb pointing upward				n/a
Using the thumb finger pointed to a direction, to request a ride or a hike				n/a
Raising one's hand/waving with an open fist to summon a taxi				n/a
Tapping one's foot/feet on the floor in a public gathering				n/a
Wiggling one's leg(s) when in a sitting position				n/a
Use of the hand (by motorists and cyclists) to signal direction of traffic				n/a

ZAIRE

		(See last page for comments on items referenced here)
Foreign tourists are welcome in the country.	yes	
The use of seat belt is mandatory.	no	
International driving license is accepted.	yes	
Foreign drivers license is accepted.	yes	
It is considered impolite to yawn in public.	yes	
Death penalty for drug trafficking is the law.	yes	
Life imprisonment for drug trafficking is the law.	yes	
Guilty until proven innocent in court is the law.	no	
Innocent until proven guilty in court is the law.	yes	
Pedestrians always have right of way.	yes	
Exit visas are required of visitors.	yes	
Crash helmet is mandatory for motor cyclist.	yes	
Hanging is used as a form of legal punishment.	yes	
Decapitation of a limb is used as a form of punishment.	no	
Caning is used as a form of legal punishment.	no	
Electric shock is used as a form of legal punishment.	no	
One is expected to stand up during the playing of the national anthem.	yes	
Crash helmet is mandatory for bicyclists.	yes	
Guests are expected to eat every thing on their plates.	yes	
Table manners are very informal.	no	
One is expected to cover one's mouth when laughing.	no	
A vertical nod of the head means YES (OK).	yes	
A horizontal shaking of the head means NO (Not OK).	yes	
Prostitution is allowed only in designated areas.	no	
One is expected to take off one's hat during playing of national anthem.	yes	
Separate seating arrangements (between sexes) are maintained at movies.	no	
Separate seating arrangements (between sexes) are maintained at churches.	no	
Uninvited visitors or guests may not be welcome, even among acquaintances.	yes	
Pets (e.g. cats, dog) are allowed in some hotels and restaurants.	yes	
Couples invited for a meal may be separated during meals according to their sex.	yes	
Punctuality is the order of business.	yes	
Automobiles are driven with headlights always turned on.	yes	
Motorcycles are driven with headlights always turned on.	yes	
Visitors with expired visa face mandatory jail time.	no	
Visitors without exit visa face jail time.	yes	
Visitors without entry visa face mandatory (automatic) jail time.	no	

ADDITIONAL COUNTRY INFORMATION

(A)	The types of gifts to avoid:	n/a
(B)	Appropriate gifts for a foreigner to give:	items on home decoration
(C)	Best time to present gifts (at the beginning or at the end of a visit?):	n/a
(D)	Best time to present gifts (on inital or later visits?):	n/a
(E)	Best place to present gifts (in private or in public?):	n/a
(F)	Number(s) with certain connotations and/or myths attached to them:	n/a
(G)	Basic shape(s) with negative connotations:	n/a
(H)	Basic color(s) with negative connotations:	n/a
(I)	Traditional greeting methods include:	n/a
(J)	Safe topics for discussion include:	travel, religion, politics, international politics, food
(K)	Best time for conversations (before, during, after meals?):	n/a
(L)	Forms of legal punishment:	hanging
(M)	Approximately length of time one could be detained by law and order authorities before being charged in court:	48 hours
(N)	January 15, 1999, for example, will normally be written as:	15/01/99
(O)	Emergency code number:	n/a
(P)	Ambulance code Number:	n/a
(Q)	Police code number:	n/a
(R)	Telephone (country) code:	n/a
(S)	Telex (country) code:	n/a
(T)	Electricity requirements:	n/a
(U)	Legal drinking age:	18 years
(V)	Systems of weights and measures:	n/a
(W)	Legal age of incarceration:	n/a
(X)	Driving side of the road:	left
(Y)	Minimum expenditure expected of foreign visitors? $	no
(Z)	Name of currency:	Zaire Currency
(Za)	Some places off-limits to foreign visitors:	military installations
(Zb)	Some places, structures and items prohibited from being photographed:	military installations

ZAMBIA	Is customary Is allowed Is permissible Is used. Is OK	Is not customary Is frowned upon	Is disallowed Is forbidden Is a crime	(See last page for comments on items referenced here)
Smoking in public	✓			
Eating in public	✓			
Not flushing public toilet		✓		
Spitting in public		✓		
Feeding animals & birds in public	✓			
Whistling in public	✓			
Drinking alcohol in public	✓			
Kissing in public		✓		
Breast feeding in public	✓			
Drunkenness (in public)	✓			
Cursing in public	✓			
Religious preaching in public	✓			
Begging (panhandling) in public	✓			
Giving money to beggars/panhandlers	✓			
Giving food/drink to beggars/panhandlers	✓			
Brushing teeth in public (other than in restrooms)	✓			
Strolling with pets in major public roads/streets	✓			
Chewing gum in public	✓			
Chewing gum in government offices		✓		
Combing hair in public (other than in toilets/restrooms)	✓			
Undressing/dressing in public		✓		
Wearing of dark glasses indoors in public places	✓			
Public display of wealth	✓			
Praying openly in public in non-designated areas	✓			
Walking bare feet in public	✓			
Chewing tobacco in public	✓			
Trimming one's finger or toe nails in public	✓			
Laughing aloud in public		✓		
Mingling of the sexes in public	✓			
Mixed bathing in public swimming pools	✓			
Distributing religious pamphlets (literature) in public/side streets	✓			

ZAMBIA

	Is customary Is allowed Is permissible Is used. Is OK	Is not customary Is frowned upon	Is disallowed Is forbidden Is a crime	(See last page for comments on items referenced here)
Dancing on side street		✓		
Nude bathing			✓	
Littering		✓		
Binge Drinking	✓			
Hitchhiking	✓			
Jaywalking	✓			
Drunk driving			✓	
Speeding			✓	
Skating on side streets (side-walk)	✓			
Graffiti painting			✓	
Pilfering			✓	
Prostitution		✓		
Haggling in the market place	✓			
Consumption of alcoholic beverages in bars and restaurants	✓			
Gambling			✓	
Possession of pornographic materials			✓	
Possession of the Christian Bible	✓			
Possession of the Moslem Koran	✓			
Possession of bullet-proof vest	✓			
Possession of toy gun	✓			
Possession of fire crackers and fireworks	✓			
Possession of prescription drugs (without doctor's note)	✓			
Possession of regulated drugs (narcotics)			✓	
Possession of firearms (by foreigners)			✓	1
Possession of pocket knife in public	✓			
Using walkie talkies	✓			
Using of "boom boxes"(loud sounding stereo system)		✓		
Using "walkman" (very small radio/cassettes with ear plugs) in public places	✓			
Using "walkman" (very small radio/cassettes with ear plugs) while driving or riding	✓			

ZAMBIA

	Is customary Is allowed Is permissible Is used Is OK	Is not customary Is frowned upon	Is disallowed Is forbidden Is a crime	(See last page for comments on items referenced here)
Use of cellular phone	✓			
Use of binoculars/periscopes other than in sports arena	✓			
Taking photographs of people (without their permission)	✓			
Taking photographs at airports, train and bus stations	✓			
Taking photographs of airports	✓			
Taking photographs of churches and synagogues	✓			
Taking photographs of religious statues	✓			
Taking photographs of public buildings	✓			
Taking photographs of bridges	✓			
Tipping (gratuity)	✓			
Tipping (when service is rendered)	✓			
Tipping (when service is not rendered)	✓			
Tipping waiters/waitresses at restaurants and hotels		✓		
Tipping taxi/cab drivers	✓			
Tipping baggage handlers, porters, door persons	✓			
Tipping of hair dressers/barbers	✓			
Overtipping	✓			
Undertipping	✓			
Spilling cigarette butt (ash) on side streets/on the floor	✓			
Men wearing lipstick		✓		
Wearing visible tattoo marks	✓			
Men painting/coloring their finger or toe nails		✓		
Cross dressing (men dressed like women & vice versa)		✓		
Walking in public without a shirt (i.e., with the upper half of the body naked)		✓		
Men wearing braided hair	✓			
Men wearing earrings	✓			
Men wearing dreadlock hair style	✓			
Homosexuality			✓	
Lesbianism			✓	

ZAMBIA

	Is customary Is allowed Is permissible Is used Is OK	Is not customary Is frowned upon	Is disallowed Is forbidden Is a crime	(See last page for comments on items referenced here)
Females covering their hair (wearing headgear) in public	✓			
Females exposing their full face in public	✓			
Females driving automobiles	✓			
Females riding motorcycles	✓	✓		
Females riding bicycles	✓			
Females smoking in public	✓			
Women wearing bras (braziers) in public	✓			
Use of lipstick by women	✓			
A woman extending her hands first when introduced	✓			
Female bashing		✓		
Females wearing trousers	✓			
Females wearing minis (short dresses)		✓		
Females wearing bikinis		✓		
Females wearing shorts		✓		
Persons of opposite sex holding hands in public	✓			
Persons of same sex holding hands in public	✓			
Handshake between opposite sex	✓			
Hugging in public by same sex	✓			
Hugging in public by opposite sex	✓			
Men and women walking side by side in public	✓			
Man walking ahead (in public), with the woman following	✓			
Woman walking ahead (in public), with the man following	✓			
Men opening doors for women		✓		
Sitting with legs crossed in the presence of elders			✓	
Talking to an elderly person with one's hat/cap on			✓	
Talking to an elderly person with hands positioned on both sides of one's waist			✓	
Blowing one's nose in public			✓	
Blowing one's nose in the presence of others	✓			
Addressing people by their title	✓			

ZAMBIA

	Is customary Is allowed Is permissible Is used. Is OK	Is not customary Is frowned upon	Is disallowed Is forbidden Is a crime	(See last page for comments on items referenced here)
Addressing people by their family name/surname/last name/given name	✓			
Addressing people by their first name/ given name	✓			2
Women going through doors first	✓			
Men helping women with their coats		✓		
Men extending their hands to women first during greetings	✓			
Taking off one's hat when entering a private home	✓			
Removing one's shoes when entering a private home		✓		
Invited guests bringing food at social gatherings		✓		
Guests bringing drinks at social gatherings	✓			
Shaking hands when leaving a small group	✓			
Shaking hands with everyone present, upon arrival at a social gathering	✓			
Eating with the right hand	✓			
Eating with the left hand		✓		
Eating with both hands		✓		3
Presenting a gift or passing on an object with the left hand	✓			
Asking a man about his wife	✓			4
Asking a woman about her husband	✓			4
Making prior appointments before a meeting or visit		✓		
Addressing an audience with one or both hands in the pocket		✓		
Carrying on conversation during meals		✓		
Females sitting with legs crossed		✓		
People discussing their wealth	✓			
Asking someone his or her age, or how old the person is		✓		
Complementing someone on his/her physical looks	✓			
Complementing someone on his/her attire	✓			
Use of both hands in handshake	✓			
In greeting, a handshake accompanied by a slight bow	✓			

388

ZAMBIA

	Is customary Is allowed Is permissible Is used. Is OK	Is not customary Is frowned upon	Is disallowed Is forbidden Is a crime	(See last page for comments on items referenced here)
Salutations such as "Good morning", "good afternoon", "Good evening"	✓			
The completion of a business deal with a handshake	✓			
Starting a negotiation session with a handshake	✓			
A gift for the host/hostess	✓			
Giving a business gift		✓		
A gift of money (use of money as gift)	✓			5
Use of flowers as a gift	✓			
Use of business cards	✓			
Accepting/presenting gifts with both hands	✓			
Burning of the country's flag			✓	
Mutilation of the national currency			✓	
Casual wearing of clothings made with colors & marks of the national flag	✓			
Wearing of look-alike military (camouflage) fatigues (attire)			✓	
Sitting on the floor (on floor mats)	✓			6
Discussion of religion	✓			
Discussion of politics	✓			
Discussion of sex		✓		
Patting/slapping someone on the buttocks		✓		
Patting/slapping someone on the back	✓			
Touching or patting someone's head/hair		✓		
Casual touching of any part of someone's body	✓			
Drinking directly out of a bottle/can	✓	✓		
Placing one's leg(s) on the table or chair		✓		

389

ZAMBIA

	Is customary Is allowed Is permissible Is used. Is OK	Is not customary Is frowned upon	Is disallowed Is forbidden Is a crime	(See last page for comments on items referenced here)
Showing the sole of one's foot (feet)	✓			
People standing very close when talking		✓		
Maintaining steady eye contact (direct gaze) when talking to someone		✓		
Kissing or exchange of kisses on the cheek		✓		
Counting money (change) in someone's palm	✓			
Finger pointing in public (in a daring manner)		✓		
Seeking attention by winking the eyes	✓			
Tapping the head to indicate someone is crazy	✓			
Twirling the head to indicate someone is crazy		✓		
Whistling as a way of requesting something/seeking attention		✓		
Using "thumbs-up" sign to mean OK	✓			
Forming a circle with the thumb and index finger (forefinger) to mean OK		✓		
Using the fingers to make a "V" sign for victory	✓			
Beckoning to someone with the index finger (forefinger)		✓		
The left to right waving of the hand with open palms facing outward to indicate "Good bye"	✓			
The use of a nod to show acknowledgement	✓			
Stopping/beckoning a taxi using a stretched hand with the thumb pointing upward	✓			
Using the thumb finger pointed to a direction, to request a ride or a hike	✓			
Raising one's hand/waving with an open fist to summon a taxi	✓			
Tapping one's foot/feet on the floor in a public gathering		✓		
Wiggling one's leg(s) when in a sitting position	✓			
Use of the hand (by motorists and cyclists) to signal direction of traffic	✓			

		(See last page for comments on items referenced here)
Foreign tourists are welcome in the country.	yes	
The use of seat belt is mandatory.	yes	
International driving license is accepted.	yes	
Foreign drivers license is accepted.	yes	
It is considered impolite to yawn in public.	no	
Death penalty for drug trafficking is the law.	no	
Life imprisonment for drug trafficking is the law.	no	
Guilty until proven innocent in court is the law.	no	
Innocent until proven guilty in court is the law.	yes	
Pedestrians always have right of way.	yes	
Exit visas are required of visitors.	no	
Crash helmet is mandatory for motor cyclist.	yes	
Hanging is used as a form of legal punishment.	yes	
Decapitation of a limb is used as a form of punishment.	no	
Caning is used as a form of legal punishment.	yes	
Electric shock is used as a form of legal punishment.	no	
One is expected to stand up during the playing of the national anthem.	yes	
Crash helmet is mandatory for bicyclists.	no	
Guests are expected to eat every thing on their plates.	no	
Table manners are very informal.	no	
One is expected to cover one's mouth when laughing.	no	
A vertical nod of the head means YES (OK).	yes	
A horizontal shaking of the head means NO (Not OK).	yes	
Prostitution is allowed only in designated areas.	no	
One is expected to take off one's hat during playing of national anthem.	yes	
Separate seating arrangements (between sexes) are maintained at movies.	no	
Separate seating arrangements (between sexes) are maintained at churches.	yes	
Uninvited visitors or guests may not be welcome, even among acquaintances.	no	
Pets (e.g. cats, dog) are allowed in some hotels and restaurants.	no	
Couples invited for a meal may be separated during meals according to their sex.	yes and no	
Punctuality is the order of business.	no	
Automobiles are driven with headlights always turned on.	no	
Motorcycles are driven with headlights always turned on.	yes	
Visitors with expired visa face mandatory jail time.	no	7
Visitors without exit visa face jail time.	no	
Visitors without entry visa face mandatory (automatic) jail time.	no	8

ADDITIONAL COUNTRY INFORMATION

(A)	The types of gifts to avoid:	items associated with witchcraft, death, sex, etc.
(B)	Appropriate gifts for a foreigner to give:	cosmetics, electronic, jewelry
(C)	Best time to present gifts (at the beginning or at the end of a visit?):	n/a
(D)	Best time to present gifts (on initial or later visits?):	depends on the occasions
(E)	Best place to present gifts (in private or in public?):	home/office
(F)	Number(s) with certain connotations and/or myths attached to them:	n/a
(G)	Basic shape(s) with negative connotations:	n/a
(H)	Basic color(s) with negative connotations:	black - bad omen, sadness
(I)	Traditional greeting methods include:	clapping of hands, shaking hands, verbal
(J)	Safe topics for discussion include:	weather, fashion, travel, art, family, religion, domestic politics, food, sports, international politics, social conditions, money
(K)	Best time for conversations (before, during, after meals?):	after a meal
(L)	Forms of legal punishment:	flogging, jailing, hanging, fines
(M)	Approximately length of time one could be detained by law and order authorities before being charged in court:	24 hrs.
(N)	January 15, 1999, for example, will normally be written as:	15/1/99
(O)	Emergency code number:	993 fire
(P)	Ambulance code Number:	992
(Q)	Police code number:	991
(R)	Telephone (country) code:	260
(S)	Telex (country) code:	95
(T)	Electricity requirements:	220 - 240 volts
(U)	Legal drinking age:	18
(V)	Systems of weights and measures:	metric
(W)	Legal age of incarceration:	18
(X)	Driving side of the road:	left
(Y)	Minimum expenditure expected of foreign visitors? $	no minimum
(Z)	Name of currency:	Kwacha
(Za)	Some places off-limits to foreign visitors:	military installations
(Zb)	Some places, structures and items prohibited from being photographed:	military installations

ENDNOTES

Item Number: COMMENTS/EXPLANATIONS

n/a: Not applicable/Not available/No response
(1)   Need license
(2)   Depends on the occasion
(3)   No/yes, depends on the type of food
(4)   Depends on the context
(5)   To the poor, not to business people
(6)   Yes, where there are no seats
(7)   Yes/no, brief detention, fine, and deportation
(8)   Detention and deportation

ZIMBABWE	Is customary Is allowed Is permissible Is used. Is OK	Is not customary Is frowned upon	Is disallowed Is forbidden Is a crime	(See last page for comments on items referenced here)
Smoking in public	✓			
Eating in public	✓			
Not flushing public toilet			✓	
Spitting in public			✓	
Feeding animals & birds in public			✓	
Whistling in public		✓		
Drinking alcohol in public			✓	
Kissing in public		✓		
Breast feeding in public	✓			
Drunkenness (in public)			✓	
Cursing in public			✓	
Religious preaching in public	✓			
Begging (panhandling) in public			✓	
Giving money to beggars/panhandlers			✓	
Giving food/drink to beggars/panhandlers			✓	
Brushing teeth in public (other than in restrooms)		✓		
Strolling with pets in major public roads/streets			✓	
Chewing gum in public		✓		
Chewing gum in government offices			✓	
Combing hair in public (other than in toilets/restrooms)		✓		
Undressing/dressing in public			✓	
Wearing of dark glasses indoors in public places		✓		
Public display of wealth		✓		
Praying openly in public in non-designated areas	✓			
Walking bare feet in public	✓			
Chewing tobacco in public	✓			
Trimming one's finger or toe nails in public		✓		
Laughing aloud in public	✓			
Mingling of the sexes in public	✓			
Mixed bathing in public swimming pools	✓			
Distributing religious pamphlets (literature) in public/side streets	✓			

ZIMBABWE

	Is customary Is allowed Is permissible Is used. Is OK	Is not customary Is frowned upon	Is disallowed Is forbidden Is a crime	(See last page for comments on items referenced here)
Dancing on side street	✓			
Nude bathing			✓	
Littering			✓	
Binge Drinking		✓		
Hitchhiking	✓			
Jaywalking		✓		
Drunk driving			✓	
Speeding			✓	
Skating on side streets (side-walk)		✓		
Graffiti painting			✓	
Pilfering			✓	
Prostitution			✓	
Haggling in the market place	✓			
Consumption of alcoholic beverages in bars and restaurants	✓			
Gambling			✓	1
Possession of pornographic materials			✓	2
Possession of the Christian Bible	✓			
Possession of the Moslem Koran	✓			
Possession of bullet-proof vest	✓			
Possession of toy gun		✓		
Possession of fire crackers and fireworks		✓		
Possession of prescription drugs (without doctor's note)			✓	3
Possession of regulated drugs (narcotics)			✓	
Possession of firearms (by foreigners)			✓	
Possession of pocket knife in public			✓	
Using walkie talkies	✓			
Using of "boom boxes"(loud sounding stereo system)		✓		
Using "walkman" (very small radio/cassettes with ear plugs) in public places	✓			
Using "walkman" (very small radio/cassettes with ear plugs) while driving or riding			✓	

	Is customary Is allowed Is permissible Is used Is OK	Is not customary Is frowned upon	Is disallowed Is forbidden Is a crime	(See last page for comments on items referenced here)
Use of cellular phone	✓			
Use of binoculars/periscopes other than in sports arena	✓			
Taking photographs of people (without their permission)		✓		
Taking photographs at airports, train and bus stations			✓	
Taking photographs of airports			✓	
Taking photographs of churches and synagogues	✓			
Taking photographs of religious statues	✓			
Taking photographs of public buildings			✓	
Taking photographs of bridges			✓	
Tipping (gratuity)	✓			
Tipping (when service is rendered)	✓			
Tipping (when service is not rendered)			✓	
Tipping waiters/waitresses at restaurants and hotels	✓			
Tipping taxi/cab drivers	✓			
Tipping baggage handlers, porters, door persons	✓			
Tipping of hair dressers/barbers	✓			
Overtipping	✓			
Undertipping		✓		
Spilling cigarette butt (ash) on side streets/on the floor		✓		
Men wearing lipstick			✓	
Wearing visible tattoo marks		✓		
Men painting/coloring their finger or toe nails			✓	
Cross dressing (men dressed like women & vice versa)			✓	
Walking in public without a shirt (i.e., with the upper half of the body naked)			✓	
Men wearing braided hair		✓		
Men wearing earrings		✓		
Men wearing dreadlock hair style	✓			
Homosexuality			✓	
Lesbianism			✓	

ZIMBABWE

	Is customary Is allowed Is permissible Is used Is OK	Is not customary Is frowned upon	Is disallowed Is forbidden Is a crime	(See last page for comments on items referenced here)
Females covering their hair (wearing headgear) in public	✓			
Females exposing their full face in public	✓			
Females driving automobiles	✓			
Females riding motorcycles	✓			
Females riding bicycles	✓			
Females smoking in public	✓			
Women wearing bras (braziers) in public			✓	
Use of lipstick by women	✓			
A woman extending her hands first when introduced	✓			
Female bashing			✓	
Females wearing trousers	✓			
Females wearing minis (short dresses)		✓		
Females wearing bikinis	✓			4
Females wearing shorts	✓			
Persons of opposite sex holding hands in public	✓			
Persons of same sex holding hands in public	✓			
Handshake between opposite sex	✓			
Hugging in public by same sex	✓			
Hugging in public by opposite sex	✓			
Men and women walking side by side in public	✓			
Man walking ahead (in public), with the woman following	✓			
Woman walking ahead (in public), with the man following	✓			
Men opening doors for women	✓			
Sitting with legs crossed in the presence of elders	✓			
Talking to an elderly person with one's hat/cap on		✓		
Talking to an elderly person with hands positioned on both sides of one's waist		✓		
Blowing one's nose in public	✓			
Blowing one's nose in the presence of others	✓			
Addressing people by their title	✓			

ZIMBABWE

	Is customary Is allowed Is permissible Is used. Is OK	Is not customary Is frowned upon	Is disallowed Is forbidden Is a crime	(See last page for comments on items referenced here)
Addressing people by their family name/surname/last name/given name	✓			
Addressing people by their first name/ given name	✓			
Women going through doors first	✓			
Men helping women with their coats	✓			
Men extending their hands to women first during greetings	✓			
Taking off one's hat when entering a private home	✓			
Removing one's shoes when entering a private home				5
Invited guests bringing food at social gatherings				
Guests bringing drinks at social gatherings				
Shaking hands when leaving a small group	✓			
Shaking hands with everyone present, upon arrival at a social gathering	✓			
Eating with the right hand	✓			
Eating with the left hand				6
Eating with both hands		✓		
Presenting a gift or passing on an object with the left hand		✓		
Asking a man about his wife				7
Asking a woman about her husband				7
Making prior appointments before a meeting or visit	✓			
Addressing an audience with one or both hands in the pocket		✓		
Carrying on conversation during meals	✓			
Females sitting with legs crossed		✓		
People discussing their wealth				8
Asking someone his or her age, or how old the person is	✓			
Complementing someone on his/her physical looks	✓			
Complementing someone on his/her attire	✓			
Use of both hands in handshake	✓			
In greeting, a handshake accompanied by a slight bow	✓			

ZIMBABWE

	Is customary Is allowed Is permissible Is used. Is OK	Is not customary Is frowned upon	Is disallowed Is forbidden Is a crime	(See last page for comments on items referenced here)
Salutations such as "Good morning", "good afternoon", "Good evening"	✓			
The completion of a business deal with a handshake	✓			
Starting a negotiation session with a handshake	✓			
A gift for the host/hostess	✓			
Giving a business gift		✓		
A gift of money (use of money as gift)	✓			
Use of flowers as a gift	✓			
Use of business cards	✓			
Accepting/presenting gifts with both hands	✓			
Burning of the country's flag			✓	
Mutilation of the national currency			✓	
Casual wearing of clothings made with colors & marks of the national flag			✓	
Wearing of look-alike military (camouflage) fatigues (attire)			✓	
Sitting on the floor (on floor mats)				9
Discussion of religion	✓			
Discussion of politics	✓			
Discussion of sex		✓		
Patting/slapping someone on the buttocks			✓	
Patting/slapping someone on the back		✓		
Touching or patting someone's head/hair		✓		
Casual touching of any part of someone's body			✓	
Drinking directly out of a bottle/can	✓			
Placing one's leg(s) on the table or chair		✓		

399

ZIMBABWE

	Is customary Is allowed Is permissible Is used. Is OK	Is not customary Is frowned upon	Is disallowed Is forbidden Is a crime	(See last page for comments on items referenced here)
Showing the sole of one's foot (feet)		✓		
People standing very close when talking		✓		
Maintaining steady eye contact (direct gaze) when talking to someone		✓		10
Kissing or exchange of kisses on the cheek	✓			
Counting money (change) in someone's palm	✓			
Finger pointing in public (in a daring manner)		✓		
Seeking attention by winking the eyes		✓		
Tapping the head to indicate someone is crazy		✓		
Twirling the head to indicate someone is crazy		✓		
Whistling as a way of requesting something/seeking attention		✓		
Using "thumbs-up" sign to mean OK	✓			
Forming a circle with the thumb and index finger (forefinger) to mean OK		✓		
Using the fingers to make a "V" sign for victory		✓		
Beckoning to someone with the index finger (forefinger)		✓		
The left to right waving of the hand with open palms facing outward to indicate "Good bye"	✓			
The use of a nod to show acknowledgement	✓			
Stopping/beckoning a taxi using a stretched hand with the thumb pointing upward	✓			
Using the thumb finger pointed to a direction, to request a ride or a hike	✓			
Raising one's hand/waving with an open fist to summon a taxi	✓			
Tapping one's foot/feet on the floor in a public gathering		✓		
Wiggling one's leg(s) when in a sitting position		✓		
Use of the hand (by motorists and cyclists) to signal direction of traffic	✓			

ZIMBABWE

		(See last page for comments on items referenced here)
Foreign tourists are welcome in the country.	yes	
The use of seat belt is mandatory.	yes	
International driving license is accepted.	yes	
Foreign drivers license is accepted.	yes	11
It is considered impolite to yawn in public.	yes	11
Death penalty for drug trafficking is the law.	no	
Life imprisonment for drug trafficking is the law.	yes	12
Guilty until proven innocent in court is the law.	no	
Innocent until proven guilty in court is the law.	yes	
Pedestrians always have right of way.	no	13
Exit visas are required of visitors.	no	
Crash helmet is mandatory for motor cyclist.	yes	
Hanging is used as a form of legal punishment.	yes	
Decapitation of a limb is used as a form of punishment.	no	
Caning is used as a form of legal punishment.	yes	
Electric shock is used as a form of legal punishment.	no	
One is expected to stand up during the playing of the national anthem.	yes	
Crash helmet is mandatory for bicyclists.	no	
Guests are expected to eat every thing on their plates.	no	
Table manners are very informal.	no	
One is expected to cover one's mouth when laughing.	no	
A vertical nod of the head means YES (OK).	yes	
A horizontal shaking of the head means NO (Not OK).	yes	
Prostitution is allowed only in designated areas.	no	
One is expected to take off one's hat during playing of national anthem.	yes	
Separate seating arrangements (between sexes) are maintained at movies.	no	
Separate seating arrangements (between sexes) are maintained at churches.	no	
Uninvited visitors or guests may not be welcome, even among acquaintances.	no	
Pets (e.g. cats, dog) are allowed in some hotels and restaurants.	no	
Couples invited for a meal may be separated during meals according to their sex.	no	
Punctuality is the order of business.	yes	
Automobiles are driven with headlights always turned on.	no	14
Motorcycles are driven with headlights always turned on.	no	14
Visitors with expired visa face mandatory jail time.	no	15
Visitors without exit visa face jail time.	no	15
Visitors without entry visa face mandatory (automatic) jail time.	no	15

ADDITIONAL COUNTRY INFORMATION

(A)	The types of gifts to avoid:	illegal things
(B)	Appropriate gifts for a foreigner to give:	electrical items e.g. videos
(C)	Best time to present gifts (at the beginning or at the end of a visit?):	beginning
(D)	Best time to present gifts (on initial or later visits?):	initial
(E)	Best place to present gifts (in private or in public?):	depends on purpose and nature of gift
(F)	Number(s) with certain connotations and/or myths attached to them:	none
(G)	Basic shape(s) with negative connotations:	none
(H)	Basic color(s) with negative connotations:	none
(I)	Traditional greeting methods include:	handshake
(J)	Safe topics for discussion include:	weather, fashion, travel, art, family, religion, domestic politics, food, sports, international politics, social conditions, money and personal wealth
(K)	Best time for conversations (before, during, after meals?):	any time
(L)	Forms of legal punishment:	jailing
(M)	Approximately length of time one could be detained by law and order authorities before being charged in court:	48 hours
(N)	January 15, 1999, for example, will normally be written as:	15/1/99
(O)	Emergency code number:	99
(P)	Ambulance code Number:	99
(Q)	Police code number:	99
(R)	Telephone (country) code:	263
(S)	Telex (country) code:	n/a
(T)	Electricity requirements:	220
(U)	Legal drinking age:	18
(V)	Systems of weights and measures:	metric
(W)	Legal age of incarceration:	18
(X)	Driving side of the road:	left
(Y)	Minimum expenditure expected of foreign visitors? $	none
(Z)	Name of currency:	Zimbabwe dollar
(Za)	Some places off-limits to foreign visitors:	state house and other public buildings
(Zb)	Some places, structures and items prohibited from being photographed:	airports, bridges, parliament building, military installations.

ENDNOTES

Item Number: COMMENTS/EXPLANATIONS

n/a: Not applicable/Not available/No response

(1) Gambling is only acceptable in Casinos.

(2) Zimbabwe is a politically stable country, wearing bullet proof clothing is not necessary.

(3) You need license from the police.

(4) In hotels, swimming pools, yes; but not in public (Zimbabwe is landlocked and does not have beaches).

(5) It is not necessary or expected but if you wish you can do so after consulting your host.

(6) It is acceptable if you are left handed.

(7) Depends on the motive of your question: If it is out of genuine concern it is acceptable.

(8) It is acceptable as long as you do not attract thieves.

(9) When chairs or seats are not available otherwise this might be taken as being rude.

(10) It really depends on the nature of discussion and with whom you are talking to otherwise it is acceptable.

(11) Acceptable for temporary periods.

(12) Long jail terms of up to twenty years.

(13) Except where there are pedestrian crossing lines or robot controlled.

(14) Only during the night.

(15) They are deported.

APPENDIX A

INTERNATIONAL GUIDE TO TIPPING*

	HOTELS	TAXIS	OTHERS
ANDORRA	10-20%	10%	YES
ANGUILLA	D	D	YES
ANTIGUA & BARBUDA	10%	D	YES
ARGENTINA	10-22%	10%	YES
ARMENIA	YES	OD	OD
AUSTRALIA	10%	D	YES
AUSTRIA	10-15%	10%	YES
AZERBAIJAN	YES	OD	OD
BAHAMAS	15%	15%	YES
BANGLADESH	5-10%	5-10%	YES
BARBADOS	10%	10%	YES
BELARUS	YES	OD	OD
BELGIUM	15%	D	YES
BELIZE	D 10%	D	YES
BENIN	D	D	D
BOLIVIA	10-23%	D	YES
BRAZIL	D	YES	
BURMA	10%	10%	YES
CAMEROON	10%	D	YES
CANADA	15-20%	15-20%	YES
CAYMAN IS	NC 10-15%	NC	YES
CHILE	10%	NC	YES
CHINA, PEOPLES REP.	F	F	F
CHINA, TAIWAN	D 10%	D 10%	YES
COLUMBIA	10%	NC	YES
COSTA RICA	10%	NC	YES
COTE D'IVOIRE	5-10%	5-10%	YES
CYPRUS	10%	NT	YES
CZECHOSLOVAKIA	OD 5-10%	5-10%	YES
DENMARK	15%	upto 15%	YES
DOMINICA	10%	D	YES
DOMINICAN REP.	10%		
ECUADOR	10%	NC	YES
EGYPT	10-12%	10%	YES
ETHIOPIA	5-10%	NC	YES
FIJI	D	D	YES
FINLAND	14-15%	NT	YES
FRANCE	upto 25%	15%	YES
FRENCH GUIANA	12 1/2%	NC	YES
GERMANY	10%	5%	YES
GHANA	YES	YES	YES
GIBRALTAR	10-12%	10%	YES
GREECE	10-15%	10%	YES
GRENADA	D	D	YES
GUADELOUPE	10-15%	YES	
GUATEMALA	10%	10%	YES

405

GUINEA	D	D	YES
GUYANA	10%	10%	YES
HAITI	NC 10%	D	YES
HONDURAS	10%	10%	YES
HONG KONG	10-15%	10%	YES
HUNGARY	OD 10-15%	YES	YES
ICELAND	NC	NC	NC
INDIA	10%	NC	YES
INDONESIA	NC 10%	NC 10%	YES
IRELAND	10-15%	YES	YES
ISRAEL	10%	NC	YES
ITALY	12-15%	15%	YES
JAMAICA	15%	10-20%	YES
JAPAN	NC 10-20%	NC	YES
JORDAN	10%	10%	YES
KAZAKHSTAN	OD	OD	OD
KENYA	10-15%	10%	YES
KOREA, SOUTH	NC 10%	NC 10-15%	YES
KUWAIT	10%	D	YES
KYRGYZSTAN	OD	OD	OD
LATVIA	NT	10-20%	YES
LIBERIA	10-15%	NC	YES
LIECHTENSTEIN	10-15%		
LITHUANIA	NC	NC	NC
LUXEMBOURG	NC 10-20%	15-20%	YES
MALAYSIA	NC 10%	NC 10%	YES
MALTA	10%	10%	YES
MARTINIQUE	10-15%	D	YES
MEXICO	7-15%	D	YES
MOLDOVA	OD	OD	OD
MONTSERRAT	10%	10%	YES
MOROCCO	10-15%	10-15%	YES
NEPAL		YES	
NETHERLANDS	15%	10-15%	YES
NEW CALEDONIA		F	F
NEW ZEALAND	NC 10%	NC	
NICARAGUA	10%	NC	YES
NIGERIA	10%	D	YES
NORWAY	15%	D	YES
PAKISTAN	5-10%	D	YES
PANAMA	10-15%	NC	YES
PAPUA NEW GUINEA	NC	NC	NC
PARAGUAY	10%	5-12%	YES
PERU	5-10%	NC	YES
PHILIPPINES	10%	D 10%	YES
POLAND	10%	10%	YES
PORTUGAL	10-15%	15%	YES
ROMANIA	NC	NC	
RUSSIA	10-15%	10-15%	YES
SAUDI ARABIA	10-15%	NC	YES
SENEGAL	10%	D	YES
SEYCHELLES	10%	D	YES
SINGAPORE	OD	10%	OD
SOUTH AFRICA	10%	10%	YES
SPAIN	5-10%	10-15%	YES
SRI LANKA	10%	D	YES

ST. KITTS	D	D	YES
ST. LUCIA	10%	10%	YES
ST. VINCENT	10-15%	10-15%	YES
ST. MAARTEN	10%	10%	YES
SURINAME	10%	NC	YES
SWEDEN	12-15%	10-15%	YES
SWITZERLAND	12-15%	12-15%	YES
TAJIKISTAN	OD	OD	OD
TANZANIA	5%	(OD) D	YES
THAILAND	D 10%	NC	YES
TOGO	OD	OD	
TRINIDAD & TOBAGO	10%	10-15%	YES
TUNISIA	10%	10%	YES
TURKEY	10-15%	D	YES
TURKMENISTAN	OD	OD	OD
UKRAINE	OD	OD	OD
UNITED KINGDOM	12-15%	10-15%	YES
UNITED STATES OF AMERICA	15%-20%	15%	YES
URUGUAY	10%	10%	YES
UZBEKISTAN	OD	OD	OD
VENEZUELA	10%	NC	YES
YUGOSLAVIA	10%	10%	YES
ZAIRE	10%	D	YES
ZAMBIA	10%	OD	YES

xxx   YES, persons who perform other services such as porters, luggage handlers, door persons, etc. may be tipped or may expect to be tipped. Tipping and amount of tip is at your discretion.

D   =   Tipping is expected. Amount of tip is at your discretion.

OF   =   Tipping is Officially Discouraged although privately welcome.

NC   =   Tipping is not customary, nevertheless welcome.

NT   =   Not usually tipped

F   =   Tipping is prohibited

APPENDIX B

INTERNATIONAL ELECTRICITY REQUIREMENTS

COUNTRIES: (Volts/AC)

AFGHANISTAN	20/50 AC	DOMINICA	220-240/50 AC
ALGERIA	110-115/50, 220/50 AC*	DOMINICAN REP.	110/60 AC
ANDORRA	125/50 AC	ECUADOR	110/60 AC
ANGUILLA	220	EGYPT	220/50, 110-120/50*
ANTIGUA	110/60 AC	EL SALVADOR	110/60
ARGENTINA	220/60 AC	ESTONIA	220/50
ARMENIA	220/50	EQUAT. GUINEA	220/50
AUSTRALIA	240 AC	ETHIOPIA	220/60 AC
AUSTRIA	220/50	FIJI	240/50 AC
AZERBAIJAN	220/50	FINLAND	220/60 AC
BAHAMAS	120/60 AC	FRANCE	220/50
BAHRAIN	220/50 AC	FRENCH GUIANA	220 & 110/50 AC
BANGLADESH	220 AC	GABON	220/240/50
BARBADOS	110/50 AC	GEORGIA	220/50
BELGIUM	220/50 AC	GERMANY	220/50 AC
BELIZE	110/220/60 AC	GHANA	220-240/50 AC
BENIN	220/50	GIBRALTAR	240-250/50 AC
BERMUDA	110/60 AC	GREECE+	220/50 AC
BHUTAN	110-220/50 AC*	GRENADA	220-240/50 AC
BOTSWANA	220	GUADELOUPE	220/50 AC
BRAZIL+	110/60; 220/60, 127/60 AC*	GUAM	120/60 AC
BRITISH VIRGIN IS	115-210/60 AC	GUATEMALA	110/60 AC
BULGARIA	220/50 AC	GUINEA	220/50
BURKINA FASO	220/50	GUYANA	110-120/60 AC
BURMA	220/50 AC	HAITI	110/60 AC
BURUNDI	220/50	HONDURAS	110 or 220/60 AC*
BYELARUS	220/50	HONG KONG++	200-220/60 AC
CAMEROON	110-220	HUNGARY	220/50 AC
CANADA	110/60 AC	ICELAND	220/50 AC
CAYMAN ISLANDS	110/60 AC	INDIA+	220/50 AC
CENTRAL AF. REP.	220	INDONESIA	220/50 AC
CHAD	220	IRAN	220/50
CHILE+	220/50 AC	IRAQ	220 DC
CHINA	110/50	IRELAND	220/50 AC
CHINA, TAIWAN	110/60 AC	ISRAEL	220/50 AC
COLOMBIA	150/60 AC, 110/60**	ITALY	220/50, 110-127/50 AC*
COMOROS	220/50	JAMAICA	110/50 AC
CONGO, REP.	220/50	JAPAN	110/50, 100/60 AC*
COSTA RICA	110/60 AC	JORDAN	220/50 AC
COTE D'IVOIRE	220/50 AC	KAZAKHSTAN	220/50
CUBA	110/60	KENYA	220/50 AC
CYPRUS++	240/50 AC	KOREA, SOUTH	110/60 AC
CZECH REP.	220/50 AC	KUWAIT	240/50 AC
DENMARK	220/50	KYRGYZSTAN	220/50

LATVIA	220/50	SPAIN	110-220/50 AC
LEBANON	110-220/50	SRI LANKA	230-240/50 AC
LESOTHO	220 AC	ST. KITTS	230/60 AC
LIBERIA	120/60 AC	ST. LUCIA	220/50 AC
LIBYA	220/50	ST. MARTIN	220/60 AC
LIECHTENSTEIN	220/50 AC	ST. VINCENT	220-230/50 AC
LITHUANIA	220/50	SUDAN	240 AC
LUXEMBOURG	220/110	SURINAME	110-115/60 AC
MADAGASCAR	220/50	SWAZILAND	240/50
MALAWI	220	SWEDEN+	220/50 AC
MALAYSIA	220/50 AC	SWITZERLAND	220/50 AC
MALI	220	TAJIKISTAN	220/50
MALTA	240/50 AC	TANZANIA	240/50/60 AC
MARTINIQUE	220/50 AC		
MAURITANIA	220/50	THAILAND	220/50 AC
MAURITIUS	220/230	TOGO	220/50 AC
MEXICO	110/60 AC	TONGA	220 AC
MICRONESIA	110/60 AC	TRINIDAD & TOB.	110/60 AC
MOLDOVA	220/50	TUNISIA 110-115/50, 220/50 AC*	
MONTSERRAT	230/60 AC	TURKEY	220/50
MOROCCO	110-120/50 AC	TURKMENISTAN	220/50
MOZAMBIQUE	220/50	TURKS & CAICOS	110/60
NAMIBIA	220/240/60	U.S.A	110-115/60 AC
NEPAL	220/50 AC	UKRAINE	220/50
NETHERLANDS ANT.	110-130/50,	UNITED ARAB EM.240/415 AC	
120/60AC*		UNITED KINGDOM	220/50 AC
NETHERLANDS	220/50 AC	URUGUAY	220/50 AC
NEW CALEDONIA	220/50 AC	UZBEKISTAN	220/50
NICARAGUA	110/60 AC	VENEZUELA	110/60 AC
NIGER	220-240/50	YEMEN, ARAB REP.	220/50 AC
NIGERIA++	220/50 AC	YEMEN, P.D.R	220/240/50
NORWAY	220/50 AC	YUGOSLAVIA	220/50 AC
OMAN	220/240/50	ZAIRE	220/50
PAKISTAN	220/240/50 AC	ZAMBIA	220/50 AC
PANAMA	110/60 AC	ZIMBABWE++	220/240/50
PAPUA NEW GUINEA	240 AC		
PARAGUAY+	220/50 AC		
PERU	220/60 AC	----------------	
PHILIPPINES	220/60 AC	* Electricity requirements vary	
POLAND	220/50 AC	in some parts of the country.	
PORTUGAL	210-220/50 AC		
PUERTO RICO	110-115/60 AC	+ Some parts of the country still use DC.	
QATAR	220/50		
REP. OF DJIBOUTI	220/50	++ In some or most parts of the country,	
CAPE VERDE	220/50	you may need three square pin	
ROMANIA	220/50	plugs.	
RUSSIA	220/50		
RWANDA	220/50		
SAUDI ARABIA	110 & 120/60 AC		
SENEGAL	110 & 220/50 AC		
SEYCHELLES	240/50 AC		
SIERRA LEONE	220/50		
SINGAPORE++	230-250 AC		
SAO TOME & PRIN.	220/50		
SOMALIA	220/50		
SOUTH AFRICA	220-230/50 AC		

APPENDIX C

INTERNATIONAL TELEPHONE DIALING CODES

<u>COUNTRY/City Codes</u>

Algeria   213
City code not required.

American Samoa   684
City code not required.

Andorra   33
Use 628 for all cities.

Anguilla   809
Dial 1 + 809 + Local Number.

Antigua   809
Dial 1 + 809 + Local Number.

Argentina   54
Bahia Blanca 91. Buenos Aires 1, Cordoba
51, Corrientes 783, La Plata 21,
Mar Del Plata 23, Mendoza 61, Merlo 220,
Posadas 752, Resistencia 772,
Rio Cuarto 586, Rosario 41, San Juan 64,
San Rafael 627, Santa Fe 42, Tandil 293

Aruba   297
Use 8 for all cities.

Ascension Island   247
City code not required.

Australia   61
Adelaide 8, Ballarat 53, Brisbane 7,
Canberra 62, Darwin 89, Geelong 52,
Gold Coast 75, Hobart 02, Launceston 03,
Melbourne 3, Newcastle 49, Perth 9,
Sydne 2, Toowoomba 76, Townsville 77,
Wollongong 42

Austria   43
Bludenz 5552, Graz 316, Innsbruck 5222,
Kitzbuhel 5356, Klagenfut 4222,
Krems An Der Donau 2732, Linz Donau
732, Neunkirchen Niederosterreich 2635,
Salzburg 662, St. Polten 2742, Vienna 1,
Villach 4242, Wels 7242,
Wiener Neustadt 2622

Bahamas   809
Dial 1 + 809 + Local Number.

Bahrain   973
City code not required.

Bangladesh   880
Barisal 431, Bogra 51, Chittagong 31,
Comilla 81, Dhaka 2, Khulna 41,
Maulabi Bazar 861, Mymensingh 91,
Rajshaki 721, Sylhet 821

Barbados   809

Dial 1 + 809 + Local Number.

Belgium   32
Antwerp 3, Bruges 50, Brussels 2, Charleroi
71, Courtrai 56, Ghent 91, Hasselt 11,
La Louviere 64, Leuven 16, Libramont 61,
Liege 41, Malines 15, Mons 65,
Namur 81, Ostend 59, Verviers 87

Belize   501
Belize City (City code not required),
Belmopan 08, Benque Viejo Del Carmen
093, Corozal Town 04, Dangviga 05,
Independence 06, Orange Walk 03,
Punta Gorda 07, San Ignacio 092

Benin   229
City code not required.

Bermuda   809
Dial 1 + 809 + Local Number.

Bolivia   591
Cochabamba 42, Cotoga 388, Guayafamerin
47, La Belgica 923, La Paz 2, Mineros 984,
Montero 92, Oruro 52, Portachuelo 924,
Saavedra 924, Santa Cruz 33, Trinidad 46,
Warnes 923

Botswana   267
Francistown 21, Gaborone 31, Jwaneng 38,
Kanye 34, Lobatse 33, Mahalapye 41,
Maun 26, Mochudi 37, Molepoloe 32,

410

Orapa 27, Palapye 42, Ramotswana 39, Selibe (Phikwe) 8, Serowe 43

Brazil   55
Belem 91, Belo Horizonte 31, Brasilia 61, Curitiba 41, Fortaleza 85, Goiania 62, Niteroi 21, Pelotas 532, Porto Alegre 512, Recife 81, Rio de Janeiro 21, Salvador 71, Santo Andre 11, Santos 132, Sao Paulo 11, Vitoria 27

British Virgin Islands   809
Dial 1 + 809 + Local Number in the following cities: Anegada, Camanoe Island, Guana Island, Josh Vah Dyke, Little Thatch, Marina Cay, Mosquito Island, North Sound, Peter Island, Salt Island, Tortola, Virgin Gorda.

Brunei   673
Bandar Seri Begawan 2, Kuala Belait 3, Mumong 3, Tutong 4

Bulgaria   359
Kardjali 361, Pazardjik 34, Plovdiv 32, Sofia 2, Varna 52

Burkina Faso   226
Bobo Dioulasso 9, Fada N'Gorma 7, Koudougou 4, Ouagadougou 3

Burma   95
Akyab 43, Bassein 42, Magwe 63, Mandalay 2, Meikila 64, Moulmein 32, Pegu 52, Prom 53, Rangoon 1

Cameroon   237
City code not required.

Canada   NPA's

Dial 1 + Area Code + Local Number.

Cape Verde Islands 238

City code not required.

Caymen Islands   809
Dial 1 + 809 + Local Number.

Chile   56
Chiquayante 41, Concepcion 41, Penco 41, Recreo 31, San Bernardo 2, Santiago 2, Talcahuano 41, Valparaiso 32, Vina del Mar 32

China   86

Beijing   (Peking)   1,   Fuzhou   591, Ghuangzhou (Canton) 20, Shanghai 21

Colombia   57
Armenia 60, Barranquilla 5, Bogota 1, Bucaramanga 73, Cali 3, Cartagena 59, Cartago 66, Cucuta 70, Giradot 832, Ibague 82, Manizales 69, Merdellin 42, Neiva 80, Palmira 31, Pereira 61, Santa Marta 56

Costa Rica   506
City code not required.

Cyprus   357
Kythrea 2313, Lapithos 8218, Lamaca 41, Lefkonico 3313, Limassol 51, Moni 5615, Morphou 71, Nicosia 2, Paphos 61, Platres 54, Polis 63, Rizokarpaso 3613, Yialousa 3513. The following cities are handled by the Turkish Telephone Network.
Use country code 90 for Turkey: Famagusta 536, Kyrenia 581, and Lefka 57817.

Czechoslovakia   42
Banska Bystrica 88, Bratislava 7, Brno 5, Ceske Budejovice 38, Decin 412, Havirov 6994, Hradec Kralove 49, Kablonec Nad Nisou 428, Karvina 6993, Kosice 95, Most 35, Ostrava 69, Pizen 19, Prague (Praha) 2, Usti Nad Labem 47, Zilina 89

Denmark   45
City code not required.

Djibouti   253
City code not required.

Dominica   809
Dial 1 + 809 + Local Number.

Dominican Republic 809
Dial 1 + 809 + Local Number.

Ecuador   593
Ambato 2, Cayambe 2, Cuenca 7, Esmeraldas 2, Guayaquil 4, Ibarra 2; Loja 4, Machachi 2, Machala 4, Manta 4, Portoviejo 4, Quevedo 4, Quito 2, Salinas 4, Santa Domingo 2, Tulcan 2

Egypt   20
Alexandria 3, Answan 97, Asyut 88, Benha 13, Cairo 2, Damanhour 45, El Mahallah (El Kubra) 43, El Mansoura 50, Luxor 95, Port Said 66,

Shebin El Kom 48, Sohag 93, Tanta 40

El Salvador   503
City code not required.

Estonia   7
Tallinn 0142

Ethiopia   251
Addis Ababa 1, Akaki 1, Asmara 4, Assab 3, Awassa 6, Debre Zeit 1, Dessie 3, Dire Dawa 5, Harrar 5, Jimma 7, Makale 4, Massawa 4, Nazareth 2, Shashemene 6

Faeroe Islands   298
City code not required.

Fiji Islands   679
City code not required.

Finland   358
Epoo-Ebbo 15, Helsinki 0, Joensuu 73, Jyvaskyla 41, Kuopio 71, Lahti 18, Lappeenranta 53, Oulu 81, Port 39, Tammefors-Tampere 31, Turku 21, Uleaborg 81, Vaasa 61, Vanda-Vantaa 0

France   33
Aix-en-Provence 42, Bordeaux 56, Cannes 93, Chauvigny 49, Cherbourge 33, Grenoble 76, Le Havre 35, Lourdes 62, Lyon 7, Marseille 91, Nancy 8, Nice 93, Paris 1, Rouen 35, Toulouse 61, Tours 47

French Antilles   596
City code not required.

French Guiana   594
City code not required.

French Polynesia   689
City code not required.

Gabon Republic   241
City code not required.

Gambia   220
City code not required.

Georgia   7
Sukhumi 88122, Tblisi 8832

Germany East   7
Berlin 2, Cottbus 59, Dresden 51, Erfurt 61, Frankfurt 30, Gera 70, Halle/Saale 46, Karl-Marx-Stadt 71, Leipzig 41, Magdeburg 91, Neubrandenburg 90, Postdam 33, Rostock 81, Schwerin (Meckl) 84, Suhl 66, Zittau 522

Germany West   49
Bad Homburg 6172, Berlin 30, Bonn 228, Bremen 421, Cologne (Koln) 221, Dusseldorf 211, Essen 201, Frankfurt 69, Hamburg 40, Heidellberg 6221, Koblenz 261, Mannheim 621, Munich 89, Numberg 911, Stuttgart 711, Wiesbaden 6121

Ghana   233
City code not required.

Gibraltar   350
City code not required.

Greece   30
Argos 751, Athens (Athinai) 1, Corinth 741, Iraklion (Kristis) 81, Kavala 51, Larissa 41, Patrai 61, Piraeus Pireefs 1, Rodos 241, Salonica (Thessaloniki) 31, Sparti 731, Thessaloniki 31, Tripolis 71, Volos 421, Zagora 426

Greenland   299
Goatham 2, Sondre Stromfjord 11, Thule 50

Grenada   809
Dial 1 + 809 + Local Number.

Guadeloupe   590
City code not required.

Guam   671
City code not required.

Guantanemo Bay   5399
City code not required.

Guatemala   502
Guatemala City 2. All other cities 9.

Guinea   224
City code not required.

Guyana   592
Anna Regina 71, Bartica 5, Beteryerwaging 20, Cove & John 29, Georgetown 2, Ituni 41, Linden 4, Mabaruma 77, Mahaica 28, Mahalcony 21, New Amsterdam 3, New Hope 66, Rosignol 30, Timehri 61, Vreed-En-Hoop 64, Whim 37

Haiti   509

Cap-Haitien 3, Cayes 5, Gonalve 2, Port au Prince 1

Honduras   504
City code not required.

Hong Kong   852
Castle Peak 0, Cheung Chau 5, Fan Ling 0, Hong Kong 5, Kowloon 3, Kwai Chung 0, Lamma 5, Lantau 5, Ma Wan 5, Peng Chau 5, Sek Kong 0, Sha Tin 0, Tai Po 0, Ting Kau 0, Tsun Wan 0

Hungary   36
Abasar 37, Balatonaliga 84, Budapest 1, Dorgicse 80, Fertoboz 99, Gyongyos 37, Kaposvar 82, Kazincbarcika 48, Komlo 72, Miskolc 46, Nagykaniza 93, Szekesfehervar 22, Szolnok 56, Varpalota 80, Veszprem 80, Zalaegerzeg 92

Iceland   354
Akureyi 6, Hafnafijorour 1, Husavik 6, Keflavik Naval Base 2, Rein 6, Reykjavik 1, Reyorarjorour 7, Sandgerol 2, Selfoss 9. Siglufijorour 6, Stokkseyri 9, Suoavik 4, Talknafijorour 4, Varma 1, Vik 9

India   91
Ahmedabad 272, Amritsar 183, Bangalore 812, Baroda 265, Bhopal 755, Bombay 22 Calcutta 33, Chandigarh 172, Hyderabad 842, Jaipur 141, Jullundur 181, Kanpur 512, Madras 44, New Dehli 11, Poona 212, Surat 261

Indonesia   62
Bandung 22, Cirebon 231, Denpasar (Bali) 361, Jakarta 21, Madiun 351, Malang 341, Medan 61, Padang 751, Palembang 711, Sekurang 778, Semarang 24, Solo 271, Surabaya 31, Tanjungkarang 721, Yogykarta 274

Iran   98
Abadan 631, Ahwaz 61, Arak 2621, Esfahan 31, Ghazvin 281, Ghome 251, Hamadan 261, Karadj 2221, Kerman 341, Mashad 51, Rasht 231, Rezaiyeh 441, Shiraz 71, Tabriz 41, Tehran 21

Iraq   964
Baghdad 1, Basiah 40, Diwanyia 36, Karbala 32, Kirkuk 50, Mosul 60, Nasryia 42

Ireland   353

Arklow 402, Cork 21, Dingle 66, Donegal 73, Drogheda 41, Dublin 1, Dundalk 42, Ennis 65, Galway 91, Kildare 45, Killamey 64, Sligo 71, Tipperary 62, Tralee 66, Tullamore 506, Waterford 51, Wexford 53

Israel   972
Afula 65, Ako 4, Ashkelon 51, Bat Iam 3, Beer Sheva 57, Dimona 57, Hadera 63, Haifa 4, Holon 3, Jerusalem 2, Nazareth 65, Netania 53, Rehovot 8, Tel Aviv 3, Tiberias 67, Tsefat 67

Italy   39
Bari 80, Bologna 51, Brindisi 831, Capri 81, Como 31, Florence 55, Genoa 10, Milan 2, Naples 81, Padova 49, Palermo 91, Pisa 50, Rome 6, Torino 11, Trieste 40, Venice 41, Verona 45

Ivory Coast   225
City code not required.

Jamaica   809
Dial 1 + 809 + Local Number.

Japan   81
Chiba 472, Fuchu (Tokyo) 423, Hiroshima 82, Kawasaki (Kanagawa) 44, Kobe 78, Kyoto 75, Nagasaki 958, Nagoya 52, Nahat (Okinawa) 988, Osaka 6, Sapporo 11, Sasebo 956, Tachikawa (Tokyo) 425, Tokyo 3, Yokohama 45, Yokosuka (Kanagawa) 468

Jordan   962
Amman 6, Aqaba 3, Irbid 2, Jerash 4, Karak 3, Maam 3, Mafruq 4, Ramtha 2, Sueeleh 6, Sult 5, Zerqa 9

Kazakhstan   7
Alma-Ata 3272, Chimkent 3252, Guryev 31222

Kenya   254
Anmer 154, Bamburi 11, Embakasi 2, Girgiri 2, Kabete 2, Karen 2882, Kiambu 154, Kikuyu 283, Kisumu 35, Langata 2, Mombasa 11, Nairobi 2, Nakuru 37, Shanzu 11, Thika 151, Uthiru 2

Kiribati   686
City code not required.

Korea   82
Chung Ju 431, Chuncheon 361, Icheon 336, Incheon 32, Kwangju (Gwangju) 62,

Masan 551, Osan 339, Osan Military (333+414), Pohang 562, Pusan (Busan) 51, Seoul 2, Suwon (Suweon) 331, Taegu (Daegu) 53, Ulsan 552, Wonju (Weonju) 371

Kuwait   965
City code not required.

Kyrgyzstan   7
Osh 33222, Pishpek 3312

Latvia   7
Riga 0132

Lebanon   961
Beirut 1, Juniyah 9, Tripoli 6, Zahlah 8

Lesotho   266
City code not required.

Liberia   231

City code not required.

Libya   218
Agelat 282, Benghazi 61, Benina 63, Derma 81, Misuratha 51, Sabratha 24, Sebha 71, Taigura 26, Tripoli 21, Tripoli International Airport 22, Zawai 23, Zuara 25

Liechtenstein   41

Use 75 for all cities.

Lithuania   7
Vilnius 0122

Luxembourg   352
City code not required.

Macao   853
City code not required.

Malawi   265
Domasi 531, Likuni 766, Luchenza 477, Makwasa 474, Mulanje 465, Namadzi 534, Njuli 664, Thondwe 533, Thornwood 486, Thyolo 467, Zomba 50, City code not required for other cities.

Malaysia   60
Alor Star 4, Baranang 3, Broga 3, Cheras 3, Dengil 3, Ipoh 5, Johor Bahru 7, Kajang 3, Kepala Batas 4, Kuala Lampur 3, Machang 97, Maran 95, Port Dickson 6, Semenyih 3, Seremban 6, Sungei Besi 3, Sungei Renggam 3

Maldives   960
City code not required.

Mali   223
City code not required.

Malta   356
City code not required.

Marshall Islands   692
Ebeye 871, Majuro 9

Mauritius   230
City code not required.

Mayotte Islands   269
City code not required.

Mexico   52
Acapulco 748, Cancun 988, Celaya 461, Chihuahua 14, Ciudad Juarez 16, Conzumel 987, Culiacan 671, Ensenda 667, Guadalajara 36, Hermosillo 621, La Paz 682, Mazatlan 678, Merida 99, Mexicali 65, Mexico City 5, Monterrey 83, Puebla 22, Puerto Vallarta 322, Rasarito 661, San Luis Potosi 481, Tampico 121, Tecate 665, Tijuana 66, Torreon 17, Veracruz 29

Micronesia   691
Kosrae 851, Ponape 9, Truk 8319, Yap 841

Moldova   7
Kishinev 0422

Monaco   33
Use 93 for all cities.

Mongolian People's Rep.   976
Ulan Bator 1

Montserrat   809
Dial 1 + 809 + Local Number.

Morocco   212
Agardir 8, Beni-Mellal 48, Berrechid 33, Casablanca (City code not required). El Jadida 34, Fes 6, Kenitra 16, Marrakech 4, Meknes 5, Mohammedia 32, Nador 60, Oujda 68, Rabat 7, Tanger (Tangiers) 9, Tetouan 96

Mustique   809

Dial 1 + 809 + Local Number.

Namibia   264
Gobabis 681, Grootfontein 673, Industria 61, Keetmanshoop 631, Luderitz 6331, Mariental 661, Okahandja 622, Olympia 61, Otjiwarongo 651, Pioneerspark 61, Swakopmund 641, Tsumeb 671, Windhoek 61, Windhoek Airport 626

Nauru Island   674
City code not required.

Nepal   977
City code not required.

Netherlands   31
Amsterdam 20, Arnhem 85, Eindhoven 40, Groningen 50, Haarlem 23, Heemstede 23, Hillegersberg 10, Hoensbraoek 45, Hoogkerk 50, Hoogvliet 10, Loosduinen 70, Nijmegen 80, Oud Zuilen 30, Rotterdam 10, The Hague 70, Utrecht 30

Netherlands Antilles   599
Bonaire 7, Curacao 9, Saba 4, Eustatius 3, St. Maarten 5

Nevis   809
Dial 1 + 809 + Local Number.

New Caledonia   687
City code not required.

New Zeland   64
Auckland 9, Christchurch 3, Dunedin 24, Hamilton 71, Hastings 70, Invercargill 21, Napier 70, Nelson 54, New Plymouth 67, Palmerston North 63, Rotorua 73, Tauranga 75, Timaru 56, Wanganui 64, Wellington 4, Whangarei 89

Nicaragua   505
Boaco 54, Chinandega 341, Diriamba 42, Esteli 71, Granada 55, Jinotepe 41, Leon 311, Managua 2, Masatepe 44, Masaya 52, Nandaime 45, Rivas 461, San Juan Del Sur 466, San Marcos 43, Tipitapa 53

Niger Republic   227
City code not required.

Nigeria   234
Lagos 1 (Only city direct dial)
Niue   683

Norfolk Island   672

Norway   47
Arendal 41, Bergen 5, Drammen 3, Fredrikstad 32, Haugesund 47, Kongsvinger 66, Kristiansund N. 73, Larvik 34, Moss 32, Narvik 82, Oslo 2, Sarpsborg 31, Skien 35, Stavanger 4, Svalbard 80, Tonsberg 33, Trondheim 7

Oman   968
City code not required.

Pakistan   92
Abbotabad 5921, Bahawalpur 621, Faisalabad 411, Gujtanwala 431, Hyderabad 221, Islamabad 51, Karachi 21, Lahore 42, Multan 61, Okara 442, Peshawar 521, Quetta 81, Sahiwal 441, Sargodha 451, Sialkot 432, Sukkur 71

Palm Island   809
Dial 1 + 809 + Local Number.

Panama   507
City code not required.

Papau New Guinea   675
City code not required.

Paragua   595
Asuncion 21, Ayolas 72, Capiata 28, Concepcion 31, Coronel Bogado 74, Coronel Oviedo 521, Encarnacion 71, Hermandarias 63, Ita 24, Pedro J. Caballero 36, Pilar 86, San Antonio 27, San Ignacio 82, Stroessner: Ciudad Pte. 61, Villarica 541, Villeta 25

Peru   51
Arequipa 54, Ayacucho 6491, Callao 14, Chiclayo 74, Chimbote 44, Cuzco 84, Huancavelica 6495, Huancayo 64, Ica 34, Iquitos 94, Lima 14, Piura 74, Tacna 54, Trujillo 44

Phillipines   63
Angeles 55, Bacolod 34, Baguio City 442, Cebu City 32, Clark Field (military) 52, Dagupan 48, Davao 35, Lloilo City 33, Lucena 42, Manila 2, San Fernando: La Union 46, San Fernando: Pampanga 45, San Pablo 43, Subic Bay Military Base 89, Subic Bay Residential Housing 89, Tarlac City 47

Poland   48
Bialystok 85, Bydgoszcz 52, Crakow (Krakow) 12, Gdansk 58, Gdynia 58, Katowice 32, Lodz 42, Lubin 81, Olsztyn 89, Poznan 48, Radom 48, Sopot 58, Torun 56, Warsaw 22

Portugal   351
Alamada 1, Angra Do Heroismo 95, Barreiro 1, Beja 84, Braga 53, Caldas Da Rainha 62, Coimbra 39, Estoril 1, Evora 66, Faro 89, Horta 92, Lajes AFB 95, Lisbon 1, Madalena 92, Madeira Islands 91, Montijo 1, Ponta Del Gada 96, Porto 2, Santa Cruz (Flores) 92, Santarem 43, Setubal 65, Velas 95, Vila Do Porto 96, Viseu 32

Qatar   974
City code not required.

Reunion Island   262
City code not required.

Romania   40
Arad 66, Bacau 31, Brasov 21, Bucharest 0, Cluj-Napoca 51, Constanta 16, Crajova 41, Galati 34, Lasi 81, Oradea 91, Pitesti 76, Ploiesti 71, Satu-Mare 97, Sibiu 24, Timisoara 61, Tirgu Mures 54

Russia   7
Magadan 41300, Moscow 095, St. Petersburg 812

Rwanda   250
City code not required.

St. Kitts   809
Dial 1 + 809 + Local Number.

St. Lucia   809
Dial 1 + 809 + Local Number.

St. Pierre & Miquelon   508
City code not required.

St. Vincent   809
Dial 1 + 809 + Local Number.

Saipan   670
Capitol Hill 322, Rota Island 532, Susupe City 234, Tinian Island 433

San Marino   39
Use 541 for all cities.

Saudi Arabia   966
Abha 7, Abqaiq 3, Al Khobar 3, Al Markazi 2, Al Ulaya 1, Damman 3, Dhahran (Aramco) 3, Jeddah 2, Khamis Mushait 7, Makkah (Mecca) 2, Medina 4, Najran 7, Qatif 3, Riyadh 1, Taif 2, Yenbu 4

Senegal   221
City code not required.

Seychelles Islands   248
City code not required.

Sierra Leone   232
Freetown 22, Juba 24, Lungi 25, Wellington 23

Singapore   65
City code not required.

Solomon Island   677
City code not required.

South Africa   27
Bloemfontein 51, Cape Town 21, De Aar 571, Durban 31, East London 431, Gordons Bay 24, Johannesburg 11, La Lucia 31, Pietermaritzburg 331, Port Elizabeth 41, Pretoria 12, Sasolburg 16, Somerset West 24, Uitenhage 422, Welkom 171

Spain   34
Barcelona 3, Bibao 4, Cadiz 56, Ceuta 56, Granada 58, Igualada 3, Las Palmas de Gran Canaria 28, Leon 87, Madrid 1, Malaga 52, Melilla 52, Palma De Mallorca 71, Pamplona 48, Santa Cruz de Tenerife 22, Santander 42, Seville 54, Torremolinos 52, Valencia 6

Sri Lanka   94
Ambalangoda 97, Colombo Central 1, Galle 9, Havelock Town 1, Kandy 8, Katugastota 8, Kotte 1, Maradana 1, Matara 41, Negomgo 31, Panadura 46, Trincomalee 26

Suriname   597
City code not required.

Swaziland   268
City code not required.

Sweden   46
Alingsas 322, Boras 33, Eskilstuna 16,

416

Gamleby 493, Goteborg 31, Helsinborg 42, Karlstad 54, Linkoping 13, Lund 46, Malmo 40, Norrkoping 11, Stockholm 8, Sundsvall 60, Trelleborg 410, Uppsala 18, Vasteras 21

Switzerland   41
Baden 56, Basel 61, Berne 31, Davos 83, Fribourg 37, Geneva 22, Interlaken 36, Lausanne 21, Lucerne 41, Lugano 91, Montreux 21, Neuchatel 38, St. Gallen 71, St. Moritz 82, Winterthur 52, Zurich 1

Taiwan   886
Changhua 47, Chunan 36, Chunghsing-Hsintsun 49, Chungli 34, Fengyuan 4, Hsiaying 6, Hualien 38, Kaohsiung 7, Keelung 2, Lotung 39, Pingtung 8, Taichung 4, Tainan 6, Taipei 2, Taitung 89, Taoyuan 33

Tajikistan   7
Dushanbe 3772

Tanzania   255
Dar Es Salaam 51, Dodoma 61, Mwanza 68, Tanga 53

Thailand   66
Bangkok 2, Burirum 44, Chanthaburi 39, Chien Mai 53, Cheingrai 54, Kamphaengphet 55, Lampang 54, Nakhon Sawan 56, Nong Khai 42, Pattani 73, Pattaya 38, Ratchaburi 32, Saraburi 36, Tak 55, Ubon Ratchathani 45

Togo   228
City code not required.

Tonga Islands   676
City code not required.

Trinidad & Tabago 809
Dial 1 + 809 + Local Number.

Tunisia   216
Agareb 4, Beja 8, Bizerte 2, Carthage 1, Chebba 4, Gabes 5, Gafsa 6, Haffouz 7, Hamman-Souse 3, Kairouan 7, Kef 8, Khenis 3, Medenine 5, Tabarka 8, Tozeur 6, Tunis 1

Turkey   90
Adana 711, Ankara 41, Antalya 311, Bursa 241, Eskisehir 221, Gazianter 851, Istanbul 1, Izmir 51, Izmit 211, Kayseri

351, Konya 331, Malatya 821, Mersin 741, Samsun 361

Turka & Caicos   809
Dial 1 + 809 + Local Number.

Turkmenistan   7
Ashkkhabad 3632, Chardzhou 37822

Tuvalu   688

Ukraine   7
Kharkiv 0572, Kyiv 044, Lviv 0322

Uganda   256
Entebbe 42, Jinja 43, Kampala 41, Kyambogo 41

Union Island   809
Dial 1 + 809 + Local Number.

United Arab Emirates 971
Abu Dhabi 2, Ajman 6, Al Ain 3, Aweer 58, Dhayd 6, Dibba 70, Dubai 4, Falaj-al-Moalla 6, Fujairah 70, Jebel Ali 84, Jebel Dhana 52, Khawanij 58, Ras-al-Khaimah 77, Sharjan 6, Tarif 53, Umm-al-Quwain 6

United Kingdom   44
Belfast 232, Birmingham 21, Bournemouth 202, Cardiff 222, Durham 385, Edinburgh 31, Glasgow 41, Gloucester 452, Ipswich 473, Liverpool 51, London (Inner) 71, London (Outer) 81, Manchester 61, Nottingham 602, Prestwick 292, Sheffield 742, Southampton 703

Uruguay   598
Atlantida 372, Colonia 522, Florida 352, La Paz 322, Las Piedras 322, Los Toscas 372, Maldonado 42, Mercedes 532, Minas 442, Montevideo 2, Parque De Plata 372, Paysandu 722, Punta Del Este 42, Salinas 372, San Jose 342, San Jose De Carrasco 382

Uzbekistan   7
Karish 37522, Samarkand 3662, Tashkent 3712

Vanuatu, Rep. of   678

Vatican City   39
Use 6 for all cities.

Venezuela   **58**
Barcelona 81, Barquisimeto 51, Cabimas 64, Caracas 2, Ciudad Bolivar 85, Coro 68, Cumana 93, Los Teques 32, Maiquetia 31, Maracaibo 61, Maracay 43, Maturin 91, Merida 74, Puerto Cabello 42, San Cristobal 76, Valencia 41

Vietnam   **84**
Hanoi 4, Ho Chi Minh City 8

Wallis & Futuna Islands   **681**

Western Samoa   **685**
City code not required.

Yeman (North)   **967**
Al Marawyah 3, Al Qaidah 4, Amran 2, Bayt Al Faquih 3, Dhamar 2, Hodeidah 3, Ibb 4, Mabar 2, Rada 2, Rawda 2, Sanaa 2, Taiz 4, Yarim 4, Zabid 3

Yugoslavia   **38**
Belgrade (Beograd) 11, Dubrovnik 50, Leskovac 16, Ljubjana 61, Maribor 62, Mostar 88, Novi Sad 21, Pirot 10, Rijeka 51, Sarajevo 71, Skopje 91, Split 58, Titograd 81, Titovo-Uzice 31, Zagreb 41

Zaire   **243**
Kinshasa 12, Lubumbashi 222

Zambia   **260**
Chingola 2, Kitwe 2, Luanshya 2, Lusaka 1, Ndola 26

Zimbabwe   **263**
Bulawayo 9, Harare 0, Mutare 20

APPENDIX D

COUNTRIES: BANKING, BUSINESS AND SHOPPING HOURS

AFGHANISTAN
Business/Shopping Hours: 8:AM - 6:AM (Sun-Thur) Businesses are closed Thursday and Friday afternoons

ALGERIA
Banking Hours: 9:AM - 4:PM (Sun-Thur) Business Hours: 8:AM - 12:Noon, 1:PM - 5:PM (Sat-Wed) Businesses are closed Thursday and Friday

AMERICAN SAMOA
Banking Hours: 9:AM - 2:PM (Mon-Thur) 9:AM - 5:PM (Fri)

ANDORRA
Banking Hours: 9:AM - 1:PM; 3:PM - 7:PM; Business Hours: 9:AM - 1:PM; 3:PM - 7:PM, Shopping Hours: 10:AM - 1:PM; 3:PM - 8:PM

ANGUILLA
Banking Hours: 8:AM - 12:00 Noon (Mon-Fri); 3:PM (Fri), Business Hours: 8:AM - 4:PM, Shopping Hours: 8:AM - 5:PM (Mon-Sat)

ANTIGUA AND BARBUDA
Banking Hours: 8:AM - 1:PM (Mon,Tue,Wed,Thur) 8:AM - 1:PM & 3:PM - 5:PM (Fri), Business Hours: 8:AM - 12:Noon & 1:PM - 4:PM (Mon-Fri), Shopping Hours: 8:AM - 12:Noon & 1:PM - 5:PM (Mon-Sat)

ARMENIA
Banking Hours: 9:AM - 6:PM, Business Hours: 9:AM - 6:PM, Shopping Hours: 8:AM - 9:PM

ARGENTINA
Banking Hours: 10:AM - 4:PM, (Mon-Fri), Business Hours: 9:AM - 6:PM (Mon-Fri), Shopping Hours: 9:AM - 8:PM (Mon-Sat)

AUSTRALIA
Banking Hours: 10:AM - 3:PM, (Mon-Thur); 10:AM - 5:PM (Fri) Banks are closed on Saturdays Business/Shopping Hours: 9:AM - 5:30PM (Mon-Thur); 8:30AM - 12:Noon (Sat)

AUSTRIA
Banking Hours: 8:AM - 12:30 PM, 1:30 - 3:30, PM (Mon, Tue, Wed, Fri); 1:30 - 5:30PM(Thur), Business Hours: 8:30 AM - 4:30 PM, Shopping Hours: 8:AM - 6:PM (Mon - Fri); 8:AM -12:Noon (Sat)

AZERBAIJAN
Banking Hours: 9:AM - 6:PM
Business Hours: 9:AM - 6:PM
Shopping Hours: 8:AM - 9:PM

BAHAMAS
Banking Hours: 9:30AM - 3:PM (Mon-Thur); 9:30AM - 5:PM (Fri)

BAHRAIN
Banking Hours: 7:30AM - 12:Noon (Sat-Wed); 7:30AM - 11:AM Thur)

BARBADOS
Banking Hours: 8:AM - 3:PM (Mon-Thur); 8:AM - 1:PM & 3:PM - 5:PM (Fri), Business Hours: 8:30AM - 4:PM (Mon-Fri), Shopping Hours: 8:AM - 4:PM (Mon-Fri); 8:AM - 12:Noon (Sat)

BANGLADESH
Banking Hours: 9:30AM - 1:30PM, (Mon-Thur); 9:AM - 11:AM (Fri-Sat)Business/Shopping Hours: 9:AM - 9:PM (Mon-Fri); 9:AM - 2:PM (Sat)

BELARUS
Banking Hours: 9:AM - 6:PM
Business Hours: 9:AM - 6:PM
Shopping Hours: 9:AM - 9:PM

BELGIUM
Banking Hours: 9:AM - 3:PM (Mon-Fri), Business Hours: 9:AM - 12:Noon & 2:PM - 5:30PM, Shopping Hours: 9:AM - 6:PM (Mon-Sat)

BELIZE
Banking Hours: 8:AM - 1:PM (Mon-

Fri); 3:PM - 6:PM (Fri) ;Business Hours: 8:AM - 12:Noon; 1:PM - 5:PM (Mon-Fri); Shopping Hours: 8:AM - 4:PM (Mon-Sat)

BENIN

Banking Hours: 8:AM - 11:AM; 3:PM - 4:PM (Mon-Fri); Business Hours: 8:AM - 12:30PM; 3:PM - 6:30PM (Mon-Fri); Shopping Hours: 9:AM - 1:PM, 4:PM - 7:PM (Mon-Sun)

BERMUDA

Business/Shopping: 9:AM - 5:PM (Mon-Sat)

BOLIVIA

Banking Hours: 9:AM - 12:Noon & 2:PM - 4:PM (Mon-Fri); Business Houre: 9:AM - 12:Noon & 2:30PM 6:PM (Mon-Fri); Shopping Hours: 9:AM - 6:PM; 9:AM - 12:Noon (Sat)

BOSNIA HERZEGOVINA

Banking Hours: 7:AM - Noon or &:AM - 7:PM; Business Hours: 8:AM - 3:30 PM; Shopping Hours: 8:AM - 8:PM (Mon-Fri)

BOTSWANA

Banking Hours: 8:15 - 12:45PM (Mon-Fri), 8:15AM - 10:45 AM (Sat); Shopping Hours: 8:AM - 6:PM (Mon-Sat)

BRITISH VIRGIN ISLANDS

Banking Hours: 9:AM - 2:PM (Mon-Fri); Business Hours: 8:30AM - 2:00PM & 4:PM - 5:PM (Mon-Fri); Shopping Hours: 8:AM - 5:PM (Mon-Sat)

BRAZIL

Banking Hours 10:AM - 4:30PM (Mon-Fri); Shopping Hours: 9:AM - 6:30PM (Mon-Fri) & 9:AM - 1:PM (Sat)

BURKINA FASO

Business Hours: 7:AM - 12:Noon, 3:PM - 5:PM (Mon-Fri); Shopping Hours: 7:AM - 12:Noon, 2:PM - 7:PM (Mon-Sat)

BURMA

Banking Hours: 10:AM - 2:PM (Mon-Fri); 10:AM - 12:Noon (Sat); Bussiness/Shopping Hours: 9:30Am - 4:PM (Mon-Sat)

BURUNDI

Business Hours: 8:AM - 12:Noon (Mon-Fri); Shopping Hours: 8:AM - 6:PM (Mon-Sat)

CAMEROON

Banking Hours: French Speaking Part: 8:AM - 11:AM, 2:30PM - 4:PM (Mon-Fri)English Speaking Part: 8:AM - 2:PM (Mon-Fri); Business Hours: French Speaking Part: 7:30AM - 12: Noon, 2:30PM - 6:PM (Mon-Fri); English Speaking Part: 7:30AM - 2:30PM - (Mon-Fri), 7:30AM - 1:PM; Shopping Hours: 8:AM - 12:30PM, 4:PM - 7:PM (Mon-Sat)

REPUBLIC OF CAPE VERDE

Banking Hours: 8:AM - 12: Noon (Mon-Fri); Business Hours: 8:AM - 12: Noon (Mon-Fri)

CAYMAN ISLANDS

Banking Hours: 9:AM - 2:30PM (Mon-Thur) & 9:AM -PM, :30PM - 4:30PM (Fri); Business Hours: 8:30AM - 5:PM; Shopping Hours: 8:30AM - 5:PM

CENTRAL AFRICAN REPUBLIC

Banking Hours: 8:AM - 11:30AM (Mon-Fri); Shopping Hours: 7:30AM - 9:PM (Mon-Sun)

CHAD

Banking Hours: 7:AM - 11:AM (Mon-Thur, Sat), 7:AM - 10:AM (Fri); Business Hours: 7:AM - 2:PM (Mon-Thur, Sat), 7:AM -12: Noon (Fri);Shopping Hours: 8:AM - 1:PM, 4:PM - 6:PM (Mon-Sat)

CHILE

Banking Hours: 9:AM - 1:PM & 2:30PM - 6:PM (Mon-Fri); 9:AM - 2:PM (Sat); Shopping Hours: 9:AM - 1:PM & 2:30PM - 6:PM (Mon-Fri)

CHINA, PEOPLES REPUBLIC

Banking Hours: varies (Mon-Sat)

CHINA, TAIWAN

Banking Hours: 9:AM - 3:30PM (Mon-Fri); 9:AM - 12:Noon (Sat)

COLUMBIA

Banking Hours: 9:AM - 3:PM (Mon-Thur); 9:AM - 3:30 (Fri); Business Hours: 8:30AM - 5:PM (Mon-Fri); Shopping Hours: 10:AM -- 7:PM (Mon-Sat)

420

COMOROS ISLAND

Banking Hours: 9:AM - 12:30PM, 3:PM - 5:PM (Mon-Fri), 9:AM - 12:30PM (Sat); Shopping Hours: 8:AM - 8:PM (Mon-Sat)

CONGO, PEOPLE'S REPUBLIC

Banking Hours: 7:AM - 2:PM (Mon-Fri); Shopping Hours: 7:AM - 7:PM (Mon-Sat)

COSTA RICA

Banking Hours: 9:AM - 3:PM (Mon-Fri); Shopping Hours: 8:30AM - 11:30AM & 2:PM - 6:PM (Mon-Fri) 8:30AM - 11:30AM (Sat)

COTE D'IVOIRE

Banking Hours: 8:AM - 11:30AM, 2:30PM - 4:PM (Mon-Fri); Business Hours: 8:AM - 12:Noon, 2:30PM - 5:30PM (Mon-Fri); Shopping Hours: 8:30AM - 12:Noon, 2:30PM - 7:PM (Mon-Sat)

CUBA

Banking Hours: 9:AM - 3:PM (Mon-Fri); Business Hours: 8:30AM - 12:30PM & 1:30PM - 5:30PM (Mon - Fri); Shopping Hours: 9:AM - 5:PM (Mon-Fri); 9:AM - 12:Noon (Sat)

CYPRUS

Banking Hours: 8:30AM - 12: Noon (Mon-Sat); Business Hours: 8:AM - 1:PM, 2:30PM - 6:PM (Mon-Fri) 8:AM -i:PM (Sat); Shopping Hours: 8:AM - 1:PM; 4:PM - 7:PM (Mon-Fri) Closed Wednesday and Saturday afternoons.

CZECH REPUBLIC

Banking Hours: 8:AM - 4:PM (Mon-Fri); Business Hours: 8:30AM - 5:PM; Shopping Hours: 9:AM - 6:PM (Mon-Fri), 9:AM - 1:PM (Sat)

DENMARK

Banking Hours: 9:30AM - 4:PM (Mon,Tue,Wed, & Fri), 9:30AM - 6:PM (Thur); Business Hours: 8:AM - 4:PM (Mon-Fri); Shopping Hours: 9/10:AM - 5:30/7:PM (Mon-Thur) 9/10:AM - 7/8:PM (Fri) 9/10:AM - 1/2:PM (Sat)

REPUBLIC OF DJIBOUTI

Banking Hours: 7:15AM - 11:45AM (Sun-Thur); Shopping Hours: 7:30AM - 12:Noon, 3:30PM - 7:30PM (Sat-Thur)

DOMINICA

Banking Hours: 8:AM - 1:PM (Mon-Fri); 3:PM - 5:PM (Fri); Business Hours: 8:AM - 1:PM & 2:PM - 4:PM (Mon-Fri); 8:AM - 1:PM (Sat); Shopping Hours: 8:AM - 1:PM & 2:PM - 4:PM (Mon-Fri); 8:AM- 1:PM (Sat)

DOMINICAN REPUBLIC

Banking Hours: 8:AM - 12:Noon (Mon-Fri); Business Hours: 9:AM - 6:PM (Mon-Fri) & 9:AM -12:Noon (Sat); Shopping Hours: 8:30AM - 12:Noon & 2:30PM - 6:PM (Mon-Fri); 8:30AM - 1:PM (Sat)

ECUADOR

Banking Hours: 9:AM - 1:30PM (Mon-Fri) Shopping Hours: 8:30AM - 12:30PM (Mon-Sat) & 3:30PM - 7:PM (Mon-Sat)

EGYPT

Banking Hours: 8:30AM - 1:PM (Mon-Thur, Sat), 10:AM - 12:Noon (Sat); Shopping Hours: 10:AM - 7:PM (Tue-Sat), 10:AM - 8:PM (Mon - Thur)

EL SALVADOR

Banking Hours: 8:AM - 12:Noon & 2:PM - 4:PM (Mon-Fri); Shopping Hours: 8:AM - 12:Noon & 2:30PM - 6:PM (Mon-Sat)

EQUATORIAL GUINEA

Banking Hours: 8:AM - 3:PM (Mon-Fri), 8:AM - 1:PM(Sat); Business Hours; 8:AM - 3:PM (Mon-Fri), 8:AM - 1:PM (Sat); Shopping Hours: 8:AM -3:PM, 5:PM - 7:PM (Mon-Sat)

ESTONIA

Banking Hours: 9:AM - 3:PM; Business Hours: 9:AM - 6PM; Shopping Hours: 9:am - 9:PM (Mon-Sat)

ETHIOPIA

Banking Hours: 9:AM - 5:PM (Mon-Fri); Business Hour: 8:AM - 12:Noon, 1:PM - 4:PM (Mon-Fri); Banks close for 3 hours for lunch

FIJI

Banking Hours: 10:AM - 3:PM (Mon-Thur); 10:AM - 4:PM (Fri) Business/Shopping Hours: 8:AM - 5:PM

FINLAND

Banking Hours: 9:15AM - 4:15PM (Mon-Fri); Business Hours: 8:30AM - 4:PM (Mon-Fri);Shopping Hours: 9:AM - 5/6:PM (Mon-Fri), 9:AM - 2/3:PM (Sat)

FRANCE

Banking Hours: 9:AM - 4:30PM (Mon-Fri); Business Hours: 9:AM - 12:Noon; 2:PM - 6:PM (Mon-Fri), 9:AM - 12:Noon (Sat); Shopping Hours: 9:AM - 6:30PM (Tue-Sat)

FRENCH GUIANA

Banking Hours: 7:15AM - 11:45AM (Mon,Tue,Thur, Fri); 7:AM - 12:Noon (Wed)

GABON

Banking Hours: 7:AM - 12:Noon (Mon-Fri); Business Hours: 8:AM - 12:Noon, 3:PM - 6:PM (Mon-Fri); Shopping Hours: 8:AM - 12:Noon, 4:PM - 7:PM (Mon-Sat)

GEORGIA

Shopping Hours: 9:AM - 7:PM

THE GAMBIA

Banking Hours: 8:AM - 1:PM (Mon-Fri); 8:AM - 11:AM (Sat); Business/Shopping Hours: 8:AM - 5:PM (Mon-Fri); 8:AM -12:Noon (Sat)

FEDERAL REPUBLIC OF GERMANY

Banking Hours: 8:30AM - 12:30PM; 1:45PM - 3:45PM (Mon-Fri), Thur-5:45PM; Business Hours: 8:AM - 5:PM; Shopping Hours: 8:AM - 6:30PM (Mon-Fri), 8:AM - 2:PM (Sat)

GHANA

Banking Hours: 8:30AM - 2:PM (Mon-Fri); Business Hours: 8:30AM - 5:PM (Mon-Fri); Shopping Hours: 8:30AM - 5:PM (Mon-Sat)

GIBRALTAR

Banking Hours: 9:AM - 3:30PM (Mon-Fri), 4:30PM - 6:PM (Fri); Business Hours: 9:AM - 6:PM; Shopping Hours: 9:AM - 1:PM & 3:30PM - 7:PM (Mon-Fri), 9:-1:PM (Sat)

GREECE

Banking Hours: 8:AM - 2:PM (Mon-Fri); Business Hours: 8:30AM - 1:30PM, 4:PM - 7:30PM; Shopping

Hours: 8:AM - 2:30PM (Mon, Wed, Sat), 8:AM - 1:30PM, 5:PM- 8:PM (Tue, Thur, Fri)

GRENADA

Banking Hours: 8:AM - 12:Noon (Mon-Fri) & 2:30 PM - 5:PM (Fri); Business Hours: 8:AM - 4:PM (Mon-Fri) 8:AM - 11:45 AM (Sat) Shopping Hours: 8:AM - 4:PM (Mon Fri); 8:AM - 11:45 AM (Sat)

GUADELOUPE

Banking Hours: 8:AM - 12:Noon & 2:PM - 4:PM; Shopping Hours: 9:AM - 1:PM & 3:PM - 6:PM (Mon-Fri); Sat mornings

GUATEMALA

Banking Hours: 9:AM - 3:PM (Mon-Fri); Shopping Hours: 9:AM - 7:PM (Mon-Sat)

GUINEA,REPUBLIC

Banking Hours: 7:30AM - 3:PM (Mon-Sat); Business Hours: 7:30 - 3:PM (Mon-Sat);Shopping Hours: 8:AM - 6:PM (Mon-Sun)

GUYANA

Banking Hours: 8:AM - 12:30PM; (Mon-Fri); Business Hours: 8:AM - 4:PM (Mon-Fri); Shopping Hours: 8:AM - 12:Noon; 2:PM - 4:PM

HAITI

Banking Hours: 9:AM - 1:PM (Mon-Fri); Business Hours: 8:AM - 5:PM (Mon-Fri); 8:AM - 12:Noon (Sat); Shopping Hours: 8:AM - 5:PM (Mon-Fri); 8:AM - 12:Noon (Sat)

HONDURAS

Banking Hours: 9:AM - 3:30PM (Mon-Fri); Shopping Hours: 8:AM - 6:30PM (Mon-Sat)

HONG KONG

Banking Hours: 10:AM - 3:PM (Mon-Fri); 9:AM - 12:Noon (Sat) Business/Shopping Hours: 9:AM - 5:PM; 9:AM - 1:Pm (Sat)

HUNGARY

Banking Hours: 8:30AM - 3:PM (Mon-Sat); Business Hours: 8:30AM - 5:PM; Shopping Hours: 10:AM - 6:PM (Mon-Fri); 10:AM - 2:PM (Sat)

ICELAND

Banking Hours: 9:15AM - 4:PM (Mon-Fri); Business Hours: 9:AM - 5:PM (Mon-Fri); Shopping Hours:

9:AM - 6:PM (Mon-Fri); 9:AM - 12:Noon (Sat)

INDIA

Banking Hours: 10:30AM - 2:30PM (Mon-Fri); 10:30AM - 12:30PM (Sat) Business/ShoppingHours:Government Offices: 10:AM - 1:PM; 2:PM - 5:PM (Mon-Sat); Non-Gov't Offices: 9:30AM - 1:PM; 2:PM - 5:PM (Mon-Sat)

INDONESIA

Banking Hours: 10:AM - 3:PM (Mon-Fri); 9:AM - 12:Noon (Sat)

IRAN

Banking Hours: 8:AM - 1:PM; 4:PM - 6:PM (Sat-Thur); Business/Shopping Hours:Gov't Office: 8:AM - 4:30PM (Sat-Wed) Non-Gov't. Offices: 8:AM - 4:30PM (Sat-Thur) Offices closed on Friday

IRELAND

Banking Hours: 10:AM - 12:30PM; 1:30PM - 3:PM (Mon-Fri); Business Hours: 9:AM - 1:PM, 2:PM - 5:PM;Shopping Hours: 9:AM - 5:30PM (Mon-Sat)

ISRAEL

Banking Hours: 8:30AM - 12:30PM; 4:PM - 5:30PM (Sun-Tue,Thur) 8:30AM -12:30PM (Wed); 8:30AM -12:Noon (Fri); Business Hours: Non-Gov't Office: 8:AM - 4:PM (Mon-Fri) Offices close early on Friday

ITALY

Banking Hours: 8:35AM - 1:35PM; 3:PM - 4:PM (Mon-Fri); Business Hours: 8:30AM - 12:30PM, 3:30PM-7:30PM; Shopping Hours: 9:AM - 1:PM, 3:30/4:PM - 7:30/8:PM

JAMAICA

Banking Hours: 9:AM - 2:PM (Mon - Thur); 9:AM - 12:Noon & 2:PM-5:PM (Fri); Business Hours: 8:AM - 4:PM; Shopping Hours: 8:30AM - 4:30PM

JAPAN

Banking Hours: 9:AM - 3:PM (Mon-Fri); 9:AM 12:Noon (Sat); Business/Shopping: 9:AM - 5:PM (Mon-Fri); 9:AM - 12:Noon (Sat)

JORDAN

Banking Hours: 8:AM - 12:30PM (Sat-Thur) Business/Shopping Hours: 8:AM - 6:PM (Sat-Thur)

KENYA

Banking Hours: 9:AM - 2:PM (Mon - Fri); 9:AM - 11;AM (1st & last saturday of month); Business Hours: 8:30AM - 4:30PM (Mon -Fri), 8:30 - 12:Noon (Sat); Shopping Hours: 8:30AM - 12:30PM, 2:PM - 5:PM (Mon - Sat)

KOREA, SOUTH

Banking Hours: 9:30AM - 4:30PM (Mon-Fri); 9:30AM - 11:PM (Sat) Business/Shopping Hours: 9:AM - 5:PM (Mon-Fri): 9:AM - 1:PM (Sat)

KUWAIT

Banking Hours: Mostly in the morning; Business/Shopping Hours: Gov't Offices: 7:30AM - 1:30PM Non-Gov't Offices: 7:30AM - 2:30PM (Sat-Wed);7:AM - 1:PM; 5:PM - 8:PM

KYRGYZSTAN

Banking Hours: 9:AM - 6:PM Business Hours: 9:AM - 6:PM Shopping Hours: 8:AM - 9:PM

LATVIA

Banking Hours: 9:AM - 12:Noon Business Hours: 9:AM - 6:PM Shopping Hours: 8:Am - 10:PM

LEBANON

Banking Hours: 8:30AM - 12:30PM (Mon-Fri); 8:30AM - 12:Noon (Sat)

LESOTHO

Banking Hours: 8:30AM - 1:PM (Mon-Fri); 9:AM - 11:AM (Sat); Business Hours: 8:AM - 4:30PM (Mon-Fri); Shopping Hours: 8:AM - 4:30PM (Mon-Fri); 8:AM - 1:PM (Sat)

LIBERIA

Banking Hours: 9:AM - 5:PM (Mon-Sat); Business Hours: 9:AM - 6:PM (Mon-Sat)

LIBYA

Banking Hours: 8:AM - 4:PM (Sat-Thur); Business Hours: 8:AM - 4:PM (Sat-Thur)

LIECHTENSTEIN

Banking Hours: 8:30AM - 12:Noon, 1:30 - 4:30PM (Mon-Fri); Business

423

Hours: 8:AM - 12:Noon, 2:30PM -
6:PM ; Shopping Hours: 8:AM -
12:15PM, 2:PM - 6:30PM (Mon-Fri),
8:AM - 4:PM (Sat)

LITHUANIA
Banking Hours: 9:AM - 12:Noon;
Business Hours: 9:AM - 1:PM, 2:PM
- 6:PM (Mon-Sat)

LUXEMBOURG
Banking Hours: 9:AM - 12:Noon;
2:PM - 5:PM (Mon-Sat); Business
Hours: 9:AM - 12:Noon, 2:PM -
5:30PM; Shopping Hours: 8:AM -
12:Noon, 2:PM - 6:PM (Mon-Sat)

MADAGASCAR
Banking Hours: 8:AM - 11:AM,
2:PM - 4:PM (Mon-Fri); Shopping
Hours: 9:AM - 6:PM (Mon-Sat);
Business Hours: 8:AM - 12:Noon,
2:PM - 6:PM (Mon-Fri)

MALAWI
Banking Hours: 8:AM - 1:PM (Mon-
Fri); Business Hours: 7:30AM - 5:PM
(Mon-Fri);Shopping Hours: 8:AM -
6:PM

MALAYSIA
Business/Shopping Hours:
8:30/9:AM - 1:PM, 2:30PM -
4:30PM (Mon-Fri); 9:AM - 1:PM
(Sat) Gov't Offices: 9:AM - 4:30Pm
(Mon-Fri); 9:AM -1:PM (Sat)

MALI
Banking Hours: 8:AM - 12:Noon,
2:PM - 4:PM (Mon-Fri); Business
Hours: 7:30AM - 2:30PM (Mon-Sat),
7:30AM - 12:30PM (Fri); Shopping
Hours: 9:AM - 8:PM (Mon-Sat)

MALTA
Banking Hours: 8:30AM - 12:30PM
(Mon-Fri), 8:30AM - 11:30AM (Sat);
Business Hours: 8:30AM - 5:30PM
(Mon-Fri), 8:30AM - 1:PM (Sat);
Shopping Hours: 9:AM - 1:PM,
4:PM - 7:PM (Mon-Fri), 9:AM -
1:PM, 4:PM - 8:PM (Sat)

MARTINIQUE
Banking Hours: 7:30AM - 4:PM
(Mon-Fri); Shopping Hours: 8:30AM
- 6:PM (Mon-Fri);
8:30AM - 1:PM (Sat)

MAURITANIA
Banking Hours: 8:AM - 3:PM (Sun-
Thur); Business Hours: 8:AM - 3:PM

(SunThur); Shopping Hours: 8:AM -
1:PM, 3:PM - 6:PM (Sun-Thur)

MAURITIUS
Banking Hours: 10:AM - 2:PM (Mon
- Fri), 9:30AM - 11:30AM (Sat);
Shopping Hours: (Varies) 9:AM -
5:PM (Mon-Fri), 9:AM -12:Noon
(Sat, Sun)

MEXICO
Banking Hours: 9:AM - 1:30PM
(Mon-Fri); Business Hours: 9:AM -
6:PM (Mon-Fri); Shopping Hours:
10:AM - 5:PM (Mon-Fri); 10:AM -
8:/9:PM

MICRONESIA
Banking Hours: 9:30Am - 2:30PM
(Mon-Fri)

MONACO
Banking Hours: 9:AM - 12:Noon,
2:PM - 4:PM (Mon-Fri); Business
Hours: 8:30AM - 6:PM; Shopping
Hours: 9:AM - 12:Noon, 2:PM -
7:PM (Mon-Sat)

MONTSERRAT
Banking Hours: 8:AM - 1:PM (Mon-
Thur); Business Hours: 8:AM -
4:PM; Shopping Hours: 8:AM -
4:PM

MOROCCO
Banking Hours: 8:30AM - 11:30AM,
3:PM - 5:30PM (Mon-Fri); Business
Hours: 8:30AM - 12:Noon, 2:30PM -
6:30PM (Mon-Fri), 8:30AM -
12:Noon (Sat); Shopping Hours:
8:30AM - 12:Noon, 2:PM - 6:30PM
(Mon-Sat)

MOZAMBIQUE
Banking Hours: 7:30 -12:Noon,
2:PM - 5:PM (Mon-Fri), 7:30AM -
12:Noon (Sat); Business Hours:
7:30AM - 12:Noon, 2:PM - 5:PM
(Mon-Fri), 7:30AM - 12:Noon (Sat)

NAMIBIA
Banking Hours: 9:AM - 3:30PM
(Mon-Fri), 8:30AM - 11:AM (Sat)
Business Hours: 8:30AM - 5:PM
(Mon-Fri); Shopping Hours: 8:30AM
- 5:30PM (Mon-Fri)
9:AM - 1:PM (Sat)

NEPAL
Banking Hours: 10:AM - 3:PM (Sat-
Thur);10:AM - 12:Noon (Sat)

NETHERLANDS

424

Banking Hours: 9:AM - 4/5:PM (Mon-Fri); Business Hours: 8:30 - 5:30PM; Shopping Hours: 8:30/9:AM - 5:30/6:PM (Mon-Fri)

NETHERLANDS ANTILLES
Banking Hours: 8:30AM - 11:AM; 2:PM - 4:PM (Mon-Fri); Business/Shopping Hours:8:AM - 12:Noon; 2:PM - 6:PM (Mon-Sat)

NEW CALEDONIA
Banking Hours: 7:AM - 10:30AM; 1:30PM - 3:30PM (Mon-Fri); 7:30 - 11:AM (Sat)

NEW ZEALAND
Banking Hours: 10:AM - 4:PM (Mon-Fri); Business/Shopping Hours: 9:AM - 5:PM (Mon-Fri)

NIGARAGUA
Banking Hours: 8:30AM - 12:Noon; 2:PM - 4:PM (Mon-Fri); 8:30AM - 11:30AM (Sat); Business/Shopping Hours: 8:AM - 5:30PM (Mon-Sat)

NIGER
Banking Hours: 7:30AM - 12:30PM, 3:30PM - 5:PM; Business Hours: 7:30AM - 12:30:PM, 3:30PM - 6:30PM; Shopping Hours: 7:30AM - 12:30PM, 3:30PM - 6:30PM

NIGERIA
Banking Hours: 8:AM - 3:PM (Mon), 8:AM - 1:30PM (Tues-Fri):; Business Hours: Gov't Offices: 7:30AM - 3:30PM (Mon-Fri) Private Firms: 8:AM - 5:PM (Mon-Fri)

NORWAY
Banking Hours: 8:15AM - 3:30PM (Mon, Tue, Wed, Fri); 8:15AM - 5:PM (Thur); Business Hours: 9:AM - 4:PM; Shopping Hours: 9:AM - 5:PM (Mon-Fri); 9:AM - 6/7:PM (Thur); 9:AM- 1/2:PM (Sat)

PAKISTAN
Banking Hours: 9:AM - 1:PM (Mon-Thur); 9:AM - 11:30AM (Sat) Business/Shopping Hours: 9:30AM - 1:PM (Mon-Thur); 9:AM -10:30AM (Sat)

PANAMA
Banking Hours: 8:30AM - 1:PM (Mon-Fri); Business Hours: 8:30AM - 12:30PM & 1:30PM - 4:PM (Mon-Fri)); Shopping Hours: 8:30AM - 6:PM (Mon-Sat)

PARAGUAY
Banking Hours: 7:AM - 12:Noon (Mon-Fri); Shopping Hours: 7:AM - 12:Noon & 3:PM - 7:PM

PERU
Banking Hours: 9:AM - 1:PM (Mon-Fri); Business Hours: 9:AM - 5:PM (Mon-Fri); Shopping Hours: 9:AM - 7:PM (Mon-Sat)

PHILIPPINES
Banking Hours: 9:AM - 6:PM (Mon-Fri); 9:AM 12:30 (Sat);

POLAND
Banking Hours: 8:AM - 1:PM; Business Hours: 8:30AM - 3:30PM; Shopping Hours: 9:AM - 8:PM

PORTUGAL
Banking Hours: 8:AM - 3:PM (Mon-Fri); Business Hours: 10:AM - 6:PM; Shopping Hours: 9:AM - 1:PM, 3:PM - 7:PM (Mon-Fri), 9:AM - 12:Noon (Some Shops)

PUERTO RICO
Banking Hours: 9:AM - 5:PM (Mon-Fri); Business Hours: 8:AM - 5:PM (Mon-Fri); Shopping Hours: 9:AM - 6:PM (Mon-Sat)

QATAR
Banking Hours: 7:30AM - 11:30AM (Sat-Thur)

REUNION ISLAND
Business/Shopping Hours: 8:AM - 12:Noon; 2:PM - 6:PM

ROMANIA
Banking Hours: 8:30 - 11:30AM; Business Hours: 8:AM - 4:PM (Mon-Fri), 8:AM - 12:30PM (Sat); Shopping Hours: 9:AM - 1:PM, 4:PM-6/8:PM

RUSSIA
Banking Hours: 9:AM - 6:PM; Business Hours: 9:AM - 6:PM; Shopping Hours: 9:AM - 9:PM (Mon-Sat)

RWANDA
Banking Hours: 8:AM - 11:AM, 2:PM - 5:PM (Mon-Fri), 8:AM - 1:PM (Sat); Business Hours: 7:AM - 12:Noon, 2:PM - 6:PM (Mon-Fri); Shopping Hours: 8:AM - 6:PM (Mon-Fri), 11:AM - 6:PM (Sat)

SRI LANKA
Banking Hours: 9:AM - 1:PM (Mon-Fri); 9:am - 11:AM (Sat)

ST. KITTS & NEVIS
Banking Hours: 8:AM - 1:PM (Mon-Fri); 8:AM - 1:PM; 3:PM -5:PM (Fri); Business Hours: 8:AM - 12:Noon, 1:PM - 4:30PM (Mon, Tues); 8:AM - 12:Noon; 1:PM - 4:PM (Wed Thur, Fri); Shopping Hours: 8:AM - 12:Noon, 1:PM - 4:PM Shops closed on Thursday afterNoons

ST. LUCIA
Banking Hours: 8:AM - 12:30PM (Mon-Thur); 8:AM - 12:Noon & 3:PM - 5:PM (Fri); Shopping Hours: 8:AM - 4:30PM (Mon-Fri); 8:AM - 1:PM (Sat)

SAN MARINO
Banking Hours: 8:30AM - 12:Noon, 2:30PM - 3:15PM; Business Hours: 8:AM - 12:Noon, 2:PM - 6:PM; Shopping Hours: 8:AM - 12:Noon 3:PM - 7:PM

ST. MAARTEN
Banking Hours: 8:30AM - 1:PM (Mon-Thur); 8:30AM - 1:PM & 4:PM - 5:PM (Fri); Business Hours: 8:AM -12:Noon & 2:PM - 6:PM; Shopping Hours: 8:AM - 12:Noon & 2:PM - 6:PM

ST. MARTIN
Banking Hours: 9:AM - 12:Noon & 2:PM - 3:PM (Mon-Fri); Shopping Hours: 9:AM - 12/12:30 & 2:PM - 6:PM (Mon-Sat)

SAO TOME AND PRINCIPE
Banking Hours: 7:30AM - 12:30PM, 2:30PM - 4:30PM (Mon-Fri); Businss Hours: 7:30AM - 12:30PM, 2:30PM - 4:30PM (Mon-Fri); Shopping Hours: 9:AM - 12:30PM, 2:30PM - 6:PM (Mon-Sat)

ST. VINCENT & THE GRENADINES
Banking Hours: 8:AM - 12/1:PM (Mon - Thur); 8:AM - 12:/1:PM & 2:/3:PM -5:PM (Fri) ;Business Hours: 8:AM - 12:Noon & 1:PM - 4:PM (Mon - Fri); 8:AM- 12:Noon (Sat)

SAUDI ARABIA
Banking Hours: 7/8:AM - 2:30PM (Sat-Thur); Business Hours: Gov't Offices: In Winter 8:AM -4:PM (Sat-Wed); In Summer 7:AM - 3:PM; During Ramadan 8:AM - 2:PM Others: 8:30AM- 1:30PM; 4:30AM - 8PM (Sat-Thur) closed Friday

SENEGAL
Banking Hours: 8:AM - 11:AM, 2:30PM - 4:30PM (Mon-Fri);Business Hours: 8:AM - 12:Noon , 3:PM - 6:PM (Mon-Fri), 8:AM - 12:Noon (Sat); Shopping Hours: 8:AM - 7:PM (Mon-Sat)

SEYCHELLES
Banking Hours: 8:30AM - 1:30PM (Mon-Sat); Business Hours: 8:AM - 12:Noon, 1:PM - 4:PM (Mon-Fri); Shopping Hours: 8:AM - 5:PM (Mon-Fri), 8:AM - 1:PM (Sat)

SIERRA LEONE
Banking Hours: 9:AM - 2:PM (Mon-Fri); Business Hours: 9:AM - 2:PM (Mon-Fri); Shopping Hours: 9:AM - 6:PM (Mon-Sat)

SINGAPORE
Banking Hours: 10:AM - 3:PM (Mon-Fri); 9:30AM - 11:30AM (Sat); Business Hours: Gov't: 9:AM - 4:30PM (Mon-Fri); 9:AM - 1:PM (Sat);Shopping Hours: 9:AM - 6:PM (Mon-Sat)

SOUTH AFRICA
Banking Hours: 9:AM - 3:PM (Mon,Tue,Thur,Fri); 9:AM - 1:PM (Wed); 9:AM -11:AM (Sat); Business/Shopping Hours: 8:30AM - 5:PM (Mon-Fri); 8:30AM - 12:Noon (Sat) Some stores

SPAIN
Banking Hours: 9:AM - 2:PM (Mon-Fri), 9:AM - 1: PM (Sat); Business Hours: 9:AM - 2:PM, 4:PM - 7:PM; Shopping Hours: 9:AM - 1:PM, 4:PM - 8:PM

SUDAN
Banking Hours: 8:30AM - 12:Noon (Sat-Thur); Business/Shopping Hours: 8:AM - 1:PM; 5:PM - 8:PM (Sat-Thur)

SURINAME
Banking Hours: 8:AM - 3:PM (Mon-Fri); Business Hours: 7:AM - 3:PM (Mon-Fri); Shopping Hours: 7:30AM - 4:PM (Mon-Fri)

SWEDEN
Banking Hours: 9:30AM - 3:PM

(Mon,Tue,Wed,Fri), 9:30AM -3:PM, 4:PM - 5:30PM (Thur); Business Hours: 8:AM - 5:PM; Shopping Hours: 9:30AM - 6:PM (Mon-Fri), 9:30AM - 1:PM (Sat), Noon - 4:PM (Sun)

SWITZERLAND
Banking Hours: 8:30AM - 4:30PM (Mon-Fri); Business Hours: 8:AM - 12:Noon; 2:PM - 6:PM; Shopping Hours: 8:AM - 12:15PM, 1:30PM - 6:30AM (Mon-Fri); 8:AM - 4:PM (Sat)

SYRIA
Banking Hours: 8:AM - 12:30PM (Sat-Thur)
Business Hours: 8:AM - 1:30PM; 4:30PM - 9:PM (Sat-Thur)

TANZANIA
Business/Shopping Hours: 8:AM - 5/6:PM (Mon-Sat)

TAJIKISTAN
Bankng Hours: 9:AM - 6:PM
Business Hours: 9:AM - 6:PM
Shopping Hours: 8:AM - 9:PM

THAILAND
Business/Shopping Hours: 8:30AM - 7/8:PM

TOGO
Banking Hours: 7:30AM - 11:30AM; 1:30 - 3:30PM (Mon-Fri); Business/Shopping Hours: 8:AM - 6:PM (Mon-Fri); Sat morning

TONGA
Banking Hours: 9:30AM - 4:30PM (Mon-Fri)

TRINIDAD AND TOBAGO
Banking Hours: 9:AM - 2:PM (Mon-Thur) & 9:AM - 12:Noon; 3:PM - 5:PM (Fri); Shopping Hours: 8:AM - 4:PM (Mon-Fri); 8:AM - 12:Noon (Sat)

TUNISIA
Banking Hours: 8:AM - 11:AM; 2:PM - 4:PM (Mon-Fri)

TURKEY
Banking Hours: 8:30AM - 12:Noon, 1:30 - 5:PM (Mon-Fri); Business Hours: 8:30AM - 12:30PM, 1:30PM - 5:30PM; Shopping Hours: 9:AM - 1:PM, 2:PM - 7:PM (Mon-Sat)

TURKMENISTAN
Banking Hours: 9:AM - 6:PM
Business Hours: 9:AM - 6:PM
Shopping Hours: 8:AM - 9:PM

TURKS AND CAICOS
Banking Hours: 8:30AM - 3:30PM
Business Hours: 8:30AM - 5:PM
Shopping Hours: 9:AM - 7:PM

UKRAINE
Banking Hours: 9:AM - 6:PM
Business Hours: 9:AM - 6:PM
Shopping Hours: 8:AM - 9:PM

UNITED KINGDOM
Banking Hours: (Varies) England & Wales: 9:AM - 3:PM (Mon-Fri) Scotland: 9:30 - 12:30PM, 1:30 - 3:30PM (Mon - Wed), 9:30AM - 12:30PM, 1:30 - 3:30PM, 3:30PM - 4:30PM-6PM (Thur) 9:30AM - 3:30PM (Fri), North Ireland: 10:AM - 3:30PM (Mon - Fri); Business Hours: 9:AM - 5:PM; Shopping Hours: 9:AM - 5:30PM

UNITED STATES OF AMERICA
Banking Hours: 9:AM - 5PM (Mon-Fr); 9:AM - Noon (Sat). Some locations have extended hours. Business Hours: 9:AM - 5PM (Mon-Fri); Shopping Hours: 9:AM -5PM (Mon-Fri); 9:AM-5PM (Sat); Noon-5PM (Sun) Some locations have extended hours.

URUGUAY
Banking Hours: 1:PM - 5:PM (Mon-Fri); Business Hours: 7:AM - 1:30PM (Mon-Fri) Summer & 12:30 - 7:PM (Mon-Fri) Winter; Shopping Hours: 10:AM - 7:PM (Mon-Sat)

UZBEKISTAN
Banking Hours: 9:AM - 6:PM
Business Hours: 9:AM - 6:PM
Shopping Hours: 8:AM - 9:PM

VENEZUELA
Banking Hours: 9:AM - 12:Noon & 3:PM - 5:PM (Mon-Fri); Business Hours: 8:AM - 12:Noon & 2:PM - 5:PM (Mon-Fri); Shopping Hours: 9:AM - 12:Noon & 2:PM - 5:PM (Mon-Sat)

VIETNAM
Banking Hours: 8:AM - 11:30AM; 2:PM - 4:PM (Mon-Fri); 8:AM - 11:AM (Sat)

WESTERN SAMOA
Banking Hours: 9:30AM - 3:PM

427

(Mon-Fri); 9:30AM - 11:30AM (Sat)

YUGOSLAVIA

Banking Hours: 7:AM - 12:Noon or 7:AM - 7:PM; Business Hours: 8:AM - 12:30PM; Shopping Hours: 8:AM - 12:Noon, 4:PM - 8:PM or 8:AM - 8:PM (Mon-Fri) 8:AM - 3:PM (Sat)

ZAIRE

Banking Hours: 8:AM - 11:30 (Mon-Fri); Business/Shopping Hours: 8:AM - 12:Noon; 3:PM - 6:PM (Mon- Sat)

ZAMBIA

Banking Hours: 8:AM - 1:PM (Mon-Fri); 8:AM -11:AM (Sat); Business/Shopping Hours: 8:AM - 5:PM (Mon-Fri); 8:AM - 3:PM (Sat)

ZIMBABWE

Banking Hours: 8:30AM - 2:PM (Mon,Tue, Thur, Fri); 8:30AM - 12:Noon (Wed); 8:30AM - 11:AM (Sat); Business/Shopping Hours: 8:AM - 5:PM

APPENDIX E

INTERNATIONAL EMERGENCY CODES

Country	Emergency #	Ambulance #	Police #
Algeria			17
Andorra		182-0020	21222
Andorra	11/15	20020	
Anguilla	999		
Antigua	999		20045/20125
Argentina			101
Austria		144	133
Bahamas		3222221	3224444
Barbados			112/60800
Belgium	900/901	906	101
Belize			2222
Bermuda			22222
Bolivia	118		110
Brazil	2321234		2436716
Columbia			12
Costa Rica	2158888		117
Cyprus	999		
Czech Republic	155		
Denmark	000		
Dominican Republic			6823000
Egypt			912644
Ethiopia			91
Fiji Islands	000		
Finland	000	002/003	
France	17	12/17	
French Guiana			18
Germany	110		
Gibraltar	199		
Great Britain	999		
Greece	100		171
Guyana	999		
Haiti	0		
Hong Kong	999		
Hungary	04		
Iceland			
(Reykavik)	11100	11166	
(elsewhere dial 02 for the operator who will then place the call)			
India		102	100
Ireland	999		
Israel			100
Italy		113	112
Jamaica		110	119
Japan		119	100

Country			
Jordan	19		
Kenya	999		
Liechtenstein		144	117
Luxembourg	012		
Malaysia	0		
Malta	99		
Maltese Island		196	191
Monaco		933-01945	17
Morocco			19
Nepal	11999		
Netherlands			
Amsterdam	559-9111	5555555	222222
(elsewhere dial 008 for the operator who will then place the call)			
New Zealand	111		
Norway		003	110011
Pakistan	222222		
Papua New Guinea			255555
Paraguay			49116
Peru	05		
Phillipines		599011	
Poland		999	997
Portugal	115		
San Marino	113		
Singapore	999		
Spain	091		
Sri Lanka			26941/21111
St. Vincent			71121
St. Kitts & Nevis	999		
St. Lucia	95		99
Suriname	99933		711111/77777
Sweden	90000		
Switzerland		144	117
Tanzania	999		
Thailand			2810372/2815051
Tunisia			243000
U.S. Virgin Is.		922	915
United States of America	411	411	411
Uruguay	401111		890
Venezuela			169/160
Yugoslavia	94		92

430

NOTES

OTHER BOOKS IN THE SERIES
FROM WORLD TRAVEL INSTITUTE
[Edition, ISBN, Page Count, Price, Availability/publication date]

Book Specification: 6 x 9, Paperback

AUTHOR: Gladson I. Nwanna (Ph.D)

Series Title: DO'S AND DON'TS AROUND THE WORLD: A COUNTRY GUIDE TO CULTURAL AND SOCIAL TABOOS AND ETIQUETTE

Edition:	ISBN#:	Pages:	Price:	Availability
EUROPE	1-890605-00-X	332	$29.99	Jan. 98
SOUTH AMERICA	1-890605-03-4	245	$19.99	Jan. 98
AFRICA	1-890605-04-2	440	$34.99	May 98
THE CARIBBEAN	1-890605-02-6	220	$19.99	March 98
ASIA	1-890605-01-8	250	$24.99	March 98
RUSSIA & THE INDEPENDENT STATES	1-890605-06-9	160	$12.99	March 98
USA, CANADA & AUSTRALIA	1-890605-08-5	75	$12.99	March 98
OCEANIA & JAPAN	1-890605-07-7	185	$15.99	May 98
THE MIDDLE EAST	1-890605-05-0	145	$12.99	March 98

INDIVIDUAL COUNTRY REPORTS ARE AVAILABLE!!!
at $7 per report per country.
Individual Country Reports can only be ordered directly from the publisher
or through the internet at **www.worldtravelinstitute.com**

COUNTRY REPORTS

[Note: Individual Country reports are currently available at $7 per country, per report. Price includes postage]

AFRICA
ALGERIA
BENIN
BOTSWANA
BURKINA FASO
BURUNDI
CAMEROON
CAPE VERDE, REP. OF
CENTRAL AFR. REP.
CHAD
COMOROS
CONGO, PEOPLE'S REP.
COTE D'IVOIRE
DJIBOUTI, REP. OF
EGYPT
ERITREA
ETHIOPIA
GABON
GAMBIA, THE
GHANA
GUINEA
GUINEA BISSAU
KENYA
LESOTHO
LIBERIA
LIBYA
MADAGASCAR
MALAWI
MALI
MAURITIUS
MOROCCO
MOZAMBIQUE
NAMIBIA
NIGER
NIGERIA
RWANDA
SAO TOME & PRINCIPE
SENEGAL
SEYCHELLES
SIERRA LEONE
SOMALIA
SOUTH AFRICA
SUDAN
SWAZILAND
TANZANIA
TOGO
TUNISIA
UGANDA
ZAIRE
ZAMBIA
ZIMBABWE

ASIA
AFGHANISTAN
BANGLADESH
BHUTAN
BRUNEI-DARUSSALEM
CAMBODIA
CHINA, PEOPLE'S REP.
CHINA, TAIWAN
CYPRUS
HONG KONG

INDIA
INDONESIA
JAPAN
KOREA, SOUTH
KOREA, NORTH
LAOS
MACAO
MALAYSIA
MALDIVES
MONGOLIA
MYANMAR (BURMA)
NEPAL
PAKISTAN
PHILIPPINES
SINGAPORE
SRI LANKA
THAILAND

EUROPE
ALBANIA
ANDORRA
AUSTRIA
BELGIUM
CROATIA
CZECH REP.
BULGARIA
DENMARK
FINLAND
FRANCE
GREECE
GREENLAND
HUNGARY
ICELAND
IRELAND
ITALY
LIECHESTEIN
LUXEMBOURG
MACEDONIA
MALTA
MOLDOVA
MONACO
NETHERLANDS
NORWAY
POLAND
PORTUGAL
ROMANIA
SAN MARINO
SLOVAK REP.
SLOVENIA
SPAIN
SWEDEN
SWITZERLAND
TURKEY
UNITED KINGDOM
YUGOSLAVIA

OCEANIA & JAPAN
AMERICAN SAMOA
COOK ISLANDS
FAROE ISLAND
FIJI
FRENCH POLYNESIA (TAHITI)

JAPAN
JERSEY CHANNEL IS
KIRIBATI
MARSHALL ISLAND
MICRONESIA
NAURU
NIEU
NEW CALEDONIA
NEW ZEALAND
PAPUA NEW GUINEA
SAMOA
SOLOMON ISLAND
ST. HELENA IS.
TUVALU
VANUATU

THE CARIBBEAN
ARUBA
ANGUILLA
ANTIGUA & BARBUDA
BAHAMAS
BARBADOS
BERMUDA
BRITISH VIRGIN
ISLANDS
CAYMAN IS
CURACAO
DOMINICA
DOMINICAN REP.
FRENCH GUIANA
GRENADA
GUADELOUPE
HAITI
JAMAICA
MONTSERRAT
NETHERLANDS
ANTILLES
ST. KITTS & NEVIS
ST. LUCIA
ST. MARTIN
ST. PIERRE &
MIQUELON
ST. VINCENT
TRINIDAD & TOBAGO
TURKS & CAICOS

MIDDLE EAST
BAHRAIN
IRAN
IRAQ
ISRAEL
JORDAN
KUWAIT
LEBANON
OMAN
QUATAR
SAUDI ARABIA
SYRIA
UNITED ARAB
EMIRATES
YEMEN
YEMEN, P.D.R.

RUSSIA & THE
INDEPENDENT STATES
ARMENIA
AZERBAIJAN
BYLERUS
ESTONIA
GEORGIA
KAZAKHSTAN
KYRGYZSTAN
LATVIA
LITHUANIA
RUSSIAN FEDERATION
TAJIKISTAN
TURKMENISTAN
UKRAINE
UZBEKISTAN

SOUTH AMERICA
ARGENTINA
BELIZE
BOLIVIA
BRAZIL
CHILE
COLOMBIA
COSTA RICA
CUBA
ECUADOR
EL SALVADOR
GUATEMALA
GUYANA
HONDURAS
MEXICO
NICARAGUA
PANAMA
PARAGUAY
PERU
PUERTO RICO
SURINAME
URUGUAY
VENEZUELA

USA, CANADA &
AUSTRALIA
CANADA
AUSTRALIA
USA

---

*Please check our website www.worldtravelinstitute.com) for a complete and updated list of available Country Reports.

433

OTHER WTI BOOKS BY THE SAME AUTHOR

Americans Traveling Abroad: What You Should Know Before You Go (2nd Ed.) Bestseller! paperback, 658 pages, ISBN: 0-9623820-7-8, $39.99 [Available at major bookstores throughout the United States. It may also be ordered from Access Publishers Network at 1-800-345-0096 or directly from the publisher-World Travel Institute].

Practical Tips For Americans Traveling Abroad: Ignore Them At Your Own Risk, paperback, 265 pages, ISBN: 1-890605-09-3, $19.99. On-line version is also available for purchase ($19.99) at **www.worldtravelinstitute.com**

ABOUT THE AUTHOR

Dr. Gladson I. Nwanna (Ph.D) is a university professor, a former consultant to the World Bank, and a veteran traveler. He has over the past 17 years traveled to numerous countries of the world, logging thousands of miles in the process.

LIBRARY RECOMMENDATION FORM

(This form should be hand delivered to your local Head Librarian or Reference Librarian)

Sir/Madam:

I regularly use the following book(s) published by **World Travel Institute**:
(1)_____ ISBN#:_____ Price $_____
(2)_____ ISBN#:_____ Price $_____
(3)_____ ISBN#:_____ Price $_____
(4)_____ ISBN#:_____ Price $_____
(5)_____ ISBN#:_____ Price $_____
(6)_____ ISBN#:_____ Price $_____
(7)_____ ISBN#:_____ Price $_____
(8)_____ ISBN#:_____ Price $_____

Your records indicate that the library does not carry these valuable and comprehensive travel reference books. Could you please place an order them for our library?

Name of Recommender:_____
Address:_____

Phone:_____

LIBRARY RECOMMENDATION FORM

(This form should be hand delivered to your local Head Librarian or Reference Librarian)

Sir/Madam:

I regularly use the following book(s) published by **World Travel Institute**:
(1)_____ ISBN#:_____ Price $_____
(2)_____ ISBN#:_____ Price $_____
(3)_____ ISBN#:_____ Price $_____
(4)_____ ISBN#:_____ Price $_____
(5)_____ ISBN#:_____ Price $_____
(6)_____ ISBN#:_____ Price $_____
(7)_____ ISBN#:_____ Price $_____
(8)_____ ISBN#:_____ Price $_____

Your records indicate that the library does not carry these valuable and comprehensive travel reference books. Could you please place an order them for our library?

Name of Recommender:_____
Address:_____

Phone:_____

ORDERING INFORMATION

MAIL OR FAX YOUR ORDERS TO:

World Travel Institute
P.O. Box 326740-1A,
Baltimore, MD 21282-2674 U.S.A.
Fax: (410) 922-8115.
Make check or money order payable to **World Travel Institute (WTI)**. We also accept,
international money orders; VISA & MASTERCARD.

Shipping/Postage Cost for books:
U.S. Residents add $4 U.S. dollars per book for postage.
Canadian Residents add $5 U.S. dollars per book for postage.
Mexican Residents add $7 U.S. dollars per book for postage.
Other Countries: add $15 U.S. dollars for airmail delivery; $7 for surface mail delivery.

Shipping/Postage Cost for Reports:
[Save on postage by ordering & downloading on-line version]
U.S. Residents reports are mailed free-of-charge.
Canadian Residents add $2 U.S. dollars for postage.
Mexican Residents add $2 U.S. dollars for postage.
Other Countries: add $5 U.S. dollars for airmail delivery; $3 dollars for surface mail
delivery.

Books may also be ordered through Access Publishers at 1-800-345-0096 ([Bookcrafters at
1-800-507-2665 after 5pm]. (BOOKS ONLY!!!). Only book orders placed directly with
publisher qualifies for the pre-publication discounts mentioned elsewhere in this document.

Remember, individual country reports are now available at $7 (U.S. dollars) per country.
Reports can only be ordered through the publisher!!! or through the web at
www.worldtravelinstitute.com

ORDER FORM

Telephone Orders: Call Access Publishers Network at 1-800-345-0096. (Bookmasters at 1-800-507-2665, after 5pm). Have Your Credit Card ready. Order any time, day or night, 7 days a week, 24 hours a day.

Fax Orders: 1-410-922-8115 (Send this form)

Postal Orders: World Travel Institute, P.O. Box 32674-1A, Baltimore, Maryland 21282-2674-8674 U.S.A.{tel: (410) 922-4903}. <u>Make check payable to WTI.</u>

☐ Please enter my order for the following books:
- **Do's and Don'ts:**

Europe	$29.99 + $____postage:	Total $____
South America	$19.99 + $____postage:	Total $____
Africa*	$34.99 + $____postage:	Total $____
The Caribbean	$19.99 + $____postage:	Total $____
Asia	$24.99 + $____postage:	Total $____
Russia/The Independent States	$12.99 +$____postage:	Total $____
USA, Canada & Australia	$12.99 + $____postage:	Total $____
The Middle East*	$12.99 + $____postage:	Total $____
Oceania & Japan*	$15.99 + $____postage:	Total $____

(* Please check availability/publication date)
(Please refer to the section containing postage/shipping information for applicable postage rates.)

- **Americans Traveling Abroad..** $39.99 + $____postage   Total $____
- **Practical Tips for Americans..** $19.99 + $____postage   Total $____
- **Do's and Don'ts - COUNTRY REPORTS:**
for the following countries at $7.<u>each</u> $____ + $____postage   Total $____
<u>List   Countries:</u>_____

_____

Sales Tax: (Maryland Residents Only) Add 5% $_____

Enclosed is my Total Payment of $_____ by

☐ Check ☐ Money Order ☐ Credit Card ☐ VISA ☐ MASTERCARD
Card Number:_____**Card Holder's Name:**_____
Expiration Date:_____**Card Holder's Signature:**_____
    ☐ This is a gift from:_____

Ship to:_____**Firm Name:**_____
Your Name:_____**Address:**_____
City:_____**State:**_____**Zip:**_____**Country:**_____

Inquiries: *All inquiries regarding your order or this book should be directed to our headquarters at the address and phone number shown above. The toll-free number is for orders only. No inquiries will be accepted at that number. <u>Note!</u> Country Reports are available through the publisher only. It cannot be ordered from Access Publisher or by calling the toll-free number shown above.*

COMMENT FORM

YOUR OPINION MEANS A LOT TO US
Please use this post card to tell us how you feel about any of our books. We are also interested in learning more about other cultural and social **do's and don'ts** of countries that you may want us to include in our data base and future editions, in particular, those we may not have included in any of our publications. Remember, we may quote you and/or use your comments, testimonials or suggestions in our promotions and future editions.

Title of Book:_____

Name:_____
Organization:_____**Position:**_____
Address:_____
City, State, Zip & Country:_____

( ) **Check here if we may quote you. Signature:**_____ **Date:**_____
[Mail your comments to WTI, P.O. Box 32674 Baltimore, MD 21282-2674, USA.]

COMMENT FORM

YOUR OPINION MEANS A LOT TO US
Please use this post card to tell us how you feel about any of our books. We are also interested in learning more about other cultural and social **do's and don'ts** of countries that you may want us to include in our data base and future editions, in particular, those we may not have included in any of our publications. Remember, we may quote you and/or use your comments, testimonials or suggestions in our promotions and future editions.

Title of Book:_____

Name:_____
Organization:_____**Position:**_____
Address:_____
City, State, Zip & Country:_____

( ) **Check here if we may quote you. Signature:**_____ **Date:**_____
[Mail your comments to WTI, P.O. Box 32674 Baltimore, MD 21282-2674, USA.]

438

Printed in the United States
52588LVS00003B/85